REALIZING RAWLS

THOMAS W. POGGE

Realizing Rawls

Cornell University Press

Ithaca and London

First published 1989 by Cornell University Press.

Library of Congress Cataloging-in-Publication Data

Pogge, Thomas Winfried Menko.
   Realizing Rawls / Thomas W. Pogge.
     p. cm.
   Bibliography: p.
   Includes index.
   ISBN 0-8014-2124-1 (alk. paper). — ISBN 0-8014-9685-3 (pbk. : alk. paper)
   1. Rawls, John, 1921–   Theory of justice. 2. Justice. I. Title.
JC578.R383P64   1989   320'.01'1—dc20   89-42879

Printed in the United States of America

FOR JOHN RAWLS,
who made it possible—
and necessary

Contents

Part Three: Globalizing the Rawlsian Conception of Justice

Acknowledgments

However critical and revisionist, this book is inspired by a deep admiration for John Rawls's theory of justice, in which I see, despite its shortcomings, a basic framework of compelling scope and moral beauty. My foremost aim was to express this vision.

My work in political philosophy has greatly benefited over the years from the critical attention it received from Rawls and later from Sidney Morgenbesser, Charles Larmore, and Bruce Ackerman. That none of them is particularly sympathetic to my approach and conclusions has made our discussions all the more valuable to me. Ackerman bears an additional responsibility: When I had abandoned plans for this book, he insisted, amicably but very firmly, that it be written. He cheerfully added that it wouldn't be great, but it would still be a good book.

The actual writing was done in the adventurous fluvial environment of Wolfson College, Oxford—a place of wonderful people and ideas that proved most inspiring and hospitable. Upon my return, I received extensive comments on the entire typescript from Charles Larmore, Andreas Føllesdal, Bruce Ackerman, and Ling Tong. Henry Richardson and Oscar Schachter provided additional feedback on Chapters 2 and 5 respectively. These benevolent critics have taught me much and, I hope, enabled me to give clearer expression to my thoughts.

Thomas W. Pogge

New York, New York

Abbreviations

Works by John Rawls are abbreviated as follows:

BLP   "The Basic Liberties and Their Priority," in S. M. McMurrin, ed., *The Tanner Lectures on Human Value*, 3 (Salt Lake City: University of Utah Press, 1982).

BSS   "The Basic Structure as Subject," in A. I. Goldman and J. Kim, eds., *Values and Morals* (Dordrecht: Reidel, 1978).

DPOC   "The Domain of the Political and Overlapping Consensus," in *New York University Law Review* 64 (June 1989).

FG   "Fairness to Goodness," *Philosophical Review* 84 (1975), 536–54.

IMT   "The Independence of Moral Theory," *Proceedings and Addresses of the American Philosophical Association* 48 (November 1975), 5–22.

IOC   "The Idea of an Overlapping Consensus," *Oxford Journal of Legal Studies* 7 (Spring 1987), 1–25.

JF   "Justice as Fairness," *Philosophical Review* 67 (April 1958), 164–94.

JFFM   "Justice as Fairness: Political not Metaphysical," *Philosophy and Public Affairs* 14 (Summer 1985), 223–51.

JR   "Justice as Reciprocity," in S. Gorowitz, ed., *Utilitarianism: John Stuart Mill, with Critical Essays* (Indianapolis: Bobbs-Merrill, 1971).

KCMT   "Kantian Constructivism in Moral Theory," *Journal of Philosophy* 77 (September 1980), 515–72.

ODPE   "Outline of a Decision Procedure for Ethics," *Philosophical Review* 60 (1951), 177–97.

PFE   "Preface for the French Edition" of TJ, English typescript (August 1986), pp. 1–6. French version in *Théorie de la justice*, trans. Catherine Audard (Paris: Seuil, 1987).

PRIG   "The Priority of Right and Ideas of the Good," *Philosophy and Public Affairs* 17 (Fall 1988), 251–76.

RAM   "Reply to Alexander and Musgrave," *Quarterly Journal of Economics* 88 (November 1974), 633–55.

RMC   "Some Reasons for the Maximin Criterion," *American Economic Review* 64 (May 1974), 141–46.

SUPG   "Social Unity and Primary Goods," in A. K. Sen and B. Williams, eds., *Utilitarianism and Beyond* (Cambridge: Cambridge University Press, 1982).

TCR   "Two Concepts of Rules," in S. Gorowitz, ed., *Utilitarianism: John Stuart Mill, with Critical Essays* (Indianapolis: Bobbs-Merrill, 1971).

TG   *Eine Theorie der Gerechtigkeit*, trans. Hermann Vetter (Frankfurt: Suhrkamp, 1975). All translations of TJ were prepared from a revised English text completed in March of 1975 (cf. PFE 1). Having checked all passages cited from TJ against their counterparts in TG, I note any relevant discrepancies.

TJ   *A Theory of Justice* (Cambridge: Harvard University Press, 1971).

WOS   "A Well-Ordered Society," in P. Laslett and J. Fishkin, eds., *Philosophy, Politics, and Society*, 5th series (New Haven: Yale University Press, 1979), first published as "A Kantian Conception of Equality," *Cambridge Review* (February 1975), 94–99.

REALIZING RAWLS

Introduction

This book is both a defense and a constructive critique of the work of John Rawls. These two aspects presuppose each other. The constructive critique is necessary to show that certain core ideas of Rawls's theory of justice can be developed in a way that makes them worth defending. After all, there is little interest in just keeping the score straight. The defense is necessary to show that these ideas have remained undamaged—and even largely unrecognized—in the barrage of criticism Rawls has provoked. The book as a whole is meant to show that Rawls offers a sound basis for progress in political philosophy as well as for political progress.

I don't aim for a comprehensive commentary on Rawls.[1] Instead, I concentrate on two central Rawlsian ideas: first, the focus on the basic structure, for moral philosophy must include, even begin from, a reflection upon the justice of our basic social institutions; second, the maximin idea that a scheme of social institutions is to be assessed by the worst position it generates, that its justice depends on how well it does by its least advantaged participants. My main interest is thus in one part of Rawls's theory, his conception of justice. I am centrally concerned with the meaning of the criterion of justice he has proposed, with the rationale for this criterion, and with its application to existing and feasible institutional schemes.

Matters peripheral to these eminently practical political concerns, however important they may be to Rawls, figure only peripherally here.

---

[1]Nor do I aim to provide a comprehensive commentary on the secondary literature on Rawls. I do cite some of these sources where it may be illuminating to see how I agree or disagree with them, but I make no effort to acknowledge and discuss every previous contribution to the issues I am concerned with. Given the amount of secondary writing on Rawls, such an endeavor would have made this book unreadable.

1

I do not, for example, treat the construct of the original position in any detail, though I do sometimes employ it to dramatize the priority concern for the least advantaged (under various institutional schemes), whom the parties take themselves to be representing. Nor do I offer an elaboration, either critical or defensive, of Kantian constructivism or of the method of wide reflective equilibrium, though I appeal to them occasionally to show that *Rawls* has reason to agree with me on some point. I avoid extensive discussion of these topics because it is not essential to my objective. I want to explicate and develop what I take to be Rawls's two most powerful and important ideas, together with their practical political implications (as I see them). All this could be done without even mentioning the "expository device" (TJ 21) of the original position, and one can fully accept my conclusions regardless of whether one accepts or rejects (or is even acquainted with) Kantian constructivism or the method of wide reflective equilibrium.

My attempt to develop a systematic and concrete conception of justice based on Rawlsian ideas goes against a popular trend in Anglo-American academia. There is a widespread sense that Rawls's work is in shambles because his critics have shown its foundations to be essentially and irremediably flawed. Since Rawls's mistake is thought to be a deep one, the collapse of his theory is said to indicate something larger, to mark the end of an era, perhaps the death of liberalism, the demise of the Enlightenment tradition, or even the bankruptcy of systematic moral philosophy. What we need is a radical reorientation in our ethical thinking, or so the story goes. Several authors have already volunteered to set the agenda for the dawning post-Rawlsian era, an agenda based on the renunciation not merely of Rawls's conclusions but of his goals and entire approach.[2]

Rather than directly confront these new agendas here, I examine one main source of their popularity, the notion that Rawls's theory has collapsed. My defense of that theory in Part One is meant to show that the obituaries are premature, that Rawls's critics have not exposed any deep flaw in his work at all; they have merely misunderstood it (albeit deeply). That Rawls's theory easily survives the common criticisms directed against it does not, of course, guarantee that it isn't deeply flawed in other ways. But judgment on its ultimate tenability is best deferred until we have a better understanding of the theory, together with its philosophical and practical implications, than has yet been achieved.

However undamaged philosophically, Rawls's work is in decline as a matter of academic politics. The critics have clearly won in the arena of public relations. We are well beyond the stage when, in Robert Nozick's words, "political philosophers now must either work within Rawls'

---

[2]Here I have in mind, for example, Alasdair MacIntyre, Bernard Williams, Michael Sandel, and Michael Walzer, who want ethics to be centrally concerned with human virtues, with ground projects and deep commitments, or with a notion of community.

theory or explain why not" (ASU 183). Today it is more common for political philosophers to make do with a brief reminder that Rawls's theory can be set aside because of its irremediable failure to come to terms with this or that fundamental difficulty.

This shift in academic prepossessions is in large part due to the work of Rawls's two most influential critics, Nozick and Michael Sandel, whom I confront in detail in Part One. I am only marginally interested in their own positions, which I make no claim to have undermined.[3] Rather, my concern is to show in all clarity how their reading and criticism of Rawls are fundamentally mistaken. Beginning in this way allows me to show that Rawls is still worth taking seriously and to correct some basic misunderstandings that are on the verge of becoming official Rawls doctrine.

Nozick and Sandel, the libertarian and the communitarian, share the most important misunderstanding of Rawls. Both fail to appreciate his distinction between justice and morality, between the focus on basic social institutions and the focus on persons' conduct and character. But in Chapter 1, when I explicate and develop this distinction and the Rawlsian focus on the basic structure, I draw upon Nozick's criticism only, because Sandel, heavily influenced by Nozick, offers nothing essentially new on this score. Sandel figures prominently in Chapter 2, because of a second, independent misunderstanding of Rawls, partly inspired by Nozick, which he has developed and grafted onto the first. This second misunderstanding involves Rawls's conception of the person as, supposedly, a barren, unencumbered self, devoid of constitutive commitments and attachments. I show that Rawls is not committed to such a conception of the person and that the tenability of his conception of justice even depends, in part, on the denial of the conception of the person that Sandel attributes to him.

The critics' success, however unjustified, has stifled what, in my view, would have been the most important upshot of Rawls's work—a broad debate about the justice of existing institutions and feasible avenues of institutional reform. Indeed, Rawls's work has a unique affinity for a concrete debate about justice because of its commitment to the primacy of the practical:

> The search for reasonable grounds for reaching agreement rooted in our conception of ourselves and in our relation to society replaces the search for moral truth interpreted as fixed by a prior and independent order of objects and relations, whether natural or divine, an order apart and distinct from how we conceive of ourselves. The task is to articulate a public

[3]Nozick has presented a crisp and interesting political philosophy of his own, and Sandel is developing his. These positions are worth studying (for some secondary literature, see, e.g., Paul, RN; Gutmann, CCL; and Larmore, PMC 121–29). My claim that Nozick and Sandel have misunderstood Rawls does not express disrespect for their positive achievements. Moreover, the mere fact that many have followed their misreadings shows that these must have some plausibility, both as readings of Rawls and in their own right.

conception of justice that all can live with who regard their person and their relation to society in a certain way. And though doing this may involve settling theoretical difficulties, the practical social task is primary. [KCMT 519]

Previous writers on justice could derive comfort from the fact that their work, whatever its political impact or lack thereof, would at least help elucidate what justice is and requires. They viewed the *truth* of a theory as independent of its popular appeal and political success, and thus considered it a great achievement to construct the just society "as a model laid up in heaven. . . . It makes no difference whether it exists anywhere or will exist" (Plato, *Republic* 592b).

Rawls can derive no such comfort, for he claims no truth for his conception beyond its potential to serve as the core of an overlapping consensus. Whether his conception of justice has this potential is not a theoretical matter that could be decided through further arguments within the theory itself. Rather, it is a practical question that can be settled conclusively only by the actual success of the conception in the role for which it was intended. Here a great deal of work remains to be done before Rawls's conception will have even a chance to succeed.

Some of this work I attempt to do here. My constructive critique of Rawls in Parts Two and Three develops his conception in a way that renders it more concrete and makes its full progressive potential more visible. Both these aims go against the trend of Rawls's later work toward abstraction, vagueness, and conservatism. I see this trend as due, in large part, to the widespread criticism of his work, which, in this decade at least, has been predominantly conservative. Rawls has been exceptionally unwilling to disagree sharply with his critics. Reluctant to claim privileged access to his work, he has shied away from saying (and showing) clearly and straightforwardly that a particular reading of it is just plain wrong. Instead, aiming for an overlapping consensus among political philosophers as well, he has made every conceivable effort to accommodate the moral positions of others, even where such accommodation has diluted the central moral statement of his own conception of justice.

With hindsight it seems fair to say that this has not been a winning strategy. It has certainly not stopped the criticism and rejection of his work; on the contrary, by showing Rawls on the defensive, it has perhaps even encouraged attack. More important, this strategy has moved the debate in exactly the wrong direction. As the political content of Rawls's conception has become more and more vague and indeterminate, attention has shifted to the philosophical underpinnings of the theory. We are back to issues in moral psychology, metaethics, and moral epistemology—to debates that are metaphysical in style, if not in substance.

Those for whom the practical social task is primary would take just the opposite approach to the subject. They would not begin with the foundations upon which a whole edifice of moral knowledge is to be erected. Instead, they would start from concrete moral issues actually in dispute and then extend their moral reflection as far afield as is necessary to reach agreement. They would not want to learn about Kantian constructivism, reflective equilibrium, and the conception of the person until they had first grasped the political content of Rawls's criterion of justice, how it is to govern social institutions and guide their assessment and reform. Other matters are important only insofar as they affect the interpretation of this criterion or its justification against competing criteria that are actually put forward in good faith.

This difference in approach has political relevance. Currently, moral and political philosophers are contributing to the general complacency about morality in various ways. Some of these contributions are scarcely avoidable. There have always been philosophers who cater to the individual and collective self-concern of their audiences, thereby turning some into eager converts and others into moral cynics.[4] What we can avoid is presenting the image of a community of experts totally and hopelessly divided on even the most fundamental questions. This image makes it far too easy for politicians, professionals, and people in general to cast moral considerations aside in situations where attending to them is liable to cause discomfort. Focusing the ethical debate on concrete issues of practical relevance would alleviate this problem in two ways: moral debates are harder to ignore when their point is to come to terms with malnutrition, homelessness, and oppression than when they exhaust themselves in speculations about ideal observers, secondary qualities, and the foundations of interpersonal comparisons; and disagreement about concrete moral issues is generally nar-

[4]Our time has perhaps more than its share of these because of the popular notion (a vulgar version of Rawls's idea of reflective equilibrium) that morality is whatever fits best with "our" reactions and intuitions—equated, in a common expression, with the moral facts. When moralists from all camps see it as their task to demonstrate that their respective theories can "account for our moral experience," we need not be surprised, at the height of what is often called the me-generation, to find philosophers proliferating all sorts of high-sounding phrases (and purported justifications) for individual and collective self-concern: agent-centered prerogatives, a robust zone of moral indifference, a cutoff for heroism, and the like. Justifications for such notions generally emphasize how very important it is to us—indeed, a matter of integrity—to be faithful to our deep projects and constitutive commitments. There is praise for loyalty to family, friends, and community and ridicule for abstract universalistic moralism supposedly producing moral saints and do-gooders who are intolerable as friends and lovers. It is transparent enough that this diversion of the agent's moral concern from those more distant to those around him and to himself will, in a world of radical inequalities, benefit the more advantaged persons and groups at the expense of the less advantaged. It shields us from moral claims invoking the extreme misery of distant others. Is this the point of such maneuvers? And if not, why hasn't their authors' (quite unexceptionable) concern for the value of deep projects and community alerted them to the fact that so many human beings, consumed by a lifelong yet often short-lived daily struggle against hunger and disease, are in no position to enjoy membership in a harmonious community or to lead a life of integrity by forming and honoring deep projects and constitutive commitments?

rower, even among philosophers, than disagreement about abstract, "foundational" questions.

At stake in the attempt to make Rawls's conception of justice more concrete, then, is its moral value by the lights of his own theory. If this theory can make no contribution to the practical tasks of facilitating agreement and alleviating injustice, then it ends up self-condemned. For in Rawls's view, the truth of a conception of justice consists in its ability to appeal and motivate. Going a little further, one might say that the point of political philosophy is not merely to show that certain principles are true, but to make them true by motivating the struggle for their gradual implementation.

Also at stake is the very meaning of Rawls's theory. An arrangement of concepts and ideas may look meaningful if it is well organized so that each of its various elements can be explained and motivated in terms of the others, but such an arrangement is not a theory if it is not pinned down to its subject matter. It is not meaningful as a whole if it does not have significant implications statable outside the language of the theory itself. If the goal is to facilitate agreement on a criterion of justice— "a public basis in the light of which citizens can justify to one another their common institutions" (KCMT 561)—then it must be made clear what this criterion means, that is, how it would assess particular institutional schemes. Rawls can plausibly reply that it is not his role as a philosopher to decide whether, say, the difference principle is satisfied in the United States. Such an investigation must surely draw upon the expertise of economists, among others. Yet it is part of Rawls's task to show how experts in other fields should go about settling such matters. Rawls must sharpen the relevant questions to clarify what sort of empirical data (and the like) are needed from other disciplines and what answers given data would entail. Similarly, in regard to his ideal well-ordered society, Rawls's conception of justice need not specify in detail what social institutions are required, but it must state clearly—in terms comprehensible to jurists, economists, and political scientists— *what is required of such institutions*. The beauty and power of Rawls's conception are wasted insofar as they cannot be imported into the political arena.

Although Rawls seems to accept this demand in principle,[5] in practice he has fallen far short of meeting it, and the gap is increasing. Let me here confine myself to a single example, one of several points extensively discussed in Part Two. Through the first principle of justice, Rawls requires that social institutions protect the freedom and integ-

---

[5]He writes: "A political conception of justice . . . needs certain guidelines of enquiry and publicly recognized rules of assessing evidence to govern its application. Otherwise, there is no agreed way for determining whether [its] principles are satisfied, and for settling what they require of particular institutions, or in particular situations. Agreement on a conception of justice is worthless—not an effective agreement at all—without agreement on these further matters" (IOC 8).

rity of the person. How do we judge whether this requirement is met? Must we look at infant mortality rates and the incidence of violent crimes? Is it relevant whether some among the poor are malnourished or starving? Rawls does not say. His silence facilitates a consensus of sorts: many can endorse the abstract requirement, interpreting it broadly or narrowly according to taste. But this is the wrong sort of consensus—or, rather, no consensus at all. To provide a shared basis for agreement on social institutions, Rawls's conception of justice must include answers to questions of this sort, and obviously, the relevant specifications must be provided in the philosophical core of the conception itself. No jurist or social theorist can answer such questions for us.

The specification of Rawls's conception of justice is a paradigmatically interdisciplinary enterprise. Philosophers cannot simply develop such a conception up to a certain point and then invite social theorists and jurists to "take over." The ideas and terminologies of the various disciplines must engage with one another. It must be assured, for example, that a particular economic measure, stated in terms that economists are familiar with and can work with, really expresses, closely enough, the assessment intended in the corresponding philosophical criterion of justice. Specification proceeds from an area that is purely philosophical to an area that is purely nonphilosophical, but along the way, it passes through an area that is genuinely interdisciplinary—an area that, I think, Rawls has for the most part failed to reach. In proposing a specification of Rawls's criterion (in Part Two), I venture into this intermediate area. Against the standards and terminologies of other disciplines, this effort is bound to appear somewhat amateurish—excusably so, I hope, given that it is merely a first sketch of how to achieve greater precision, an invitation for cooperation and not an attempt to go it alone.

I have argued that Rawls's conception must be specified to make clear what his criterion of justice *means*, how it is to be used to assess the institutions of a particular social system and to guide their reform. Rawls's conception of justice must also be developed in two further dimensions to make it sufficiently concrete. One task is to clarify the domain of this conception. Rawls offers it for the assessment of the institutional scheme of a society that is (as he variously puts it) "self-contained," "more or less self-sufficient," or "a closed system isolated from other societies" (TJ 457, 4, 8). "At some level there must exist a closed background system, and it is this subject for which we want a theory. We are better prepared to take up this problem," he further suggests, "for a society (illustrated by nations). . . . If we are successful in the case of a society, we can try to extend and to adjust our initial theory as further inquiry requires" (BSS 70 n. 8; cf. TJ 8). In the modern world there are no self-contained national societies; a closed background system exists only at the global level. The question, therefore, is whether Rawls's conception, if it applies at all, applies to open national societies (as Rawls seems to prefer) or to the closed social system of humanity at large (as I maintain in Part Three).

The other additional task is to sketch how the transition toward juster social institutions is to be brought about. The ultimate political import of a conception of justice consists in showing that persons ought to do certain things. Like specification, this task is essentially interdisciplinary. It must draw upon the knowledge of historians and social scientists and upon the practical experience of jurists and politicians to determine which institutional reforms are feasible, which policies would be effective, and how such reforms and policies might be initiated. But it also, to a significant extent, calls for philosophical reflection. A conception of justice may affect what we ought to do in at least three ways: we ought to help reform existing social institutions so as to render them more just; we ought to mitigate and alleviate the plight of those deprived and disadvantaged by existing unjust institutions; and we ought to accept certain constraints upon our conduct and policies that anticipate the ideal of just ground rules toward which we are striving. Philosophical reflection is required to resolve (1) conflicts of moral considerations within and across these three categories; (2) competitions among these moral considerations with respect to scarce resources of time, money, and energy; and (3) conflicts and competitions among such considerations of justice and other considerations. The problem of implementation is addressed—albeit neither systematically nor at length—in Parts Two and Three.

I have mentioned two kinds of abstractness in Rawls that I want to avoid: abstract philosophical theorizing (e.g., about Kantian constructivism) and abstract moral requirements that are too vague to settle the more interesting political controversies about institutional injustices. These must be distinguished from another kind of abstractness, embodied in Rawls's focus on basic social institutions, which is of great fertility and importance. To understand this abstractness, begin with the ultimate, concrete question of ethics—How ought I to live?— central to which is the question of how I ought to conduct myself toward others. For us the question arises in the context of a pervasive structure of ground rules purporting to regulate human interactions. We find ourselves as participants in an ongoing institutional scheme. This preexisting scheme of ground rules is of crucial importance in at least two ways. First, the relevant ground rules are at least partly constitutive. They determine who we are (mother, juror, doctor, delegate, convict, candidate, prince, or priest) and what our actions mean (buy or sell, command or promise, vote or veto, marry or divorce, apply or appeal) in the network of human interaction. Without an understanding of the ground rules we would lack the very terms in which to reflect upon our conduct. Second, the evolution of these ground rules has made our social world highly complex and interdependent. The effects of my conduct reverberate throughout the world, intermingling with the effects of the conduct of billions of other human beings (as illustrated by market transactions). Thus, many morally salient features of the situations of human beings (persistent starvation in northeastern Brazil, civil war in El Salvador, famine in India) arise from the confluence of the often very remote effects of the conduct of vast numbers of human beings. We as individuals have no hope of coping with such complexity and interdependence if we take the existing ground rules for granted and merely ask "How should I act?" or "What should I do differently?" We can cope only by attending to this all-pervasive scheme of ground rules which shapes the way persons act and co-determines how their actions, together, affect the lives of others.

Here, then, is the fruitful abstraction in Rawls's approach. In order to cope adequately with the question of how to live, one must, at least in the modern world, abstract from this question and reflect upon the basic ground rules that shape us, upon the social context in which we all act. Such reflection cannot proceed piecemeal. We cannot just reflect separately upon the ethics of each role and office, because to do so would take for granted the existing differentiation into roles and offices, would blind us to the *joint* effects of how these roles and offices are conceived. Nor can we attend to institutions one by one (marriage, property, the nation-state, the market), because these institutions, too, interpenetrate in their effects. The problem is analogous to that of seeking to optimize some process of production. Even if it is true that each part of the process is designed in the best possible way, *given* the way the other parts are designed, it may still be possible to improve the entire process greatly by redesigning all parts together or (more important) by altering its very structure (including its division into parts). We must, then, reflect upon social institutions and the roles and offices they involve *as one scheme*, against the background of feasible alternative schemes. This reflection is highly abstract, but without it we cannot even begin to understand what we are doing to others, how we are involved in their lives, and what concrete responsibilities we might have toward them. As I see it, Rawls's work is important for achieving this abstraction, yet weak in making it relevant to the concrete political issues before us. The abstraction is crucial, but it must be brought back down to earth.

This focus on the basic structure, combined with the priority concern for the least advantaged, makes Rawls a radical thinker. My remarks about his (increasing) conservatism are thus meant in a relative sense. It seems that in working out his two central ideas (as I have called them), Rawls has been resisting their progressive power every step of the way. To some extent he has done this by leaving his conclusions abstract and vague where further development would have made them more controversial and critical of the status quo. And where he did argue toward somewhat more definite conclusions, his arguments seem bent—bent on ensuring that these conclusions would be as bland, traditional, and mainstream American as possible.

While Rawls is then both a radical and a conservative, I will try to be faithful to the radical core of his conception, countering the many (and individually often minor) conservative stipulations that threaten to obscure the great progressive potential of his principal ideas. Thus it is not essential to my goal here that Rawls should fully agree with my conclusions. Of course, insofar as I try to explicate and defend his position, especially in Part One, it matters that I should do so correctly, that what I reject as misunderstandings really are misunderstandings. But insofar as I make his criterion of justice more concrete, my overriding concern is to develop the two central ideas in a plausible way. I would certainly be pleased and encouraged if Rawls were to find some of these developments attractive, and I would rethink my conclusions if he gave reasons to reject them, but these are my attitudes to the responses of any reader.[6] My deepest allegiance here is not to Rawls but to his foremost ideas. These ideas have a life and power independent of Rawls, which is testimony, surely, to the greatness of both.

Rawls's most important conservative stipulation is that his focus on major social institutions is to exclude the institution of the nation-state. Rawls follows tradition in treating national borders as moral watersheds. Only within a national territory and the population it defines does he view the focus on the least advantaged as appropriate. He thereby circumvents a crucial moral question, which his theory ought to *answer*, namely whether the institutionalization of national borders really has this magical moral force of shielding us from (or reducing the force of) the moral claims of "foreigners." The practical importance of this question is enormous, seeing that the institution of the nation-state is a crucial contributor to the current institutional production of extreme deprivations and inequalities.

Rawls's conservatism is exemplified also in his specification of the maximin idea and in his remarks about implementation.[7] The most important example here is how Rawls lets his lexical priority of the basic liberties (the first principle of justice) undermine his priority concern for the least advantaged. This problem arises even apart from the stunning lack of interest in basic social and economic needs that is reflected in Rawls's discussions of the lexical priority. As it stands, the lexical priority of the basic liberties will support two of Rawls's conclu-

---

[6]Still, it would be of some historical interest if one could get Rawls to be more specific about his own views, if only in response to the specifications proposed by others.

[7]The discussion of Part Two deals with some of these matters in detail. As for the asserted conservative drift in Rawls's writings, one might mention, for example, the notable dilution of the requirements that institutions must maintain the fair value of the political liberties (§12.4) and fair equality of opportunity (§14.7). One might also point out that remarks deploring existing violations of his second principle—common in TJ and sometimes rather strongly worded (e.g., TJ 78, 87, 226, 279, 300, 536)—are absent from the later writings.

sions: the fulfillment of its participants' basic liberties should be the primary criterion for identifying the least advantaged under some institutional scheme, and enhancing the basic liberties of the least advantaged should be the most urgent imperative guiding the reform of an institutional scheme. But Rawls draws the further conclusion that reforms involving an enhancement of basic liberties are *always* the most urgent, even when they involve an expansion of the basic liberties of the more advantaged (whose basic liberties are already more complete or better protected) at the expense of advancements in the socioeconomic position of the least advantaged. As I demonstrate in some detail (§11.3.1, cf. §11.2.1), this conclusion is a clear violation of the maximin idea.

Making Rawls's central ideas more concrete in a way that corrects for his conservative tendency, I hope to leave the reader at the end with reasonably clear theses about where our world is now as far as justice is concerned, how we are morally related to existing injustices, and what a just institutional scheme and progress toward it might look like. These conclusions stand opposed to the smug consensus that truly grievous injustices exist only in the past or in distant lands and so need not concern us here and now. I conclude that we are advantaged participants in an institutional scheme that produces extreme poverty on a massive scale so that many persons are born with no realistic prospects of a life without hunger, malnutrition, and oppression. The scheme is imposed upon these, its most disadvantaged participants— and imposed not by fate or nature but by other, more advantaged participants, ourselves included. Current injustices are no less severe than those suffered by earlier disadvantaged groups, and our responsibility for these injustices is no less than that of earlier more advantaged groups. But because of the vastly greater differentiation and complexity of the prevailing institutional scheme, the injustice and our responsibility for it are both much more opaque.

Clearly, the plight of the least advantaged is due to *social* realities. It is not natural, for most of them, like most of us, are perfectly capable of leading healthy and successful lives if given a chance to escape from their prison of poverty. But then we are not like slaveholders, who embody and live out the injustice of slavery in the violence and cruelty they visit upon their slaves. We lead ordinary, civilized lives, and nothing we do seems to have a major or even minor negative impact upon the lives of the disadvantaged. And so, paradoxically, the relevant social realities take on the appearance of anonymity—seem to be produced and reproduced without a trace of human agency.

Rawls's focus on basic social institutions and their effects makes it possible to clarify how injustice can be systemic, can exist without being traceable to any manifestly unjust actions by individuals or groups. Our causal contribution to the suffering of the poor is extremely indirect and intermixed with the causal contributions of others. It is quite infeasible for us to adjust our conduct so as to avoid such effects. And here again, Rawls's institutional approach is crucial for showing the alternative to such an (infeasible) adjustment of our conduct. We must initiate institutional reforms toward a scheme that, however differentiated and complex, does not tend to engender the severe poverty and oppression so typical of our current world. Those presently most disadvantaged have virtually no means for initiating such reforms. We do. And our responsibility vis-à-vis existing injustices hinges upon our ability to initiate and support institutional reforms.

The ultimate goal of such reforms is a fully just global institutional scheme, defined, perhaps, by reference to the two principles. Our responsibility, however, in no way depends on whether such a fully just scheme is practicable or realistically attainable. Yes, Rawls's criterion can be used to design a blueprint of ideal institutions that would be perfectly just. But much more important for now is its role in the comparative assessment of alternative feasible institutional schemes. Perhaps we will never reach a scheme whose worst social position is optimal. But we don't need the assurance that such a scheme is reachable in order to recognize that we ought to support institutional reforms that *improve* the worst social position, just as one does not need the assurance that one can reach perfection for undertaking to become a better human being.

PART ONE

DEFENDING
THE MAIN IDEAS

CHAPTER 1

Nozick and the Focus
on the Basic Structure

1. The Problem of Justice

It is John Rawls's ambition to present a conception of justice for the basic structure of a self-contained social system. To get an intuitive idea of what this means, I bring in Robert Nozick's work, including his reading and criticism of Rawls. I am especially interested in Nozick's claim that Rawls's approach begs important questions, particularly against historical entitlement theories of distributive justice, in which ownership rights are defined recursively and operate as side constraints.

1.1. We can quickly get to the core of Nozick's attack on Rawls by accepting a challenge he raises (ASU 167n, 204–5) which Rawls has not taken up, the challenge to examine the plausibility of competing conceptions of justice in a surveyable, small-scale context. To accommodate Rawls, and without prejudice to Nozick, let us imagine a closed and self-contained group of persons, perhaps sharing a small isolated island, a collectivity that is reproducing itself over time, with contemporaries widely scattered in age. For now, we can make the simplifying assumption that any social order we consider for this group would be understood and generally complied with. To keep matters even more simple, let us leave aside most of the basic features of the social order and focus on the details of the group's institution of private property.[1] In taking for granted that this primitive, agrarian economy prominently involves this institution in some form, we presuppose a commitment

[1]We can then largely rely, for the moment, on Rawls's difference principle in its simplest form—covering only the single good, income—to bring out what is distinctive about his full criterion of justice, which is merely a more complicated maximin criterion, addressing a wider range of social goods with a priority ordering among them.

15

Rawls and Nozick share and can concentrate immediately on what is controversial between them.

We can further eliminate the more abstruse patterned principles Nozick entertains—that property should be distributed according to persons' moral merit, usefulness to society, need, intelligence, race, or some mixture or combination of these, or so as to match some anonymous profile. Against this uncontroversial background, let us consider some important parameters of the definition of property rights, especially what kind of items are ownable, how one comes to own such items, and what rights one has when one owns them. Let me give a thin sketch of the economic order Nozick would envision for our island, followed by an equally thin countersketch more Rawlsian in spirit.

Nozick defines the set of ownables quite widely, including even persons within its scope: "I believe that . . . a free system will allow [a person] to sell himself into slavery" (ASU 331). He allows slavery because he is convinced, contrary to the American Declaration of Independence, that all rights should be alienable.[2] Still, a person is an ownable of a special kind, in that she is initially self-owned when she comes of age (ASU 289, 331, 38f). That her parents or their owners owned all the ingredients to her "production" does not, *in this one case*, entail that they own the product. Persons can become slaves only by alienating themselves.

Concerning control of the island's pivotal natural resource—land— Nozick advocates these main rules: All land is subject to acquisition by the first comer, who thereby gains full, exclusionary control over it, including the right to transfer any or all of his rights as owner to some other person(s) of his choice. A legitimate landholding is then defined recursively as one that arose from a valid first acquisition through any number of valid transfers.

Someone with Rawlsian leanings might propose the following alternative ground rules. There is to be no institution of slavery; persons cannot alienate themselves or come to be owned in any way. All land is subject to appropriation by the first comer, who thereby gains full, exclusionary control over it. As owner, he is free to relinquish ownership over (a portion) of his land at any time (through exchange, gift, or bequest), but he controls the assignment of only 80 percent of the land he relinquishes. The remaining 20 percent is assigned (perhaps via some lottery mechanism) to young persons from landless families or, should there be no landless families, to young persons from families with the lowest landholdings per capita. Thus, a legitimate landholding is again defined recursively as one that arose from a valid first acquisition through any number of applications of the change-of-ownership rules. Our Rawlsian prefers these ground rules to Nozick's, because they can be expected to engender less, and less severe, poverty.

---

[2]It may well be Nozick's view that is historically more typical in this regard. Cf., e.g., Tuck, NRT 29, 49, 54, 147–48.

1.2. I pursue this dispute to the next higher level in §3, examining how Rawls and Nozick might disagree about what sorts of considerations should resolve the lower-level dispute about a just social order for our island, but first we must characterize precisely what the dispute is about. In particular, we must keep sharply distinct, as Nozick does not, *our* subject, *how the ground rules of a social system ought to be assessed/designed,* from the (secondary) subject of how actors (individuals, associations, the government) may and should act within an ongoing scheme whose terms are taken as fixed. The former of these subjects, *justice,* is concerned with the moral assessment and justification of social institutions; the latter, *morality,* with the assessment of conduct and character.

Both Rawls and Nozick are essentially concerned with the first subject, but Nozick expends much effort attacking a view that is not Rawls's. While Rawls seeks to consider ground rules from a higher level, Nozick often casts their dispute as one about which ground rules it is permissible to infringe under what circumstances. Though his arguments in this vein are not relevant to Rawls's project, they are likely to have a significant rhetorical effect upon the unwary reader. Let me give three prominent examples.

First, Nozick frequently conjures up the horror of *redistribution,* the idea that some authority (the government, say) will come along, whenever it pleases, to take away part of what you own in order to devote it to some purpose it deems worthy. But our Rawlsian's proposal regarding landownership is not redistributive in this sense. It envisions no mechanism that makes ad hoc corrections and improvements in the distribution of land that has emerged in accordance with the rules of first acquisition and change of ownership. Rather, it envisions a particular *content* for these rules, which determine how (patterns of) landholdings arise in the first place. No property is taken from someone and given to another. A landowner controls his entire property up to the moment when he relinquishes it; no land is taken away from him. His designated assignee receives 80 percent of the land in question; no land is taken away from her either, because she never owned the full plot to begin with. Now one may think that what is taken away is the landowner's power to dispose of *all* his property as he deems fit. But no such power exists (and thus could be taken away) under the Rawlsian's practice. All land is held, from the very beginning, on the public understanding of the change-of-ownership rules. No one need hold land on these terms, but those who do are bound by them.[3]

Second, Nozick often complains that Rawls begs the question against all *entitlement* theories of distributive justice (e.g., ASU 199, 203–4, 207,

---

[3]This constraint is structurally analogous to limitations that figure in Nozick's own scheme: "My property rights in my knife allow me to leave it where I will, but not in your chest" (ASU 171). "Each owner's title to his holding includes the historical shadow of the Lockean proviso on appropriation" (ASU 180). Again, no one need own things on these terms, but those who do are bound by them.

215). Straightforwardly understood, this complaint is false. The economic structure our Rawlsian is proposing also revolves around a notion of entitlement. It, too, features a recursive definition of legitimate landholdings, involving rules of first acquisition and change of ownership. Relinquished entitlements are transformed, in accordance with the change-of-ownership rules, into new entitlements of the chosen assignee and of some other person(s). And again, as in Nozick, the proposal stipulates that existing entitlements may not be infringed for the sake of, for example, distributional considerations.[4]

Third, Nozick offers reasons for conceiving of rights as *side constraints* (ASU 28–34), in contrast to a conception of rights as goals which would urge agents to act so as to maximize the weighted sum of rights fulfillment overall. On the latter view, one should, despite a right of innocents not to be killed, kill innocents when doing so secures a greater gain in terms of rights (for example, saves more innocents from being killed) elsewhere. But the side-constraint conception of rights, which Rawls can and does accept, again fails to advance Nozick's case for a particular specification of property rights (ASU 172–73). It implies that *if* we end up accepting the property rights Nozick proposes, then no land can be taken by the landless (or given them by some official authority) without the consent of its owner. But this implication, again, is irrelevant to our subject, namely, what side constraints should be recognized or, more specifically, how property rights are to be specified to begin with. Choosing the practice proposed by our Rawlsian does not mean that the rights of landowners are violated for the sake of fulfilling the right to an initial plot of land. Rather it means that the conflict between these two *purported* rights is resolved by recognizing the latter and correspondingly institutionalizing an adjusted version of the former. The proposal is *not* that the Nozickian property rights of the landowners should be violated but that such rights should not exist. Our Rawlsian finds insufficient the reasons supporting a right to reassign all one's land, and so rejects *ab initio* the economic institutions Nozick favors.[5]

[4]Yet Nozick's complaint may also have another sense, that Rawls is begging the question against the claim that "historical-entitlement principles are fundamental" (ASU 202). Here, the point is not that Rawls is biased against all ways of specifying property rights as historically recursive but rather that we are to identify the correct specification of property rights without any reasons or, at any rate, without the kind of reasons Rawls deems relevant. This issue will be central in §§3–4.

[5]Analogues to these three points can be made about an income-tax-funded welfare scheme. There is no *redistribution* under the historical entitlement rules of such a scheme, because under these rules persons are entitled only to their *net* income (which alone is distributed to them in the first place). Income taxes would represent part of your property, which is being taken away from you, only if you were entitled to your gross income, which, under the scheme, you are not. Though the tax portion may still be physically in your possession, it is (when due) no longer yours but rather belongs to the orphans, unemployed, etc., who are entitled to it under the scheme. Of course, that Nozick's three complaints are irrelevant to the critique of these (or any other) institutional schemes does not show that these schemes are just, only that their justice must be decided on the basis of different considerations, which I will begin to discuss in §3.

1.3. In response to Nozick's affirmation of a particular specification of rights, Rawls would not offer remarks on a different *subject*, claiming that these Nozickian rights (and whatever entitlements they give rise to) should sometimes be overridden by other moral considerations (cf. BSS 65). Instead, he would adduce reasons on a higher *level* against accepting Nozick's specification of property rights in the first place. It may help to fix the distinction between the two levels terminologically by contrasting the *rights* specified as part of an institutional scheme with the *values* appealed to in the comparative moral assessment of alternative institutional schemes.[6] Values may conflict and then require trade-offs and sacrifices. But whatever liberties and rights (side constraints) are specified by the chosen institutional scheme are designed to be compatible with one another from the start. The question of whether to violate someone's right in order to fulfill the rights of others should in principle never arise.[7]

It is likely, for example, that Nozick would value both freedom of movement and the chance of exclusionary control over land. It is not possible for both values to be fully incorporated into one institutional scheme, however. Among the various possibilities of sacrifice and compromise, Nozick favors a scheme under which persons have full exclusionary control over whatever land they own, as well as a correspondingly limited right to freedom of movement. Though the *value* of freedom of movement is sacrificed in part, the limited *right* to freedom of movement that emerges from the trade-off is not subject to violation for the sake of other rights.[8] Similarly, the Rawlsian's scheme, though it

[6]Nozick's failure to appreciate this distinction confuses not only his long discussion of Rawls but also his development of his own theory. Thus, consider his view (ASU chap. 4) that some borders may be crossed (i.e., some rights may be violated) without consent, provided that compensation is paid. Offhand this view must seem incomprehensible. If I am at liberty to do X without your consent provided I pay you compensation, then you have *no* right that I refrain from doing so, and hence my doing it crosses no border at all. But the mistake *is* comprehensible, because Nozick, operating on a single level, has no intelligible alternative. What am I paying you compensation *for* if no right violation (border crossing) is involved in my action?

The difficulty disappears if we understand Nozick's proposal as resolving, on the higher level, a competition between values. Should there be a right not to have X done to one without one's consent or a liberty to do X to others without their consent? Given strong reasons in favor of each, one might, rejecting both, be drawn to a compromise of the sort Nozick proposes. Let there be a liberty to-do-X-with-consent-or-side-payment, and a right not-to-have-X-done-to-one-without-consent-and-without-side-payment. In this compromise, the side payment compensates *not* for violation of a *right* (it enters into how the right is formulated in the first place) but for abridgment of a *value*, the value of controlling whether others do X to oneself. One does not get such control, but the institutionalized side payment tends to make less unpleasant and less frequent the occasions on which X is done to one without one's consent.

[7]But such conflicts will, of course, arise in practice. Even the most rational legal structure cannot fully anticipate all possible conflict scenarios or preempt all possible disputes about its own interpretation.

[8]A value, even where it is abridged, might still be partly realized, through consent. In Nozick's scheme, persons can buy or exchange trespass rights; in the reverse scheme, landowners can buy their neighbors' promise not to trespass. Still, Coase's theorem notwithstanding, the choice of scheme will make an enormous difference in human

compromises certain values, features (more limited) property rights that may not be violated for the sake of other rights. *Neither* scheme is or involves a "utilitarianism of rights," whose rules require or permit that persons violate the rights of others whenever doing so produces a net gain for rights fulfillment overall (cf. ASU 28). And *both* schemes could be justified through a *balancing of values*, determining which institutional structure (including an interpersonally consistent equal package of recognized rights and liberties) yields the best lives for individuals.[9]

1.4. Still leaving aside the moral substance of Rawls's conception of justice, let me now expound somewhat more precisely its subject, the basic structure of a self-contained social system. My exposition of the two key notions involved departs from Rawls's own in two minor respects.

1.4.1. I prefer to speak of the basic structure of a *social system*, rather than, as Rawls, of a society. He explicates this notion as follows: "Let us assume, to fix ideas, that a society is a more or less self-sufficient association of persons who in their relations to one another recognize certain rules of conduct as binding and who for the most part act in accordance with them. Suppose further that these rules specify a system of cooperation designed to advance the good of those taking part in it. . . . [A] society is a cooperative venture for mutual advantage" (TJ 4).[10] This explication seems narrow, for there are surely many historical societies (standardly so-called) whose rules fail either to be designed for mutual advantage or to be recognized as binding by all participants. For example, the rules may be designed for the advantage of a minority, and compliance by the remaining participants may be due to coercion or religious superstition.[11] Now Rawls is free, of course, to exclude such cases from his inquiry, leaving open whether and how such social systems can be assessed as more or less just. But as his frequent use of slavery as an example of a social institution makes clear, this is not his intention. Seeing that Rawls is unclear about the scope of his inquiry in

terms, as can be seen by comparing, e.g., the position of the landless poor under these two alternative schemes.

[9]This statement fits with what Nozick says when he is clear about the distinction between the two levels. In discussing how his principles of appropriation and rectification should be formulated, he remarks about the latter (which governs adjustments of holdings in light of past infractions of his acquisition or transfer principles), "Whatever difficulties [the entitlement theorist] has in applying the principle of rectification to persons who did not themselves violate the first two principles are difficulties in balancing the conflicting considerations so as correctly to formulate the complex principle of rectification itself; he will not violate moral side constraints by applying the principle" (ASU 173, cf. 146, 180–81). My point is that such balancing of considerations is required throughout—in the formulation of *all* side constraints or other institutional features.

[10]I think Rawls is here defining what a society *is*. Were he already making assumptions about what a society ought to be, I would not need to object to this passage.

[11]This problem is first noted by Wolff, UR 77–79. It is also discussed in Beitz, PTIR 130–32, 150 n. 52, though Beitz takes Rawls to assume that, to be a society, a social system must be mutually advantageous (rather than be *designed for* mutual advantage).

this respect, I am starting out with the concept of a (self-sufficient) social system, which is broader than Rawls's official notion of a society. Correspondingly, I am also broadening his expression "social cooperation" to allow that the economic interactions within a social system may be largely coercive rather than genuinely cooperative and that the most important social interactions may take place outside the economic sphere.[12] My initial focus, then, is on a comprehensive and reasonably self-contained system of social interaction. I am not denying the possibility that there are some such systems to which Rawls's conception of justice is not plausibly applicable, but we do best to confront this possibility later (§23), when his conception is before us in developed form.

1.4.2. What, then, is the *basic structure* of a self-sufficient social system? Rawls leaves this notion not merely vague but also ambiguous. Let me explain by elaborating one of its two senses in Rawls, how I understand the term *basic structure*. I will then defend my choice by contrasting it to the other sense in which Rawls uses the term.

In *A Theory of Justice* the basic structure of a social system is defined as "the way in which the major social institutions distribute fundamental rights and duties and determine the division of advantages from social cooperation" (TJ 7). Social institutions are a species of social practices and thus are in some ways analogous to games and rituals (TJ 55; cf. TCR 175 n. 1; JF 164 n. 2). So the term *institution* is used here in a sense that—allowing the (redundant) addition of "social"—contrasts with its other sense of organization or corporation (as in "institution of higher learning"). For this latter sense of *institution*, Rawls uses the term *association*.

Not every collective activity, however regular, constitutes a social practice. It is further required that the relevant rules be generally known and understood by those participating in the activity. A practice involves a system of rules and procedures that "defines offices and positions with their rights and duties, powers and immunities, and the like" (TJ 55). This system may include ways of dealing with rule violations—for example, procedures for determining violations, a list of admissible excuses, penalties, and so forth. Moreover, some of the rules governing the activity must be *constitutive* rules, which stipulate roles and moves that could not exist (under their relevant descriptions) outside of the activity in question (goalkeeper, to checkmate, etc.).[13] A

---

[12]Cp. Höffe, PG 326–28.

[13]Rawls states this second requirement and then illustrates it with baseball terminology as follows: "The rules of practices are logically prior to particular cases. . . . Given any rule which specifies a form of action (a move), a particular action which would be taken as falling under this rule given that there is the practice would not be *described as* that sort of action unless there was the practice. In the case of actions specified by practices it is logically impossible to perform them outside the stage-setting provided by those practices, for unless there is the practice, and unless the requisite properties are fulfilled, whatever one does, whatever movements one makes, will fail to count as a form of action which the practice specifies" (TCR 189). I have weakened this condition by assuming that

game, for example, may involve various roles (batter, umpire), with each role envisaging various game-dependent moves that occupants of this role may or must make in certain contexts.

There seems to be no very clear way of defining social institutions within the domain of social practices. If games and rituals are not normally thought of as institutions, it is presumably because they are, at least in modern Western culture, marginal to the ongoing competition over control of conduct and resources. Though persons' behavior within a game or ritual may be subject to moral critique, such practices themselves are much less so, assuming that participation can easily be declined, risks are limited, and so on.[14] Institutions, by contrast, do call for moral assessment. For this subject Rawls reserves the term *justice* as "the first virtue of social institutions" (TJ 3) or, perhaps better—to bypass the side issue of how to individuate institutions—as the first virtue of institutional schemes.[15]

Given this notion of the basic structure, Rawls's project is to develop a conception of justice (or the central part thereof) that assesses the *most important* institutional features of any *self-contained* (TJ 457) or *all-inclusive* social system (BSS IV). These essential features of a closed system's institutional scheme—"the political constitution, the legally recognized forms of property, . . . the organization of the economy, and the nature of the family" (BSS 47), whose effects are "profound and pervasive, and present from birth" (TJ 96)—Rawls refers to as its basic structure (TJ §2, BSS). I will also say that the basic structure consists of the, largely constitutive, *ground rules* that shape a society, or of the *terms of social interaction* that significantly involve or at least affect all its participants. These ground rules define the society's central procedures, bodies, and offices, and they regulate the assignment of benefits and burdens (rights and duties, powers and immunities, goods and services) to participants in general and to the occupants of special roles.

In broad outline, the basic structure consists of a society's basic mode of economic organization; the procedures for making social

---

only *some* rules of the practice need have this character (there might be a rule in baseball that forbids players to bite or kick others). This point is relevant to Rawls's subject of a social system's basic structure. Some of the conduct rules in such a system may merely restate natural duties, which persons have toward one another irrespective of any practices they may jointly participate in—criminal-law prohibitions against cruelty (TJ 114) or against harming the innocent (TJ 109), for example.

[14]Compare the distinction Rawls makes in another context between "a practice in which there is no option whether to engage in it or not, and one must play" and "a practice in which there is such an option, and one may decline the invitation" (JR 242; cf. JF 179).

[15]This focus is characteristic of Rawls's work from the beginning: "Throughout I consider justice only as a virtue of social institutions. . . . The principles of justice are regarded as formulating restrictions on how practices may define positions and offices, and assign thereto powers and liabilities, rights and duties. Justice as a virtue of particular actions or of persons I do not take up at all" (JF 164–65; cf. TJ 7).

choices through the conduct of, or interactions among, individuals and groups, and limitations upon such choices;[16] the more important practices governing civil (noneconomic and nonpolitical) interactions, such as the family or the education system; and the procedures for interpreting and enforcing the rules of the scheme. The first category includes a specification of what kind of items can be owned and by whom, how ownership is gained and lost, but not the internal organization of particular economic associations such as firms or unions, which only some participants are involved in. Similarly, the last category might include a specification of the ways and circumstances in which infractions of social rules are to be protested, determined, punished, deterred, or preempted but not the internal organization of the judiciary or the full details of criminal trial procedures. Among the institutional features that, where they exist, are part of the basic structure are the use of money, "competitive markets, private property in the means of production, and the monogamous family" (TJ 7), rules governing the use of force, slavery (TJ 248), the division of powers, parliamentary democracy, judicial review, a tax-funded welfare system, and compulsory primary education.[17]

This notion of a basic structure, an elaboration of the account in *A Theory of Justice*, conflicts with a narrower understanding of the term which dominates Rawls's discussion in "The Basic Structure as Subject." There the basic structure is defined in terms of "an institutional division of labor between the basic structure and the rules applying directly to individuals and associations" (BSS 55). "The role of the institutions that belong to the basic structure is to secure just background conditions against which the actions of individuals and associations take place" (BSS 53). By this narrow construal, Rawls's examples of private property in the means of production and the monogamous family would not be included, because it is not their role, even ideally, to preserve just background conditions. The basic structure of a developed society might then include little more than its welfare and school systems, and some historical societies, organized around rules that apply directly to individuals and associations, would lack a basic structure altogether.

In what follows, I work with the first, wider sense of the term *basic structure*. In a way, this choice reflects no disagreement with Rawls, because it leaves undisputed his reasons for thinking that special mechanisms are needed to preserve a fair distribution of bargaining power among the participants in a social system. I also believe, how-

---

[16]Here a basic structure may allow for choices through which features of itself are changed.

[17]The notion of the basic structure, like many other important concepts, retains a certain vagueness, which it would be futile to try to remove completely. The notion may surely be significant and penetrating even without a sharp line between practices that are and those that are not part of the basic structure.

ever, that Rawls's narrowing of the notion was a strategic mistake, because he was thereby accepting the way Nozick wants to structure the contrast between their two approaches. What I have in mind can become clear only gradually, as I develop the contrast in a way that differs from Nozick's and Rawls's presentations. But one quick way of sketching my worry is this: On the narrow understanding of the term, Rawls's enterprise—to develop a conception of justice that provides a criterion for the moral assessment of alternative basic structures— either begs the question by assuming that social systems *ought* to have a basic structure or has nothing to say about social systems that lack a basic structure. The latter, more charitable verdict would render Rawls's approach parochial, as he himself seems to concede when he suggests that (only?) when we opt for a social-contract doctrine and (only?) "once we think of the parties to a social contract as free and equal (and rational) moral persons [are there] strong reasons for taking the basic structure as the primary subject" (BSS 48). "The libertarian doctrine . . . has no place for a special theory of justice for the basic structure" (BSS 52). This parochial character of Rawls's approach is close to what Nozick is suggesting. The construct of the original position at best provides a suitable standpoint for ranking institutional schemes that are organized in accordance with (what Nozick calls) *patterned* principles. It is unsuitable for a fair assessment of the libertarian institutions Nozick favors (ASU 198–204).

On the wide notion of basic structure which I am presupposing, *any* comprehensive social system has a basic structure and thus falls within the purview of Rawls's conception of justice.[18] The basic structure of Nozick's minimal state, for example, consists of certain prohibitions against force and fraud, certain rules of acquisition, transfer, and rectification of holdings, and some basic mechanisms of adjudication and enforcement.[19] Rawls and Nozick can then be seen to be operating

---

[18]This wide notion is not fully displaced in Rawls's later work. It still appears, for example, at BSS 55, where he varies the expression with "institutional form" and "social structure," suggesting that every social system has such a core of basic institutions.

[19]Nozick discusses some other basic structures in which the same rules and prohibitions are combined with different methods of adjudication and enforcement—involving an *ultra*minimal government, protection agencies, and individuals (respectively). As we shall see, Rawls's conception of justice is applicable even to the last of these. Nozick's state of nature can be understood as a basic structure, provided the rules and practices he postulates for it are sufficiently known and honored to enable reasonably settled expectations about how persons will interact. Thus it is false, I think, that "anarchist theory, if tenable, undercuts the whole subject of political philosophy" (ASU 4)—at least if one allows that Rawls's question is in political philosophy. Anarchists oppose institutional schemes involving governmental authorities and coercion, but this is not opposition to institutions as such. In fact, anarchist theorists typically make detailed proposals of practices, procedures, rules, and norms that are to regulate and pervade the entire social system. These are anarchist basic structures (in my wide sense of this term). Nevertheless, some intercourse is clearly not regulated by shared institutions whose justice could be assessed (paradigmatically, the first contacts between two civilizations). Rawls contends that even in such contexts each person's conduct is morally constrained by certain natural duties (cf. Chap. 2, n. 17).

within the same arena of possibilities, offering competing approaches to the same subject, the justice of institutional schemes.[20]

1.5. Once this focus on a social system's basic structure has been fully understood, it has a strong claim to primacy within moral reflection quite apart from whether one believes in social contracts or free and equal moral personhood. The reason is that we cannot, conceptually or causally, evaluate what we are doing to others without understanding the structure of the ground rules that give meaning to our actions and omissions and determine their (often remote) repercussions. Nor can we simply take these ground rules for granted. To some extent the choice of ground rules, the way we structure human interaction, is up to us collectively, and the consequences of this choice are of the greatest moral significance. Confronted with the question of how one ought to conduct oneself within a social context, therefore, one cannot simply follow the prevailing social institutions but must examine these from a moral point of view. Where they are just, they should be complied with and supported. Where they are unjust, one should see how one might contribute to their reform and perhaps help mitigate some of their consequences. And where (just) institutions are lacking altogether, the task is to help bring them about.

This crucial contrast between two moral subjects, dealing respectively with institutions and with conduct, is not the contrast between macro- and microcontexts, though many have followed Nozick (ASU 167n, 204–5) in supposing otherwise. Understood generally, Rawls's criterion of justice is applicable, in the limit, to the design of ground rules regulating the cooperation of two persons stranded together on an isolated island or to the assessment of ground rules that may have emerged between them. If it is inapplicable to how parents should allocate resources to the education of their children, how teachers should grade their pupils, or how firms should remunerate their employees, the reason is not that these are small-scale issues but that they raise questions about conduct within institutions rather than about institutions themselves. Rawls's criterion is also inapplicable to the design and assessment of the institutional structure of associations (such as firms) and subsystems (such as national education systems), no matter how large these may be. This must be so on pain of inconsistency, as there is every reason to believe that the global criterion and the local criteria are not cosatisfiable. The entire self-contained social system can be organized so as to optimize the worst position it tends to generate, or each part of this social system might be organized so as to optimize the worst position within that part, but we cannot have it both ways, because the two requirements would in practice conflict with each other.

---

[20]Though *basic structure* is somewhat more restrictive than *institutional scheme* in regard to institutions included, this difference will not matter in what follows. I will generally prefer *institutional scheme*, because it is more descriptive and not peculiar to Rawls.

The crucial point, then, is that Rawls focuses on the fundamental "rules of the game" and not on what moves players are morally free or constrained to make within a particular game in progress. To stay with the metaphor for a moment, the question is not whether in an ongoing poker game those who have won a great deal shouldn't (be made to) give some of their winnings to those who have lost nearly all they had. The question is whether we ought not rather play some other game that does not, time and again, produce destitute losers. This question may seem silly in the context of games that persons can join and quit at will, but it is of considerable urgency in regard to the framework of basic social institutions, whose participants are born into it and shaped by it, cannot quit at will, and are subject to violent coercion when they try to ignore its rules.

1.6. The common misunderstanding of Rawls's project has various sources. Frequently his term *institution* is associated with a special kind of actor, such as a government or other authority.[21] This association is somewhat encouraged by his narrow use of the term *basic structure* in "The Basic Structure as Subject." The case of our simple island economy (or even that of the poker game) may help show how Rawls's question can arise even in very small-scale social systems whose relevant practices could quite conceivably work without any authorities or officials.

The misunderstanding is perhaps further encouraged by a reluctance to accept that social institutions or basic structures can exist (be quantified over) and can have moral properties. But I don't believe Rawls's approach, properly understood, has such implications. In developing a conception of justice (in his sense), one is not committed to thinking of social institutions as things that, like persons, are responsible for certain morally salient aspects of reality. (In fact, thinking this way invites the mistaken assumption that insofar as institutions are responsible, persons are not.) Rather, one can allow that talk about social institutions may be shorthand for (much more complex) talk about expectations and modes of interaction prevalent in some social system and, correspondingly, that a critique of some institution as unjust can be cashed out as a critique of conduct as wrong (namely, the conduct of those who inaugurated, perpetuate, or are in a position to reform the mode of interaction in question).

Even with such reducibility, the distinction between justice and morality is significant and fruitful. This may be overlooked if—perhaps led on by the fact that the adjectives *just* and *unjust* can also apply to (individual and collective) agents and their conduct—one conceives the reducibility simplistically, that is, thinks of institutional injustice as simply the aggregate of many homologous interpersonal "injustices"

---

[21]This misreading is unbelievably common. Even a close reader such as Sandel speaks of "the aims institutions pursue" (LLJ 75) and so on. See also Raz, MF 66–67, 101–4.

committed by (individual or collective) agents. I have already suggested how this view is misleading. The *social* injustice blacks have suffered as victims of the *institution* of slavery does not consist of a multitude of wrongs committed against them by their ("unjust") slaveholders. We cannot combat this injustice by stealing and protecting slaves or through attempts to reform slaveholders (perhaps by urging them to release their slaves or at least to give them better treatment). We must reform *institutions*. Only when the relevant legal and political system ceases to recognize property rights in persons is the social injustice overcome. Likewise, when Rawls claims that economic inequalities prevailing in developed Western societies are unjust (TJ 226, 279), he is not envisaging that—thanks to a change of heart among the rich or to interventions by third parties—wealth is to be transferred or redistributed to the poor. Rather, the point is to change the economic institutions that govern the distribution of resources (and give rise to excessive inequalities) in the first place.

Correspondingly, the responsibility for such unjust institutions and the task of reforming them are not confined to slaveholders or to the rich but rather fall upon all participants in the social system (though perhaps in proportion to the benefits and advantages they enjoy under the unjust scheme and surely in proportion to the opportunities they have of supporting institutional reform). Spelled out in this way, the focus on a social system's basic institutions represents a way of addressing (and thus assumes) a special type of moral responsibility, the joint responsibility that the participants in an institutional scheme have for its justice.

Now one might think that, so understood, the subject of justice will largely preempt the subject of morality. Once the ground rules are given, individuals and groups ought simply to abide by them, at least so long as these ground rules are just; it is only when ground rules are unjust, or partly lacking, that morality comes into play. But this view, somewhat encouraged by Rawls's earlier baseball analogy (TCR), is a substantial overstatement. Even when a just and complete scheme of ground rules exists, it does not supersede morality. Institutional ground rules principally govern external conduct (generating duties of justice in Kant's sense)[22] and thus largely leave aside our inner lives. Morality (or ethics) addresses questions of character, maxims, virtues, intentions, sentiments, and the like, which would be important even (or rather, especially) in a perfectly just world. Next, a just institutional scheme provides only a general framework for interaction. Morality is relevant to how we act within the considerable leeway left by such a framework. Not everything the ground rules permit is of equal moral quality. Finally, morality supplies independent reasons for action which may conflict with just ground rules in special cases. Even par-

[22]See Kant, KPW 132–33.

ticipants in a (nearly) just institutional scheme may in special circumstances have moral reasons not to comply with particular obligations that properly arose within it (cf. §9.5).[23]

2. The Relevance of Patterns

2.1. Let us begin the discussion of possible criteria for assessing feasible basic structures by asking what relevance patterns might have for our subject. This inquiry should further illuminate our distinction between two types of moral assessment, as well as the character of Rawls's project and of Nozick's misunderstanding of it.

With an eye to economic institutions especially, Nozick postulates a fundamental division between *patterned* and *unpatterned* principles of distributive justice (ASU 155–60). He favors unpatterned principles, which specify procedures through which holdings can be acquired (initially or from others) and then, so to speak, let the chips fall where they may. Patterned principles, by contrast, involve the idea that some distributions of income or wealth are better than others—for example, that holdings (at any moment or over time) should be roughly equal, should reflect how hard people work, or should be above a certain threshold. Nozick opposes patterned principles, because they require meddling in consensual economic interactions ("between consenting adults") whenever these interactions would otherwise upset the favored pattern. They lead to "head-on clashes . . . [with] moral side constraints on how individuals may be treated" (ASU 173; cf. the tale of Wilt Chamberlain, ASU 161–64). And he sees Rawls as prepossessed in favor of patterned principles, "for people meeting together behind a veil of ignorance to decide who gets what, knowing nothing about any special entitlements people may have, will treat anything to be distributed as manna from heaven" (ASU 199; but cf. TJ 88).

The mistake here is that the parties in the original position are to decide *not* who gets what but rather which criterion will govern the choice of economic institutions that regulate who gets what. According to Rawls, such a criterion should be sensitive to what sorts of patterns various alternative economic schemes tend to generate. Nozick fails to appreciate that any pattern preference might be deemed relevant in two different ways. One might propose its incorporation into the ground rules, as a requirement upon the participants (officials) to work for improvements in the prevailing distribution of holdings by adjusting their own economic activities and by interfering with those of

---

[23]For examples of how such intrapersonal conflicts may arise even in a basically just society, see Feinberg, RI 120–24. Rawls once had the ambition of extending his contractarian conception "to the choice of more or less an entire ethical system . . . including principles for all the virtues" (TJ 17, cf. 109, 130; BSS II), to be titled "rightness as fairness" (TJ 17, 111).

others. Such a proposal conflicts with the particular ground rules Nozick advocates and more generally with the idea that economic ground rules should be procedural. Alternatively, the pattern preference may be brought to bear upon the assessment (and design) of ground rules. What is proposed in this case is that we be guided in ranking institutional schemes by the pattern of holdings each tends to produce. Such a proposal does not conflict with the idea of procedural ground rules. Whether it supports the particular ground rules Nozick advocates depends on what pattern preference is proposed and on empirical data about the patterns of holdings that various alternative institutional schemes (Nozick's included) tend to generate.

Rawls's difference principle might indeed be described as "patterned." It does involve the idea that some patterns are better than others. But it is a pattern preference in the second sense. Rawls employs it as a criterion for the assessment (and design) of ground rules. He does not want it to be incorporated into the content of those rules themselves. In fact, like Nozick, he wants the economic ground rules to be procedural. If they are just, that is, tend to generate a better pattern of holdings than any feasible alternative institutions would, then there is no need for official interference and participants need not worry about the impact of their economic activities upon the overall pattern of income and wealth (cf. TJ 87–88; BSS 54). So the difference principle does not select a pattern as such; it selects an institutional scheme on the basis of the pattern it tends to produce. Hence fluctuations in the pattern a just economic scheme generates are not reasons for interfering (through redistributions) with the workings of this scheme.

Moreover, in making this selection, the difference principle functions rather differently from the other "patterned" principles that Nozick lumps together with it. From examining an economic scheme with the pattern of holdings it tends to produce, one can tell how close it comes to equality or to holdings being proportional to IQ or moral worth. Yet one cannot tell whether it satisfies the difference principle or even whether it does well or poorly. This assessment essentially depends upon what other schemes are feasible and what patterns they would tend to generate. What economic scheme is preferred and what sort of pattern the preferred scheme tends to produce depend upon the full range of feasible institutional alternatives. This point underscores the conclusion of the previous paragraph: Rawls is not committed to some pattern. He seeks to be committed, like Nozick, to a particular institutional scheme and to the acceptance of whatever particular distributions this scheme may generate over time. But he wants to base this commitment upon an examination of the patterns that various alternative schemes tend to produce. He holds that institutions should be assessed or chosen *via* their patterns.

2.2. If we assess social institutions via the patterns they tend to produce, we must ultimately compare entire basic structures, because the best way of setting one parameter of the basic structure may not be independent of how its other parameters will have been set. The value of certain rights a person has under one institution, for example, may depend on whether he has certain other rights conferred by another. It would also be implausible, in comparing alternative schemes, to proceed piecemeal through the various kinds of goods whose distribution is presumed to matter. If two goods—income and wealth, for example—are unequally distributed, it will often be relevant whether the same participants are disadvantaged under both distributions. While there is plenty of room for abstractions and simplifications of various kinds, the ultimate idea must then be to compare entire basic structures by reference to the *master pattern* each tends to produce. Here a master pattern contains information about the overall value some institutional scheme has for each of its participants.

2.3. That institutional schemes can engender patterns is an idea Nozick himself appeals to in the context of his discussion of invisible-hand explanations, which explain "some overall pattern or design" as the unintended result of the uncoordinated activities of persons coexisting within a certain environment (ASU 18). Let me show how the idea of patterned principles in Rawls's sense can be presented as an extension of this point of Nozick's.

A homicide rate is a simple example of a pattern that emerges as the by-product of the uncoordinated activities of many individuals. It is not intended or brought about by anyone. Such rates and the way they vary from country to country cannot be explained by reference to the motives and beliefs of individual agents, though these are crucial to the explanation of particular homicides. The social phenomenon of homicide calls then for explanation on two distinct levels: for *macro*explanations of its rates of incidence and for *micro*explanations of particular instances. Neither type of explanation can fully preempt the other. Individuals' motives cannot account for statistical patterns, and the explanation of a statistical pattern does not account for why the phenomenon was manifested in *these* instances rather than in others.[24]

Now suppose, for the sake of the argument, it became known that strictness of handgun legislation is one main factor in the true macroexplanation of homicide. (Assume it explains some sizable part of national differentials in homicide rates, and don't worry about whether such legislation is important enough to be part of the basic structure.) It would then be true that *if* we have moral reason to prefer a lower over a higher homicide rate, then we have moral reason to support stricter

---

[24]Nozick offers this refutation of methodological individualism: "If there is a filter that filters out (destroys) all non-P Q's, then the explanation of why all Q's are P's (fit the pattern P) will refer to this filter. For each particular Q, there may be a particular explanation why *it* is P, how it came to be P, what maintains it as P. But the explanation of why all Q's are P will not be the conjunction of these individual explanations, even though these are all the Q's there are, for that is part of what is to be explained" (ASU 22).

rather than laxer handgun legislation. Once we come to understand what rough patterns various alternative sets of rules would engender, we can bring our moral valuations of these patterns to bear upon our moral assessment of alternative sets of rules. For example, we can use our new knowledge to construct a moral critique of existing handgun legislation. Such a critique would be dependent upon a particular macroexplanation of the homicide rate (involving reference to institutional factors), just as the condemnation of a particular killing is dependent upon a particular microexplanation (involving the killer's actions and intentions). Nozick's own distinction between micro- and macroexplanations can then serve as a bridge. It can facilitate appreciation of the parallel distinction between two subjects of moral reflection: institutional schemes, which can be more or less just or unjust, and conduct, which may be right or wrong in degrees. And it can make clear how patterns may play a valid role in the *former* type of assessments.

Let me add two clarifications. First, these two types of assessment, just like Nozick's two types of explanation, do not preempt each other. Faulting institutional factors for a high murder rate need not at all exonerate the criminals, nor is denouncing all murders and murderers tantamount to condoning laxity of gun control.[25] And faulting institutional factors can again be taken as shorthand for ascribing a responsibility that all citizens share. Even though each and every murderer is fully accountable for his act, the citizens in a democracy may also bear an additional collective responsibility for some fraction of all homicides if these are attributable to the lack of adequate handgun legislation, for example, or to an unjust distribution of police protection.[26]

Second, I have so far merely tried to show *how*, in a Rawlsian view, the moral valuation of patterns enters—via information about what patterns alternative institutional schemes tend to engender—into the moral debate about the assessment of such schemes. It is a separate question whether such considerations, once they have entered, will be weighty enough to affect our assessments—that is, in the case at hand, whether they can overturn the belief in a person's right to own firearms or in a majority's right to set risk levels for the population at large.

2.4. Let us extend these thoughts to economic issues, to which Nozick's distinction between patterned and unpatterned principles is chiefly addressed. I begin by sketching an argument that could have motivated the supporters of the New Deal. Suppose they believed that (1) there is moral reason to prefer a pattern of holdings with less rather

[25]Nozick explicitly accepts the related point that two persons can each be fully responsible for a single murder (ASU 130).

[26]Here and in the sequel I assume that it would be objectively wrong not to do what one can easily do toward the reform of unjust features of an institutional scheme for which one shares a collective responsibility. I do not mean, however, to prejudge the question whether and to what extent one is blameworthy for not being aware of this responsibility or for being aware but ignoring it. These issues I leave aside because they would lead us too far beyond my main topic: the moral assessment of social institutions.

than more severe poverty and also (2) there are feasible alternative economic schemes (besides the laissez-faire scheme prevailing in the 1920s) that would tend to engender less severe poverty. Assume such New Dealers further believed that the moral reason resulting from (1) and (2) is not neutralized by other moral reasons favoring the existing scheme over alternatives engendering less severe poverty. They would then conclude that the prevailing scheme is unjust against the background of superior alternatives. What does this conclusion mean for individuals? In particular, does it entail that the poor have a right to a certain minimum income, with corresponding obligations on the part of others?

Asserting such a right in this context could be triply misleading. First, as a matter of terminology, rights are best specified by reference to an institutional scheme. Under the scheme prevailing in the 1920s no right to a minimum income existed. Second, the formulation may suggest that under a just alternative scheme persons would have a right to a certain minimum income. But this need not be so. The just scheme would be one that, somehow or other, tends to engender less severe poverty. It may not include the right in question if—however unlikely under modern conditions—this right is infeasible or if there are more effective alternatives for preventing severe poverty. Is the point, then, that the poor have a *moral* right to a certain minimal income? In a sense, yes. But third, the "right to" formulation suggests that what is at issue is a positive moral right that would give the poor a claim, against all of humankind, to be helped in their need. But no such claim is at issue. I appeal to a *negative* moral right, a claim the poor had against American citizens, specifically, who were collaborating in the imposition of an unjust economic scheme that tended to produce more severe poverty than is morally justifiable. To be sure, Americans presumably had to *do* something ("positive") toward institutional reform in order to avoid violation of the negative moral right in question. But in the context of practices, it does not follow that their duty to act is therefore a positive one. The negative duty not to abuse just practices may demand positive action, as when one must act to keep a promise or contract one has made. Similarly, the negative duty not to collaborate in the imposition of unjust institutions may also demand positive actions (with the sometimes possible alternative of withdrawing altogether from participation in the unjust scheme).[27]

All this suggests how our Rawlsian can begin to support the alternative specification of landownership rights against Nozick's. I left their

[27]While his conception of justice, I think, strongly suggests it, Rawls does not acknowledge such a negative right and duty but merely speaks of a natural duty to uphold and to promote just institutions (TJ 115, 334), which he classifies as *positive* (TJ 109). This leaves him unable to explain why one's responsibility for the injustices of a social system is greater when one is a participant in that system. This difference *is* explained by the negative duty I postulate, together with the ordinary view that "negative duties have more weight than positive ones" (TJ 114).

dispute in a standoff, showing how neither protagonist could reasonably take his specification of property rights for granted and then accuse the opponent of advocating a scheme under which the correct property rights would be routinely violated. We now have a consideration that might break the standoff. As Nozick understands, his set of rules would engender a certain rough pattern of holdings, reasonably stable over time: "Heavy strands of patterns will run through it; significant portions of the variance in holdings will be accounted for by pattern-variables" (ASU 157). Now it is quite possible that under his libertarian ground rules our island economy would tend to be dominated by two or three large family estates where the remaining landless population would spend their lives as laborers or serfs.[28] The Rawlsian's scheme, by contrast, would keep land widely distributed and would thus ensure that those who do end up landless can at least choose among many competing employers and sellers of agricultural produce. In short, the available evidence from history and social theory may suggest that Nozick's scheme would have feudalistic features and that the Rawlsian's scheme would tend to engender a competitive market economy in which the worst positions, especially, would be much superior to that of serf.

2.5. I have said that Rawls's topic—moral reflection upon basic institutions—is crucial for gaining a moral orientation, for understanding what we are doing to others. Social institutions play a large role in determining both the meaning and the effects of our conduct. The considerations of the last few pages bring out two further reasons why this topic is so important.

First, institutions are a central factor in determining the conditions prevailing in some social system. This is easily appreciated through comparative studies of national societies that differ in social institutions (for example, form of government, legal system, organization of military and police forces, educational facilities, system of land tenure, specification of property rights, or tax structure). Such institutional factors condition the conduct of the various actors—citizens, officials, associations, and governments—by shaping their values and options and by fixing their "pay-off matrix," that is, the schedule of incentives and disincentives they confront. In this way they determine (in a rough statistical way) morally significant aggregate features of the social system, such as the level and distribution of basic freedoms, opportunities, political influence, health care, education, work satisfaction, self-respect, culture, poverty, crime, life expectancy, infant mortality, child abuse, suicide, and so forth. The pattern so engendered already reflects the fact that some persons try, within their means, to help alleviate conditions they consider objectionable. While such efforts may certainly make a great difference, it does not seem reasonable or realistic

[28]Compare here Nozick's endorsement of "private towns" (ASU 270n, cf. 322–23).

to expect that they could multiply to the point where they would fully offset strong countervailing tendencies endemic to an institutional scheme. In any case, one should explore the alternative strategy that goes beyond such remedial transactions demanded or encouraged by morality, aiming for a new institutional scheme that would tend to engender a more acceptable pattern (and thus would reduce the need for remedial transactions). Such attempts at institutional change would seem to hold out the greatest hope that our combined moral efforts will accumulate into lasting progress. Concentrating exclusively on private attempts to improve a prevailing pattern, one can at best hope that continuing efforts will maintain the social system somewhat above its equilibrium point (where it would be if everyone acted self-interest-edly). By contrast, institutional change, as exemplified by the abolition of slavery or by the New Deal, can move this equilibrium point itself, thereby also bringing further institutional reforms within reach. Moral efforts are likely to be of enduring historical significance only when they can become cumulative in this way.

This first new reason may suggest that institutional reform is being recommended for its effectiveness alone, that it is merely a different (and better) way of doing something moral by making the world a little better. But this conclusion misses a crucial point concerning the *ground* of the duty to take an interest in institutional matters. An argument founded on morality would seek to show that persons in general have positive claims against one another—for example, to be rescued, fed, or defended. Such an argument would go against the grain of the Anglo-American moral and legal tradition, in which it is often denied that persons have duties to protect and aid other persons in distress: it's a good thing to help those who might otherwise drown or starve or be murdered, but it isn't very wrong not to, especially if the trouble, expense, or risks involved aren't negligible. I am not challenging this view here. The moral responsibility I am speaking of is founded on *justice* and involves persons' *negative* claim not to be made victims of unjust institutions.

This thought indicates the second new reason for the importance of Rawls's topic, that (advantaged) participants in an institutional scheme share a responsibility for the justice of the scheme. If the scheme is unjust, one may be implicated with others in a collective wrong whose victims have unjust institutions imposed upon them. Since, as a moral person, one wants to avoid being involved in such wrongs, one has reason to reflect upon the justice of social institutions.

Such reflection is especially needful because injustices may not be obvious. The connection of excessive deprivations and disadvantages to the institutional scheme producing them may be opaque. The injustice of an institutional scheme tends to be most manifest when the radical inequalities it produces are clearly "on the books," are, for example, explicitly incorporated into the legal code. The injustice tends to be least obvious when the radical inequalities it produces are neither explicitly nor even implicitly called for by the prevailing ground rules but have merely, as an empirical matter, come about pursuant to them.

Thus the injustice of the institution of slavery (as it existed in the United States) is comparatively obvious. Not only were some forced to live in a highly dehumanizing condition, but this condition of slavery was "official," explicitly incorporated into the American political and legal system (in voting rights, fugitive slave laws, and so forth). Because of its distinctly institutional or systemic character, it is also especially evident that the moral problem concerned not slaveholders alone but even those American citizens who neither owned slaves nor benefited from slavery. These were not unconcerned bystanders, as their Swedish contemporaries may have been—merely aware of enslavement and in a position to do at least a little bit about it. Rather, they shared a responsibility for the injustice; they had a *negative* duty to stop cooperating in its imposition, for example, by helping to end slavery through institutional reforms.[29]

The other end of this spectrum can be exemplified, once again, by the laissez-faire institutions preceding the New Deal. Suppose these engendered severe disadvantages—in terms of nutrition, education, health care, etc.—for those born into the lower classes, whose plight was the systematic correlate of an unconstrained market scheme in which the income of many households was determined solely by the vagaries of supply and demand for the kinds of labor their members could sell. Unlike slavery, this scheme did not (explicitly or implicitly) call for excessive deprivations and disadvantages. Yet it did in fact consistently engender them. It is on the basis of this fact, and against the background of at least one accessible alternative scheme that would not tend to produce similarly radical inequalities, that one can reject the relevant economic scheme as unjust and conclude that many persons at the time were impoverished (rather than merely poor), were starved (rather than merely starving). And this conclusion in turn supports the judgment that the advantaged participants in this scheme, insofar as they perpetuated it (or even resisted its reform), shared a responsibility for its injustice. They had a *negative* duty not to collaborate in the imposition of unjust institutions, which in practical terms means that they ought to have planned and promoted institutional reform.

It is possible that in our complex and functionally highly differenti-

[29]In such clear cases it is also most obvious that reforms cannot be blocked by the argument that a liberation of slaves would violate the entitlements of their present owners and is therefore excluded by moral side constraints. Perhaps entitlements that arose pursuant to legally valid but unjust rules should not be simply disregarded. The unjust rules were not uniquely the slaveholders' responsibility, and so there may be reasons why citizens at large should compensate slaveholders for their loss. There is no reason, however, why the slaveholders should have the option to retain their slaves in preference to appropriate compensation. No one can have a claim that unjust institutions should exist or continue, and the slaves (and their progeny) have a continuing negative claim not to be forced to endure unjust conditions.

ated world, injustices of this sort are quite prominent, especially if I am right (in Part Three) to extend the Rawlsian project to the *global* basic structure. It is not easy to convince oneself that our current global order, assessed from a Rawlsian perspective, is moderately just despite the widespread and extreme deprivations and disadvantages it engenders. Even if we limit our vision to our own advanced Western society, it is hardly obvious that the basic institutions we participate in are just or nearly just. In any case, a somewhat unobvious but massive threat to the moral quality of our lives is the danger that we will have lived as advantaged participants in unjust institutions, collaborating in their perpetuation and benefiting from their injustice.[30]

3. The Consequentialism of Rawls's Conception of Justice

3.1. If his ground rules did really tend to engender a degenerate form of feudalism, Nozick might well regret it. But he would not reconsider his commitment to libertarian ground rules. Why not? We have seen that Nozick's insistence on (property) rights conceived as side constraints, with the correlative rejection of redistributive interferences, cannot be a good reason, because Nozick's antifeudalist preference can still be relevant to the question of what rights (or institutions generally) there should be in the first place. When brought to bear upon *this* question, the pattern preference *cannot* collide with property rights, for the choice of a scheme of such rights is still at issue. Can we attribute to Nozick another rationale that would explain his indifference to the kind of empirical argument our Rawlsian proposes?

At times Nozick seems quite unwilling to entertain any deeper rationale or justification for his view, insisting instead that "historical-entitlement principles are fundamental" (ASU 202). The suggestion is that it is not good enough for Rawls's criterion to favor procedural ground rules (such as a specification of property rights as historically recursive). The problem Nozick sees is that Rawls would have derived these ground rules from higher-level considerations: "Rawls' construction will yield approximations of [the precisely correct principles] at best; *it will produce the wrong sorts of reasons for them*" (ASU 202, my emphasis, cf. 203–4, 215). But what is Nozick's alternative? Are we to take it as just plain obvious that the rights *he* proposes express "the precisely correct principles"? And what if some alternative specification of rights (perhaps that of our Rawlsian) is recommended as obvious as well? The debate might become rather dull.

But perhaps Rawls and Nozick are not so far apart. Rawls, too,

---

[30]This sentence, I realize, goes against everyone's favorite moral conviction, namely, that there is nothing seriously wrong, morally speaking, with the lives we lead. I assume this conviction is not self-verifying, can be subjected to rational examination, and may well be untenable. Still, I don't pretend that the considerations adduced so far are sufficient to undermine it.

believes that we have certain moral fixed points, on all levels of generality, which any conception of justice must by and large accommodate. Thus, although all rights must be derivable from the relevant higher-level considerations (those reflected in the original position), the failure of such a derivation would in many cases be more likely to make us doubtful about Rawls's construct of the original position than about the right in question. So Rawls would agree that some rights are fundamental in the sense that we would reject any conception of justice that did not—under modern conditions anyway—firmly entail these rights. But he would not, of course, agree that Nozick's favorite property rights are fundamental.

Nozick, too, could provide some rationale for his account of rights, or so I suggest. Just as Rawls agrees with Nozick that ground rules should be procedural, Nozick can agree with Rawls that the endorsement of a particular set of ground rules can be justified, or at least motivated, by appeal to a (master-)pattern preference. In one sense this point is trivial. Nozick can say that he prefers the institutional scheme under which certain rights and liberties are distributed in exactly the way provided for by the ground rules he favors. What I am suggesting, however, is a more interesting scenario in which Nozick would offer an independent notion of personal freedom, for example, and would then proceed to argue that the ground rules he favors would produce an optimal distribution of personal freedom so conceived. This scenario might then get some debate going by putting Nozick into conflict with Rawls over what considerations should be deemed relevant, and *how* relevant, to the moral assessment of alternative basic structures. Nozick would accept the invitation to justify his favored ground rules through a "patterned" criterion of distributive justice that involves what I earlier called a systematic balancing of values. For present purposes, we can analyze each such patterned criterion by asking three main questions about it:

Who is a participant, a unit of moral concern, or where should we look for information?

What goods and ills are morally significant and what is their comparative significance, or what information must we look for and how does this information determine a participant's position (intrapersonal balancing/aggregation)?

How should one rank the distributions of positions that alternative institutional schemes might generate among their participants (interpersonal balancing/aggregation)?

Answers to the first two questions determine what information is needed for the comparative assessment of institutional schemes. Answers to the last two questions determine how that information is to be evaluated so as to arrive at this assessment. Taken together, the three answers constitute a pattern preference.

3.2. Let us try to locate Nozick's view and its contrast to Rawls within the framework of this analysis. It is clear, I think, that they do not seriously differ in respect to the who-question. Nozick is somewhat more open to the claims of animals (ASU 35–42), but in essence they share the commitment to humanism and individualism. For both of them, the appropriate units of moral concern are individual human persons.

We can also say, at least within the framework of this analysis, that it is not helpful to characterize the dispute between Rawls and Nozick as being centrally about the relative moral importance of freedom and equality. Freedom and equality figure in the answers to different questions—what and how, respectively—and therefore do not compete. Yes, Nozick is willing to tolerate even extreme inequalities in holdings, when these are produced by his libertarian ground rules. But this is not, I think, because he cares so little about equality, but because he does not view holdings as a significant aspect of that personal freedom whose distribution matters for the design of an institutional scheme. With regard to the aspects of individual freedom he does recognize, Nozick is, as we will see, at least as egalitarian as Rawls. And Rawls, for his part, is no less committed to freedom than Nozick is. Not only does he give lexical priority to certain basic liberties; he even wants to formulate his second principle of justice so that both principles together are tantamount to the requirement "to maximize the worth to the least advantaged of the complete scheme of equal liberty shared by all" (TJ 205; cf. BSS 41).

The substantive divergence between Rawls and Nozick must then concern the what-question, reflecting differences about the meaning of personal freedom and the relative moral significance of various aspects thereof. Here I see as the crucial difference their conflicting views about the moral relevance of the distinction between established and engendered pattern features. By *engendered* pattern features I mean ones that, like income differentials in a free-market system, are not directly called for in the relevant rules and procedures but merely foreseeably come about through them. They are a subset of the larger class of social phenomena an institutional scheme engenders (this class may also include its birth rate, homicide rate, degree of political apathy, and so on). In assigning causal responsibility for such phenomena to (particular) social institutions one will often have to rely on complex and somewhat speculative empirical generalizations, which must also deal with such background factors as culture and natural environment. Goods and ills are *established* when they are directly called for in the (written or unwritten) rules and procedures of the social system, even if they are not specifically assigned to particular persons or natural classes of persons. Legal exclusion of the poorest 20 percent from political participation is an established inequality. By contrast, the same differential in rights to political participation counts as engendered if the minimum-income requirement is defined so that it is in principle possible that all should meet it.[31] By establishing certain disadvantages, a basic structure may engender further burdens, as when gender-sensitive inheritance laws have resulted in an inferior economic position for women.

Nozick gives considerable moral significance to this distinction. I take him to hold that in designing an ideal institutional scheme,[32] we should be primarily or even exclusively concerned with the distribution of established goods and ills and, more particularly, with the distribution of established freedom. We need not be concerned (or we need be much less concerned) with the distribution of engendered goods and ills. There is a great difference, morally, between a scheme under which some are assigned inferior property rights and a scheme under which some come to have inferior property rights pursuant to procedural ground rules that do not call for this inequality.

Rawls, by contrast, maintains that we should assess feasible schemes of economic institutions in light of the overall patterns each would tend to generate (and should design an economic scheme accordingly). Economic ground rules and entire basic structures are to be judged by their effects. But not by their effects alone. To some extent morally significant goods and ills are directly called for by prevailing institutions, are part of the scheme rather than effects of it. Rawls takes benefits and burdens of both kinds to be on a par. It makes no difference to the assessment of an institutional scheme whether given deprivations forseeably existing under it are established or engendered. Either way, their incidence would be, in a broad sense, a consequence of (the choice of) a particular institutional scheme. Let us call a criterion of justice *broadly consequentialist* if and only if it assesses institutional schemes exclusively on the basis of their consequences, broadly conceived, that is, if it takes equal account of goods and ills established and of equivalent goods and ills engendered by such schemes.[33]

Such a broadly consequentialist approach involves two subsidiary topics. One must settle on specific goods and ills whose distribution is

---

[31]Admittedly, there are borderline cases, as when those earning less than the mean income are excluded. It is just barely possible that all have the same income, and so the exclusion might (implausibly) seem to count as engendered. Despite such problematic possibilities, I hope the distinction is clear enough in realistic scenarios and for the role it will play in what follows.

[32]In contrast to Rawls, Nozick shows little interest in how to rank institutional schemes that are less than just by his standards. I assume he would say that in assessing such a scheme we must normally be much more sensitive to the restrictions on freedom it calls for than to restrictions on freedom it effects.

[33]The justice of an institutional scheme is, in Sen's phrase, "given by the goodness of its consequent states of affairs" (WAF 175). Calling Rawls's conception broadly consequentialist is somewhat at odds with current usage in philosophy, which, strongly influenced by Rawls himself, would encourage us to characterize Rawls's conception as deontological. My attempt at revision is motivated by the idea, to be developed later in this section, that we should reserve the terms *deontological* and *consequentialist* for a deeper and more important distinction than the one Rawls emphasizes.

to be incorporated into the Master Pattern[34] and on a way of weighting and aggregating information about such goods and ills (for purposes of ranking particular institutional schemes via their master patterns). And there needs to be a broadly empirical inquiry, involving social theory and comparative historical investigations, aimed at estimating what master patterns various feasible basic structures would tend to produce.

3.3. Calling Rawls a consequentialist requires clarification of his relation to utilitarian conceptions of justice which he so forcefully attacks.

3.3.1. This task can conveniently be begun by examining how his contractarian conception in *A Theory of Justice* differs from the utilitarian view he had sketched earlier.[35] This essay employs our division of subjects in a somewhat different way. Rawls envisions a social system whose institutions are to be justified on utilitarian grounds but whose participants are to comply with these (optimal) practices irrespective of utilitarian considerations. Let me discuss a central weakness in Rawls's earlier indirect utilitarianism and how it is overcome in his later conception.

3.3.1.1. A utilitarian assessment of social practices poses the notorious problem of explaining why an actor, and officials in particular, should feel constrained to honor a rule of a practice even though violating it *in this case* would clearly be better in terms of aggregate utility. Yes, the going practice is the best possible one, and it would be worse if actors in general had such discretion, but if only utility ultimately matters, why should one not maximize utility just this once? Further utilitarian considerations will not help, nor does it seem possible to resolve the substantive problem by appeal to the meaning of concepts ("rule," "practice," "authority," etc.).[36] What one would have to claim is that utility is somehow an inappropriate value to appeal to in justifying one's conduct in such a case. This claim raises new questions: what other values are relevant, and why aren't they relevant also to the assessment of practices? But the central problem is to explain how utility can simultaneously be valuable (so that in designing practices we should be guided by it) and not valuable (so that we should ignore it in decisions about compliance with a practice).

3.3.1.2. This problem could be solved if a suitable substitute were provided for utility as the value upon which the assessment of social institutions is to turn. What is valuable about the provisions and effects

---

[34]"Master Pattern" is capitalized here to indicate that I am talking about the *schema* of variables provided by a criterion of justice rather than about the concrete master patterns that particular institutional schemes tend to produce and via which they are assessed by this criterion.

[35]In TCR. Rawls may not actually have *held* that utilitarian view when he wrote this essay (cf. TCR 176).

[36]See Lyons, UR 126–30. Rawls clearly saw the problem but apparently believed he had solved it (TCR 191 n. 25). For a recent "solution," see Johnson, AMA.

of an institutional scheme should be defined in such a way that individuals *cannot* affect it (except, of course, through their role in institutional change). This, I think, is the idea of the later Rawls. He attempts to define his Master Pattern (via which basic structures are to be assessed) in terms of features that persons cannot affect by their conduct within the practices of an ongoing social system. Personal efforts, though they can mitigate (or aggravate) the *effects* of injustice, cannot reduce (or increase) the injustice itself, cannot alter the fact that some institutional scheme unjustly fails to establish certain rights or tends to engender certain inequalities.

3.3.1.3. This strategy is strengthened by conceiving the Master Pattern so that perfection is possible. Under a utilitarian criterion, the best basic structure will be the one that tends to produce the most utility. But even this optimal structure still leaves indefinite room for further improvement; there is no limit to how much utility there might be. Even under perfectly just institutions, the question can therefore arise whether one should violate the ground rules for the sake of a net increase in utility. In Rawls's later conception, by contrast, the values underlying the assessment of basic structures can be invoked to justify violating the rules of existing institutions only when such violation comes in response to some injustice.

Suppose, for example, that the institution of slavery in some social system is unjust because the position of slaves is much worse than any position must unavoidably be (modulo the prevailing natural environment and level of economic development). Suppose that, under such conditions, a citizen were to help a slave escape from her master. Such an action would not make the structure of the slaveholding society any more just (even the escapee is still legally unfree, may be recaptured, etc.), but it may still be justifiable to break the rules in this way so as to shield one slave from unjustifiable harms she would otherwise suffer. So far, Rawls's later conception agrees with his earlier one. It differs in that, when the existing basic structure is fully justifiable (in that the worst position it tends to produce is superior to the worst positions feasible alternative schemes would tend to produce), then there are no unjustifiable burdens of the relevant kind to shield others from. The values underlying Rawls's criterion of justice are fully accommodated, "exhausted," cannot (logically) be satisfied to an even greater degree, and hence cannot justify any violation of the institutions that they also justify.[37] Rawls's later criterion of justice is *satiable*.[38] This quality is often overlooked; readers take this criterion (and especially the differ-

---

[37]It may still be a morally good thing, of course, to help those worse off than oneself. But this assessment now involves a *separate* value—enshrined, perhaps, in a principle of morality—which can plausibly be subordinated to the values in terms of which the basic structure is justified (so that the concern to help others is an insufficient reason for violating the terms of just practices). Moral reasons based on utility, by contrast, cannot be so subordinated; all that can matter are the quantities involved.

[38]The term *satiable* is borrowed from Raz (MF 235–44).

ence principle) to require that the least advantaged should be as well-off as possible. This reading is mistaken. Only *the basic structure inso-far as it generates inequalities* is required to optimize the position of those least advantaged by those inequalities (cf. §§14.1, 14.3).

3.3.1.4. Through these revisions Rawls arrives at values for the assessment of institutions that cannot come into conflict with themselves in the way the earlier value of utility could. This is the first step toward realizing an aim that, I believe, Rawls had earlier failed to achieve, namely, to sketch an *overall* moral conception that is (in what for Rawls is the most important sense of this word) *deontological*. Just institutions confer rights that give persons "an inviolability founded on justice that even the welfare of society as a whole cannot override" (TJ 3). In his second attempt Rawls has succeeded in taking a broadly consequentialist approach to the choice of social institutions (and natural duties) that is compatible with a strictly deontological assessment of actors participating in these institutions (bound by these natural duties). The entire conception is a successful version of *indirect* consequentialism—successful in that the broadly consequentialist justification of the ground rules does not corrupt the strictly deontological status these ground rules are to have for (individual and collective) actors. Hence nothing is lost if this justification is fully public. The willingness of actors to give precedence to the institutional ground rules over the pursuit of any social or individual goals is sustained rather than subverted by their full understanding of the deeper consequentialist considerations that unify and support those ground rules.

3.3.2. There are two further important departures from his earlier view—these explicitly emphasized in *A Theory of Justice*—that move his criterion of justice itself in a recognizably deontological direction. Rawls defines a deontological (or non-teleological) conception as one "that either does not specify the good independently from the right, or does not interpret the right as maximizing the good. . . . Justice as fairness is a deontological theory in the second way" (TJ 30, cf. 24). He then emphasizes two ways in which his criterion of justice, unlike the utilitarian one, does not interpret the right as maximizing the good.

First, in using a simple function for aggregating the good of different persons (sum ranking or averaging), the utilitarian criterion is insensitive to how goods and ills are distributed. Institutions generating the most extreme inequalities in utility are required by justice, so long as the greater welfare of some outweighs the greater suffering of others as compared to more egalitarian alternative schemes (TJ §5). Against this criterion Rawls seeks to present a distribution-sensitive criterion on which an institutional scheme may permit inequalities only insofar as doing so raises the worst position as against those under all feasible more egalitarian alternative schemes. This modification by itself is enough to make his later conception of justice deontological by Rawls's lights: "If the distribution of goods is also counted as a good, perhaps a higher order one, and the theory directs us to produce the most good (including the good of distribution among others), we no longer have a teleological view in the classical sense. The problem of distribution falls under the concept of right as one intuitively understands it, and so the theory lacks an independent definition of the good" (TJ 25, cf. 210–11). But then, such a broad definition would also classify as deontological a quasi-utilitarian criterion that gives no weight to the well-being of the worst-off 5 percent, say.

Second, Rawls argues that a utilitarian criterion relies on an inappropriate conception of the good as happiness or the satisfaction of rational desire. This way the justice of institutions comes to depend excessively upon the desires that happen to be dominant at the time (TJ 447–51).[39] Moreover, certain goods (such as basic rights and liberties) are much more valuable than their contribution to a person's utility may suggest (TJ 207). To accommodate these points, Rawls postulates a "thin theory of the good," embodied in his conception of social primary goods (TJ §60). Only this thin, objective notion of the good is appealed to in the assessment of feasible alternative basic structures. Rawls takes this departure as a further reason for thinking that his conception is deontological in that it "does not interpret the right as maximizing the good. . . . (Here I suppose with utilitarianism that the good is defined as the satisfaction of rational desire.)" (TJ 30, cf. 396). Yet again, this definition seems excessively broad; it would classify as deontological a criterion requiring that institutions maximize gross national product.

3.4. To sum up, by defining the right as "maximinning the thin good"—that is, as demanding that inequalities be arranged so as to optimize the worst representative share of social primary goods— Rawls's conception of justice reflects a broadly consequentialist approach. Feasible alternative basic structures are to be assessed by reference to the distribution of social primary goods each of them tends to produce, regardless of the extent to which this distribution is established or engendered. (Obviously the effects of social institutions must be described in a rough, statistical way, involving general tendencies, probability distributions, and the like.) Moreover, Rawls's construction precludes any spillover of the values informing the assessment of institutions to the subject of conduct assessment. In this way the ground rules justified through his criterion of justice can be morally determinative, and his entire construction is in this sense deon-

---

[39]Here utilitarians might reasonably reply that they do not take existing desires for granted but treat desires as a dependent variable that, as far as possible, is to be adjusted for the sake of the greatest happiness. The choice of an institutional scheme will importantly involve attention to what sort of desires various alternative schemes would tend to engender in people. Utilitarians prefer, other things equal, institutions that generate easily satisfiable desires whose pursuit will produce intrapersonal and social harmony, thereby in turn supporting those institutions. In this respect utilitarians need not differ from what Rawls says about his own conception (TJ §9 and chap. 8).

tological. Finally, the parameters of Rawls's broadly consequentialist approach are set so as to yield a criterion of justice that itself has a deontological flavor, in two respects: Its preeminent concern for the worst position ensures that the needs and vital interests of even small minorities cannot be outbalanced by the greater good of the many. And by incorporating a thin account of the good, Rawls's criterion partially disconnects the assessment of social institutions from whatever desires and conceptions of the good may be empirically prevalent (because of natural or social factors).[40]

3.5. I have said that one important difference between Rawls and Nozick is that Rawls's conception is broadly consequentialist, and Nozick's is not. Let me now try to incorporate this contrast between them into a more complex framework that extends the deontological/ consequentialist distinction from conceptions of morality to conceptions of justice.

A deontological morality typically gives considerable weight to two distinctions: between what persons *do* and what they merely let happen; and within the domain of what they do, between what they *intend* and what they merely foresee (or should foresee). The point of both distinctions is that some X is morally more important than some Y. But the distinctions may be drawn in various ways. The difference in moral importance may obtain always or only sometimes. And Y may be weighted less heavily than X or may be relegated to the status of a tie breaker (X has lexicographical priority), or information about Y may be disregarded altogether. There are then at least $2 \times 3 = 6$ ways in which each distinction might be incorporated into a conception of morality. To make clear what is demanded of such a conception for it to count as deontological, we must then specify not merely that it must recognize the two differentials in moral importance but also how prominent these two differentials must minimally be. I propose that a conception of morality is deontological if and only if it holds *both* that (a) any harm an agent does is always more important than any harm that agent merely lets happen (so that the latter can figure at most as a tie breaker in the assessment of conduct), and that (b) harm an agent intends and does, sometimes at least, has more weight than equivalent harm the agent does but merely foresees (or should foresee). To be fully consequentialist, a conception of morality must deny both (a) and (b). Such conceptions will typically not recognize the two differentials at all.[41]

---

[40]As my objections suggest, it is probably futile to look for a sharp demarcation of the extension of "deontological" in this last sense. It is enough that criteria of justice may be more or less deontological in this sense, depending on *how* they define the good and on *how* they are sensitive to its distribution. Rawls's criterion does not merely satisfy the minimum conditions for being deontological (in his excessively broad sense). It is, as I would put it, much more significantly deontological than my two competing sample criteria (requiring, respectively, the maximization of gross national product and the maximization of utility for the best-off 95 percent).

[41]It is notoriously difficult to draw clear distinctions between what agents do and what they merely let happen, and between what they intend and what they merely foresee, partly because the same conduct can be reported and intended under different descrip-

In analogy, a conception of justice is deontological if and only if it holds *both* that (A) any benefits and burdens an institutional scheme brings about are always more important than any goods and ills it merely lets happen (so that the latter can figure at most as a tie breaker in the assessment of institutions), and that (B) within the domain of what an institutional scheme brings about, benefits and burdens it establishes have, sometimes at least, more weight than equivalent benefits and burdens it foreseeably engenders. A conception of justice is fully consequentialist only if it denies both (A) and (B). Again, such conceptions will typically not recognize the two differentials at all.

3.5.1.1. Let me sketch how Nozick's views can be motivated, in part, by attributing to him the two deontological commitments. Human life is exposed to a wide range of natural contingencies, such as genetic handicaps, illnesses, accidents, and other misfortunes not socially induced. Such contingencies restrict our options. Thus it may seem that in evaluating the prospects for personal freedom under some institutional scheme, one must take into account to what extent such restrictions are mitigated through this scheme. Nozick, however, disputes the relevance of this consideration. One rationale for his opposition is provided by (A): abstracting from natural restrictions on freedom, we should assess institutional schemes by reference to the "institutional" freedom each tends to generate. Thus Nozick thinks that when an institutional scheme requires the healthy to support the handicapped, it introduces (rather than mitigates) an inequality. It restricts the freedom of the former and confers benefits upon the latter. A scheme that requires no such support, by contrast, involves no morally significant inequality, because the special hardships suffered by the handicapped are natural restrictions on their freedom and hence do not count in the assessment of institutional schemes. The intuitive idea is that we ought not conflate the question whether an institutional scheme is just between its participants with the question whether the world at large (the institutional scheme included) is just between those same persons.

3.5.1.2. Nozick's libertarian scheme imposes servitude upon slaves and excludes persons from things, such as land, held by nonconsenting owners. Under it the freedom of large segments of the population is likely to be very severely restricted.[42] But Nozick shows no interest in an empirical examination of this issue, and a strong version of (B) provides one rationale for this reluctance. In assessing an institutional scheme by reference to the distribution of benefits and burdens it produces, we should care much more about established than about engendered benefits and burdens. We should concentrate on the restrictions on personal freedom that the scheme directly calls for and be much less concerned with restrictions that (depending on how people interact)

---

tions. I need not worry about this difficulty here, since my task is to clarify the analogous distinctions in the domain of justice.

[42]Such arguments have been advanced, for example, by G. A. Cohen, CFP. See also Cohen's more general critique of Nozick in RNWC.

may or may not be imposed under the scheme (though they predictably will be). In the libertarian scheme it is intended only that persons should have the freedom to alienate their rights over land and even over themselves and also that there should be institutional mechanisms enforcing whatever particular entitlements may come about through such transactions. But the ground rules do not "intend" any particular entitlements so generated. They do not prescribe that some should be slaves or be landless, nor do they prescribe any particular distributional feature of the pattern of holdings they engender. Even though it may be a statistical certainty that the scheme produces (widespread) slavery or a (large) landless class, the rules do not mandate that (many or) anyone at all should occupy these social positions. The restrictions on the freedom of such persons, however severe, common, and predictable, are merely an incidental consequence of the libertarian scheme. Hence, Nozick could conclude by appeal to a strong version of (B) that these restrictions are morally insignificant for the assessment of his scheme, at least in this case, where the restrictions the scheme does directly prescribe are the correct ones.[43]

3.5.2.1. Rawls shares with Nozick the commitment to (A). He confines his attention to the benefits and burdens of social interaction (e.g., TJ 4–5). His criterion of justice governs the distribution of *social* primary goods alone, rather than the joint pattern emerging when the distribution of social primary goods is superimposed upon that of natural goods and ills. In applying this criterion, "we are not required to examine citizens' psychological attitudes nor their comparative levels of well-being" (SUPG 163). Correspondingly, his contracting parties are concerned with citizens' *social* positions, or *shares*, and not with their overall *situations*, or *standard of living* (in Sen's sense). They care about the least advantaged, not about the least well. Some readers, overlooking this point, have supposed that the parties are concerned with all factors affecting the lives of those they represent, which has given rise to many mistaken counterexamples, about how institutions must be designed so as to optimize the quality of life of those most sick, feeble, ugly, or retarded.[44] Yes, the account of social primary goods is meant to reflect a conception of human needs (RAM 643; WOS 15; FG 554; SUPG 172–73). But these are the *standard* needs of the participants in a given social system. Throughout, Rawls leaves aside differences among persons that affect how useful a given bundle of social goods

[43]I add this proviso because Nozick, having said nothing about the comparative assessment of less-than-just schemes, is liable to think that the distinction in (B) may otherwise be irrelevant. He may believe, for example, that an inequality in *initial* shares of rights is equally unjust irrespective of whether the inequality is established (as in an aristocracy) or engendered (e.g., through market trading in the rights of future persons).

[44]This misunderstanding receives some encouragement when Rawls occasionally refers to the least advantaged as the "least fortunate." To be sure, natural handicaps make it more likely that one is among the least advantaged, but whether one is or not is determined without reference to such handicaps.

will be to each. In their commitment to (A) Rawls and Nozick stand together against such fully consequentialist conceptions of justice as utilitarianism or the capabilities approach recently set forth by Sen.[45]

3.5.2.2. Yet Rawls denies (B). His criterion of justice ranks basic structures on the basis of information about the overall pattern of social primary goods they tend to generate. Rawls explicitly develops his conception in consequentialist terms: "The basic structure is to be arranged to maximize the worth to the least advantaged of the complete scheme of equal liberty shared by all" (TJ 205), for example, and "the parties . . . strive for as high an absolute score as possible" (TJ 144).[46] His criterion of justice is ultimately concerned with the institutional freedom persons actually enjoy, and he evaluates the foreseeable distribution of such freedom without asking to what extent it is established or engendered by social institutions. Rawls, therefore, pays much more attention than Nozick does to the *effects* of institutional schemes. I see this as a central divergence between them: Nozick's conception of justice is deontological in my sense, whereas Rawls's, because of its rejection of (B), is broadly consequentialist. But then, because of its commitment to (A), Rawls's conception of justice is not fully consequentialist. Let me call conceptions of justice that are committed to (A) but not to (B) and likewise conceptions of morality committed to (a) but not to (b) *semiconsequentialist* conceptions. This term should not give rise to confusion, at least if it is true that no significant moral conception instantiates the inverse combination: a commitment to (B) but not to (A), to (b) but not to (a).[47]

[45]A conception of justice committed to (A) ipso facto employs an *objective* criterion for interpersonal comparisons, whereas the criterion employed by fully consequentialist conceptions may be either subjective, as with utilitarianism, or objective, as in Sen (EW, SL, WAF). Sen's conception is fully consequentialist (in my sense) because it evaluates a person's bundle of benefits and burdens in light of particular features of this person (notably capabilities, disabilities, and special needs). It is objective, because no account is taken of particular interests or preferences. See Scanlon, PU 656–58, and SC 197–201, for this subjective/objective distinction.

[46]On the other hand, Rawls also says that "the conception defined by these principles is not that of maximizing anything" (TJ 211), but he is here speaking in rejection of the narrower idea that social institutions should be designed so as to "maximize the sum of intrinsic value or the net balance of the satisfaction of interests" (ibid.) in a distribution-insensitive way. Rawls believes that in developed societies certain established benefits and burdens are of paramount importance. Yet he gives these no special weight from the start but rather argues for this result. The priority of the first principle is defended by demonstrating the special importance of certain goods for citizens and is thus not based on the idea that established goods are more important *as such* (TJ §26, §33). That this is so is confirmed by his first principle of justice, which is concerned with only *some* established goods (certain basic rights and liberties) and also with engendered inequalities in the well-protectedness of these rights and liberties and in the worth of the basic political liberties. I discuss these matters further in Chapter 3.

[47]By proposing analogous tripartite typifications for conceptions of justice and conceptions of morality, I don't mean to suggest that reasons for preferring a semiconsequentialist conception of justice, say, have analogues in the domain of conceptions of morality. It is perfectly conceivable that the most reasonable combination will consist of a semiconsequentialist conception of justice coupled with a fully consequentialist or deontological morality.

4. Nozick's Deontological Alternative

4.1. Let me develop the suggested justificatory background for Nozick's views a little further by looking more closely at what he could say in support of his Orwellian conclusion that if we are firmly committed to freedom, we must endorse ground rules that recognize and enforce slavery.[48]

For Nozick, slavery involves total and unlimited perpetual unfreedom. Slaves have no control over their own lives, and are legitimately subject to every conceivable form of sadistic or sexual perversion—may be worked to death, eaten alive, tortured, and so forth.[49] Evidently, Nozick does not think that this sort of unfreedom disqualifies the ground rules he proposes. Nor would he be taken aback, I suppose, if historians and social theorists predicted that the institutional scheme of our Rawlsian would produce a world of many more options to choose and lives to lead, that under Nozick's constitution a slave economy would emerge on our island and few persons, being neither slaves nor slaveholders, would have the independence and incentives to commence novel ventures—to trade, compose, invent, explore, rhyme, research, and perform. Against objections of these kinds, Nozick can appeal to a strong version of (B): the ground rules he is advocating do not call for slavery; they do not prescribe that any particular persons or groups or proportion of the population should be slaves; they don't even mandate that there be any slaves at all; and therefore, since the burdens associated with slavery, though predictable and officially enforced, are entirely engendered, the costs of its recognition are morally insignificant in comparison to the gains. For the benefits slavery confers are established: Every person is assigned the liberty of selling himself into slavery if he so chooses. And everyone (so long as he has not sold himself) has an opportunity to own slaves, by acquiring an

---

[48]Cf. ASU 331. Concerning the question of how ground rules should be designed, I see no evidence that Nozick recognizes any values beyond freedom. It is true, he "feel[s] more comfortable" with a capitalist system, because the circulation of assets within it is "largely reasonable and intelligible" and correlated with persons' success in "serving others and winning them as customers" (ASU 159). But I think he would endorse the same entitlement structure even if people under it made transfers in less appealing ways. If so, the point has no weight against freedom considerations. Elsewhere Nozick appeals to the "familiar social considerations favoring private property," but he adds immediately, "These considerations enter a Lockean theory to support the claim that appropriation of private property satisfies the intent behind the 'enough and as good left over' proviso, *not* as a utilitarian justification of property" (ASU 177; cf. Locke, STG §41). Those for whom there is no land left to appropriate are allegedly compensated by the superior options they have under Nozick's scheme. Acceptable property schemes must satisfy this condition, but Nozick would deny that, beyond this threshold, such schemes are the more acceptable the better they satisfy it (i.e., the better the worst option set they engender).

[49]This is so because Nozick—in contrast to Locke—declares that his "nonpaternalistic position holds that someone may choose (or permit another) to do to himself *anything*" (ASU 58, his emphasis). Slaves are those who have transferred *all* their rights for the remainder of their lifetime.

existing slave from her present owner or a self-owned person from herself. In light of these two options, slavery, as envisaged by Nozick, should clearly be recognized in "a free system."

One may question whether having these two options really constitutes a benefit. Is not the first option rather a liability, given that the decision to sell oneself may well turn out to have been a dreadful mistake? Nozick would say that the possibility—even probability—of mistakes does not count against slavery, because, when she was still self-owned, the slave had the liberty to sell herself into some more limited form of dependence, or not to sell herself at all. It would be paternalism pure and simple to second-guess or disallow such choices. Even if some slaves, or even all, would have had more freedom and a better life if they had not sold themselves, we cannot count this differential against Nozick's institution of slavery. The loss of freedom suffered by a slave does not count, because it came about pursuant to free choice (whether rational or otherwise).[50]

But there are nonpaternalistic arguments as well. To invoke a commonplace from game theory, the recognition of slavery will create the very emergency situations in which selling oneself could be rational. Consider a sick person who has managed to reach a doctor but is too poor or weak to make it to the next physician alive. The doctor, who can easily cure her, is in a position to exact any price. He can demand all things she owns. If slavery is recognized, the patient's situation is much worse, as he may demand *her* in addition. In this case, the patient has no reason to be grateful that she had the liberty to sell herself: The need to use this option arose only because she had it in the first place.[51]

---

[50]This reply also explains why the "Lockean proviso" does not protect slaves against mistreatment. Though persons are owed compensation (by whom?) insofar as their options are inferior to the standard state-of-nature options (ASU 178–79n), their options are valued *ex ante*. Compare the situation of an uninsured rider without helmet who is badly hurt in a self-caused motorcycle accident; she has no right to compensation even if her options now are much less valuable than the standard state-of-nature options. It was her own free choice to ride without helmet and insurance (and a choice that it would have been wrong to deprive her of).

[51]Medical expertise, not being a natural resource, does not fall under Nozick's "Lockean proviso" (cf. ASU 181, the cases of the medical researcher and the surgeon). The following trialogue is then a realistic scenario within Nozick's libertarian society. A police officer comes upon a couple struggling with each other, the man evidently trying to rape the woman.

Woman: Please, sir, please help me.

Officer (*to man*): Hey, you, let her go at once!

Man: Don't get involved.

Officer: I must. You are violating this woman's right not to be assaulted.

Man: No, I'm not. She is my slave. Here are the papers, signed by herself.

Woman: But I was coerced into signing. He said he would not treat my father if I refused to sign.

Officer: That's not coercion but at most duress. He was at liberty not to treat your father or to ask compensation for treating him.

Woman: But my father is dead!

Man: The contract says only that I would try to save him, and I did.

Moreover, the institution of slavery provides incentives for would-be slaveholders to try to *entrap* another in a situation that makes it rational to sell herself. One can lure her into a life-threatening situation and then offer to rescue her, one can pay others to boycott her and then offer to save her from starvation, and so forth.[52] All these examples show how it may be quite a burden to be too free (by having the liberty to sell oneself).

Here it does not help much to insist (cf. ASU 331) that if someone finds it dangerous to have the option to sell herself, then she can enter a contract disabling this option, that is, give away this liberty. (Could her pursuer buy this contract from those with whom it was made, and when he has her in a desperate situation, quickly restore her liberty to sell herself by releasing her from the promise?) One may doubt that such contracts could be permissible in a libertarian society. If they were, couldn't you and your friend make a similar contract, promising each other that neither of you will ever sell your house, thereby protecting yourselves against potential creditors? But even if such contracts were recognized, they would not help in all cases. For example, a slaveholder would find it easy to make the children of his slaves his property: When such a child comes of age (before she can make any disabling contracts), he can threaten to mistreat her parents if she will not give herself over as his slave. He also has every opportunity to determine her upbringing, to mold her abilities, desires, and ambitions so that she will accept slavery rather than be chased away from the only place she knows. The children of slaves, at the very least, are likely to be much better off without the option of selling themselves, but does having the option reduce their *freedom* (as Nozick conceives this notion)?

4.2. Let us step back from the exchange at this point, to examine more generally what sort of a conception of distributive justice Nozick might have presented had he cared to systematize considerations like the foregoing into a justificatory background for his view analogous to the one Rawls develops. In addition to their differing views about the moral relevance of the distinction between established and engendered pattern features, there is a second important difference within the what-component. This difference concerns the option space in terms of which a person's freedom is described. For Rawls, this option

---

Officer (*to Woman*): I'm sorry, ma'am, but I cannot help you.

Man: But you can help *me* in forcing her to fulfill her contractual obligations. She has already scratched me. See if you can tie her hands.

(*Officer ties Woman's hands, she screams for help as she is being raped. . . .*)

Man (*to Officer*): I'm glad the police are protecting citizens' rights. Isn't she great? My sons will have lots of fun with her when I bring her home.

[52]Note that such entrapment need not run afoul of the Lockean proviso. We may suppose that there is enough unowned land so that she could have grown food during the summer. She has come, however, to rely on making and selling tools, for which she now cannot, suddenly, find any customers.

space is largely structured by social institutions. His basic liberties cover such conventional options as voting, marrying, worshiping, making a speech, having access to the media, and so on. This emphasis is closely associated with his insistence on the *constitutive* aspect of social practices.

Nozick, though he too views the distribution of freedom as regulated by social institutions, thinks of freedom itself as a nonconventional good. The options of the various individuals are located within a preexisting space. They are, in the first instance, options with respect to chunks of space-time, physical objects, and persons. There are, in addition, second-order options, that is, options to make certain changes in the distribution of first-order options (for example, gaining an option or depriving another of one), as well as third-order options, and so on up. While ground rules bring into being new kinds of relations between persons and options—persons can now have options *legitimately*, can be entitled to them—they do not alter the space of possible options or the possible options themselves. Therefore, seeing that a given universe of space-time, objects, and persons fixes the space of possible options, Nozick tends to think of freedom as a constant-sum good. For Rawls, by contrast, the space of possible options is a function of existing social institutions. Institutional reforms will change the shape and structure of this space, make it larger or smaller or (when they are significant) incommensurable altogether.[53]

This brings us to the third component, the how-question, which concerns the demands Nozick makes on the distribution of established freedom. He strongly emphasizes a formal constraint, namely, that a set of ground rules should restrict persons' (legitimate) options so as to achieve a complete ordering of claims, or *interpersonal consistency*. This demand is brought out especially in his arguments (ASU 28–35) for seeing rights as side constraints that—by means of a boundary, line, or hyper-plane (ASU 57)—define a moral space for each individual (thereby restricting the options of others).[54]

In addition, Nozick seems committed to three substantive constraints. First, persons' option spaces should be not only mutually exclusive but also exhaustive. Person's options may be restricted *only* insofar as is necessary for interpersonal consistency. The rights and liberties of the various individuals together must "fill the space" (ASU

[53]Nozick would recognize, of course, that the set of ownable objects of value may fluctuate, that the total of wealth produced may be affected by the choice of ground rules. But he would deny, I think, that this choice could affect the shape and structure of the space of possible options. This idea of a fixed space is compatible with carving the space up in very complicated ways, as when persons have partial control over some thing, e.g., over some aspect or time slice of it, or through voting rights or veto powers.

[54]Such imaginative reflection about freedom in spatial metaphors is prominent before Nozick, e.g., in Hobbes, Locke, and Kant. It also appears in Rawls's reference to liberties as "a framework of legally protected paths" (BLP 40). For an illuminating way of extending the metaphor in terms of railway lines, switches, and locomotives, see Feinberg, ILS.

238); freedom must not be wasted. This *exhaustiveness* constraint provides a straightforward rationale for one of Nozick's views, his ("non-paternalistic") rejection of inalienable rights. Suppose some person, P, inalienably had some right, R. Then no one could legitimately have the higher-order option of divesting P of R; some bit of freedom would go to waste. This idea may motivate Nozick's opposition to deep rights (for example, the right to hold property) that define the permanent framework within which superficial rights (for example, to this piece of property) arise and lapse. All rights are on a par. For each right or liberty there is a deeper right or liberty to change its ownership, and so on, ad infinitum.

Insofar as the distribution of legitimate options is the result of the exercise of higher-order options, it is engendered and hence of little moral significance, if any. The universal alienability of rights and liberties, as required by the exhaustiveness constraint, therefore reduces the morally important part of Nozick's view to the key question of the *initial* distribution of options and restrictions (on all levels). This question can be formulated from the perspective of either the subjects or the objects of rights. What are the initial rights and liberties of the various persons, which spring into existence at the moment of social birth (but are then immediately salable and thus instantaneously on a par with the new person's infinitely malleable holdings) or what are the initial rights and liberties relating to each piece of the universe (chunk of space-time, physical object, or person)?

Second, there must be no inequalities in established freedom. While persons' liberties may have the same object (all can be at liberty to appropriate this thing, for example), this is not possible for rights such as property rights. But persons can and should have symmetrical rights, as when each has certain rights with regard to *his own* body. We may call this the *equality* or the *maximin* constraint. Given the constant-sum nature of Nozick's good, these two formulations don't differ in respect to the design of ideal ground rules. They do differ in how they rank less-than-ideal ground rules, but we do not have Nozick's views on this topic. Let me note that Nozick offers no comment on, or rationale for, his egalitarian commitment—a somewhat amusing lack, given his complaints about a dearth of valid arguments for equality (ASU 223, 233). Why shouldn't some people *start out* as slaves; why shouldn't some be able to acquire more property than others through the same acts; and why shouldn't men need the consent of a female relative to transfer property? Proponents of such inequalities could tell Nozick (in analogy to what he tells us at ASU 239–41) that his hang-up with certain *equal* rights is the historical product of *envy*, which has rankled away for generations in those born less excellent.

Third, as far as options (on all levels) with respect to persons and their actions are concerned, persons should have initial rights to the options relating to themselves in preference to symmetrical options relating to others. Let's call this the *relatedness* constraint.

4.3. My quick sketch of a justificatory background for Nozick's views was meant to bring out the absence of dramatic structural disparity in how he and Rawls approach political philosophy. The disagreement is one in substance. Yet it may look structural (ASU 203) because Rawls and Nozick have worked out different halves of their conceptions. Rawls has concentrated on the higher level of abstraction, on supporting a criterion for assessing alternative sets of ground rules. This criterion has the form of a pattern preference. Basic structures are to be ranked by the distribution of social primary goods each tends to produce. Nozick, by contrast, has developed a set of ground rules, showing their inner coherence and their implications for the social system as a whole. These ground rules are purely procedural, that is, do not require the participants to orient their conduct toward any particular pattern preference. It is clear that Rawls, despite his pattern preference on the higher level, can and does favor procedural ground rules. And it is clear that arguments Nozick might give for his choice of ground rules could be construed as a pattern preference, though Nozick may not wish to restate them in this way.

To bring out this last point somewhat dramatically, let us imagine, as a vivid image equivalent to my conjectured justificatory background for Nozick's views, a Nozickian analogue to the original position.[55] As in Rawls's own construction, representatives of persons would be asked to choose a criterion of justice for the design and assessment of basic social institutions. They would meet behind some veil of ignorance so that they know nothing about their "clients' " particular characteristics. In representing their clients' interests, such parties would again be extremely risk-averse. But, in contrast to Rawls's construction, these parties would be given to know that their clients care (almost) exclusively about their personal freedom insofar as it is directly called for by an institutional scheme and care much less, if at all, about further ways in which (the choice of) an institutional scheme might predictably affect their institutitional freedom. Each deliberator would assume that her client wants as large as possible a share of established freedom so conceived. (Because of the constant-sum character of the relevant good, we need not worry whether shares would be understood in relative or absolute terms.) In an initial situation so described, the parties would then choose a criterion that ranks each basic structure by the worst share of established freedom.[56]

---

[55]As Rawls says, "The contractarian method is a useful way of studying ethical theories and of setting forth their underlying assumptions" (TJ 16). "We may conjecture that for each traditional conception of justice there exists an interpretation of the initial situation in which its principles are the preferred solution" (TJ 121).

[56]Rawls has now settled on viewing the parties and the citizens they represent as distinct (SUPG 165, BLP 19–21), whereas in TJ the prospective participants themselves were generally pictured as entering the original position. In a sense, "it makes no difference either way" (KCMT 525), but I follow Rawls's later style by distinguishing between the parties and their clients (my term) because doing so makes it easier to keep separate two sets of "psychological" assumptions. As we will see, Rawls's picture of the

4.4. The rationale I have sketched for Nozick's views does not solve his problems, of course, but it highlights them. These problems are of three main kinds: how plausible are the key values underlying Nozick's ground rules which can be identified by analyzing their potential rationale, how clear are these background values, and are they sufficient to derive the views Nozick has put forth? Though I cannot discuss these questions in detail, let me offer a few comments on each.

4.4.1. Under the first heading, let me briefly suggest two internal reasons for departing from Nozick's deontological commitment in the direction of a broadly consequentialist alternative (cf. §10.4.1). The first reason arises from Nozick's advertisement (in ASU pt. 3) of his proposed social system as a "framework for utopia," featuring "a wide and diverse range of communities which people can enter if they are admitted, leave if they wish to, shape according to their wishes; a society in which utopian experimentation can be tried, different styles of life can be lived, and alternative visions of the good can be individually or jointly pursued" (ASU 307). The merits of such a free framework are to be an independent source of support for the minimal state with its particular economic institutions (ASU 333). They can lend such support, however, only if it is empirically true that Nozick's ground rules would indeed engender such a framework. I have already suggested reasons for believing that Nozick's rights would lead instead to a feudal system (with slavery) offering a very narrow range of diverse communities and opportunities for experimentation. Should this be so, then the merits of Nozick's framework for utopia would furnish independent reasons *against* his libertarian institutions. Nozick rushes to assert that his are "the precisely correct principles" (ASU 202) without examining this possibility, and he can do so by heavily discounting the engendered effects of his scheme. But this defense has two drawbacks. If bad data don't count for much, good data can't count for much either. Thus, even if his libertarian institutions did tend to engender his framework for utopia, that they did so could not be much of a reason in their favor. Moreover, it appears from Nozick's lyrical celebration of the framework-for-utopia idea, that he himself might be quite uncomfortable with abandoning this ideal so easily for drab feudalism, if that is what his favorite ground rules would likely produce. After all, it is possible that a modified scheme of institutions would in fact tend to engender and sustain something like the social ideal he envisions.

Just as Nozick is not sensitive to what sort of social world his ground rules would tend to engender given full compliance, he also pays no attention to whether there would *be* compliance. A second reason for moving in a broadly consequentialist direction is then that Nozick's disregard for engendered phenomena leads him to ignore the empirical question of whether his libertarian ground rules would work as intended or could even sustain themselves. They might tend to en-

---

parties as amoral, rational maximizers (inspired by neoclassical economics) is quite unlike his conception of the prospective participants whom the parties represent.

gender a good deal of noncompliance, as compared to many differently organized social systems—rampant corruption among minimal-government officials, frequent private feuds and civil wars, and a high crime rate (born, perhaps, of the desperation of large numbers of people). It is possible that the institutions of the minimal state constitute only a minimal improvement over the Lockean state of nature. Nozick ignores such possibilities; and, again, he can do so by heavily discounting the engendered effects of his scheme. But he thereby risks endorsing a society whose members enjoy less personal freedom (as Nozick himself defines it) than the members of differently organized societies that he condemns as unjust. These dangers of ignoring how the choice of ground rules affects compliance is a further reason against designing an institutional scheme by looking only at what the "rules of the game" call for, rather than also at how they would actually work in practice.

These two internal objections to Nozick bring out an important point. My projecting a pattern preference and especially an analogue to the original position behind Nozick's views may well have looked like begging the question in favor of broadly consequentialist criteria of justice: "Once we look at institutional schemes from the perspective of their prospective participants, the discounting of engendered benefits and burdens does indeed come to look silly. Faced with some given prospect of being excluded from education, one will, of course, not care whether this is due to an official prohibition (based on gender or descent) or a conditional effect of the rules (based on engendered parental poverty, say). But what this fact shows is not that deontological conceptions of justice are untenable but that the contractarian perspective begs the question against them." I can now respond that adopting the perspective of prospective participants is not an arbitrary move. Nozick himself appeals to this perspective in part 3 of *Anarchy, State, and Utopia*, and it is unclear what else one can plausibly appeal to if one cares at all to give a justification of the ground rules one favors.

Consider how the second deontological commitment loses its plausibility once it gets transferred from the domain of conceptions of morality to that of conceptions of justice. When we are assessing the conduct of those who shaped the education system in question, it may well matter to us whether they intended that the scheme should effectively exclude some proportion of all children (as they must have if the exclusion is gender-based). It is plausible to assess their conduct by more than its consequences. But it is not plausible, I suggest, to assess the relevant education system itself by more than its consequences. Once it is known effectively to exclude some given proportion of all children, then the desire to have access to an education, which potential participants are presumed to have, counts equally against both schemes.[57]

[57]This is not to deny that there may be other reasons for preferring one of the two schemes. In one of the two cases, the exclusion may come on top of many other

This line of thought exposes Rawls's semiconsequentialism to an attack from the opposite direction. If prospective participants do not care whether given benefits and burdens are established or engendered, why should they care whether given differences in welfare are due to natural or institutional factors? Faced with some given prospect of being less well educated than others, why should one care whether it is because of social factors (official prohibitions or high tuition fees) or a natural handicap (blindness, say) that is not evened out through social institutions? Rawls makes what appears to be an arbitrary stipulation by giving his parties to know that their clients care exclusively about their share of social primary goods. So how can I protest if Nozick were to make an equally arbitrary stipulation, namely, that his parties are given to know that their clients care exclusively about their established share of personal freedom?

My answer has two parts, which correspond to two ways in which it may be implausible to truncate the account of the individual good— from a fully consequentialist (goods and ills, or welfare) to a semiconsequentialist (benefits and burdens) to a deontological one (established benefits and burdens). Such truncations may be seen as *irrational*, because all may end up intuitively worse off if certain information is disregarded, or they may be seen as *unfair* because of their distributional implications. I will discuss both objections as they apply to the two truncations.

Rawls's disregard of natural inequalities does not expose him to the charge of irrationality, because, though he ignores interpersonal differentials in needs, he does not ignore human needs as such. On the contrary, his account of social primary goods is specifically designed to reflect optimally the more vital *standard* needs of human beings, or so, at least, he claims.[58] Nozick's disregard of engendered pattern features does expose him to the charge of irrationality, because *everyone's* desire to enjoy a framework for utopia and a high level of compliance may be better fulfilled under competing institutional schemes.

It could be said that Rawls's attempt to secure an acceptable share of social primary goods for every participant treats some participants, namely, those who suffer special natural handicaps, unfairly. Rawls can reply (with Nozick's approval) that it is not the role of an institutional scheme to even things out in the interest of the overall justice of the human universe (the institutional scheme included). What persons may reasonably demand of an institutional scheme is only that it should situate them fairly *as participants* vis-à-vis the others. Society's response to the blind objector would then be that, by hypothesis, the amount of resources devoted to his education represents a share that

---

disadvantages and therefore be less tolerable, or the financially based exclusion may provide valuable incentives to parents to work harder. A broadly consequentialist approach can be sensitive to such matters, but it will weigh the educational disadvantage equally in the two cases.

[58]I will examine this claim critically in Chapters 3 and 4.

would be fair for a normal, sighted participant. His natural handicap, though no fault of his own, is in no way a consequence of social institutions (or any other social factors, for that matter). Therefore the claim for additional resources he addresses to his fellow participants can appeal only to morality, not to justice. The Rawlsian parties' selective concern with shares of benefits and burdens, however unintuitive psychologically, at least has a *philosophical* rationale.[59]

But the same is not true of Nozick's further truncation of the good to shares of established benefits and burdens. The person excluded from education because of parental poverty is not handicapped but disadvantaged. In her case the inequality *is* a consequence of the (choice of) institutional scheme. She is treated worse than others *by the scheme*. She can then demand that the inequality be justified to her—perhaps through some balancing of values modeled in a contractarian situation. Her claim may be outweighed, but it cannot be discounted.

4.4.2. Under the heading of clarity, a pervasive problem for any attempt to give a precise justificatory background suitable for libertarian views derives from the fact that the objects of rights and liberties can be described in many different ways. To illustrate, let us ask how abstract the formulation of rights may be for purposes of the equality constraint. Take the simplest case of two subjects and one thing. The exhaustiveness constraint entails that the thing must be usable and ownable. The equality constraint entails that initially neither subject owns and both may use the thing. How then can it come to be owned? The standard solution is, of course, that both subjects have a second-order liberty to help themselves, through "first appropriation," to an exclusionary property right in the thing (which extinguishes the other's liberty to use it). How can this simple symmetrical solution cope with the real-world fact that subjects come into being at different times? In appropriating some thing, does Senior do so pursuant to a liberty to appropriate this thing or pursuant to a broader liberty to appropriate unowned things in general? If the former, the equality constraint would require that the arrival of a new subject extinguish all property rights, so that for every thing, the new person has an equal initial liberty to use and appropriate it. If the latter, the equality constraint is satisfied even if there is nothing left unowned upon which Junior could exercise liberties to use and appropriate.

Both these formulations are implausible extremes of concreteness and abstraction, and this implausibility motivates the search for an intermediate solution. For example, Junior must have an initial liberty to appropriate stuff that is equivalent to the stuff Senior had the initial liberty to appropriate; Senior must leave "enough, and as good" for Junior (Locke, STG §33, cf. §27). But libertarians typically want to justify

[59]Whether this rationale can undermine the idea that each feasible basic structure should be assessed via the worst quality of life that would exist under it is another matter. Later, I develop Rawlsian responses to this and other fully consequentialist views in various contexts, including the especially troublesome case of medical needs (§10.4.1–2, §§14–16).

a world in which everything is owned and in which new subjects (some of them owning nothing) will find no use for their initial liberty to appropriate. So they favor another intermediate formulation of the equality constraint. Junior must have initial established rights and liberties that are at least equivalent to the initial established rights and liberties of Senior.

But opting for one of the intermediate solutions does not remove the unclarity, given the vagueness of the notion of equivalence. A relaxed notion of equivalence can make the equality constraint very weak indeed, as when the liberty to seek employment in a capitalist economy is offered as a substitute for earlier persons' liberties to appropriate large tracts of land (Locke, STG §37; Nozick ASU 175–82). A demanding notion of equivalence can yield quite radical conclusions, as in the case of Bruce Ackerman's theory of justice (SJLS), which also differs from Nozick's in its acknowledgment of goods other than freedom.

4.4.3. Besides clarification, the proposed justificatory background needs considerable specification before it can single out any particular ground rules (such as the ones Nozick proposes). Very different schemes satisfy all the constraints so far imposed upon the distribution of established freedom. A scheme might, for example, define a more limited second-order liberty of appropriation. The appropriation of a piece of land would leave intact certain liberties of trespass, and (some of) the rights it confers would be limited to the appropriator (that is, would be nontransferable by him, as under the Rawlsian's change-of-landownership rules). Alternatively, persons might have an initial liberty to gain ownership of a plot of land for the next planting season by organizing some open and fair bargaining procedure through which such plots are distributed. More radical still, persons might have an initial liberty to use and consume everything, together with a second-order right not to be deprived of this liberty without their consent. In this anarchist world, people would "own" what they swallow and maybe what they wear but would share everything else when asked to. Private property, in plots of land for example, would be possible in principle (as mandated by the exhaustiveness constraint) through unanimous consent, but it would be extremely unlikely and also highly unstable because of the appearance of new persons.[60]

Under all three proposals the liberty of unilateral appropriation is defined as more limited, so that it would give rise to less extensive, less

[60]This instability raises the cute question whether the exhaustiveness constraint requires that plot futures be ownable today (in which case the instability would not exist as alleged). In Nozick's scheme plot futures are ownable today. A property owner by first appropriation owns all future stages of the object as well. But is it reasonable to make this a *requirement* on schemes of ground rules? To do so would be strange in the case of the scheme discussed in the text because those in the present generation, by giving up liberties meaningless to them, could constrain the liberties of future generations. If everyone now consents that Nozick should now own Manhattan-in-2080, then Nozick's great-granddaughter will, in 2080, have the right to exclude everyone else from the island.

exclusionary, or less enduring property rights. Such a modification seems attractive if there is reason to prefer a more egalitarian distribution of engendered freedom. Given Nozick's endorsement of equality in the distribution of established freedom, it seems that this preference should exist at least as a secondary principle (tie breaker). But the main point of sketching these alternative possibilities was to show that— consistent with my conjectured constraints, however clarified—there are indefinitely many and very different ways of specifying the initial package of rights and liberties to be assigned to the participants in libertarian institutions.[61]

4.5. Before concluding this section, I must briefly address an objection. It may be said that Nozick, instead of accepting a justificatory background involving a pattern preference, can bring in a structurally different justificatory background that appeals to historical facts. Whereas for Rawls the justice of a basic structure hinges on a forward-looking (broadly consequentialist) assessment of it and its feasible alternatives, Nozick asserts that its justice cannot be assessed apart from information about how this scheme came about. For him, the justification of particular social institutions is historically recursive just like the justification of a particular distribution of holdings. Thus, institutional changes (for example, from a barter to a money economy or from protective agencies to the minimal government) are legitimate only if they actually came about through legitimate processes (for example, through an invisible-hand process or through a mandatory attempt to safeguard moral rights that would otherwise have been violated). He might then reject competing ground rules more Rawlsian in spirit because they could not (or not plausibly) have come about through a sequence of legitimate transitions from an original state of nature constrained only by Nozickian rights (cf. ASU 280–90).

This appeal to history can move but it cannot fill the gap in Nozick's account. His favorite institutions, even with their historically recursive justification, still hang in midair so long as it has not been shown which ground rules were valid at the very beginning.[62] Instead of challenging

---

[61]Nozick once entertains shaping "the precise contour of the bundle of property rights"—a special case—with an eye to the most efficient internalization of externalities (ASU 280). We should choose property rights so that productive exchanges are encouraged at low transaction costs. Inasmuch as productive exchanges are ones that make both sides subjectively better off, this proposal comes perilously close to a utilitarian criterion for assessing institutions. Moreover, it would seem to favor a specification of property rights that tends to engender more egalitarian patterns of holdings. For productive exchanges of the relevant kind actually to occur, the parties without right must have the funds to buy off (part of) the rights of the opposite party, and this consideration supports assigning the right to the generally poorer party. (Consider the choice between a purported right to pollute and a purported right to veto pollution in one's area. The latter option is superior for purposes of internalizing externalities if it is more likely that industrialists have the funds to buy pollution entitlements from their neighbors than that residents have the funds to buy pollution limitations from industrialists.)

[62]There is considerable unclarity even about what he takes these original ground rules to be in the economic sphere. Most often it seems that these are his principles of

his proposed ground rules, one would now challenge his proposed *original* ground rules, including rules for their valid revision. The core idea of such a negative strategy is clear enough, and I will confine myself to a few brief illustrations. Concerning the original ground rules, how can we settle, for example, whether the world was originally unowned or owned collectively? Can we decide on philosophical grounds and, if so, which? Or can we decide by appeal to history and, if so, how? Concerning rules for the valid revision of the original ground rules, both Nozick and Locke suggest that such revisions must be mutually beneficial. (Must *everyone* under the new scheme be better off than *anyone* was under the old one? How could it be shown that they were? Or is some weaker condition sufficient; and which might this be?) Both emphasize that private appropriation of some plot of land on the terms *they* propose will tend to improve the shares of all (including those who will not own land) as against a state without private land-ownership.[63] But the same could be said, with greater plausibility perhaps, about many other revised sets of ground rules that would permit less extensive, less exclusionary, or less permanent private appropriation than theirs do. Again, how do we decide among various such revisions? On philosophical grounds? Or by appeal to historical facts about how property rights and other institutions actually emerged? And what if they emerged differently in Egypt, Greece, Rome, etc.?

Those who want to assert that there is *one* obvious set of (original) ground rules will have to defend "obvious" answers to these and many other such questions. The Rawlsian, favoring what I have called a broadly consequentialist assessment of social institutions, can maintain the ground on the higher level by merely blocking such assertions. Perhaps the best way to succeed at this negative task is to confront the various proffered descriptions of supposedly obvious or natural institutions with one another, to make clear how hopeless is the project of legitimating one particular set of (original) ground rules as morally fundamental. And so long as no such scheme has been so legitimated,

---

acquisition, transfer, and rectification of holdings. But if so, then there would be no reason for Nozick to try to "rebut the claim that . . . no natural right to private property can arise by a Lockean process" (ASU 177). This right wouldn't need to arise, because it would exist *ab initio*. I don't think this passage is just a slip on Nozick's part. Rather, I believe (in elaboration of n. 6) that Nozick takes the institution of private property to have *arisen*, because he wants to reaffirm the Lockean proviso but can make sense of it only as some kind of compensation requirement. If property rights had existed at the very beginning, then the Lockean proviso would seem to him to have no rationale. Nozick can solve this supposed problem by assuming, with Locke, that the institution of private property *developed* in a world that originally belonged to humankind in common. If so, then the proviso has a rationale: it ensures that the emergence of this institution makes no one worse off by guaranteeing to everyone a share of initial freedom that is no worse than the initial such share under the original ground rules. This reading of Nozick conflicts with R. P. Wolff's assertion that Nozick views the world as originally *unowned* (see DMS 101 n. 9).

[63]Cf. Locke, STG §§37, 40, and 41; ASU 177.

nothing has been shown to preempt or constrain Rawls's pattern preference (as applied to the ranking of such schemes).

Independently and in addition, there are reasons against accepting the very idea that the justification of economic institutions should have to fit the historically recursive mold. The problem is that such a conception of justice is highly inflexible and unadaptable to the enormous range of social and environmental conditions to which human beings have been and might be—sometime, somewhere—exposed. Rights that seem obvious within a small-scale social system may make a large-scale one entirely unmanageable. A specification of property rights that is plausible for an agricultural society may, in a hunting society, lead to extinction from starvation. Variations in technology, culture, and population density define an enormous space of possibilities. Reflecting on this point drains away yet more of whatever plausibility Nozick's conception may have. The original ground rules he proposes don't look so bad in the state of nature Locke describes, in which vast tracts of fertile land are available to be brought under cultivation and the Rawlsian's change-of-landownership rules (besides being pointless) would far exceed existing administrative capacities. Of course, I could describe another state of nature in which things would be otherwise, but even waiving this objection, why should we now have to justify our institutions by reference to some base-line scheme that would have been plausible at the beginnings of human history? And if we do, why is Nozick's argument a justification for the minimal state rather than the reductio ad absurdum of his specification of original rights?

A theory envisioning a historically recursive assessment of institutional schemes vastly overburdens us with morally significant considerations. One must not merely design a scheme suitable for a particular social system at a particular time in history. In designing such a scheme one must also be concerned that this scheme can plausibly have come about through a sequence of legitimate institutional changes from the original scheme, that the original and all intermediate schemes be suitable to their respective social conditions, that all other schemes that might plausibly have legitimately emerged (or might yet so emerge) from the original scheme also be suitable under all sorts of social and natural conditions, and that no alternative specification of the original scheme should generate a tree of accessible schemes that seems more acceptable on the whole than the tree generated by Nozick's own original scheme. Given these fantastic complexities, one may come to appreciate why Nozick is tempted—even at the expense of decoupling the third part of *Anarchy, State, and Utopia*, which holds out the promise of a "framework for utopia"—by the quicker route of declaring his specification of original rights "fundamental" by insisting that his are "the precisely correct principles" (ASU 202). If these principles (perhaps through some plausible sequence of legitimate institutional changes) lead to massive slavery, serfdom, starvation, or noncompliance, then there is perhaps reason to violate some rights here and there—"to avoid catastrophic moral horror" (ASU 30n)—but certainly not reason to change one's mind about the principles themselves.

4.6. Rawls in *A Theory of Justice* also aims for a theory that is applicable to social systems under very different social and natural conditions. But he wants to assess the justice of a basic structure by how it works now, without regard to its history. Through his broadly consequentialist mode of assessment, Rawls gains a good deal of security against shocking surprises, for instance, that the most repugnant schemes can be just and the most beneficial ones unjust on account of their genesis. Employing a thin notion of the human good, Rawls makes the justice of an institutional scheme turn on how its least advantaged fare in comparison to the least advantaged under feasible alternative basic structures.

Rawls's pattern preference would entail a low ranking for Nozick's ground rules. If Nozick protests that his ground rules are somehow natural or obvious, he is unlikely to prevail. There are just too many pretenders to these attributes, and only if there were some convergence upon one set of ground rules might these be used to test (and reject) the Rawlsian criterion. Absent such convergence, it seems more promising for Nozick to extend his conception to the higher level so as to prevent Rawls from maintaining that ground by default. Doing so, I have suggested, would lead him to defend a conception of justice that in its balancing of values, is structurally similar to Rawls's own. This balancing, however, would not be broadly consequentialist, because Nozick in constructing his Master Pattern would give much less weight to the benefits and burdens that are the effects of an institutional scheme than to equivalent benefits and burdens it calls for.

This chapter has done little to defend the particular criterion Rawls proposes for assessing alternative basic structures. My main concern was to make plausible the very idea of such a criterion, the idea of thinking about institutional schemes in terms of distributional patterns. I have also tried to gain some initial credibility for the semiconsequentialist approach to the subject of the basic structure. Such an approach is concerned with the distribution of benefits and burdens an institutional scheme tends to produce, irrespective of the extent to which it establishes or engenders them.

CHAPTER 2

Sandel and the
Conception of the Person

5. Natural Endowments

Misunderstandings of Rawls's treatment of natural endowments have been so routine that a clear (though somewhat critical) defense of it seems useful for this reason alone. My discussion of natural endowments serves two additional purposes as well: it allows me to clarify a further important aspect of Rawls's focus on the basic structure, and it constitutes a small-scale prelude to the discussion of Rawls's infamous conception of the person, which, supporting the account of social primary goods and the maximin idea, plays a crucial role in his conception of social justice.

5.1. The severe criticisms of Rawls's treatment of natural endowments center around the mistaken idea that the difference principle, as defended in *A Theory of Justice*, permits or even requires that persons be used as means for the benefit of others. This interpretation thrives on Rawls's claim that his is "a conception of justice that nullifies the accidents of natural endowment" (TJ 15). It is confirmed by his advertisement of the difference principle as an agreement to regard the distribution of natural endowments as a "common," "collective," or "social asset to be used for the common advantage" (TJ 101, 179, 107). And it finds further support when Rawls announces that "no one deserves his place in the distribution of native endowments" (TJ 104, cf. §48), that such endowments are "arbitrary from a moral point of view" (TJ 312, cf. 72, 75, 102). These phrases may easily mislead, and then inspire horror in righteous hearts. Let us further develop Rawls's conception of justice so as to provide the context in which these phrases can be correctly understood and their defensibility examined. I begin the first task by peeling away three layers of potential misunderstanding.

5.1.1. It has been supposed that control over one's natural endowments is itself up for consideration, that Rawls is examining the natural distribution of special gifts and handicaps against the background of other, perhaps more desirable alternative patterns. On this supposition, the consistent proposals for Rawls to make would involve involuntary organ transplants (Nozick, ASU 206–7), coownership by others of exceptional natural endowments (giving them a right to decide how these should be employed),[1] or at the very least a "head tax" (ASU 229n) to be imposed upon the better endowed. The supposition, however, is mistaken: "Greater natural talents are not a collective asset in the sense that society should compel those who have them to put them to work for the less favored" (RMC 145). "We have a right to our natural abilities" (BSS 65). This much is enshrined in Rawls's first principle.

We should recall here that Rawls's conception of justice is only *semi*consequentialist. *Natural* primary goods, such as "health and vigor, intelligence and imagination" (TJ 62), fall outside the master patterns by which feasible alternative basic structures are assessed. "The natural distribution is neither just nor unjust" (TJ 102). Rawls is concerned only with the distribution of *social* primary goods, which is regulated by the basic structure. All and only inequalities in this distribution require justification: "A hypothetical initial arrangement in which all the social primary goods are equally distributed . . . provides a benchmark for judging improvements" (TJ 62). Hence there is no reason, not even a reason overridden by other considerations, why the use of persons' endowments should be decided collectively, or natural inequalities be offset by social ones.

The fact of natural inequalities may provide another sort of reason for departing from an equal distribution of social primary goods. Perhaps all shares could be larger if special rewards were offered for the development and exercise of special talents. In this case, however, the resulting social inequalities would be justified by reference to the preferred distribution of *social* primary goods they make possible (and *not* by reference to a preferred distribution of welfare or of primary goods overall). Information about natural inequalities—though it plays no normative role within Rawls's criterion of justice, does not figure in the Master Pattern—is still needed in an empirical role. It codetermines how this criterion can be satisfied.

There is then no disagreement about whether the better endowed should have and control their superior natural gifts. Rawls does not

---

[1]Sandel has it that Rawls's text is not merely inconsistent with but is self-consciously arguing against the view "that I have certain privileged claims with respect to [my endowments], a bundle of rights, while not unlimited, at least more extensive with respect to my assets than any bundle of rights anyone else may have with respect to them" (LLJ 96; cf. Nozick, ASU 282–92). On this reading, Rawls would be urging that every compatriot should have as much of a say as you do in deciding how *your* endowments will be developed and exercised.

question that they should. The only controversy is over what advantages they are to be offered for developing and exercising their special endowments.

5.1.2. The second misunderstanding once more involves the distinction of moral subjects: the assessment of institutions and the assessment of conduct. How we feel about a preference for some patterns over others depends upon the role it is assigned in moral argument. Appeal to the same pattern preference may seem perfectly sensible and also quite outrageous, depending on whether it is meant to justify the ranking of one institutional scheme above another or the infringement of rights under some (reasonably just) existing institutional scheme. The second misunderstanding consists in assuming that Rawls's valuation of income patterns, which reflect the natural distribution of endowments, is to be applied within an ongoing economic scheme whose terms are taken for granted. Rawls is viewed as suggesting that we should try to factor out the part of a person's holdings that is due to natural endowments, and therefore undeserved, as a fit candidate for redistribution. Against this position Nozick can quite convincingly argue that something may be legitimately one's own even though what one used to obtain it (and what one used to obtain *that*, etc.) are not "deserved, *all the way down*. . . . Some of the things he uses he just may *have*, not illegitimately" (ASU 225).

Taking natural endowments to be among these things one just *has*, Nozick sketches this argument:

1. People are entitled to their natural assets.
2. If people are entitled to something, they are entitled to whatever flows from it (via specified types of processes).
3. People's holdings flow from their natural assets. Therefore,
4. People are entitled to their holdings.
5. If people are entitled to something, then they ought to have it (and this overrides any presumption of equality there may be about holdings). (ASU 225–26)

This argument is entirely unexceptionable. Only it leaves open what those "specified types of processes" should be via which holdings flow from natural endowments. And it is precisely this issue, and this issue alone, that Rawls's reflections about natural endowments are meant to address. There is no question that persons are entitled to whatever they acquire under just processes, no matter what role their endowments may have played in this acquisition (cf. TJ 103). What Rawls disputes is that persons, in virtue of their endowments, are entitled to or deserve *any particular specification of these processes* (cf. TJ 104)— something Nozick would dispute just as vigorously. Once again, the valuation of the relevant pattern features (income differentials reflecting diverse natural endowments) is meant to influence the assessment of *institutions*. It is not intended to inspire rectificatory interference with the holdings that have arisen under some existing institutional scheme.

5.2. These two misunderstandings out of the way, we can begin delineating the main issue: How are economic institutions to be designed and assessed (the relevant "types of processes" to be specified)? What is the meaning and plausibility of Rawls's view that institutional schemes should regulate differentials in the social rewards for developing and exercising natural endowments so as to optimize the worst representative share of social primary goods?

Let me give a crude illustration of Rawls's position, based, once again, upon his difference principle in its simplest form (where it governs only income) as applied to the economy of a small self-contained society. To further simplify matters, I assume that there are only two levels of endowment: eighteen specially gifted persons ("the exceptionals"), capable of working in the complex job, and fifty-four normally endowed persons ("the normals"), who can work only in the simple job. I consider four alternative economic schemes, under which the income for one hour of work in the complex job is the market price of such labor minus, respectively, 0, 40, 50, and 60 percent. The income for one hour of work in the simple job is the market price of such labor plus some percentage, which is chosen so that the total flow of supplementary income (that is, of "negative" income taxes in the simple job) exactly balances the total flow of taxes raised in the complex job. Suppose empirical studies show the patterns that the four alternative schemes would engender to be roughly as shown in Table 1 (stating in each column the data for the complex job first).[2]

For each scheme, the first value in row [A] is exogenous. All other values are calculated, except for those in rows [B], [F], and [H]. These are stipulated in accordance with three straightforward empirical assumptions about variations across schemes. First, as regards [F], average working hours for each group under each scheme are such that groups with higher net income rates [D] have more leisure [F] and earn more income [G]. Second, as regards [H], an increasing proportion of the exceptionals prefer to work in the simple job as the ratio between the two net income rates [E] decreases (from S_4 to S_6). Third, as regards [B], the divergence in gross incomes is negatively related to the labor supply ratio [J]. The market price of labor in each job is a function of the relative scarcity of such labor. These three tendencies combine to make S_5 rather than S_6 the scheme preferred by the difference principle. Although tax rates are highest under S_6, the least advantaged under S_5

---

[2]For simplicity I am keeping prices and price vectors fixed, assuming that all dollar figures are fully comparable across schemes. See Gibbard, DG, for a discussion of this problem. The income-tax schemes envisaged in this illustration may exemplify the workings of (what Rawls calls) the transfer branch (TJ 276–77) and the second part of the distribution branch (TJ 278–79). Let me note Rawls's suggestion that "a proportional expenditure tax may be . . . preferable to an income tax" (TJ 278). I chose income tax schemes because they afford a more familiar and perspicuous illustration.

Table 1. Alternative economic schemes and the difference principle

	S_0		S_4		S_5		S_6	
[A] Tax rate	0%	0%	−40%	44%	−50%	60%	−60%	64%
[B] Gross income rate per hour ($)	110.00	13.00	82.00	16.00	90.00	15.00	96.00	14.40
[C] Tax per hour ($), [A]×[B]	0.00	0.00	−32.80	+7.04	−45.00	+9.00	−57.60	+9.22
[D] Net income rate per hour ($), [B]+[C]	110.00	13.00	49.20	23.04	45.00	24.00	38.40	23.62
[E] Net income rate ratio, from [D]	8.46		2.14		1.88		1.63	
[F] Average working hours per week	20	60	26.4	41.0	28	40	32.4	40.5
[G] Average net income per week ($), [D]×[F]	2,200.00	780.00	1,298.88	944.64	1,260.00	960.00	1,244.16	956.45
[H] Number of workers	18	54	18	54	16	56	12	60
[I] Total working hours per week, [F]×[H]	360	3,240	475.2	2,214	448	2,240	388.8	2,430
[J] Labor supply ratio, from [I]	0.111		0.215		0.200		0.160	
[K] Total tax bill per week ($) [A]×[B]×[I]	+/− 0		+/− 15,586.56		+/− 20,160.00		+/− 22,394.88	

are nevertheless better off (have a higher net income rate [D]—work less [F] and earn more [G]) than the least advantaged under any of the alternative schemes.[3]

5.3. While it is quite clear that the Rawlsian criterion would entail a preference for S_5, Rawls makes it difficult to understand what this preference means. Consider his formulations in explication of the difference principle: "Those who have been favored by nature . . . may gain from their good fortune only on terms that improve the situation of those who have lost out" (TJ 101); "the more fortunate are to benefit only in ways that help those who have lost out" (TJ 179); "no one gains or loses from his arbitrary place in the distribution of natural assets . . .

[3]As the example makes clear, Sandel goes wrong in believing that the scheme ranked highest by Rawls's conception "nullifies the *effect* of these differences [in natural fortune]" (LLJ 69). In S_5 those working in the complex job have considerably more income and more leisure than their fellows working in the simple job. Moreover, they prefer their complex job (unavailable to the normals), as is witnessed by the fact that they could switch at any time. There is no question that they have—on top of their better endowment, which is irrelevant for Rawls—a better social position than the normals. It may seem that a weaker claim is true. A just scheme is such that *some* of the exceptionals just barely prefer the complex job; some of them (in S_5) would switch into the simple job if the net income rate ratio were reduced a little bit further. But one must be careful with such statements. Rawls's criterion compares long-term schemes (existing "in perpetuity," as it were). So the table does not illustrate how actual persons, having convex indifference curves between income and leisure which reflect decreasing marginal utility for both goods, would adjust their economic behavior to tax-rate fluctuations. Rather, the assumption is that persons have grown up in "their" scheme, that their preferences and indifference curves (etc.) have been shaped by it. There is no guarantee that persons in S_5 would adjust to *short-term* changes in income tax rates as shown in the table.

without giving or receiving compensating advantages in return. . . . In justice as fairness men agree to share one another's fate" (TJ 102). These formulations invite the third misunderstanding. Granted, it might be said, S_5 is so organized that nothing is taken away from the exceptionals or *re*distributed. It's all done automatically and on a schedule announced in advance. But the question remains: Why should the exceptionals owe the normals *any* compensating advantages? In return for what? Yes, the exceptionals are free to work in the simple job, and they have to pay only if they choose to exercise their superior endowments, but by what right may this condition be imposed upon them? Why should they be forbidden to exercise their superior endowments *without* helping the normals? How is this way of using people (or their talents or their work) for the benefit of others made acceptable by the fact that it's built into the rules of the game, rather than imposed by officials in an ad hoc manner?

This line of criticism is beautifully captured in Nozick's image of the exceptionals being *harnessed* to serve others, "and 'harnessing' is an appropriate term—as it would be for a horse harnessed to a wagon which doesn't *have* to move ever, but if it does, it must draw the wagon along" (ASU 229n). What Nozick wants to conclude is that Rawls's conception of justice, by favoring institutional schemes under which the exceptionals are harnessed, encourages the use of some persons as means for the benefit of others.

When persons are harnessed, however, only their *work and efforts* are immediately used. Nozick's path to his conclusion requires then two further steps: to use persons' work and efforts is to use their natural endowments, and to use their natural endowments is to use *them*. Nozick explicitly asserts the second of these steps: "Why we, thick with particular traits, should be cheered that (only) the thus purified men within us are not regarded as means is . . . unclear" (ASU 228). And denying Nozick's point—insisting that using the special gifts of the exceptionals (the strength of a horse) as means is not tantamount to so using the exceptionals *themselves* (the horse *itself*)—indeed seems to put too much weight on rather too subtle a distinction. Still, Nozick asserts only the second step, as if it were enough, and Sandel follows him in this, presenting the same half argument, albeit in greater detail (LLJ 77–78). But why should it be so obvious that when persons are harnessed (so that some of their efforts will benefit others) their endowments are used as means?

Nozick and Sandel are liable to defend their conclusion by pointing out that Rawls himself has spared them the trouble of arguing for the first step, since he freely admits to it. His common-asset formulations, even if they don't mean that we ought to have joint control over the development and exercise of our collective endowments, entail at least that such endowments, insofar as they *are* exercised, may be used as means for the common good. As they see it, Rawls is arguing this way:

(1) Natural endowments may be regarded as a common asset.
(2) Hence, the talents and abilities of (or "residing in") the exceptionals may be used as means.
(3) Hence, the work and efforts of the exceptionals may be used as means, or harnessed.
(4) Hence, an income tax scheme like S_5 may be instituted.[4]

If Rawls were really arguing in this way, then Nozick and Sandel would indeed need to show only how (1) or (2) presupposes that *persons* may be used as means.

Their reading, however, is mistaken; Rawls makes no such argument and does not endorse any of propositions (1)–(3). My discussion will concentrate on (3), for by showing that, despite appearances, Rawls is not invoking (3) in any relevant sense, I can destroy the ordinary rationale for attributing (1) and (2) to him. At the end I will look again at Rawls's common-asset formulations to show how the Nozick-Sandel reading of them goes wrong and how they should instead be understood.

5.4. The second misunderstanding viewed Rawls as encouraging officials to take away some of people's earnings and pass them along to the less fortunate. I said in response that Rawls is discussing the *scheme* under which earnings arise in the first place. He addresses himself to the deepest basis of economic entitlements and thus cannot be criticized in a way that already takes some entitlement-producing processes for granted. To say that with Rawls in charge people get less than they are entitled to begs the question Rawls is raising, by assuming we already know what people are entitled to.

The third misunderstanding is similar to the second in that it again reflects the failure to understand Rawls's focus on the basic structure. The charge is that under the scheme Rawls favors, S_5, people are entitled to less than they ought to have. This objection can be embellished by adding that people ought to have what flows from their work and efforts, but it still begs the question, this time by assuming we already know what flows from people's work and efforts and that this is what they ought to have.

But is not Rawls himself saying that the exceptionals, if they want to exercise their special talents, must "help" the normals, must "improve their situation" and "give them compensating advantages"? And does this requirement not presuppose that we *do* know what flows from their work and efforts, namely, their entitlements under S_5 *plus* whatever "help" was diverted to those in the simple job?

In two of the three passages quoted at the beginning of §5.3, Rawls formulates more carefully, saying that the more fortunate may gain

---

[4]For Nozick, this argument shows how low even the most able defenders of income taxes must sink, whereas Sandel would perhaps be willing to entertain *other* arguments in support of such taxes, at least within local communities.

only *on terms* that improve, may benefit only *in ways* that help those who have lost out. These formulations suggest an alternative reading, which alone makes them meaningful as a paraphrase of the difference principle. On this reading, the implicit reference of such comparative expressions as "gain," "improve," "help," "giving compensating advantages" is *not* to the (smaller) share the normals would have if the exceptionals did less work in the complex job. Instead, the implicit reference is to the (smaller) share of the normals *as it would exist under alternative schemes*. It's not that the preferred economic scheme is rigged so that those in the complex job cannot but help those in the simple job. Rather, Rawls's criterion of justice is such that its selection of an economic scheme will (maximally) help—that is, improve—the lowest social position. Thus S_5 is preferred over S_6 because the ("*inter-schemic*") gain in the complex job is associated with a compensating gain in the lower job. (The "in return" is meaningful if we approach S_5 from Rawls's equal-income benchmark.)

This reading makes the sentences at issue continuous with how we must construe the principle they are intended to explicate. The difference principle assesses institutional schemes with an eye to the inequalities each tends to produce, which are to be "to the greatest benefit of the least advantaged" (TJ 302). Rawls does not mean to endorse the scheme in which benefits are largest, with benefits defined in a way *internal* to each scheme. If this were his point, then he would have to prefer S_6, under which the income supplement in the simple job is highest both in relative and in absolute terms (64 percent or $9.22 per hour or $22,394.88 in total, as compared to 60 percent or $9.00 per hour or $20,160.00 in total under S_5). But Rawls intends to favor the scheme under which those in the simple job have the largest share, and so he must have in mind a notion of benefit *across schemes*. At issue are not the benefits *concrete persons* derive from others' actions within a scheme but the benefits *abstract* (or "representative") *groups* derive from the existence of one scheme rather than another. In this sense we may say that workers in both jobs benefit from the selection of S_5 rather than S_6.

5.5. The difficulty of grasping Rawls's point is increased by two factors. First, in making such comparisons across schemes, he presupposes that the same groups would exist under different schemes. In one sense this presupposition is clearly false, for had S_6 really been in force, some persons would now be working in a different job.[5] Since Rawls never addresses this problem, it may seem that his comparisons must involve groups within the same scheme. The presupposition, however, is not problematic *for Rawls*, because he is concerned only with the group of the least advantaged under each scheme and does not care to what extent their memberships would overlap. What is to be

---

[5] Or altogether different persons would have been born (cf. Parfit, RP, chap. 16).

optimized through the choice of an economic scheme is never the position of the presently poorest persons (as if one could keep track of concrete individuals across hypothetical schemes) but always the smallest share, that is, in the simplest case, the floor of the income hierarchy.

Second, Rawls moves freely back and forth between (what I call) the *intra*schemic and *inter*schemic senses of such terms as *benefit* and *advantage*. That institutional inequalities must be to the advantage of the least advantaged, for example, means that the scheme must be chosen so that those *intra*schemically most disadvantaged will enjoy an *inter*schemic advantage over those (*intra*schemically) most disadvantaged under feasible alternative schemes. Likewise, his criterion selects the scheme that benefits most those whom it benefits least (Rawls uses both expressions). The share of this group is inferior to the shares of all other (existing) groups and yet superior to the (hypothetical) worst share under any feasible alternative scheme.

5.6. The interschemic construal of the comparative terms ("greatest," "gain," "improve," etc.) dissolves the accusation that Rawls himself explicitly favors a scheme under which some are harnessed for the benefit of others. Rawls is not running afoul of his own insistence that persons must not be regarded as means (TJ 183). I can then continue in his behalf the strategy I have embarked upon in §4.5 (cf. §4.6)—the strategy of blocking any assertion of an obvious economic scheme or of conditions that economic schemes must obviously satisfy.[6]

[6]Consider here the complaint that under schemes Rawls would favor people's activities will have positive and negative externalities (on account of the tax system). Such a scheme will allow that I can act to benefit myself in ways that make you worse off or (as in S_5) that you cannot do certain things without benefiting me. But why should this be inadmissible? After all, this much is true of every market scheme we know. My income may be very significantly affected by others' economic activities that don't involve me at all. It would be ridiculous to say that they are harnessed to me just because I benefit (as a shareholder, perhaps) every time they buy a new car ("They don't *have* to buy a new car ever, but if they do, they must generate some gain for me"). Another external attack might charge that under what Rawls considers a just economic scheme persons would not be receiving their marginal products. (This idea seems to me already disqualified on economic grounds. There is no guarantee that if factor inputs are multiplied, each with its marginal product, and the results are added, the sum will equal total production.) But a person's marginal contribution depends in various ways upon contextual factors that cannot reasonably be attributed to this person (cf. TJ 308). Moreover, is it really obvious that those who cannot contribute (the aged, orphaned, handicapped, etc.) *ought* to be receiving their marginal product, i.e., nothing? Do they not also have some claim on the material world that is a main source of economic values? Only a *morally appealing* notion of what "flows from" a person's work or efforts could overturn or constrain the Rawlsian pattern preference.

Finally, Nozick suggests that the appropriate way of settling on an economic scheme is through an unconstrained collective bargaining session between the exceptionals (as a team) and the normals (ASU 193–95). In such a session the exceptionals would be fools to agree to S_5. They could make a counterproposal under which the simple job is taxed so as to fund an income supplement for the complex job. The bargaining would likely converge toward a mild proposal of this form (rather than S_0) because, Nozick tells us, the normals have more to lose, vis-à-vis S_0, from a breakdown of social cooperation. But once again

Let me add that the intraschemic construal suggested by the harnessing image is unsound even in strictly economic terms, because tax rates have an impact on gross incomes. Consider the complaint against S_5 or against currently existing schemes that what is paid in income tax and spent on the needs of others represents (unjustly) redistributed income. In keeping current gross incomes fixed, this complaint presupposes the very income tax scheme it rejects. If the challenged tax really did not exist, then gross incomes (and average working hours) in all jobs would be different. Gross incomes represent not the market price of our labor simpliciter but the market price of our labor within some particular institutional scheme.

To be coherent, the complaint must then be formulated in interschemic terms. But, so formulated, it has considerably less intuitive appeal. Critics may advocate their favorite alternative economic scheme and point out that relative to *it*, a scheme favored by the difference principle would be using or exploiting the better endowed.[7] But this complaint reduces to the commonplace that some schemes are better for some groups and others for others. Relative to S_0, S_5 raises the prospects of the normals while lowering those of the exceptionals. But this complaint presupposes, and hence cannot support, a preference of S_0 over S_5, for it is equally true that, relative to S_5, S_0 raises the prospects of the exceptionals while lowering those of the normals. It is unlikely that there is a feasible scheme under which no group would lose relative to *any* feasible alternative scheme, and if there were such a scheme (weakly Pareto-superior to *all* alternatives) then Rawls's criterion would favor it in any case.

5.7. With the three misunderstandings clarified, there is no basis left for believing Rawls has any need for proposition (3), that the work and efforts of some may be used as means for the benefit of others. Thus he has no reason to assert what the Nozick-Sandel reading takes him to assert, "that everyone has some entitlement or claim on the totality of natural assets (viewed as a pool)" (ASU 228), "that the least advantaged may share in the resources of the fortunate" (LLJ 70). And if he has no reason to assert (1) or (2), then he also need not be at pains to show that by regarding "the distribution of natural talents as a common asset . . .

---

such reasoning presupposes that unconstrained bargaining is the right method for arriving at *morally* acceptable terms of cooperation. Why should a discussion about justice have to yield the same result as a bargaining session among unequal self-interested groups? (Rawls has a lovely footnote on how this is implausible even in microcases [TJ 134 n. 10].) Nozick can insist that accepting S_5 would be foolish on the part of the exceptionals, but he thereby is demonstrating only that they would be fools (in Nozick's sense) to talk about justice at all, rather than to exact the best terms they can get (the Melian dialogue). He does not show that S_5 is unjust or that under S_5 the exceptionals are used as means.

[7] So Nozick (ASU 228–29): "In a free society, people's talents benefit others, and not only themselves. Is it the extraction of even more benefit to others that is supposed to justify treating people's natural assets as a collective resource?"

not *persons* but only 'their' *attributes* are being used as means to others' well-being" (LLJ 78; cf. ASU 228).[8]

6. Natural Endowments and Desert

6.1. Rawls claims that his conception of justice nullifies the accidents of natural endowment. This does not mean that endowments are to be equalized or that an economic scheme must not offer greater rewards to those better endowed. The point is that the better endowed have no special claims upon the construction of the criterion of social justice. This point has two important corollaries: when the appropriate terms of economic cooperation are negotiated (for example, in the original position), it is morally inappropriate for endowments to be a factor in the participants' bargaining position;[9] and natural endowments do not reflect an intrinsic moral worth that would set bounds on the terms an economic scheme may offer for their development and exercise. This second corollary will be central to the present section.

Given the constraint upon its construction, Rawls arrives at a criterion of (economic) justice that does not mention natural endowments. It ranks economic schemes solely with regard to the income distribution (specifically, the lowest incomes) they tend to produce. How the development and exercise of endowments should be rewarded is a secondary issue, to be settled by reference to this criterion (and empirical facts). Endowments play no role in specifying what an economic scheme is supposed to achieve, though they do of course play a role in how it can best achieve this.

Thus, in the correct reading of the common-asset formulations, Rawls's pattern preference requires that economic institutions be such that the inequalities they generate tend to maximize, interschemically, the minimum share. This preference leaves wide open the kind and extent of inequalities the favored scheme would allow. In particular, the rewards this scheme offers to persons with special gifts depends on how useful and how widespread these are and also on how the development and exercise of these gifts would be affected by alternative reward schedules.[10] By thus adjusting the (choice of) economic scheme

---

[8]Nor need Rawls accept Sandel's invitation to go over to the communitarian camp "by questioning the sense in which those who share in 'my' assets are properly described as 'others'. . . . If the difference principle is to avoid using some as means to others' ends, it can only be possible under circumstances where the subject of possession is a 'we' rather than an 'I', which circumstances imply in turn the existence of a community in the constitutive sense" (LLJ 79–80).

[9]This corollary is explicit in a parallel passage: "The idea of the original position is to set up a fair procedure so that any principles agreed to will be just. . . . Somehow we must nullify the effects of specific contingencies" (TJ 136). Compare the final paragraph of n. 6.

[10]For example, if there were a feasible scheme under which almost all the exceptionals would greatly enjoy the complex job and would choose to work in it even though it pays

to the distribution of natural endowments (and of human dispositions), one regards as a common asset *this distribution*, not the particular endowments themselves or what flows from their exercise within some economic scheme. One might say that this *fact* of differential endowments is used as a means.

Stated in the abstract, the distinction I propose here may seem to have an air of sophistry, so let me offer an illustration of its significance. A travel company operating with run-down accommodations, unsafe flights, hidden charges, and the like may be said to use the needs and desires of its customers as means for its own enrichment. This use may well be, as Nozick and Sandel would insist, tantamount to using these customers themselves merely as means. By contrast, consider a travel company that charges different prices for identical services provided at different times of the year (off-peak, high season, etc.), so as to equalize demand. In this case it is the distribution of customer interests and desires, the fact that customers are different in various relevant respects, that is used as a means. Though the end motivating the policy may be the same in both cases (maximization of profit, say), it seems clear that only the first policy can reasonably be said to use customers as means. This distinction concerning (the choice of) policies has an analogue, I believe, as regards (the choice of) social institutions. Here Rawls's suggestion is analogous to the second kind of policy. By adjusting the terms offered for the development and exercise of endowments, institutions make this fact serve the Rawlsian imperative of justice, that social inequalities must be to the greatest benefit of those most disadvantaged by them.

This reading is confirmed by looking once more at the sentences upon which the Nozick-Sandel reading so heavily relies: "The difference principle represents, in effect, an agreement to regard the distribution of natural talents as a common asset and to share in the benefits of this distribution whatever it turns out to be" (TJ 101) and "the two principles are equivalent, as I have remarked, to an undertaking to regard the distribution of natural abilities as a collective asset so that the more fortunate are to benefit only in ways that help those who have lost out" (TJ 179). Both passages confirm that it is the *distribution of* natural endowments that is to be regarded as a common or collective asset.[11] Nozick and Sandel simply ignore what Rawls is saying. Nozick, after quoting the former passage, speaks of "treating people's natural

---

no more than the simple one, then this scheme would be preferred because both jobs would have a higher net income rate than the simple job under S_5. Table 1, on the contrary, is based on the assumption that under *all* feasible schemes some of the exceptionals prefer the complex job only for its greater rewards. On this assumption, S_5 engenders the highest minimum net income rate.

[11]Such formulations occur also in the post-TJ writings. Rawls describes what is to be used for the common benefit as "the natural distribution of abilities" (RMC 145; RAM 647), "natural contingencies" (WOS 17), and "natural differences" (KCMT 551). Rawls's point is correctly noted, for example, in Martin, RR 77.

assets as a collective resource" (ASU 228–9). Sandel, after quoting both, paraphrases them by saying that Rawls "regard[s] people's natural assets as common property" (LLJ 78).[12]

With this point cleared up, a number of further issues raised by Nozick and Sandel turn out to be irrelevant. Thus Sandel, again drawing upon Nozick, spends a good deal of effort (LLJ 96–103) on the question whether, if endowments do not belong to those who "have" them, it follows that they belong to society or humankind at large, or whether they might belong to no one at all? This question reappears in his later discussion of affirmative action (LLJ 135–47), where he writes: "The arbitrariness of an individual's assets argues only against the proposition that the individual owns them or has a privileged claim to their benefits, not in favor of the proposition that some particular society owns them or has a privileged claim with respect to them. And unless this second proposition can be established, there would seem no grounds for favoring a utilitarian dispensation of such assets and endowments rather than just letting them lie where they fall" (LLJ 141). Rawls, far from seeking to establish the second, has no reason to deny the first proposition. Within the option space available in a just social system, persons should have the right to develop or not to develop, to exercise or not to exercise, their endowments as they wish and should be entitled to the full benefits offered for their efforts in this regard. The question Rawls and Ronald Dworkin are raising is whether having greater endowments should entitle persons to anything *else*, such as a higher income, preferential treatment by university admission boards, and so forth.

In Sandel's case, the misreading is all the more puzzling in view of his exemplarily clear grasp of the philosophical issue. He writes: "In order for me to deserve the benefits associated with 'my' superior intel-

---

[12]Ironically, Sandel does not quote the third occurrence of the expression, a sentence in which Rawls does indeed suggest the common-property view: "By accepting the difference principle, [the less fortunate] view the greater abilities as a social asset to be used for the common advantage" (TJ 107). This careless phrasing, cited by neither Nozick nor Sandel, would count in favor of their reading, at least if there weren't the two parallel sentences and if there were any other indications that Rawls regards people's natural endowments as "common property." Still, it must be noted that by the time of Sandel's writing Nozick's interpretation had become widespread, presumably in large part because Rawls has never explicitly repudiated it. Even so sympathetic and knowledgeable a commentator as Scanlon writes: "As Rawls says, the terms of this principle are equivalent to an undertaking to regard natural abilities as a common asset" (RTJ 203)—after correctly quoting Rawls's statement that the *distribution* of natural abilities is to be so regarded (RTJ 199). The common-asset formulations are not only infelicitous, thus inviting the misunderstanding I have discussed. They are also undistinctive in that they fit *any* broadly consequentialist criterion for assessing basic structures. Even conceptions of justice concerned with the income of the better endowed or general happiness or the flourishing of the arts and sciences, for example, would treat the distribution of endowments as a common asset by demanding that institutions affecting the development and exercise of natural endowments be designed so as optimally to satisfy the chosen criterion.

ligence, say, it is necessary both that I possess my intelligence (in some non-arbitrary sense of possession), *and* that I have a right (in a strong, pre-institutional sense of right) that society value intelligence rather than something else. But on Rawls' account, neither condition holds" (LLJ 77). Here Sandel understands that in order to deny the conjunction, one *does not need* to deny more than the second condition.[13] How does he get the idea that Rawls, whose aim is to argue "from widely accepted but weak premises" (TJ 18), *unnecessarily* invokes the shocking common-property claim? One might be tempted to think that Sandel, so close a reader of Rawls, falls for Nozick's interpretation only because it fits so wonderfully into his overall attack on Rawls's (or "the liberal") conception of the person (to be discussed in §§8–9).

6.2. While this may be so, it would be unfair to claim that Sandel is taking a few sentences out of context and then using them to support a perverse construal of Rawls's position. This is closer to what Nozick does, brilliantly. Sandel manages to connect these misreadings in a systematic way and ends up with a reasonably coherent account of large portions of Rawls's text, as we can see in a discussion of the third quotation of my opening set (§5.1), the assertion that "no one deserves his place in the distribution of native endowments" (TJ 104), that such endowments are "arbitrary from a moral point of view" (TJ 312). To make things more vivid, let us personify the doubt Rawls is addressing in these phrases. Suppose an exceptionally gifted person, Genius, has lodged this complaint against the difference principle: "Perhaps it would be nice, other things equal, to arrange a scheme of economic institutions so that the inequalities it produces tend to optimize the smallest representative share. But other things are not equal. I am a lot more talented than most, and I deserve these talents together with the greater income that flows from them. It is not right that the possibility of (intraschemically) benefiting from one's endowments should be incorporated into the economic scheme only insofar as such incorporation (interschemically) enhances the smallest share."

To cope with this complaint, it would be enough to challenge Genius's presupposition that something—naturally, as it were—"flows from" her talents. Rawls makes this response, as Sandel appreciates. Rawls, however, is denying another link in Genius's argument as well, namely, that she deserves her talents. So Rawls, whether he needs to or not, does burden himself with a stronger commitment. To explain what Sandel takes this commitment to be, let me conjecture how he would construe the argument by Genius that Rawls is entertaining and responding to:

---

[13]I say "here" because Sandel isn't always this clear. There are two equally clear parallel passages (LLJ 72, 143), but more common are claims like this: "The difference principle *must* presuppose . . . that I am the guardian of assets to which the community as a whole has some prior title or claim" (LLJ 97, my emphasis).

(a) I have endowments.
(b) One deserves whatever endowments one has; which is to say: it is proper that one have them, it would be wrong for one to be deprived of them, and so forth.
(c) I deserve my endowments [from (a) and (b)].
(d) Hence, I deserve the goods that flow from the development and exercise of my endowments.

Sandel acknowledges that Rawls denies the transition from (c) to (d), and that this denial is enough to turn away the complaint. Still, Sandel finds him disputing (c) as well, repeatedly denying that "the person with greater natural endowments deserves those assets" (TJ 103). Because he denies (c), Rawls is committed to denying either (a) or (b), because these together imply (c). But how could Rawls possibly deny either, if both seem so plausible? The ingenious answer Sandel attributes to Rawls is that (a) and (b) are both true, but that they do not employ the same sense of "to have" and therefore do not imply (c): "Rawls' argument from arbitrariness undermines desert not directly, by claiming I cannot *deserve* what is arbitrarily given, but indirectly, by showing that I cannot *possess* what is arbitrarily given, that is, that 'I', *qua* subject of possession, cannot possess it in the undistanced, constitutive sense necessary to provide a desert base" (LLJ 85). This answer powerfully supports Sandel's chief thesis about Rawls's conception of the person, condensed into the refrain: "On Rawls' conception, the characteristics I possess do not *attach* to the self but are only *related* to the self, standing always at a certain distance. This is what makes them attributes rather than constituents of my person; they are *mine* rather than *me*, things I *have* rather than *am*" (LLJ 85).

This impressive reconstruction of Rawls's treatment of desert goes wrong by misconstruing the sense in which Rawls is speaking of desert. According to Rawls, for one to deserve something entails that it is proper that one have it. But it means more. Desert, for Rawls, is *moral deservingness*, a reflection of one's moral worth in virtue of which alone one can Deserve anything. This may not be the ordinary sense of the term. Rawls suggests as much when he occasionally speaks more fully of *moral* desert and, once, when he has the broader sense in mind, talks of people being "deserving in the ordinary sense" (TJ 74). Still, there can be no doubt that the stronger, narrower notion is the one he is using.[14] It follows that many things deserved in the ordinary sense are not Deserved in Rawls's. You may have worked all your life on your autobiography and thus deserve the National Book Award, but you would still not Deserve it in Rawls's sense, unless your efforts somehow testified to your superior *moral* worth.

[14]For example, Rawls writes, "there is a tendency for common sense to suppose that income and wealth, and the good things generally, should be distributed according to moral desert. Justice is happiness according to virtue" (TJ 310).

6.3. With this narrower sense of *Desert* in mind, we can also understand Rawls's claim that the distribution of natural endowments is morally arbitrary. Rawls is not saying that there is no moral reason to leave endowments where we find them—of course there is—but that differences in endowments do not, within the conception of social justice, signify differences in moral worth. This claim does not presuppose that native endowments are a matter of luck or fortune. Even if people had to have worked very hard to be bright or athletic, these traits would still be arbitrary from a moral point of view. Those who don't care to become bright or athletic through hard work are not therefore to be considered *morally* inferior (as far as our shared public conception of justice is concerned). So in Rawls's terminology the two locutions express the same distinction: something we have is morally arbitrary just in case our having it is not Deserved.

Given this distinction, there are two different ways in which a practice or a set of natural rights and duties may specify something as a person's due. If something is due you in the wider sense, then you ought to have it, it is right that you have it, and it would be wrong for you to be deprived of it. I have been expressing this sense of "due" by speaking—with Nozick—of your being *entitled* to something. One might stretch this term by including under the label of entitlements also undesirable things that are due you, such as a debit or a punishment. In this stretched sense, being entitled to something does not entail that you have a choice whether to receive it or not. You may or may not have such a choice.

Something is due you in the narrow sense only if you are entitled to it in virtue of your moral Deservingness, that is, in virtue of a moral quality of yourself or a moral quality of something you have done. Your due in this sense presupposes Desert (moral Deservingness) on your part. It would not be unnatural to speak of desert in connection with most of your entitlements (salary, awards, vacations) and in other contexts as well (good luck, ill-behaved children, an accident), but we must stick to the narrow notion because it is the one Rawls is using.

Keeping this notion of Desert in mind, let me give a countersketch of the argument by Genius that Rawls is entertaining and responding to:

(a) I have endowments.
(B) One Deserves whatever endowments one has, which is to say, one's endowments reflect one's moral worth, are a sign of moral Deservingness.
(C) I Deserve my endowments (from (a) and (B)).
(D) Hence, I am entitled to the goods that flow from the development and exercise of my endowments.

Here (D) is equivalent to (d), the conclusion of the previous argument sketch. Let me note three points about this reconstruction of the complaint Rawls seeks to block. To begin with, since (C) is stronger than (c), the last step of the reasoning has become much more plausible. If Genius is morally more worthy than others less well endowed, then one may be tempted to believe—as Rawls thinks common sense is tempted (n. 14)—that she should have a higher income too. And thus my countersketch makes more comprehensible why Rawls should have seen the need to complement his denial of the last step by denying its starting point as well.

Next, Rawls's denial of (C) is fully consistent with (a), (b), and (c), with what, on my reading, Rawls simply takes for granted: persons have their natural endowments in a thick, constitutive sense and are fully entitled to (exercise control over) them. There is no question that Genius's talents must not be destroyed or tampered with or taxed and that she must not be coerced to develop or exercise them.[15] The denial of (C) gives no support to Sandel's view that Rawls thinks of endowments as only tenuously connected to their "repository" or "guardian" (LLJ 97), so that "it matters little how some came to reside in you and others in me" (LLJ 74).

Finally, the premise Rawls challenges is (B), claiming that it is no *moral* distinction to be gifted, that the better endowed are not for this reason more worthy, morally: "Surely a person's moral worth does not vary according to how many offer similar skills, or happen to want what he can produce. No one supposes that when someone's abilities are less in demand or have deteriorated (as in the case of singers) his moral deservingness undergoes a similar shift" (TJ 311). It seems quite likely that Nozick and Sandel, had they appreciated his point, would have agreed with Rawls. Nozick, at any rate, is constrained to agree, for under his own scheme rewards are determined by existing market demand, and so Genius would be unable to earn rewards for exercising her talents if people were either unable or unwilling to pay her for such exercise. So Nozick and Rawls are here in full agreement. While Genius has every right to earn any special rewards for the exercise of her talents that may be offered under the preferred scheme (and is surely fully entitled to whatever rewards she may have so earned), she has no claim that there be a scheme under which such rewards are offered, let alone rewards of any particular kind or magnitude. Of course, Rawls and Nozick disagree about what economic schemes are just. They merely agree that the answer to this question is not constrained by claims of moral worth based on natural endowments. Sandel, on the other hand, believes that this answer *is* constrained by some claims of moral worth and Desert. I discuss his view in cases where such claims have a more plausible basis than natural endowments (§7.3), but first, let us bring the whole topic of natural endowments to a conclusion.

[15]There is one passage I must discount as a slip: "No one deserves his greater natural capacity. . . . But it does not follow that one should eliminate these distinctions. There is another way to deal with them" (TJ 102). Nozick rightly asks (ASU 229), what if there weren't another way to deal with them? Rawls has corrected the slip in the German translation (TG 122).

6.4. Rawls holds that economic schemes should be ranked on broadly consequentialist grounds, specifically, according to the worst social position each tends to produce. Whether and to what extent the favored economic ground rules would lead to differentials in income (etc.) based on differentials in natural endowments is left open by Rawls, to be settled through the difference principle in light of empirical conditions. This approach is subject to two main sorts of attack on behalf of the better endowed: one insists that the practices and processes that are to regulate economic interaction should be chosen in a way that reflects the *superior bargaining position* of the better endowed; the other maintains that the better endowed, in virtue of their *greater moral Deservingness*, ought to receive special rewards (of a certain relative or absolute magnitude) for the development and exercise of their endowments. These attacks may be used to assert that there are morally obvious processes (which are to be chosen regardless of the pattern they would yield) or that the chosen economic scheme or the distribution it would produce must satisfy certain moral constraints.

I have discussed how Rawls can block these attacks. He can resist the assertion of morally obvious practices and processes and reject the claim that persons Deserve their natural endowments. Neither of these defenses relies on any particular conception of the self, let alone on the assertions Sandel attributes to Rawls—that "the various natural assets with which I am born may be said to 'belong' to me in the weak, contingent sense that they reside accidentally within me, but this sense of ownership or possession cannot establish that I have any special rights with respect to these assets or any privileged claim to the fruits of their exercise. In this attenuated sense of possession, I am not really the owner, but merely the guardian or repository of the assorted assets and attributes located 'here' " (LLJ 82). The dispute about Rawls's treatment of natural endowments turns out, upon examination, to have nothing at all to do with the debate about his conception of the person.

These defenses show that there is no moral reason why a just economic scheme or the income distribution it generates should reflect our differential natural endowments in one way or another or not at all. It is important to note that this result defends *any* pattern preference that does not mention natural endowments, not merely Rawls's in particular. Yet the result is not therefore insignificant. In the abstract, the maximin criterion, as epitomized in the difference principle, is highly plausible and intuitive. Even Nozick concedes, "If *somehow* the size of the pie wasn't fixed, and it was realized that pursuing an equal distribution somehow would lead to a smaller total pie than otherwise might occur, the people might well agree to an unequal distribution which raised the size of the least share" (ASU 198, cf. 231). But if, as I have argued, the way the size of the pie isn't fixed cannot (justifiably) have any moral bearing on our pattern preference in matters of justice, then Nozick could be persuaded to accept whatever economic process does best by the difference principle. Among pattern preferences that do not mention natural endowments Rawls's criterion might well win out almost by default.

7. Desert

7.1. Ground rules regulate the distribution of benefits and burdens among individuals and associations on the basis of various predicates that are true of them or of their conduct. I will say that ground rules are *moralized* insofar as the predicates they invoke are predicates of moral evaluation. Thus, when ground rules classify certain kinds of conduct as right or wrong or certain kinds of persons or associations as morally better or worse, then any benefits or burdens attached to such predicates are (positive or negative) sanctions that, when correctly applied, are *Deserved* by their recipients. Conversely, ground rules are *unmoralized* insofar as the predicates they invoke are nonmoral. Any benefits or burdens attached to such predicates—(dis)incentives, for example—are viewed as merely deserved, not Deserved. In such cases the *moral* quality of persons or their conduct is not at issue.[16]

Let me give a simple illustration of the distinction. Take, in our culture, a law that imposes some tax on interest income. This law is partly unmoralized. There is nothing morally unworthy about earning interest, and so the tax is not a punishment. In this the tax is akin to the interest itself, which also is merely earned, not Deserved. Investing one's money for interest is no better or worse, morally, than spending it or keeping it under one's pillow. Yet suppose the law makes it an offense to evade the tax. It would then, in this respect, be moralized. It is wrong to earn interest without paying the tax, and any fine for doing so is a punishment.

This distinction makes Rawls's task harder than it may initially appear. He is offering us the original position together with arguments about how parties so situated would go about regulating human interaction. Here Rawls seeks to show that they would adopt a particular set of natural rights and duties[17] and a criterion of justice for the assess-

---

[16]The distinction drawn here is purely descriptive. So I leave open what moral or nonmoral predicates may be important in or may be incorporated into the ground rules of a given society. Moreover the distinction is not entirely sharp. A parking ticket may (in our culture) be a borderline case, in that it can be viewed as a Deserved punishment for having done something wrong or also as a mere disincentive morally on a par with a parking fee.

[17]Rawls presents his account of natural duties in TJ §§18, 19, and 51. Natural duties "hold between persons irrespective of their institutional relationships" (TJ 115) and include the duties not to be cruel, not to harm or injure the innocent, to show respect, to help those in need, and to contribute to the establishment of just institutions (TJ 109, 114–15, 334, 337–39). It is sometimes overlooked that the account of natural duties is also chosen through the original position (TJ 116, 334, 338). Thus, like the criterion of justice, it

ment of institutional ground rules. He then invites us to check these natural duties and some basic structures that might plausibly satisfy his criterion of justice under stipulated empirical conditions against our considered judgments. Is what Rawlsian institutions would specify as a person's due consistent with what we intuitively believe one ought to have or receive? Yet an affirmative answer to this question is not enough, for not only must a person's due by Rawls's lights match what we intuitively think is due, but the two senses of *due* must match as well. Even if what persons are entitled to, pursuant to Rawls's natural duties and under Rawlsian ground rules, is consistent with what we think persons should be entitled to, there may still be disagreement about which of these entitlements should involve Desert. And even this is not all. We must also be satisfied that Rawls is right about which Deserts and mere entitlements are natural and which institutional, that is, which arise between persons generally (even in the absence of shared institutions) and which arise only among participants in an ongoing practice or institutional scheme.

These two crosscutting distinctions (moralized/unmoralized and natural/institutional) yield four categories of entitlements, namely, benefits and burdens that persons (a) Deserve according to a natural law (such as a punishment for cruelty); (b) Deserve under the terms of an institutional scheme (such as a fine or a jail sentence); (c) are entitled to according to a natural law but do not Deserve (minimal respect and nonviolence, perhaps); or (d) are entitled to under the terms of an institutional scheme but do not Deserve (salaries, taxes, goods and services paid for, etc.), which Rawls refers to as *legitimate expectations* (TJ §48). Rawls says nothing about entitlements of the first kind, presumably because these are superseded, once reasonably just institutions exist, by entitlements of the second kind. Still, he can say that, even when a Deserved punishment is meted out in accordance with a civil law, what is being punished can always be viewed as also the transgression of a natural duty, minimally, the duty to comply with just institutions (TJ 115, 334). In this sense part of the moral force of all institutional ground rules derives from our natural duties.

7.2. We have seen how Rawls sought to reject (my version of) Genius's complaint against the difference principle by denying that a conception of justice should count natural endowments as a *moral* distinction. This denial raises the question whether persons (or their conduct) have other qualities that do reflect their moral worth and thus might give the more Deserving valid claims to benefits that an economic scheme satisfying the difference principle might leave unmet. In this vein Rawls denies that "a man deserves the superior character that

---

is to rest upon an appeal to our considered judgments rather than upon such metaphysical premises as were prominent in the natural-law tradition. The account is then consistent with Rawls's recent emphasis that his quest is for a moral conception that is "political not metaphysical" (JFPM; IOC).

enables him to make the effort to cultivate his abilities . . . for his character depends in large part upon fortunate family and social circumstances for which he can claim no credit" (TJ 104).[18] The reason Rawls gives here for the denial is not a good one. It suggests that he requires Desert itself to be Deserved "all the way down" (cf. Nozick, ASU 225), with the result that there is no Desert at all. Rawls counteracts this impression by insisting that entitlements arising under the criminal law do involve Desert (TJ 314–15). But then Sandel can ask with some plausibility how a criminal can Deserve her inferior character if it depends in large part upon *un*fortunate family and social circumstances (LLJ 91–92). The reason Rawls gives would then suggest that the economic and penal systems are, *pace* Rawls, opposites of each other—two unmoralized systems of incentives and disincentives (respectively), which are designed to steer conduct in the interest of maximizing economic efficiency and the effectiveness of ground rules generally.

Even if the reason Rawls gives is not a good one, his contention itself seems plausible enough (at least if Desert is understood in his narrow sense). Persons who put scant effort into their careers, perhaps because they care little for material wealth or prefer to concentrate their energies upon other projects, are not for this reason morally less worthy. Of course, higher incomes will generally be earned by those who make special efforts to develop and exercise abilities for which greater rewards are offered. But these higher incomes are merely earned, not Deserved, because such efforts at self-improvement are not considered (within our public conception of justice) a form of *moral* excellence. That they are not is one reason persons who make special efforts to develop and exercise unrewarded abilities have no valid grounds for complaint. That some have trained themselves to juggle six balls or to recite the *Iliad* implies nothing about their (moral) Deservingness.

7.3. But the objection may be renewed one last time. Even if Rawls is right thus far, surely there are *some* forms of moral excellence. Clearly, some persons are morally better human beings than others, and might not these persons raise a valid complaint against an economic scheme that is just by Rawls's criterion, if their incomes under this scheme do not reflect their superior moral character? Let me sketch such a complaint.

(A*) Courtney has a superior moral character.
(B*) One Deserves whatever moral character one has, which is to say, one's moral character reflects one's moral worth, is a sign of moral Deservingness.
(C*) Courtney Deserves her superior moral character.
(D*) Courtney is entitled to greater economic rewards.

---

[18]Cf. TJ 312, where the willingness to make an effort is ascribed to superior endowments.

In this case, at last, Rawls's first line of defense is surely overwhelmed, for he cannot deny (C*). That (as Rawls insists) criminals *Deserve* punishment implies that they are morally less worthy on account of their actions (and intentions). So surely it is possible that Courtney is morally *more* worthy on account of *her* actions (and intentions), at least more worthy than the criminals.

Rawls is right to emphasize that "the concept of moral worth does not provide a first principle of distributive justice . . . because it cannot be introduced until after the principles of justice and of natural duty and obligation" (TJ 312). Nevertheless, surely we could settle on the natural duties and the civil and political aspects of a just basic structure first, use these results to define the idea of morally (more or less) worthy citizens and human beings, and then choose an economic scheme under which (insofar as is feasible) income reflects moral worth. In this case the economic and penal systems would once again be opposites of each other, but they would both be moralized, two systems of (respectively) positive and negative sanctions that play a secondary role in the reinforcement of duties and ground rules independently defined.

In the face of this complaint, Rawls is thrown back upon his second line of defense, which denies the steps from (C) to (D), and from (C*) to (D*): Even persons who are genuinely Deserving ought not therefore to be entitled to larger shares of social primary goods. A basic structure under which some good or bad deeds go unrequited is not unjust for this reason. Though Rawls is clearly committed to this view, he does not seek to support its intuitive plausibility. But I think it would not be too hard to do so. It may be enough to imagine a social system in which cash prizes are paid to those who do not break any laws for five years or in which all moral wrongs (lies, for example) incur fines, to see that this is not what we would think justice *requires*.

7.4. This second line of defense also shields Rawls's belief that the distribution of income and wealth should be regulated, by and large, by unmoralized ground rules. Again we must rely on conjecture as to how he would support this belief. The natural duties and the civil and political ground rules of a just basic structure impose simple, "binary" constraints on persons' conduct. No moral distinctions are made (by these rules) within the vast arena of permissible conduct. Participants are not asked to strive for the greatest moral excellence as measured on some open-ended scale but are merely enjoined to refrain from certain specified wrongs. Complying with these natural duties and social practices to perfection does not then require fantastic feats of moral fortitude. Rather, the relevant rules are so designed that compliance is quite possible and can reasonably be expected from any ordinary person, which suggests that there is little or no reason for institutionalizing any positive sanctions at all. Such sanctions might even subvert the standing of the rules by diverting attention away from the moral reasons for honoring them, might impede the development of a sense of justice. Punishments will of course be needed, and some of these may take the form of fines. Still, these will be rare, and organizing the entire economic reward system around them would entail that most persons would receive (and Deserve) the equal maximum income of a law-abiding citizen. Against such a scheme Rawls can plausibly ask: Why not "unmoralize" economic benefits so as to allow income differentials (among law-abiding citizens) insofar as these benefit everyone? Thus collective rationality makes it plausible to prefer an economic scheme under which income is generally conceived as merely earned, not Deserved.

Nozick would wholeheartedly agree with this conclusion. Economic sanctions attached to (moralized) ground rules should not play a central role in the distribution of income and wealth.[19]

7.5. One cannot tell whether Sandel would agree, because he has not yet presented his own conception of justice. Still, let me briefly trace where his criticisms of Rawls go wrong. As we have seen, Sandel fails to appreciate the distinction between Desert and desert, the stronger and weaker notions. This misunderstanding leads him to construe Rawls's distinction between Desert and legitimate expectations as one between preinstitutional and institutional entitlements. But even correcting for such terminological differences, Sandel is wrong to claim that Rawls makes "a dramatic departure from traditional conceptions" in presenting "a theory of justice . . . ruling out desert altogether" (LLJ 86). "The principles of justice do not mention moral desert, because, strictly speaking, no one can be said to deserve anything. . . . on Rawls' view, *people have no intrinsic worth*, no worth that is intrinsic in the sense that it is theirs prior to or independent of or apart from what just institutions attribute to them" (LLJ 88).

This diagnosis is false because Rawls's conception of justice incorporates a notion of Desert connected to the moralized part of a just basic structure (the ground rules insofar as they admit of violation). So there is an institutional notion of Desert that contrasts with the (institutional) notion of legitimate expectations. There is a preinstitutional notion of Desert as well. Violations of natural duties—cruelty or injury of an innocent, for example—do detract from a person's moral worth or Deservingness (and will expose that person to punishment within, and maybe also apart from, any institutional scheme).

Perhaps Sandel would think this too thin a notion of preinstitutional Desert. He appeals to the classical idea of the virtues, defining various (perhaps correlated) dimensions of moral excellence. Maybe his idea is that persons should be treated in accordance with their scores in these dimensions or in overall moral excellence, but how is this idea to be

---

[19]Compensation for "border crossings" is owed under *unmoralized* ground rules. It is not wrong to cross and pay. See Chap. 1, n. 6; and Nozick, ASU, chap. 4.

incorporated into the basic structure of a social system? Would Sandel prefer a society in which, say, the right to rule is reserved for the most virtuous? This sort of traditional conception raises familiar problems, such as how we reach agreement on a specification of the virtues and on procedures for selecting those who excel in them.[20]

I conclude that Rawls's conception can and does incorporate the distinctions between natural and institutional and between moralized and unmoralized ground rules. Hence he has both a preinstitutional and an institutional notion of Desert—which notions, moreover, are even stronger than Sandel's (and thus more sparingly invoked). Sandel is then mistaken in claiming that Rawls dispenses with Desert, and so there is no reason to saddle Rawls with the reason Sandel predictably provides for this supposed denial: "No one can be said to deserve anything (in the strong, pre-institutional sense), because no one can be said to possess anything (in the strong, constitutive sense)" (LLJ 92f). It is not true that Rawls is presenting "a theory of justice without desert and a notion of the self as essentially dispossessed, or barren of constituent traits" (LLJ 92). Let us, nevertheless, investigate the second conjunct of this claim as well.

8. The "Deontological" Self

8.1. So far I have shown how, once his Nozickian misreadings of "common asset," "moral arbitrariness," and "desert" are corrected, large parts of Sandel's attack dissolve. The starting points of Rawls's argument are quite mainstream and hardly warrant the surprise and hostility they have evoked. Persons should control the development and exercise of their own natural endowments within the option space available in a just social system. The assessment and design of social institutions should not be influenced by the idea of bargaining based on knowledge of differential endowments or by the idea that those who have or develop or exercise greater endowments are therefore morally more worthy. Moreover, institutions regulating the distribution of income and wealth should be conceived as unmoralized, that is, should not be designed to achieve a correlation between income and moral

[20]But perhaps Sandel was merely misexpressing his objection. Perhaps he would not want the parties in the original position to supplement their account of natural duties with an account of natural virtues. Such additional moral notions, though conceived as preinstitutional, would still be ones we construct rather than find. They would leave us "inhabitants of a world without *telos*, . . . unconstrained by an order of value antecedently given . . . the author of the only moral meanings there are" (LLJ 177). Against this, he might insist on a truly natural telos, part of the fabric of the universe, through which we can discern the natural order of human affairs and the place each of us occupies in this order. But then Sandel also seems to want a community-relative telos, intersubjective rather than objective, that is constitutive of how the community members conceive of their identity. At least he suggests as much by denying that "we cannot know one another, or our ends, well enough to govern by the common good alone" (LLJ 183).

worth. Since neither these commonplace views nor any conclusions anyone has nonfallaciously drawn from them have even mildly exciting implications for our self-conception as persons, Sandel's most important source of evidence for attributing to Rawls a particular notion of the self is entirely unproductive.

Still, Rawls is offering an explicit conception of the person, and we should therefore see whether Sandel accepts Rawls's self-understanding on this point or presents plausible reasons to depart from it. This undertaking presents a new task, namely, to understand the idea of a "deontological" self, which Sandel claims to have discovered in Rawls's conception of justice.

8.2. Sandel describes how he has discovered this idea as follows: "The original position is the fulcrum of the justificatory process in that *it* is the device through which all justification must pass. . . . [W]hat issues at one end in a theory of justice must issue at the other in a theory of the person, or more precisely, a theory of the moral subject. Looking from one direction through the lens of the original position we see the two principles of justice; looking from the other direction we see a reflection of ourselves" (LLJ 47–48). Sandel's central discovery is that for Rawls the self, or subject, is prior to its ends. Sandel links this priority with five further priorities: of the right over the good, of justice over other values, of the contract over the principles it generates, of plurality over unity, and of principles of justice over the choice of conceptions of the good.[21]

Sandel's general idea is that "deontological" liberals, by asserting certain moral priorities, must presuppose certain other, nonmoral priorities that he wishes to expose as embarrassing. To his credit, Sandel is clear throughout that Rawls does not himself assert the nonmoral priorities Sandel ascribes to him. Thus he recognizes, for example, that Rawls's phrase "the self is prior to the ends which are affirmed by it" (TJ 560) asserts a moral priority (persons are to constrain their pursuit of ends by principles of right and justice) and that he, Sandel, must *show* that Rawls *implicitly* presupposes a nonmoral priority of the self over its ends (LLJ 19–20).

Much less clear, however, are Sandel's attempts to demonstrate Rawls's supposed implicit presuppositions. One problem is that he never states with any precision what he means when he speaks of priority in a nonmoral sense. Here the adjectives he employs to refer to the deeper and revealing nonmoral priorities he claims to have discovered in Rawls are of little help. Sandel alternates between "foundational," "metaethical," and "epistemological," of which the latter is by far the most frequent, for example: "The independence of the self . . . is

---

[21]It remains unclear why and how, according to Sandel, these priorities hang together. Do they resemble or suggest or imply each other? Sandel's standard way of asserting the connection is in vague sentences of the form "As X is prior to Y, so V is prior to W." The five further priorities are so likened to the first at LLJ 7, 20, 120, 133, 157, respectively.

above all an epistemological claim" (LLJ 182, cf. 12, 20) and "this is the epistemological priority that deontological ethics carries over into a moral priority" (LLJ 156) and so on.[22]

Often, nonmoral priority is explained as some kind of independence: X is prior to Y if X (or the notion of X) is independent of, or derived independently from, Y (the notion of Y). As I understand Sandel, such independence obtains if no change in (the notion of) Y makes a difference to (the notion of) X, if the latter can be understood without any understanding of the former. Using the word "priority" in this way is puzzling because Sandel is not concerned that the independence be unilateral (and were it mutual, X and Y would be prior to each other, an odd possibility). Thus he asserts that for Rawls justice is "prior in the sense of independently derived" (LLJ 16). But one would think that the priority of justice over other values (benevolence etc.) requires not only that it should be independent of them but also that *they* should *not* be independent of *it*. Sandel does not worry whether the independence is mutual.[23]

But even this strange notion of priority as independence might work to Sandel's advantage. A moral conception deriving the right independently of the good must specify it, he assumes, without appeal to what we know about human needs and ends—on the basis of the bare notion of a self (perhaps characterized solely by rationality and agency). If such a moral conception also requires actors to give primacy to constraints of the right (including just ground rules), then, Sandel reasons, it is at least implicitly committed to the preeminence of this bare notion of the self. This thought establishes the sought connection between a deontological moral conception and a "deontological" self (cf. LLJ 6–7). He concludes: "If the claim for the primacy of justice is to succeed, if the right is to be prior to the good in the interlocking moral and foundational senses we have distinguished, then some version of the claim for the primacy of the subject must succeed as well. This much seems clear" (LLJ 7).

We may leave aside whether this diagnosis is true of Kant[24] and, if so,

[22]The adjective *epistemological* is ubiquitous in the text and predicated of the other five priorities as well (LLJ 16, 22, 23, 53, 115, 133, 156). As Sandel recognizes, Rawls always uses *priority* in the sense of "*moral* priority." The further nonmoral notion(s) of epistemological, metaethical, and/or foundational priority, though supposedly implicit in Rawls, are introduced by Sandel. It is, therefore, Sandel's responsibility to clarify this notion or these notions.

[23]The problem recurs when Sandel says that for Kant "the right is prior to the good . . . in that its principles are independently derived" (LLJ 2). He makes the same assertion about Rawls. But in neither case does he deny the converse by excluding the possibility of *mutual* independence. He does not assert that for Kant and Rawls the notion of the good does *not* receive its content independently of that of the right. This is not to deny that with a somewhat more precise notion of independence such an assertion could be sustained for Kant (and perhaps Rawls as well). For Kant, happiness (the satisfaction of natural inclinations) is good only when it derives from the attainment of *permissible* ends and only insofar as it is proportional to the person's virtue (disposition to act *from duty*).

[24]Kant surely asserts the *moral* priority of the right over the good. By claiming that Kant's conception of right relies upon a notion of human needs (TJ 338, WOS 19), Rawls

whether such a "primacy of the subject" would be an embarrassment. Sandel is certainly wrong to claim (LLJ 18) that "the right is derived independently from the good" *by Rawls*, who explicitly asserts the opposite: "It should be noted that deontological theories are defined as non-teleological ones, not as views that characterize the rightness of institutions and acts independently from their consequences. All ethical doctrines worth our attention take consequences into account in judging rightness. One which did not would simply be irrational, crazy" (TJ 30). So Rawls endorses no independence of justice or the right from the good. His criterion of justice incorporates an account of social primary goods that reflects a notion of the moral subject as a being with certain needs and interests (cf. WOS 15). We must conclude, then, that Sandel fails in his first attempt to saddle Rawls with a conception of the self as barren and disencumbered.

8.3. In a further attempt to reveal Rawls's commitment to the priority of the self, Sandel attributes to Rawls the view "that I can never fully be constituted by my attributes, that there must always be some attributes I *have* rather than am. Otherwise, just *any* change in my situation, however slight, would change the person I am" (LLJ 20). Sandel freely admits that "this account is not offered by Rawls himself . . . [but] a reasonable reconstruction of the perplexities he seeks to address" (LLJ 20). We are not told where Rawls addresses such perplexities, but the view attributed to him is so far harmless enough.

Later Sandel strengthens his claim (LLJ 54–59): Rawls is really committed to the view that *all* of a person's attributes stand outside the self. As evidence, he cites two passages from section 22 of *A Theory of Justice*, where Rawls says that the parties in the original position are to "try to advance their conception of the good as best they can" (TJ 128). This does not mean, Rawls adds, that each person's conception of the good is assumed to be egoistic. The (unknown) interests the parties are to promote "are not assumed to be interests in the self," though they are, "as they must always be, interests of a self" (TJ 127, 129). Here, Sandel exclaims, "we find the key to Rawls' conception of the subject, . . . the notion of the self as a subject of possession. . . . To say that I possess a certain trait or desire or ambition is to say that . . . I am distanced from it in a certain way—that it is *mine* rather than *me*" (LLJ 55). But in the passages Sandel quotes (and elsewhere) Rawls says nothing at all about possession, let alone about possession in the "attenuated" as opposed to the "undistanced, constitutive sense" (LLJ 82–85). He merely says that interests are always the interests *of* a self. Whereas possession may sometimes function as "a distancing notion" (LLJ 54), it is far from clear that "of" must always function in this way. Talk about the interests *of* a self or *of* Michael Sandel hardly excludes

---

has denied, however, Kant's commitment to the "epistemological" priority, the other half of Sandel's reading of Kant. Rawls may well be mistaken on this point, but Sandel has done nothing at all to show that he is.

the possibility that some of these might be what Sandel calls *constitutive* interests.[25]

8.4. Sandel draws further conclusions. Since for Rawls "the identity of the agent is barren of constituent traits so that no aim or desire can be essential to it" (LLJ 164), a Rawlsian self is incapable of genuine choice and can only weigh desires against one another in the way of a hedonist: "The good is nothing more than the indiscriminate satisfaction of arbitrarily-given preferences, regardless of worth" (LLJ 168). Readers might think, Sandel foresees, "that Rawls could escape this apparent collapse of this account of agency" (LLJ 163) by suggesting that persons might have second-order desires. This is indeed possible, in the sense that some of the agent's desires may be desires about desires. But since all desires are equally outside the self, second-order desires would be no more essentially connected to the self than first-order desires are. Hence they could not be authoritative but would simply be weighed in "a slightly more complicated estimate of the relative intensity of pre-existing desires, first- and second-order desires included" (LLJ 164).

It is only on the second to last page of his book that Sandel informs us of what should have dissolved all this unreal speculation; he quotes Rawls's "concession" that "citizens in their personal affairs, or within the internal life of associations, . . . may have attachments and loves that they believe they would not, or could not, stand apart from; and they might regard it as unthinkable for them to view themselves without certain religious and philosophical convictions and commitments" (KCMT 545).[26] Unfortunately, Rawls's explicit statements to this effect were not noticed in time to mitigate the powerful impression evoked in Sandel by his reading of "of" and thus to block his elaborate tale of the empty self and the "impoverished theory of the good" (LLJ 165).

In restricting his remarks to "citizens in their personal affairs, or

[25]It may be fun to follow Sandel's story one step farther here. Since in Rawls's conception the self is entirely "unencumbered" and barren of attributes, any two selves are qualitatively identical. Rawls must then rely on our bodies to distinguish our various selves: "On Rawls' view of the moral subject, every individual human being is a moral subject, and every moral subject is an individual human being" (LLJ 52). This is yet another failure of Rawls's theory, according to Sandel, for Rawls must assume "that the bounds of the subject unproblematically correspond to the bodily bounds between individual human beings. But this claim is never defended by Rawls, only assumed" (LLJ 80). Sandel suggests (LLJ 62–63) that it would have been better had Rawls allowed for the possibility of selves who embrace more ("a family or community or class or nation") or less ("a plurality of selves within a single, individual human being") than a physically individuated person. It will be interesting to see Sandel work out his vision of a criterion of justice and of social institutions suitable for such entities. In doing so, however, he should perhaps avoid speaking of inter- and intrasubjective conceptions of the self (LLJ 62–63), as such talk would seem to confirm rather than contest Rawls's point that "for reasons of clarity among others" (TJ 264) we should recognize as the basic notion of a subject that of an individual human being.

[26]Apparently Sandel views the relevant passages as a concession because Rawls hopes, as he adds in a footnote, that they will clear up some objections made by Bernard Williams. I show in the next section, however, that Rawls is here merely reiterating what even in TJ is an integral part of his theory.

within the internal life of associations" (KCMT 545), Rawls creates the impression that Sandel is right at least in the very limited sense that in "public life . . . no loyalty or allegiance could be similarly essential to our sense of who we are . . . , no devotion to city or nation, to party or cause, could possibly run deep enough to be defining" (LLJ 182, cf. 179). Yet consider how Rawls continues after the quoted sentence about our nonpublic attachments and loves: "But none of this need affect the conception of the person connected with society's public conception of justice and its ideal of social cooperation" (KCMT 545). This is a statement about how *citizens* are to be conceived and treated in political contexts, from the point of view, as it were, of the basic structure of a well-ordered society. Such a basic structure stands apart from all more particular political commitments and also views citizens as detached from whatever such commitments they may have. Thus a person's deepest loyalties, commitments, and self-understandings do not affect his status as participant in the basic structure—his basic rights and duties and so forth.[27] And this statement is compatible with citizens' having deep self-understandings and convictions *even of a political sort*. Citizens may understand themselves as political feminists or may have strong convictions about the common good. To be sure, *all* such constitutive commitments are subject to a categorical sense of justice (to be discussed in §9), and some political and nonpolitical convictions will be excluded by Rawls's conception of justice fully spelled out. But many of the political convictions most deeply held today can be equally deeply held in a well-ordered Rawlsian society. The standard issues concerning technologies and the environment; budget allocations to education, health care, science, and the arts; the school curriculum; special taxes on tobacco or gasoline; speed limits; etc. are hardly fully settled by Rawls's criterion of justice. These must be decided through the political process as matters of pure procedural justice.[28] Given their categorical sense of justice, persons will have a sufficient moral motive to comply with even those outcomes of this process that go against their deeply held convictions. This does not mean that they have no such convictions, that they won't deeply identify with some political cause and continue the attempt to convince others of its merits.

8.5. Two further aspects of Sandel's reading may be worth examin-

[27]"When citizens convert from one religion to another, or no longer affirm an established religious faith, they do not cease to be, for questions of political justice, the same persons they were before. There is no loss of what we may call their public identity, their identity as a matter of basic law. In general, they still have the same basic rights and duties; they own the same property and can make the same claims as before" (JFPM 241). This, of course, was written after, and partly in response to, Sandel, but it is anticipated at BLP 83 and also, I believe, fully consistent with KCMT.

[28]To be sure, Rawls says that "the political process is a case of imperfect procedural justice" (TJ 229)—clearly true in that legislation can be more or less just by the lights of his criterion of justice. Still, this criterion leaves many important decisions open, and in respect to this open space, the political process is an instance of pure procedural justice, designed so that the law will, within the constraints of justice, reflect citizens' desires and preferences. See §13.5 herein; and also Gutmann, LE 173–83.

ing. Sandel believes Rawls begs the question against communitarianism by describing the parties in the original position as mutually disinterested, that is, as seeking to promote their own client's (unknown) conception of the good regardless of how this affects the lives of others. As Sandel understands (LLJ 42), the assumption of mutual disinterest does not mean that persons in real life are mutually disinterested. Rawls merely wants the basic structure of society to be arranged in accordance with a criterion that can be justified on the basis of undemanding, commonly shared assumptions. In reference to this ambition, Sandel correctly points to the relativity involved in calling such assumptions weak (LLJ 45–46). The assumption of mutual disinterest indeed demands little of those who see the primary function of social institutions as providing a framework within which people can choose and lead their own lives, safely, effectively, and with a minimum of restrictions and interferences. But it demands a great deal of those who, like Sandel, want the entire social system, not merely associations, to be a community in a strong sense. Such a community presupposes a set of defining values and loyalties that is "constitutive of the shared self-understandings of the participants and embodied in their institutional arrangements, not simply an attribute of certain of the participants' plans of life" (LLJ 173). So why shouldn't the parties be informed that their clients have an overriding desire to live in this sort of a comprehensive community?

But this suggestion is still incomplete. Somehow the parties must be given or be enabled to derive the *content* of those "shared self-understandings" that are to play a constitutive role both in shaping the community's institutions and in the identities of its members. Once this content is incorporated into the original position, however, it is unlikely that more than a small minority of us would be pulled into the argument and thus be persuaded by it to support institutional change toward the communitarian basic structure that would best embody and inculcate the particular values that are to be constitutive. It is this empirical fact—that there is not even a remote chance that we might freely come to share a specific vision of the good and to arrange our basic institutions in accordance with it—that makes the Sandelian alternative stipulation more demanding. Rawls's vision of a well-ordered society, by contrast, is tailor-made for a social system in which disagreement over values (including community values) is widespread. It can appeal to noncommunitarians and also to all communitarians realistic enough to accept what for them is admittedly second best, a noncommunitarian institutional framework within which communitarian associations can thrive. Within such a framework, Sandel's community may flourish and grow, but its growing strength would never shift the basic framework itself in the direction of Sandel's favored values and self-understandings.

Essentially the same reply can be made to the milder proposal—first rejected by Sandel (LLJ 11–12), but later resurrected in a different guise (LLJ 44–46)—that the parties should be endowed with benevolence or love of humankind, that is, the desire that others should be successful in the promotion of their conception of the good as well. As Sandel notes only much later (LLJ 171), Rawls has another plausible reply to this suggestion as well, namely, that it would make no difference. The veil of ignorance already ensures that the parties cannot safeguard and promote the interests of their own clients without promoting those of all others as well. All participants are virtually represented in the deliberations of every contractor.

8.6. This response Sandel again finds revealing: "Even in the face of so noble a virtue as the love of mankind, the primacy of justice prevails, although the love that remains is of an oddly judicial spirit" (LLJ 171). This remark is representative of another pervasive strand of Sandel's reaction to Rawls's work, the complaint that justice is a remedial virtue, a virtue "not absolutely, as truth is to theories, but only conditionally, as physical courage is to a war zone" (LLJ 31, cf. 168–72), and would it not be nice to do without courage and enjoy peace and tranquility instead? This theme is played repeatedly. There is the heartrending story about an ideal family situation governed by spontaneous affection, which deteriorates to the point where "parents and children . . . dutifully if sullenly abide by the two principles" (LLJ 33). Similarly disturbing is the imagined close friend who "insists on calculating and paying his precise share of every common expenditure" and is extremely reluctant to accept any "favor or hospitality" (LLJ 35). Finally, "intimate or solidaristic associations" would also seem to get along well without too great an emphasis on justice (LLJ 30).

But then Rawls has praised justice as the first virtue *of social institutions* (TJ 3) and not as the most noble personal virtue or human sentiment. He is concerned with such issues as the organization of the economy, of government and political participation, and of the legal and penal systems. Such issues are not made obsolete by "circumstances of benevolence, or fraternity, or of enlarged affections" (LLJ 32), for the sentiments of benevolence and love can hardly, on a large scale, pervade human interactions so thoroughly as to render shared institutions unnecessary. For one thing, even if everyone genuinely seeks to realize the common good, people are likely to disagree about what this is concretely.[29] Hence practices and procedures of settlement are not dispensable even in a world of saintly altruists, though they may be among close friends or within a family.

Now Sandel might well accept the indispensability of such practices and procedures; his demand might then be that some *analogue* of benevolence or fraternity should displace justice as the foremost virtue

---

[29]This point is due, I believe, to Kant. See also Larmore, PMC 175 n. 71, who cites Michael Taylor, CAL 26–32.

of *social institutions*. But this idea is surely very different from, and much more complicated than, the idea that peace and tranquility should displace physical courage as a virtue of *persons* and thus cannot be illuminated by this vague analogy. One wants some sketch, at least, of Sandel's favored benevolent or fraternal economy, penal system, or political process, together with some assurance that these would not give rise to the pathologies characteristic of previous (philosophical and political) attempts to construct such institutions. Sandel fails to address these issues.

9. Rawls's Conception of the Person

9.1. Having found no tenable grounds for Sandel's view that Rawls is implicitly committed to a conception of citizens as mean-spirited "strangers" (LLJ 183) and barren selves, let us examine what Rawls himself has to say about his conception of the person and its role within his conception of justice.

Rawls is centrally concerned in this and other matters to argue from weak premises. This ambition counsels, first of all, against relying on too thick or rich a conception of the person. If a highly specific conception of the person is involved in constructing his criterion of justice, then this criterion is liable to be rejected by those who find this specific conception of the person unappealing. Rawls himself has quite effectively used this strategy against utilitarianism. By postulating a shared highest-order preference function, utilitarians presuppose that there is only one rational good for human beings (SUPG 173–83). They assume that, if doing sports in one's spare time makes persons happier than reading, then persons ought to (be educated to) prefer sports over reading. Moreover, by demanding that this (subjective) good be maximized, utilitarians view persons as mere containers for this good. In whom utility occurs and how it is distributed are morally immaterial (RAM 645). The utilitarian criterion can reasonably be rejected by anyone who does not share, and does not want to live under institutions that reflect, this view of persons as locations for the occurrence of valuable subjective states.

But then it is not clear that a thin or abstract conception of the person can avoid such problems. To see why, suppose someone has proposed an elaborate conception of the person, rich with stipulated features (such as needs and interests) A through F. Assume also that various criticisms are directed against this conception, challenging features D, E, F as empirically inaccurate or morally unconvincing. In response to such criticisms, one might try to retreat to common ground, by retracting the assertion of features D, E, F and arguing from a thin or abstract conception of the person defined by the uncontroversial features A, B, C. But is one now relying on weaker premises?

With regard to strictly deductive arguments in logic, mathematics, and geometry, the answer would be affirmative. But in practical reasoning, when decisions must be made "in light of" given premises, matters are otherwise. Here conclusions may be upset by the introduction of additional premises. Consider, for example, the case of a criminal trial, where the jurors are asked to decide between conviction and acquittal on the basis of various facts asserted during the trial. In this sort of situation, no neutrality can be had by simply discounting alleged facts that are controversial among the jurors. For suppose that some alleged facts favoring the defendant are disputed and that the jurors must either include these alleged facts among their premises and acquit or exclude them and convict. In this case, the latter course cannot be said to be neutral between them or to rely on weaker premises, because the former course implicitly also invokes a disputed premise, namely, that no further facts favoring the defendant have been established.[30]

Essentially the same point can be made about the quest to attain some measure of procedural neutrality.[31] Thus, acceptance of Rawls's criterion of justice may hinge on whether we accept and incorporate into the original position the richer or the thinner conception of the person. In choosing the thinner conception, we do not get a clearly more neutral argument or one based upon unequivocally weaker premises, because we are making the strong and controversial assumption that A, B, C are the *only* features of persons relevant to a political conception of justice.[32] We thereby snub all those who believe that persons' general benevolence, say, or general nonbenevolence should be included among the premises. Genuine procedural neutrality would be achieved not by leaving controversial premises aside but—at best—only by showing that a conclusion follows irrespective of how these assertions are treated, that the argument goes through no matter whether D, say, is asserted, denied, or left open. Unfortunately, one will rarely be able to show this. Nor is it promising to seek the conception of justice that incorporates *the most neutral* conception of the person.[33] Many tenable conceptions of justice will be undominated and hence incommensurable in this regard.

[30]Similarly, the neutral ground among an atheist, an agnostic, and a believer is decidedly *not* agnosticism. Rather, neutral ground among these three includes whatever it would be reasonable to accept from any of the three perspectives.

[31]"Metaprocedural neutrality" might be more precise, because Rawls is here concerned not with the neutrality of rules and procedures but with neutral ways of justifying such rules and procedures. For the distinction between neutrality of outcome and neutrality of procedure, see Raz, MF 114–15 (who falsely ascribes to Rawls a neutrality-of-outcome view [MF 117–24]); and Larmore, PMC 42–47. Rawls's own discussion of the neutrality issue (PRIG V) follows Larmore, who argues that in disputes about the justice of shared institutions one should be willing to retreat with others to neutral or common ground (PMC 50–68). I am not questioning Larmore's account of why one should do this, and to what extent—only his suggestion of what it would mean to retreat to neutral ground.

[32]This point, as I have said, is due to Sandel (LLJ 45–46).

[33]Cf. Larmore, PMC 68.

9.2. Rawls's conception of the person comprises whatever empirical and (especially) normative claims about human beings are implicit in various features of the original position—for example, the publicity condition on adoptable criteria of justice, the construction of the original position "so that it is a situation in which the maximin rule applies" (TJ 155), the rationality of the parties, and the description of those the parties represent (including the account of social primary goods). The most important challenges to Rawls's conception of the person concern the last of these features.

Rawls stipulates that the parties in the original position "know . . . that they prefer more rather than less primary goods. . . . [These] are things which it is supposed a rational man wants whatever else he wants. . . . With more of these goods men can generally be assured of greater success in carrying out their intentions and in advancing their ends, whatever these ends may be" (TJ 93, 92). While the choice of this account (for the purpose of interpersonal and interschemic comparisons) may be "founded on the facts of psychology" (FG 538), it is surely not determined by these facts and thus reflects some broadly moral attitudes toward these goods and toward the role they should play in a successful human life. Those who find reason to disagree significantly with Rawls's account of social primary goods and to diverge from the attitudes it expresses may reasonably reject his conception of justice (at least if they can point to another sharable basis for agreement).

This point is particularly obvious in regard to the priority Rawls gives in this account to certain basic rights and liberties. One set of these fall under the general heading of freedom of thought and conscience (TJ §33). Now if the parties were deliberating in behalf of persons who care primarily about utility (one's own or that of others), they might not want the rights and liberties of this set to be very extensive. The suppression of certain beliefs and practices may well raise each position, particularly the lowest (interschemically as evaluated in terms of utility), if the frustrations resulting from abridgments of the relevant rights and liberties are outweighed by satisfactions gained directly (from seeing unpopular doctrines suppressed) or through intermediate social or economic factors. But on Rawls's account the parties deliberate differently. They "must assume that they may have moral, religious, or philosophical interests which they cannot put in jeopardy unless there is no alternative. . . . [They] must choose principles that secure the integrity of their religious or moral freedom. They do not know, of course, what their religious or moral convictions . . . [and obligations are or whether] they think of themselves as having such obligations. The possibility that they do suffices for the argument. . . . They cannot take chances" (TJ 206–7, cf. 151–52, §82; BLP 25–26).

The argument of this passage crucially hinges upon constitutive interests and commitments of just the sort Sandel thinks Rawls is denying. Though he can concede that some persons may organize their lives around the idea of maximizing utility, Rawls *must* insist that persons "may have attachments and loves that they believe they would not, or could not, stand apart from; and they might regard it as unthinkable for them to view themselves without certain religious and philosophical convictions and commitments" (KCMT 545). Whoever is convinced that this is not, or ought not to be, a significant feature of human personality can reasonably reject the importance Rawls attaches to freedom of thought and conscience.

9.3. But Rawls does not merely inform the parties that their clients have constitutive interests; he also gives them to know, more specifically, what the most important of these interests are. The parties represent *moral* persons, "characterized by two moral powers . . . the capacity for an effective sense of justice . . . [and] the capacity to form, to revise, and rationally to pursue a conception of the good. Corresponding to the moral powers, moral persons are said to be moved by two highest-order interests to realize and exercise these powers. By calling these interests 'highest-order' interests, I mean that . . . [they] are supremely regulative as well as effective. This implies that, whenever circumstances are relevant to their fulfillment, these interests govern deliberation and conduct" (KCMT 525).[34]

Clearly these are very substantial stipulations. A brief reflection on the actual persons we know is likely to press upon us the question of how relevant Rawls's criterion of justice can be to *our* world if it has been adopted in behalf of moral persons so conceived. If Rawls aims for a comparative assessment of basic structures by how suitable each would be for persons having the two highest-order interests, and if these interests are and will be quite rare in actual fact, then Rawls's criterion, and the ranking of feasible basic structures based upon it, would seem to be discredited.

Let me consider two possible responses to such doubts. Rawls could say that persons born into a self-contained society governed by his criterion of justice would be more likely to become moral persons. Perhaps so, but there would remain a significant number of persons in whom the "highest-order" interests would not be supremely regulative. Moreover, utilitarians could equally well argue that persons born into a self-contained society governed by the principle of utility would be more likely to come to have a highest-order preference function.[35]

Rawls could also say that his conception of the person is to serve only

---

[34]Rawls's talk of highest-*order* interests may mislead by suggesting a parallel with second-order desires, which are desires about desires and need not be regulative with respect to first-order desires. Highest-order interests are not about but are regulative with respect to other interests. Rawls also stipulates that moral persons, as represented by the parties, have "a higher-order interest in protecting and advancing their conception of the good" (KCMT 525).

[35]Here Rawls may still claim some advantage, assuming that *our* considered judgments here and now would go against a highest-order preference function while supporting at least the *ideal* of moral personality (as he defines it).

for developing a *political* conception of justice: "Within different contexts we can assume diverse points of view toward our person without
contradiction so long as these points of view cohere together when
circumstances require" (KCMT 545; cf. JFPM 232 n. 15). But the coherence condition sharply limits the usefulness of this strategy as a
response to the difficulty. For consider again the possibility of a utilitarian making the same response to Rawls's criticisms. Rawls would
probably counter this by showing how conceiving of persons as having
a highest-order preference function cannot neatly be confined to political philosophy but would also affect the way persons in the envisaged
utilitarian society would view themselves outside the political realm,
especially if the operative conception of justice and the reasons for it
are required to be public (the publicity condition, [cf. TJ 133, 182]).
Persons' conceptions of their public and private roles must "cohere
together." The analogous counter would, I believe, defeat the response
in Rawls's behalf as well. If citizens—even in Rawls's most favored
society—would frequently set aside their (supposedly) "highest-order"
interests for the sake of other interests and commitments, then Rawls's
ranking of basic structures is based upon an empirically false assumption. Therefore, if the two highest-order interests really are "supremely
regulative as well as effective" (KCMT 525), then the desire to honor just
institutions must constrain and (in case of conflict) override even our
most constitutive *private* loyalties, commitments, and attachments,
whether personal, religious, or ethical. The conception persons are to
have of their public role constrains how they can conceive of themselves from other points of view.

   The two responses I have considered do little to defend the stipulation of the two highest-order interests or to mitigate the conclusion
that this stipulation makes Rawls's conception of the person very demanding. In addition, it seems that Rawls does not even need to affirm
this model of moral personality in order to derive his criterion of social
justice; in *A Theory of Justice* the two moral powers are introduced
only near the end (in very rudimentary form [TJ 505, 561]), long after the
parties have adopted their criterion of justice in its final statement (TJ
302–3). And Rawls may then seem to endorse far too controversial a
conception of the person, thereby making his criterion of justice excessively vulnerable. Instead of basing the account of social primary goods
upon this conception (KCMT 525–26; SUPG 165; JFPM 224 n. 2), he
should have defended social primary goods as the relevant all-purpose
means necessary for pursuing the interests and plans persons in modern democratic societies are in fact likely to have. Such a more broadly
based defense would have been compatible with allowing that some
persons will have the two highest-order interests while others will have
no broad moral allegiance to the basic institutions of the social system
(complying perhaps on prudential grounds) or will care very little for

the capacity rationally to revise their conception of the good.[36] By relying on a more neutral conception of the person, this argument would have had wider appeal. So why does Rawls insist on the two highest-order interests instead?

9.4. If there is a good answer, then it must be that Rawls considers the more demanding stipulation necessary for another purpose (other than establishing a preference in the original position for his criterion). But *what* purpose? The simplest explanation is that Rawls was carried away by Kantian predilections. The conviction, even pathos, in his endorsement of the first highest-order interest is certainly not unrelated to his strong attraction to Kant: "The sense of justice . . . reveals what the person is, and to compromise it is not to achieve for the self free reign but to give way to the contingencies and accidents of the world" (TJ 575). He adds that by acting from a sense of justice, we express "our nature as moral persons" (TJ 574). This appeal, however, cannot be to a universal "we" but only to those who will share the Kantian aspiration to the free reign of the self.[37] That Rawls's most favored society is designed for Kantian spirits will *for them* surely count in its favor but is bound to alienate others who are less than enthusiastic about the ideal of free reign for the self. Rawls's appeal to Kant does not provide the kind of broadly based and powerful argument that so demanding a stipulation requires. Is there another way of providing such an argument?

9.4.1. Let me begin with the stipulated interest in a sense of justice. There is surely something morally disturbing about an institutional scheme that, relying on self-interested motivations, would work with equal effectiveness in a nation of intelligent devils.[38] But is this disturbing enough to stipulate a *highest-order* interest? There is, I think, an even more broadly based and compelling argument for moral citizenship. Rawls wants to show not merely that his criterion of justice indicates a morally plausible way of organizing social interaction but also that a social system satisfying this criterion would be well-ordered, which for him requires *stability*. That a social system is "stable with respect to its conception of justice . . . means that . . . its members

[36]In TJ, this capacity is not included within the second moral power (TJ 505, 561). Apparently Rawls owes the idea of including it to Buchanan (KCMT 526 n. 5; SUPG 165 n. 6), who bases Rawls's social primary goods on the interest "to maintain an attitude of critical revisability toward one's own conception of the good" (Buchanan, RRC 399). Perhaps foremost among the problems with this idea is that one must show not merely that rational persons have this interest but also that its relative strength and importance are very great. Buchanan defends only the former.

[37]We can see that Rawls is aware of this limitation by appreciating that the word *nature* must be understood neither empirically nor teleologically but as denoting an individual person's character: About "those who find that being disposed to act justly is not a good for them . . . one can only say: their nature is their misfortune" (TJ 576). So the sense of justice expresses the nature of only some, not all human beings.

[38]The image is from Kant's essay "Perpetual Peace" (KPW 112–13).

acquire . . . a sufficiently strong and effective sense of justice, one that usually overcomes the temptations and stresses of social life" (RAM 634). This is a considerably stronger requirement than that of *equilibrium*, which is satisfied even if "individuals comply with the institutional scheme solely as a means to their separate concerns . . . from self- or group-interested motives" (TJ 455).

Here, then, is a partial rationale for Rawls's decision to invoke stronger premises. If we believe that human beings are indeed capable of a regulative and effective sense of justice and if we care strongly that our criterion of justice and the institutions it favors should have a tendency toward stability (that is, toward engendering such a supporting sense of justice), then it is reasonable to stipulate that "other things equal, the persons in the original position will adopt the more stable scheme of principles" (TJ 455).[39] Now one may well think that the more intuitive way of embedding the concern for stability would be given by the stipulation that the parties' clients value an effective sense of justice *in one another*, rather than each only in him- or herself as the first highest-order interest suggests. In a later essay, Rawls does indeed explain the parties' preference for an institutional scheme that engenders an effective sense of justice by emphasizing how persons living under stable institutions will be more successful in advancing their determinate conceptions of the good, whatever these may be (BLP 31–32). There is, I believe, no serious tension between these two accounts of the parties' reasoning, because behind the veil of ignorance the two stipulations are equivalent. Still, the second account (in BLP, published after KCMT) may have the advantage of making more perspicuous how the parties' rational deliberations represent *our own* moral reflections.

9.4.2. Why then should the parties have so decisive a preference for stability over other forms of social equilibrium? I suggest that stability enables a good that is otherwise unattainable. Stability makes certain features of the basic structure immune to the shifting distribution of bargaining power within the social system in question. To see what is at stake, consider that an institutional scheme must cope with the assurance problem.[40] Persons' prudential and moral reasons for accepting their fair share of the burdens of social cooperation are undermined when there are no assurances that others are complying as well. This problem can generally be solved through mechanisms for detecting and penalizing noncompliance (TJ 270, 240). There is, however, also a deeper version of the assurance problem. Here the relevant suspicion is not that others may be shirking their responsibilities under the scheme but that major groups may be seeking through their legitimate political and economic power to shift the terms of the institutional

---

[39]Thus, even if two conceptions of justice have equally strong tendencies toward equilibrium, the parties prefer the one that relies more on stability (a sense of justice) rather than on sanctions and (dis)incentives.

[40]This problem is clearly stated in "Perpetual Peace" (Kant, KPW 121n).

scheme itself in their favor. This suspicion tends to dispose other groups to use *their* legitimate power in similar ways so as to block any advances by those whom they suspect and, if possible, to weaken their position as well. As the *situated* assurance problem threatens pervasive noncompliance with existing ground rules, so the *fundamental* assurance problem threatens pervasive and unrestrained competition over what the ground rules will be.

While, on the one hand, the fundamental assurance problem cannot be solved through institutional mechanisms, it may, on the other hand, seem much less threatening. Suppose that each major group accepts the going scheme only prudentially, as the best it can for now exact from the others, and that there are significant shifts in the distribution of bargaining power among these groups or in their values and interests. Even then, a breakdown of order is less likely than an adaptation of the scheme to the altered circumstances. Even while the going scheme would undergo substantial changes, order would be preserved through an underlying *modus vivendi* (cf. JFPM 247; IOC), according to which the going terms of interaction will tend to reflect a *dynamic* bargaining equilibrium. The continuity achievable through such a modus vivendi is quite weak, however, as the going terms are liable to change without limit. In fact, it is precisely because its terms are flexible that a modus vivendi can endure over time. As the bargaining power or the values and interests of the various groups change, the institutional distribution of benefits and burdens is adjusted so that the scheme continues to be rationally acceptable to all. Thus, when a group's power has increased, so that it now has more to gain and less to lose from a (partial) breakdown of orderly relations, it will prudently press for more favorable terms. And other groups will prudently accede to its demand— weakened groups being obliged to accept less favorable terms because of their increased vulnerability or decreased threat advantage.

9.4.3. It is important to note that while the competition among groups is effectively constrained at each moment by the going terms of the scheme, there are no restraints on the terms themselves. There are no limits on how weak or strong a group may become through shifts in the distribution of power as reflected in and compounded by shifts in the terms of the modus vivendi. And this absence of limits indicates the reason for insisting on a sense of justice. The features characterizing a just basic structure can be preserved only if each major group within the social system will support them even when it is in a position to exact new terms more favorable to itself. A truly enduring just scheme presupposes a widespread and deep moral allegiance to its basic terms, so that each of at least the influential social groups can be relied on to honor them even when they significantly conflict with its moral or religious convictions or with its political or economic interests. Only in this way can all be assured that the terms of the scheme will not be unjustly shifted against them, that they will not be forced into a declining spiral of fading power and deteriorating terms of participation. Such assurance, in turn, radically reduces the temptation to seek unjustly to shift the scheme's terms in one's favor (cf. §19.2 and §20.4).

9.4.4. Rawls has, then, a crucially important reason for favoring a basic structure that has a strong tendency to engender a normally overriding moral allegiance to itself. The stipulation of the first highest-order interest can be justified through the preference for a social system whose basic ground rules are "taken off the political agenda,"[41] are not themselves objects of the political and economic competition they are to regulate. The realization of this preference requires persons who, despite a wide diversity of conflicting values and interests, share an area of value overlap (cf. TJ 387–88), who have an overriding allegiance to this "kernel of political morality"[42] and to its institutionalization, and who know all this about one another. The aspiration toward such a social system with such persons is partly a matter of collective rationality, but it is also moral in three distinct respects. First, each social group will consider it *morally* important to protect its values and way of life, and for many such groups stability is the only feasible or at least the most reliable way of ensuring that its conception of the good will survive, will be available to be known, reaffirmed, and continued by whoever may choose to do so. Second, individuals and associations may also recognize *other* groups as having a valid claim that *their* values and form of life should remain accessible within the social system, and ensuring stability is then the best way of discharging this collective responsibility vis-à-vis other groups in general. Here stability is a way of assuring that we, as members of one group, will never be forced to choose between the security of our own conception of the good and the moral claims of others to live in accordance with theirs. Third, a kernel of political morality would also engender greater social peace and harmony than has been displayed by any of the large societies we are familiar with from history, and such peace and harmony are of moral value for their own sake.

The argument I have suggested Rawls can give in defense of his stipulation of the first highest-order interest has this schematic form:

(1) An ideal social system should be in *stable* equilibrium through a widespread, strong and effective sense of justice.
(2) Hence we should aim for a basic structure that tends to produce in its participants the first highest-order interest.
(3) And therefore we should seek to develop and implement a conception of justice that is hospitable to basic structures with this tendency and acceptable to persons who have the first highest-order interest.

[41]Rawls credits Stephen Holmes with suggesting this phrase and idea (IOC 14 n. 22).
[42]TJ 221. A political morality comprises, I assume, a conception of justice and criteria for assessing conduct (and character) in the political domain.

9.4.5. The preference for stability may also furnish the most broadly based and most compelling argument for stipulating the second highest-order interest in realizing and exercising the capacity to form, to revise, and rationally to pursue a conception of the good. Social institutions under which this interest is widespread would engender a strong and lasting allegiance to a kernel of political morality that allows a wide range of diverse and even mutually incompatible conceptions of the good. For contrast, consider a social system in which persons are primarily motivated by their interest in protecting and advancing their own particular conception of the good. In such a system the shared political morality is liable to change in response to shifts in the relative strength of the groups supporting the various conceptions of the good. There is little concern to preserve space for values and ideals currently out of favor. Hence the adherents of each group must fear that, should their numbers decline temporarily, there would be pressures on the basic structure to change so as to make a resurgence of their values less likely or even impossible. This fear in turn tends to produce in each group a strong determination to maintain and increase its strength. The fear and determination tend to undermine the groups' moral allegiance to the existing social institutions. This problem is avoided when the second highest-order interest is widespread. In that case, many persons will want the social system to be open to, and even to foster, a wide diversity of values and projects, so as to provide a rich background against which persons can form and change their own conceptions of the good. And the adherents of each particular way of life will then be assured that an openness for, and understanding of, their particular conception of the good will be preserved *by others,* even if their own strength should dwindle.

Both highest-order interests, then, play an important role in preventing the inevitable competition between rival values and interests from broadening into a competition over the terms of the basic structure itself. This role indicates an important reason why persons living together under a shared institutional scheme should—for the sake of their particular conception of the good, whatever it may be—want these highest-order interests in one another. This prudential reason, reinforced once again by the three moral reasons, should lead *us* to want our conception of justice and the basic structure(s) it favors to engender these highest-order interests and to be appropriate for persons having them. The original position is to be designed accordingly.

9.4.6. If Rawls wants to make a convincing case for his stipulation of the two highest-order interests, then he must present a rationale of this sort, whose appeal is independent of any particular conceptions of the good. Rawls fails to supply such a rationale in *A Theory of Justice.* Some eleven years later, he sketches one by saying that the parties seek to engender the highest-order interests *as means* to protect and advance the determinate conception of the good of those they represent (BLP 27, 29–32). But immediately thereafter he goes right back to a highly partisan Kantian rationale: "The role and exercise of [the moral] powers (in the appropriate instances) is a condition of good. . . . [Citizens'] just and honorable (and fully autonomous) conduct renders them, as Kant would say, worthy of happiness; it makes their accomplishments wholly admirable and their pleasures completely good" (BLP 49).[43]

9.4.7. The stipulation of the highest-order interests will of course affect how the content of the favored conception of justice is argued for within the constraints of the original position. The argument will reflect the thinking of persons who value their shared categorical allegiance to a lasting kernel of political morality and their shared interest in preserving the space for a wide range of diverse conceptions of the good. These persons are not we, but the members of the well-ordered society correlated with Rawls's conception of justice. But the argument still touches us insofar as we, upon reflection, would aspire to such a social system, would want to see our conception of the good and way of life better protected, would want to participate in institutions that satisfy the two principles of justice, and would want to be and live among persons who, however different in other ways, share a categorical commitment to maintain the justice of their shared basic institutions. Some people here and now may see neither rational nor moral reasons for finding this aspiration plausible and will, perhaps reasonably, reject Rawls's conception of the person, although they might have accepted a more neutral one sufficient for deriving his criterion of justice. But losing them cannot be helped, because a more neutral conception of the person would not support the ambition for a stable, harmonious, and enduringly just social system.

9.5. Let me conclude with some remarks on how Rawls's insistence on a supremely regulative and effective sense of justice might come to terms with the doubts first voiced by Bernard Williams in "Persons, Character, and Morality."[44] The worry is that once we reserve a special dignity or supremacy for moral motivations we will not be able to account for the significance and structural importance that can attach to our other constitutive commitments (Williams, ML 2). Thus Williams

---

[43]On this question of different rationales for Rawls's stipulations, see also Galston, MPLT, and Larmore, PMC 118–30. Larmore suggests that rather than appeal to a narrowly Kantian (or Aristotelian) conception of the good life, Rawls should base his stipulations upon a retreat to neutral ground, upon the common denominator of the conceptions of the good actually affirmed in the relevant society at a given time. As should be clear from the text, however, this proposal fails to resolve the fundamental assurance problem. Groups must fear that a decline in their power may induce a shift in this common denominator, making the institutions based upon it less supportive of (or even hostile to) their values. I have argued for solving this problem by invoking yet a third kind of rationale that appeals to the value of *stability*, viewed as a condition for the long-term security of *any* conception of the good.

[44]First published in 1976, and reprinted in Williams, ML 1–19.

thinks we ought "to allow more room than Kantianism can allow for the importance of individual character and personal relations in moral experience" (ML 5). Four considerations mitigate this concern as addressed to Rawls's conception. First, what is to take motivational precedence over our deep loyalities, attachments, or ground projects is a *political*, rather than a general and comprehensive morality (cf. IOC 3– 4). What Rawls stipulates is an allegiance only to the criterion of justice, to the basic structure insofar as it is justified by this criterion, and to legislative, judicial, and administrative decisions insofar as they are rendered pursuant to justified procedures and accord in content with the criterion of justice.

Second, the political morality is specifically conceived so as to be compatible with, and protective of, a wide range of diverse and often mutually incompatible religions, personal values, and ethical doctrines (of the more general and comprehensive kind).

These two considerations show that the occasions on which the sense of justice would come into conflict with other constitutive commitments are likely to be rare, at least in comparison to alternative, non-Rawlsian basic structures. This fact is welcome, because a regulative and effective sense of justice, though it must be determinative, need not be our supreme or preeminent commitment. It need not be ranked above commitments that do not conflict with it.[45]

Third, Rawls's theory is an exercise in ideal theory. So even if it were true that persons as they now are have some constitutive commitments that may conflict with an allegiance to a just institutional scheme, it would not follow that such conflicts would occur under that scheme.[46] The reason, as Williams himself points out, is that a person's constitutive commitments are "in good part . . . formed within, and formed by, dispositions which constitute a commitment to morality" (ML 12)—in this case to the political morality Rawls is proposing. This consideration shows how one need not deny either the crucial role of constitutive commitments in a worthwhile human life or the fundamental importance of such commitments once they have been formed. Both these points are compatible with the hope that in the context of an

[45]If one accepts this point, as Rawls seems to do (IOC 17), then one might consider revising Rawls's talk of the two highest-order interests. A preeminent interest in one's own salvation, for example, poses no problem so long as a conflict between it and the (lesser) interest to develop and exercise one's sense of justice is impossible (or at least only very remotely possible). Thus one may prefer to speak of a *determinative* rather than a highest-order interest and call it "regulative in the political domain" rather than "supremely regulative." This proposal also avoids the misleading association of "highest-order" with "second-order" (see n. 34 above).

[46]Compare: "We do not consider the strains of commitment that might result from some people having to move from a favored position in an unjust society to a less favored position . . . in this just society. Rather, one is to ask what strains arise from the ongoing conditions of the society one is putting to test. . . . The strains of commitment test applied to cases of hypothetical transition from unjust societies is irrelevant" (RAM 653). Rawls is here retracting the last few lines of TJ 176 (cf. TG 202–3). See also Shue, BJ 607.

ongoing just basic structure, persons would tend either not to form certain commitments or to understand their constitutive commitments as limited from the start so that the possibility of such conflicts is largely excluded. Given widespread moral allegiance to a just regime, persons might, for example, be unwilling to form a friendship with a notorious tax cheat or might refuse to understand such a friendship as obligating them to help cover up their friend's fraudulent activities.

It may nevertheless happen, of course, that a deep and long-standing commitment comes into conflict with political morality. Such conflicts would be much more difficult than Williams's case (ML 17–18), in which someone, unable to rescue both of two endangered persons, gives precedence to the one who is his wife. It would be a case where the agent's loyalty to his wife would require him to violate just rules, to break a law, to bribe a judge, or such like. It is not obvious that one should want to be a person who would, even in a perfectly just society, do such things if one's wife turned out to be in the Mafia, say. I feel that at this point Williams overstates the significance of constitutive commitments when he writes (about the rescue case): "It might have been hoped by some (for instance, by his wife) that his motivating thought, fully spelled out, would be the thought that it was his wife, not that it was his wife and that in situations of this kind it is permissible to save one's wife," as the latter reasoning "provides the agent with one thought too many" (ML 18). But the second thought is not out of place in the contexts relevant here, for example, the Mafia case. Even if she is one's wife, one may still ask whether it is right to violate a just practice for her sake. This much seems perfectly compatible with having a character.

Fourth, the sense of justice need not be determinative for all persons all the time. "There can come a point at which it is quite unreasonable for a man to give up, in the name of the impartial good ordering of the world of moral agents, something which is a condition of his having any interest in being around in that world at all" (ML 14). Indeed, such a point may come. Yet one need not say, I think, that he is *justified* in refusing to give it up, but at most, in Williams's phrase, that "some situations lie beyond justifications" (ML 18). Moreover, the possibility of such situations is quite compatible with the feasibility and desirability of a well-ordered society, in which most persons most of the time will have a categorical sense of justice so that the enduring justice of the basic structure is manifestly assured. Such assurance is undermined not by a few persons such as Williams describes but by powerful religious, political, or economic groups struggling to shift the accepted political morality in accordance with their particular interests or values.

DEVELOPING RAWLS'S CRITERION OF JUSTICE

CHAPTER 3

The First Principle
of Justice

10. The General Parameters

Rawls proposes a criterion of justice that ranks feasible alternative basic structures by the minimum representative lifetime share of social primary goods each of them tends to generate. In this section, I analyze this proposal into eight main elements, which may be grouped into our familiar three components, the who-, what-, and how-questions of §3.1. While I discuss some of these elements elsewhere (as indicated in Table 2), the present section is intended only to introduce them briefly in one place. The remainder of Part Two focuses on the core of the what-component, the specification of Rawls's semiconsequentialist account of the individual good, which is to inform all interpersonal and interschemic comparisons in matters of social justice.

Table 2. The main elements of Rawls's criterion of justice

Who	Humanism	§10.2
	Individualism	§10.3
What	Semiconsequentialism vs. deontology	§10.4.1, §3.5.2.2, §4.4.1
	Semiconsequentialism vs. full consequentialism	§10.4.2, §3.5.2.1, §4.4.1, §16
	Freedom, social primary goods	§10.5, §9.4, §§11–17
	Lifetime *ex post* shares	§10.7
How	Maximin	§10.1
	Representative groups	§10.6, §17.5

10.1. Let me begin with the key element within the how-component, Rawls's commitment to the maximin idea. In analogy to the biblical idea of morality— "Whatever you have done to one of the least of these my brethren, that you have done to me" (Matthew 25:40)—the ranking of feasible alternative basic structures is to depend upon the worst social position each of them tends to produce. All information about better positions is left aside as irrelevant. Thus Rawls invites us to think of "the two principles as the maximin solution to the problem of social justice. . . . [T]he two principles are those a person would choose for the design of a society in which his enemy is to assign him his place. . . . [T]hat the two principles of justice would be chosen if the parties were forced to protect themselves against such a contingency explains the sense in which this conception is the maximin solution" (TJ 152–53). As these remarks indicate, Rawls's argument from the original position is divisible into two steps. The first of these links the description of the original position with the parties' employment of the maximin rule, and the second presents the criterion of justice he proposes as "the maximin solution to the problem of social justice." After some brief comments about the first step, I concentrate on the discussion of the second, which brings in the other elements of his criterion of justice.

Rawls's use of the maximin idea has provoked a flood of criticism.[1] These appear quite devastating if one takes literally Rawls's professed aim "to characterize [the initial] situation so that the principles that would be chosen, whatever they turn out to be, are acceptable from a moral point of view. . . . Thus justice as fairness is able to use the idea of pure procedural justice from the beginning" (TJ 120). This statement seems to indicate that Rawls's entire argument would collapse if the parties' employment of the maximin rule were refuted. In the same section, however, Rawls suggests the opposite picture as well: "The procedure of contract theories provides, then, a general analytic method for the comparative study of conceptions of justice. One tries to set out the different conditions embodied in the contractual situation in which their principles would be chosen. In this way one formulates the various underlying assumptions on which these conceptions seem to depend" (TJ 121–22). Here, Rawls suggests that one begins with a particular criterion of justice and then constructs one's initial situation accordingly: "We want to define the original position so that we get the desired solution" (TJ 141); "the original position has been defined so that it is a situation in which the maximin rule applies" (TJ 155).

Each of these two pictures is overdrawn and at odds with Rawls's method of reflective equilibrium. Of the original position and his maximin criterion, neither is conceived prior to and independently of the other. The point is rather to fit them closely into each other while arguing for the specification of each on independent grounds as far as

---

[1]For some early examples, see Sen, CCSW chaps. 9 and 9*; Pettit, TJ 312–14; Nagel, RJ 10–12; Hare, RTJ 102–7; Arrow, SOUN 250–51; Musgrave, MULT; and Harsanyi, CMP. Rawls provides some defenses and elaborations in RMC and RAM.

possible (cf. TJ 20). Hence Rawls's failure to establish a tight connection between his original position and his favored criterion would not destroy his case for the latter. He could still try to redescribe the original position in a way that preserves the plausibility of this "expository device" (TJ 21) while also redeeming his claim that the parties would employ the maximin rule (and choose his favored criterion). Rawls's argument would be defeated only if every description of the initial situation that could yield his preferred criterion were morally implausible.

But let us not rush to speculate about how the original position might best be redescribed. For it is far from clear that such revision is needed. It is Rawls's claim that a "constellation of weaker and more basic conditions on the original position, each with its appropriate pedigree or justification . . . , when one considers their combined force, would lead reasonable people to choose as if they were highly risk-averse" (RAM 649).[2] Rawls has given at least six grounds for this claim, but his critics have almost exclusively concentrated on only two of these: that there is reason, behind the veil of ignorance, for sharply discounting probability estimates (TJ 154) and that choosing in accordance with the maximin rule ensures an acceptable minimum position above which there is little to gain and below which there is much to lose (TJ 154–55).[3] Let me briefly recapitulate the remaining four reasons.

Third, "the parties want their decision to appear well founded to others" (TJ 173). What is meant, I suppose, is that the parties should choose in the spirit of a trustee investing money for a ward. This attitude is indeed appropriate because in shaping basic institutions the parties (and *we*) are determining the various social positions that persons will be born into, without choice.[4] Fourth, the benchmark of

[2]I take the original position to incorporate the following six features: (1) the conception of the parties as mutually disinterested and rational in the narrow sense of decision theory and economics (e.g., TJ 144–45); (2) the characterization of those the parties represent as individuals, free and equal moral persons with two highest-order interests and a conception of the good (KCMT 525–26); (3) the restriction on information through the veil of ignorance (TJ §24); (4) the formulation of the parties' task, to reach a stable agreement on a criterion for assessing the basic structure of a self-contained social system existing in the circumstances of justice (TJ §§2, 22); (5) the list of alternatives supplied to the parties (TJ §21); and (6) the formal constraints of the right—generality, universality, publicity, ordering, and finality (TJ §23).

[3]Rawls cites Fellner, PP 140–42, as showing that these conditions make it appropriate for the parties to choose in accordance with the maximin rule. He follows Fellner in splitting the second condition into two, though the point must be that the potential gains are small *relative to* the potential losses.

[4]Compare here Rawls's remarks that the parties have a responsibility toward the persons they represent (BLP 21, 26) and also the passage about "the parties' concern for the next generation" (TJ 208f), for which I see no other rationale. It has been objected that this consideration requires the parties to know that those they represent are risk-averse, but this is not so. Suppose the parties were given to know that, on the contrary, those they represent are entrepreneurs or gamblers by temperament. Even with this stipulation,

equality, together with the concern for the least advantaged, appropriately expresses the political conception of the person, our aspiration for a society of free and equal citizens (RMC 144–45). Fifth, a maximin criterion is much easier to apply, for it is concerned only with the worst share. It is especially suitable as a public criterion because one can more easily understand it and check whether it is satisfied (TJ 517; RMC 143–44).[5]

Finally, the parties' choice is to be a binding agreement that persons should be able to keep without too much difficulty. When Rawls's maximin criterion is satisfied, the "strains of commitment" are relatively weak because everyone will benefit from existing inequalities vis-à-vis the benchmark of equality, and the worst share, in particular, will not be worse than necessary so as to allow other shares to be higher than they could otherwise be. That even the worst social position will be reasonably acceptable (compared to the worst social position under any alternative basic structure favored by other criteria) is of some moment because "the parties must decline all risks each possible outcome of which they cannot agree in good faith to accept" (RAM 653). Moreover, weak strains of commitment are a necessary prerequisite for the crucially important good of stability (TJ 175–78, 498–99; RMC 144).

In view of these additional positive reasons (and the defenses developed in §6.4) let me then assume that the case for maximin is still plausible and concentrate on the second step: "If the original position has been described so that it is rational for the parties to adopt the conservative attitude expressed by [the maximin] rule, a conclusive argument can indeed be constructed for these principles" (TJ 153). There are many different ways in which a maximin criterion might be specified, however, depending on how one sets various further parameters. In this section and the next I will present and partly discuss these further elements of Rawls's particular maximin criterion. The discussion will suggest various ways of revising the Master Pattern upon which the maximin ranking of feasible alternative basic structures is to be based.

10.2. Rawls is committed to humanism and thus denies that a conception of justice should include animals as well: "Those who can give justice are owed justice" (TJ 510).[6] Rawls seems also to deny that

---

they would have reason to choose conservatively, for they would then want to preclude that those they represent will be born into a social position in which gambling and enterprise are, for lack of means, out of the question. A trustee who lost her ward's inheritance on a high-risk commodity option contract can hardly justify this gamble to him (now of age) by pointing out that *she* gambled because she knew that *he* was going to be a risk-taker—and likewise for one of Rawls's parties whose client is born into slavery.

[5]For Rawls's statement and defense of the publicity condition underlying this argument, see TJ 133; KCMT 537–41, 553–54.

[6]He also argues that "it would be unwise in practice to withold justice" from that small minority of human beings who lack the capacity for moral personality. "The risk to just institutions would be too great" (TJ 506).

animals have moral rights (that we owe them morality), for he says that
we have "duties of compassion and humanity *in their case*" (TJ 512, my
emphasis). While this second tenet is controversial,[7] the first is more
secure. Animals would be suffering an injustice if they were excessively
disadvantaged participants in social institutions or unreasonably excluded from such institutions altogether. But neither is the case. Animals cannot participate in basic institutions because they cannot
understand political decision making, legal rights, markets, money,
marriage, and the like. If we should nevertheless take them into account in the design of our social world, we are bound by a collective
duty of morality.

10.3. Rawls takes the relevant participants in social institutions,
represented by the parties in the original position, to be individual
persons.

10.3.1. One alternative stipulation is that the ultimate units of moral
concern include groups, and in his first statement of his conception of
justice Rawls did indeed stipulate that the parties also represent "nations, provinces, business firms, churches, teams, and so on" (JR 245, cf.
248–49).[8] He has since come to the view that one should not postulate
groups with representable interests over and above those of its members: "For reasons of clarity among others . . . we want to account for the
social values, for the intrinsic good of institutional, community, and
associative activities, by a conception of justice that in its theoretical
basis is individualistic" (TJ 264). A further, decisive reason supporting
this change is that the inclusion of "suprapersonal" units would be
incompatible with Rawls's insistence on the primacy of (the subject of)
the basic structure. If we are to begin moral philosophy with the
reflection upon our most basic institutions, then we can hardly take for
granted that these are to regulate the interactions among business
firms and churches. What kinds of associations exist is itself a function
of the design of basic institutions.[9]

10.3.2. In roughly the opposite direction goes the demand for the
admission of "subpersonal" units. Sandel's idea of "a plurality of selves
within a single, individual human being" (LLJ 63) can hardly be useful
for the design and assessment of institutions, but one might consider
time slices of individual human beings. This idea raises various ques-

---

[7]See, for example, the essays in Singer, DA.

[8]The admission of groups is still urged by van Dyke, JFG, ISE. Cf. also Sandel's criticism
of Rawls, outlined in Chap. 2, n. 25, herein.

[9]One might object, for analogous reasons, to Rawls's invitation to picture the parties as
representing "heads of families" (TJ 128). This idea plays a very limited role in TJ. It
motivated the conclusion that the parties care for members of future generations. (It does
not mean that each household, regardless of size, has only one representative in the
original position.) Rawls wanted that conclusion for purposes of an account of justice
between generations. He has since withdrawn this account (BSS 70 n. 11). Correspondingly, he has also abandoned talk of heads of families in favor of cleanly individualistic
language.

tions: how "thick" should the slices be, and should persons be sliced individually (by age) or together on certain fixed dates? The problems of incorporating this idea into the institutional structure of a modern society are evident, but more damaging is the problem that these human slices would themselves want to be taken into account as complete persons, would want to be able to save for and borrow against future income, and the like.

10.4. There are two main alternatives to the semiconsequentialist element of Rawls's conception of justice.

10.4.1. Rawls departs from deontological conceptions of justice by holding that equivalent benefits and burdens should be weighted equally, regardless of whether they are established or engendered by social institutions. In the comparative assessment of basic structures the perspective of its potential participants is decisive, or so a broadly consequentialist approach maintains.

10.4.2. Within such an approach, the alternative to semiconsequentialism is full consequentialism, which holds that a conception of justice must pay attention not only to the distribution of social goods but also to differences in persons' physical and mental constitutions. We should consider shares not in the abstract but in relation to the particular persons whose shares they are. This kind of objection to Rawls can be specified in two ways, pointing toward two roughly opposite kinds of fully consequentialist conceptions of justice.

10.4.2.1. One might argue that relevant positions should be defined as including capabilities, needs, good looks, tastes, preferences, or desires, so that natural differences are *compensated for*. Those whose lives are worse because of their inferior physical or mental constitution should, other things equal, have a superior share of benefits and burdens; institutions should optimize the worst quality of life (or standard of living, in Sen's phrase). The appropriate criterion for assessing social institutions might then be either maximin utilitarianism or some measure combining social and natural primary goods. In response to this objection, Rawls has stressed the need for "workable criteria for interpersonal comparisons which can be publicly and, if possible, easily applied" (SUPG 169). He has also pointed out that he conceives persons, in virtue of their second moral power, as free to choose and as responsible for their own final ends and preferences. They can be expected to have "adjusted their likes and dislikes over the course of their lives to the income and wealth they could reasonably expect" (SUPG 169).[10] But these remarks address only the easier cases, bypassing the difficult question of how to cope with those manifest and objective interpersonal differences in needs for and capacities to take advantage of social primary goods for which persons are not themselves responsible and to which they can adjust themselves only with great difficulty, if at all.

[10]Cf. also Scanlon, SC 185–90.

The serious problem for Rawls is the contention that for purposes of identifying the worst position, special gifts and natural handicaps (special disabilities or needs) should be taken into account.[11] This idea is perhaps most compelling in cases such as blindness or special medical needs, which Rawls leaves aside (e.g., KCMT 546; SUPG 168). But it poses a general challenge to his assumption that for purposes of assessing basic structures, the participants' positions should be defined solely in terms of benefits and burdens of social interaction.

10.4.2.2. On the other hand, one might argue that positions should be defined so that natural differences are *corrected for*. When a basic structure generates unequal shares of social primary goods, these give rise to questions of justice only insofar as they cannot be explained by reference to differences in endowments (or motivation).[12] On this view, the least advantaged are those whose shares fall farthest short of the shares of others similarly motivated and endowed. There are two problems with this view. Defining the benchmark of equality as a state in which persons' shares of social primary goods match their natural endowments implicitly presupposes that greater endowments *should* entitle persons to larger shares; this is the kind of claim whose merits were questioned in §6.2–4. Moreover, the institutional schemes favored by the proposed criterion would be likely to engender considerable strains of commitment, as natural handicaps and social disadvantages would powerfully aggravate each other. Those with a weak physical and mental constitution would in addition have the smallest minimum share of social primary goods.

The second challenge is perhaps not so serious, but it helps me bring out how Rawls's semiconsequentialism is a plausible intermediate point between two fully consequentialist extremes. To illustrate, let me sketch how the difference principle in its simplest form (symbolizing Rawls's maximin criterion) would evaluate an income distribution against a background of diverse natural attributes. On Rawls's proposal, positions are assessed straightforwardly in terms of income alone. Thus he rejects, on the one hand, the idea of defining them in terms of <income + natural attributes>—in which case equality of income for persons working equally hard would require special justification because it would disadvantage the naturally more gifted (whose greater gifts are not rewarded) vis-à-vis the naturally handicapped. And he rejects, on the other hand, the idea of defining positions in terms of <income relative to natural attributes>—in which case equality of

---

[11]For this criticism, see Sen, EW; and WAF 195–200. Rawls has replied that "we can in principle expand the list to include other goods, . . . even certain mental states such as the absence of physical pain" (PRIG 257). But so far Rawls seems unwilling to move from a semi- to a fully consequentialist criterion, though he has lately preferred to speak of primary goods rather than social primary goods.

[12]As regards differences in motivation, this view articulates a plausible point, which, I will argue in §17.2, can be accommodated through the difference principle, at least if leisure time is included among the social primary goods.

income for persons working equally hard would require special justification because it would disadvantage the naturally handicapped (to
whom other human goods are less accessible) vis-à-vis the naturally
gifted. On Rawls's proposal, justification is required insofar as institutions generate *unequal* incomes for persons working equally hard; the
disadvantaged are those with the lowest incomes, regardless of their
specific natural capabilities or needs.

10.5. In Rawls's conception of justice, all intra- and interschemic
comparisons are to be made in terms of shares of social primary
goods—certain basic liberties and opportunities, income and wealth,
powers and prerogatives of offices, and the social bases of self-respect
(TJ 62, 92). Rawls holds that the parties in the original position have
reason to conclude that those they represent prefer more of these
goods to less (TJ 93, 142–43, 253, 260, 396, 433–34). But he changes his
mind about their basis for this conclusion. In *A Theory of Justice* the
account of social primary goods is said (TJ 92) to follow from the "thin
theory of the good," featuring the Aristotelian Principle and rational life
plans (TJ §§60–65). Later, this account is linked to the highest- and
higher-order interests of free and equal moral persons (KCMT 525–26).
In both cases, the argument, though somewhat sketchy, is clearly
related to the value of personal freedom.

10.5.1. It may be objected that persons ultimately care not about
social primary goods but, for example, about happiness or utility. Interpersonal and interschemic comparisons should therefore be made in
terms of the utility value of shares, as calculated by means of general
formulas (which, consistent with semiconsequentialism, would leave
aside interpersonal differences). Rawls can reject this proposal on the
ground that utility is just one end among others. Some will attach great
importance to it, while others will cherish wisdom, love, or art. The
distribution of these goods is not directly regulated by the basic structure—and could not plausibly be at any rate—and so there is no need
to settle their relative importance. A conception of justice should as far
as possible avoid taking a stand on such differences about the good life.
It can do so by describing shares in terms of goods that overlap closely
with the benefits and burdens that actually get distributed in the
course of social interaction as regulated by the ground rules (are "at the
disposition of society" [TJ 62]). Further assumptions about what the
value of these goods consists in are to be avoided because such assumptions would needlessly make the conception of justice more
controversial.

The same goes for further assumptions about what such goods
should best be used for. Shares are to be described in very general
terms. Instead of asking whether people travel and read books, for
example, it is better to ask whether they have the freedom to travel and
read, and income sufficient to exercise this freedom. Instead of asking
whether they have access to unspoiled nature, it is better to ask

whether they have liberties of political participation that allow them an equal say about matters of environmental quality. This way, Rawls's conception of justice respects persons' freedom in that it "does not look behind the use which persons make" (TJ 94; cf. SUPG 169–72) of the general all-purpose means at their disposal. It takes these means themselves as fundamental and defines relevant positions in terms of them.

10.5.2. But one may still challenge Rawls's approach at this point without abandoning his respect for freedom. Different institutional schemes will engender different attitudes and will thus affect the ways in which persons will use their freedom. Perhaps persons would cherish art and would support art through private and political efforts under some institutional schemes but not under others. Rawls is committed to the view that such differences should not play a role in constructing a conception of justice. It should not be presumed ahead of time that art ought to be cherished.

10.5.3. Even if Rawls were right about how an account of social primary goods should be constructed, he might still be mistaken about what particular goods should be included or about how they should be weighted relative to one another. I will discuss several such issues in §§11–12 and §§15–17.

10.5.4. Finally, Rawls's way of bringing the maximin idea to bear upon his account of social primary goods may also seem problematic. For even if the parties employ the maximin rule and assume that the persons they represent prefer more social primary goods to less, it does not follow that they would favor whatever basic structure offers the best minimum share. It must also be assumed that Rawls's social primary goods have no significant negative externalities. Even while each person is better off with more rather than less, it may still be true that each is worse off if all have more than if all have less. (Compare, even if each is safer with a gun than without one, it may still be true that each is less safe if all have guns than if none do.) I try to resolve this problem in §13.5 and Chapter 4 through a particular view of the basic political liberties and the political process.

10.6. Rawls modifies the maximin idea by stipulating that interschemic comparisons are to be based upon *representative* shares, that is, in the first instance, upon the social position of the least advantaged representative group. One reason behind this stipulation seems to be that one cannot reasonably estimate for various feasible alternative schemes what *the* worst individual share would be. It would be quite difficult to find this share even within an actually existing scheme. And even if one could find it, this share would probably be affected by various peculiarities—such as its "owner's" family background, bad luck, disabilities, personal dispositions (for example, to laziness or crime), and so on—and thus would reveal little about the prevailing basic structure (cf. TJ 96). For these reasons the parties can more effectively safeguard the interests of those they represent by basing their interschemic comparisons upon some larger least advantaged group (under each scheme).[13] I find this kind of reasoning convincing in regard to *engendered* (intra- or interschemic) inequalities in social primary goods, such as inequalities in income and wealth, in the fair value of basic political liberties, or in the security of other basic liberties. The reasoning is less convincing in regard to partly *established* inequalities however. When some are explicitly excluded from certain constitutional guarantees or legally barred from certain opportunities, the number of persons so disadvantaged is much less relevant. But then we cannot treat established and engendered inequalities differently—at least if I am right to argue (§§2.2, 11.2.1) that the criterion of justice must consider the distribution of overall shares rather than the separate distributions of various goods.[14] Here the more important considerations seem to point in the direction of representative groups, and the countervailing considerations can be accommodated by stipulating that representative groups are reasonably small or that representative shares are the geometric (rather than arithmetic) mean of the shares of the members of the corresponding representative group.

10.7. Rawls specifies a social position in terms of a *lifetime* share of social primary goods: "The least advantaged are defined as those who have the lowest index of primary goods, when their prospects are viewed over a complete life. This definition implies that social mobility is not considered a primary good. Individuals actually born into this group have some likelihood of improving their situation and of belonging to the more favoured; but whatever this likelihood is, it is irrelevant, since the least advantaged are, by definition, those who are born into and who remain in that group throughout their life" (SUPG 164). The last sentence, I suggest, cannot be taken literally, because it would leave us with an empty group if in some social system the likelihood of

[13]It sometimes sounds as though Rawls has more principled reasons for focusing on the least advantaged representative group rather than person (TJ 98)—similar to the parties' principled reasons for focusing on social primary goods rather than utility. If so, I do not see what they might be (see end of §17.5). The notion of representative groups raises the questions how such groups are to be defined and how the representative prospects of each group are to be determined on the basis of empirical data about their members (cf. Scanlon, RTJ 193–94). These questions, hardly touched upon by Rawls, play a crucial role in settling how egalitarian his maximin criterion really is. Suppose, for example, we are trying to find out what the income of the least advantaged is in the United States today and whether it could be raised by reforming economic institutions in respect to the income inequalities they generate. Here, it makes an enormous difference how this least advantaged group is defined—whether it comprises, say, 40 percent or 2 percent of the population and whether its representative share is defined as the arithmetic mean, median, or geometric mean of the shares of its members (cf. §17.5).

[14]Rawls does seem to want it both ways. At least he speaks of "representative individuals" specifically "in applying the second principle" (TJ 64), thus running into the further problem that the distribution of first-principle goods is to some extent engendered—as regards the well-protectedness of persons' basic liberties, for example, or the fair value of their political liberties. In these matters the considerations against focusing strictly upon individual persons would seem at least as strong as in the case of income and wealth.

upward mobility were 100 percent. It would lead to the absurd conclusion that a scheme under which the least advantaged earn $5.00 an hour all their lives is, other things equal, to be preferred to a scheme under which *everyone's* net income rate gradually increases with age, say, from $4.50 to $30.00. It is evident, I trust, that the upward mobility under the latter scheme must count in its favor.

I suggest that Rawls means to address the question whether persons' social positions are to be evaluated *ex post* or *ex ante*.[15] Should we care about those whose lifetime expectation or prospect for social primary goods (a probability-weighted average) is worst or about those who would actually have the worst share of social primary goods over a lifetime? Under a scheme with a lot of social mobility, representative *expected* lifetime shares may not differ much between those born into different classes. Yet *actual* lifetime shares may differ quite significantly, so that those (from all class backgrounds) who fail in their careers are very badly off. Under such a scheme, the worst representative *ex ante* position (prospective shares of those born into the lowest class) would be much superior to the worst representative *ex post* position (the worst actual shares). I interpret Rawls's statement about the irrelevance of social mobility to mean that he is opting for the *ex post* perspective.[16] The least advantaged are defined as those who would actually turn out to have the worst shares of social primary goods over a complete life.[17]

Another alternative to the *ex post* perspective is the view that a criterion of justice should be concerned not with lifetime shares at all but only with the distribution of *initial* shares or *starting* positions (at coming of age, say). The preferred institutional scheme is the one that generates the best minimum initial share. This view differs from the *ex ante* perspective in that it disregards social mobility. It does not matter for the assessment of an institutional scheme to what extent initial inequalities will tend to be compounded (through centrifugal tendencies) or to be washed out. This matters very much on the *ex ante* perspective and matters at least somewhat on the *ex post* perspective.

[15]For a brief discussion by an economist, see Kanbur, SL 59–69.

[16]Rawls often speaks of expectations, (life) prospects, and even starting positions, but I believe these expressions are meant to emphasize that he is concerned not with the particular shares of concrete individuals but with *representative* shares. Moreover, the alternative schemes we consider in reflecting upon institutional reforms are normally hypothetical. We ask from the standpoint of *prospective* participants how they would do under some scheme. So my interpretation can account for Rawls's talk of prospects: He is thinking of the actual shares we can *expect* to exist (e.g., from the vantage point of the original position) if this or that scheme is chosen, not of the expected shares (probability-weighted averages) under some given scheme. Let me add that any criterion of justice involving (*ex post* or *ex ante*) lifetime shares must say something about intrapersonal aggregation in the case of goods such as income. For example, is the same lifetime income worth more if it comes as a more even flow? Rawls does not address this issue.

[17]The idea of persons moving from one representative group to another is then senseless because each person has only one actual lifetime share. Social mobility is taken into account in calculating persons' shares and in sorting them into representative groups.

Both alternative proposals can be semiconsequentialist by agreeing with Rawls that established and engendered inequalities (in expected shares or starting positions) should be considered on a par. Yet both are somewhat deontological in spirit, in that persons themselves are assigned a much larger responsibility for their success in life. Still, neither alternative goes to Nozickian extremes, and that in at least two respects. First, under Nozick's libertarian scheme some may (subject to the Lockean proviso) start out in dire poverty without any realistic prospect of ever improving their condition. Nozick is not concerned with starting positions insofar as they are engendered, or with prospects for social mobility. Second, under Nozick's scheme persons may risk or alienate all their initial rights. The *ex ante* perspective, however, will favor inalienable rights when this improves persons' prospects. Even the starting-position view may well do likewise on the grounds that an initial bundle of alienable rights can be improved upon by transforming some of the rights it contains into inalienable ones. The second-order liberty to risk or alienate one's basic rights is not advantageous, quite apart from paternalistic considerations about the likelihood of mistakes. It endangers agents by providing various nasty incentives to others to try to bring them under their control.

Still, the two alternative views, like Nozick's, pay much less attention than does Rawls to how persons' lives actually turn out under alternative schemes, whether through the agent's own failures and achievements or through contingent factors. Both may favor a scheme under which some persons *end up* very badly off indeed, which would be justified to such persons by pointing out that they started out either reasonably well off (starting position) or with reasonably good prospects of success as witnessed by all the others from their background who "made it" (*ex ante*).

There are two main kinds of argument against these views. First, considering alternative institutional schemes from the (risk-averse) standpoint of a prospective participant, one cannot plausibly ignore the possibility of ending up very badly off or be concerned with this possibility only in proportion to its likelihood. It is thus implausible for the parties to be indifferent to how their clients' lives actually turn out. Of course, if the parties deliberated in a risk-neutral fashion, the *ex ante* and *ex post* perspectives would be equivalent. But since they are risk-averse, they must be concerned to optimize the worst lifetime shares rather than the worst expected lifetime shares, let alone the worst initial shares.

Second, the two alternative criteria of justice would also be risky in that they would largely give up the fourth and sixth advantages Rawls claims for the maximin idea. They might favor schemes that engender radical economic inequalities, which would frustrate Rawls's aspiration for a shared notion of equal citizenship and would also induce extreme strains of commitment as persons whose position had gravely deteriorated would be strongly tempted not to abide by the ground rules when all they could now expect is a life of abject poverty. Such schemes would be less likely to endure and unlikely to engender a widespread categorical sense of justice. These are important reasons for describing the parties so that their risk-averse concern extends to the entire lives of their clients.

Yet one may think that the Rawlsian *ex post* perspective is too conservative in favoring institutional schemes that prohibit almost all forms of gambling and (voluntary) economic risk taking. In considering any liberty to take risks, Rawls's parties pay very little attention to those who gamble and win, for they will be underrepresented among the least advantaged. They focus disproportionately upon those who gamble and lose, whose *ex post* position is likely to be worse than the worst position under the alternative institutional scheme without the liberty. That these losers wanted to gamble and were free not to is simply ignored.

This objection may seem to take an extreme view of what it would mean to opt for the Rawlsian *ex post* perspective. It does not mean that every lottery ticket persons might purchase must be considered *ex post* and that lotteries must therefore be prohibited. Rawls can say that buying a lottery ticket does not reduce one's net income but is one way of spending one's income, like buying a movie ticket. There is no reason why consumption decisions of either kind should be prohibited.

But I think the objection can be stated in a plausible form. Take the case of a society in which a certain middling position is open to everyone but may be declined in favor of a riskier career that offers a higher (*ex ante*) expectation but also involves some danger of falling below the middling position. Here the position of those who are unsuccessful in the risky career can be measured in three different ways: one might ascribe to them the representative share of the middling position, which is the optimal no-risk share attainable antecedent to their career choice; one might use the expected share of the risky career, which is their *ex ante* prospect before their career turns out one way or another but after it is chosen; finally, taking the *ex post* perspective, one might ascribe to them the (poor) share they actually had after having chosen the risky career. Those objecting to Rawls's view might say: "Let us take one of the *ex ante* perspectives in this case so that such risky careers need not be prohibited. We should have faith that people can understand that they became poor as a consequence of their own choice, and that their low economic position will therefore not tempt them into noncompliance."

This objection is plausible in principle, I think, but there are limits to its plausibility in such cases. First, taking the *ex ante* perspective is implausible when the risk taking is not fully voluntary—if the no-risk share is not (or not understood to be) genuinely available or when the risks involved in the risky career are not understood and accepted.

Second, taking the *ex ante* perspective is also implausible when the worst *ex post* share of those who fail in the risky career is very bad, so that the equal-citizenship and strains-of-commitment arguments clearly come into play. Where *radical* deprivations and inequalities are at stake, we must take the *ex post* perspective.

These considerations suggest an intermediate solution that makes the choice of perspective depend in part upon the severity of the potential inequalities at issue. Rawls's conception of justice is already committed to a suitable notion of significance through which this idea can be incorporated and made more concrete—his lexical prioritization of the two principles (within the special conception of justice). My conjecture, then, is that when the lexical ordering of the principles applies, first-principle goods and opportunities should always be defined in an *ex post* fashion, while all other goods should be defined in an *ex ante* fashion for cases of voluntary exposure to risk and in an *ex post* fashion otherwise.[18] I consider this conjecture a plausible working hypothesis that must redeem itself by fitting together with the remaining elements of Rawls's criterion of justice.

11. The Split into Two Principles of Justice

11.1. I have analyzed into its main elements Rawls's *general* conception of justice, which treats all social primary goods as commensurable: "All social primary goods . . . are to be distributed equally unless an unequal distribution of any or all of these goods is to the advantage of the least favored" (TJ 303). Ultimately, however, Rawls wants to defend a specification of the general conception that divides these goods into two categories, each governed by its own criterion. This *special* conception of justice is to apply under "reasonably favorable conditions" (BLP 11); the general conception is to apply under all other conditions. The introduction of the special conception raises several further issues.

11.1.1. Although both the general and the special conceptions are maximin criteria, it is, strictly speaking, the disjunctive combination of general and special conceptions that, according to Rawls, constitutes "the maximin solution to the problem of social justice" (TJ 152). It is thus important how the domains of the two conceptions are delimited, that is, how "reasonably favorable conditions" are defined—a question Rawls largely evades. This topic includes the question whether two conceptions are really necessary or whether one of them is superior under all conditions (cf. §12.8.4).

---

[18]Even with this conjecture, the liberty to take extreme risks or the assignment of basic rights through (involuntary) lottery could still be justified under very extraordinary circumstances, namely, when the worst actual lifetime shares (taking outcomes of risk taking or the lottery into account) are no worse than the worst shares would be under any feasible alternative scheme. This view is continuous with the justification Rawls entertains for the institution of slavery (TJ 248).

11.1.2. Conversely, seeing the great diversity of possible conditions, one may ask why the parties shouldn't adopt a large number of conceptions, each fine-tuned to a specific set of social conditions. I think Rawls could plausibly resist this idea, arguing that the parties have reason not to want a long list of conceptions. Too complicated an agreement is likely to be misapplied in practice even by conscientious persons and is generally unsuitable as a public criterion by which citizens can assess their common institutions. So the parties may well prefer Rawls's proposal of only two conceptions—and this not merely as an acceptable approximation but as the best way of safeguarding the interests of those they represent under foreseeable worst-case scenarios.

11.2. Let us consider whether the special conception is, under reasonably favorable conditions, a plausible maximin criterion. It reads as follows (BLP 5):

> FIRST PRINCIPLE: Each person has an equal right to a fully adequate scheme of equal basic liberties which is compatible with a similar scheme of liberties for all.
>
> SECOND PRINCIPLE: Social and economic inequalities are to satisfy two conditions. First, they must be attached to offices and positions open to all under conditions of fair equality of opportunity [the opportunity principle]; and second, they must be to the greatest benefit of the least advantaged members of society [the difference principle].

Underlying this special conception is the idea that "the social structure can be divided into two more or less distinct parts, the first principle applying to the one, the second to the other. They distinguish between those aspects of the social system that define and secure the equal liberties of citizenship and those that specify and establish social and economic inequalities. . . . [T]he distinction between fundamental rights and liberties and economic and social benefits marks a difference among primary social goods that one should try to exploit. It suggests an important division in the social system" (TJ 61, 63). Assuming that each basic structure can be so analyzed into two jointly exhaustive and nonoverlapping parts, Rawls proposes that over a certain range of conditions the maximin criterion governing the assessment of entire basic structures should consist of two maximin criteria governing the assessments of these two parts. This way, each basic structure receives one score based on the worst position it generates in terms of basic rights and liberties and another score based on the worst representative socioeconomic position it generates. Of course Rawls must assign weights to these two scores so as to enable a unified ranking of alternative basic structures. But even before asking how the two scores are to be aggregated, I can state two objections right away.

11.2.1. With the split into two criteria, the distributions of the two kinds of goods are assessed independently of each other. Important information about each basic structure is disregarded. It cannot come into view whether inequalities of the two kinds tend to *compensate* or *aggravate* one another, but this information is indispensable if the quest is for the maximin solution to the problem of social justice. To clarify the objection let me symbolize the evaluation of a social position by an ordered pair of numbers that represent the position's first-principle score and socioeconomic score, respectively. Suppose basic structure ONE has two relevant groups with scores <80,70> and <30,20>, while basic structure TWO has two relevant groups with scores <80,20> and <30,70>. We may assume that other things and also the size of all four groups are equal. In this case, the two basic structures would be ranked as equals by Rawls's split criterion; both principles of justice are equally well or ill satisfied. But the parties would obviously prefer a criterion yielding a preference for basic structure TWO because both relevant social positions under TWO are clearly superior to the worst position under ONE.[19]

We see here that the special conception—though it is in one sense, as its name is meant to suggest, a limiting case of the general conception, in which specific weights are attached to the various social primary goods relative to each other—is also more than just a special case of the general conception. The general conception would always yield a preference for TWO over ONE, no matter how the two scores are weighted (so long as neither kind of social primary goods is disregarded entirely).

11.2.2. A related difficulty derives from Rawls's view that "as far as possible the basic structure should be appraised from the position of equal citizenship. . . . The problems of adjudicating among the fundamental liberties are settled by reference to it" (TJ 97). By contrast, a maximin criterion would be sensitive to what alternative specifications of the basic liberties would mean for the various socioeconomic classes, and surely the interests of the rich and the poor might be opposed in regard to, say, how freedom of the press should be specified, how political speech should be regulated (cf. BLP 73–74), or how judicial proceedings should be financed. What is the preference of "the representative equal citizen" in such cases?[20]

This problem is somewhat mitigated by Rawls's qualification that differential effects of a set of equal basic liberties "may be left aside . . . if social and economic inequalities are just" (TJ 97).[21] This suggests

---

[19]Rawls may respond with the empirical claim that the distributions of the two kinds of goods will in fact correlate. This claim, however, is historically doubtful (as in the case of European Jewry) and, at any rate, not something he could ask his risk-averse parties simply to take for granted.

[20]This difficulty is extensively discussed in Hart, RLP III. In his elaborate response to Hart, Rawls attempts to elucidate the notion of the representative equal citizen by reference to the two highest-order interests. This response makes his idea more determinate, but it does not, I believe, resolve the difficulty.

[21]May they really? Suppose an economically just society encounters an emergency in which conscription is necessary. Can we say that basic liberties are *equally* restricted if everyone may avoid conscription through making a large payment? I suspect such a

(though it does not entail) that they may not be left aside when social and economic inequalities are not just. But when Rawls actually discusses the specification of basic rights and liberties in the United States, he does so from the standpoint of equal citizenship (BLP), even though he clearly believes that the second principle is not satisfied (TJ 279).

The problem has an analogue in the socioeconomic sphere. How are we to compare incomes across institutional schemes if these have different price vectors? This is evidently an extremely complicated problem, which I cannot address in any detail.[22] Still, the intuitive idea must be to construct some standard basket of goods and services and then ask how many such baskets could be bought with the lowest representative income under each scheme. The problem is how to construct this standard basket—from the standpoint of "the equal citizen" or from the standpoint of the least advantaged. In the former case, we would be guided by what persons in general tend to consume in the two schemes. In the latter case, we would be guided by what the poor would tend to consume and might, therefore, weight the price of basic foodstuffs more heavily and that of airline tickets less heavily, for example. Once the question has been clearly stated, it is hard to see how risk-averse contractors (or maximin philosophers) can allow interschemic income comparisons to be made from the standpoint of the representative (average) citizen rather than that of the least advantaged. And the same holds, for analogous reasons, for interschemic comparisons of alternative specifications of basic rights and liberties.

11.3. For reasonably favorable conditions Rawls proposes a serial or lexicographical ("lexical") ordering of the two scores, so that first-score differentials always override second-score differentials. The reason he gives is that "the interests of liberty . . . become stronger as the conditions for the exercise of the equal freedoms are more fully realized. Beyond some point it becomes and then remains irrational from the standpoint of the original position to acknowledge a lesser liberty for the sake of greater material means and amenities of office" (TJ 542). The parties adopt the special rather than the general conception for such conditions because, on the basis of their limited knowledge, they find it rational to assume that those they represent will, under these conditions, take an incommensurably greater interest in basic rights and liberties than in all other social primary goods. Rawls need not claim that the parties know this assumption to be true, though he sometimes seems to think that he must (BLP 83 n. 87). It is enough that it be the most sensible one to make for the parties who seek to safeguard the interests of those they represent under foreseeable worst-case sce-

---

possibility would be acceptable only if economic positions were strictly equal. I can appeal here to ordinary ideas about wartime rationing, which are presumably not based on the belief that social and economic inequalities are unjust.

[22]See Gibbard, DG, for a discussion of this problem.

narios. Perhaps the parties know only that their clients, given their two highest-order interests as stipulated by Rawls, will under reasonably favorable conditions attach very great importance to the basic liberties relative to social and economic benefits and burdens. If the dangers of underestimating this importance are greater than those of overestimating it, it may well be rational for them to make the assumption of infinite weight, especially when this assumption obviates the need for weighting and balancing diverse goods and thus results in a criterion that is easier to apply and more suitable as a public criterion (all of which tends to raise the worst social position).

Evidently, the serial ordering has very considerable advantages as a simplifying device. It neatly resolves cases where the two principles are not cosatisfiable. As Rawls understands it, it also guides our efforts toward institutional reform: "When we come to nonideal theory, we do not fall back straightway upon the general conception of justice. . . . [T]he ranking of the principles of justice in ideal theory reflects back and guides the application of these principles to nonideal situations. It identifies which limitations need to be dealt with first" (TJ 303, cf. 246) in that it "requires us to satisfy the first principle in the ordering before we can move on to the second, the second before we consider the third, and so on. A principle does not come into play until those previous to it are either fully met or do not apply" (TJ 43, cf. 244). This lexical priority, however, also raises a number of serious difficulties for Rawls's claim to be presenting the maximin criterion of social justice.

11.3.1. Let me again represent the evaluation of a social position by an ordered pair. Suppose that when the first principle is satisfied, the first number will be 100 for all positions. Now take a basic structure generating two positions with scores $<80,70>$ and $<30,20>$. Here the last quotation would suggest that one need not worry about the second-principle score of the least advantaged (unjustly low, let us suppose), so long as some first-principle scores have not reached 100. By contrast, a maximin criterion would demand that political efforts and social resources be devoted to raising the second-principle score of the least advantaged when such efforts do not detract from improving their first-principle score. All principles should always be "in play." More important, both quotations entail that feasible improvements in the first-principle score of the more advantaged (for example, larger press freedoms for the South African whites) must take precedence over feasible improvements in the second-principle score of the least advantaged (for example, better education for the South African blacks). But the parties' maximin rule would lead them to prefer a criterion favoring precisely the opposite priority.[23]

---

[23]It is uncontroversial that feasible improvements in the first-principle score of the least advantaged take precedence over everything else. What is at issue here is a secondary priority.

Rawls gets into this problem, I believe, because he does not properly distinguish two different roles of the lexical priority. Initially he takes it to be a *design priority*. Our ultimate goal, as envisioned by the special conception, is to satisfy the first principle completely (which presupposes the achievement of what I call *truly* favorable conditions), no matter how its satisfaction may constrain the distribution of second-principle scores. This design priority does not clash with the preeminent concern for the least advantaged. The reason is that a basic structure under which the first-principle goods of some or all are abridged ipso facto produces a worst social position that is inferior to the worst social position under any basic structure that completely satisfies the first principle.[24] For purposes of designing an ideal institutional scheme, the requirements of the second principle are then *subject to* those of the first and invalidated in cases of *inconsistency*.[25]

Without proper argument for the transition, Rawls also understands his lexical priority in the quite different sense of an *implementation priority*. For purposes of reforming a less-than-just institutional scheme under reasonably favorable conditions, feasible reforms demanded by the second principle must *give way to* those demanded by the first, when demands of the two kinds stand in *competition* (on account of scarce resources). Given the parties' assumption of a preeminent interest in first-principle scores, this move is unobjectionable when the competition is between interests of the same representative group. But in other cases the parties would clearly prefer a criterion in which (in the allocation of scarce resources available for institutional reform) the priority concern for the worst representative share overrides the lexical priority of first-principle over second-principle scores.

11.4. Before discussing further difficulties, we must look more closely at Rawls's overall rationale for his two principles. Here it turns out that the two parts of the basic structure aren't so distinct after all. The goods falling under the two principles are both separated and united by the *different* contributions they make to the *same* supreme value. Rawls marks this difference by distinguishing between the *freedom* persons have, thanks to their basic rights and liberties (an enumeration of which is appended to the first principle [TJ 61]), and the *worth of this freedom*, as estimated through second-principle scores.

The interplay between the two principles is envisaged as follows:

> Freedom as equal liberty is the same for all; the question of compensating for a lesser than equal liberty does not arise. But the worth of liberty is not

---

[24]This assumes, of course, that it really is rational "from the standpoint of the parties in the original position" (TJ 542) to give, under reasonably favorable conditions, infinite weight to first-principle goods relative to social and economic benefits and burdens.

[25]Thus the opportunity principle, for example, is construed as requiring only that institutions come as close to maintaining fair equality of opportunity as is feasible without abridgment of basic rights and liberties.

the same for everyone. Some have greater authority and wealth, and therefore greater means to achieve their aims. The lesser worth of liberty is,
however, compensated for, since the capacity of the less fortunate members of society to achieve their aims would be even less were they not to
accept the existing inequalities whenever the difference principle is satisfied. . . . Taking the two principles together, the basic structure is to be
arranged to maximize the worth to the least advantaged of the complete
scheme of equal liberty shared by all. [TJ 204–5]

Rawls reaffirms this idea eleven years later:

The basic liberties are specified by institutional rights and duties that
entitle citizens to do certain things, if they wish, and that forbid others to
interfere. The basic liberties are a framework of legally protected paths and
opportunities. Of course, ignorance and poverty, and the lack of material
means generally, prevent people from exercising their rights and from
taking advantage of these openings. But rather than counting these and
similar obstacles as restricting a person's liberty, we count them as affecting the worth of liberty, that is, the usefulness to persons of their liberties.
Now in justice as fairness, this usefulness is specified in terms of an index
of the primary goods regulated by the second principle of justice. . . . The
basic structure of society is arranged so that it maximizes the primary
goods available to the least advantaged to make use of the equal basic
liberties enjoyed by everyone. [BLP 40–41]

I believe Rawls's general idea is to conceive worth of freedom (what
ultimately matters) as a function of three components: the *public recognition* of certain basic freedoms (the public understanding that it is
legitimate for me to travel along certain paths); their *protection* (the
maintenance of these paths as secure highways); and the *means* at
one's disposal (my ability to obtain food and boots, a car and gasoline,
without which I could not travel on even the best and safest highway).
Let us say that the first component determines (*formal*) *legal freedom*;
that the first two components together determine *effective legal freedom* (Rawls: freedom); and that all three components together determine *worth of freedom* or (as I also say) *worthwhile freedom*.[26]

While the third component is relegated to the second principle,
Rawls's first principle governs *both* of the other components, reflecting
the realization that basic rights and liberties protect our freedom only
insofar as they are themselves well-protected, that is, upheld and enforced. Thus the first principle requires not merely formal but effective
legal freedom: "It is the institution as realized . . . which is just or
unjust" (TJ 55). "Whether the basic structure guarantees equal liberty of
conscience, or freedom of thought, is settled by . . . how they are
actually interpreted and enforced" (SUPG 163). Unfortunately, Rawls
makes no attempt to say *how* this issue is to be settled. Take the

---

[26]Normally, the distribution of the first component is largely established, that of the
other two largely engendered, but there are exceptions.

integrity of the person, for example. Suppose this is guaranteed by laws against homicide, rape, assault, drunk driving, and so on. What else is required for the integrity of the person to be sufficiently well protected? What if 60 percent of all women are raped, or 4 percent of all black men murdered within ten years of reaching age sixteen? What if 3 percent of the population meet their deaths in car accidents? Without a clue how to answer such questions, we cannot tell whether the first principle is satisfied in a given social system and hence do not know what political priorities Rawls's conception would set for its institutional reform.

My conjecture in §10.7 achieves somewhat more specificity, though perhaps at the price of implausibility. Effective legal freedom is evaluated *ex post*. The disadvantaged are those whose basic rights and liberties are actually ill protected. It is not enough that certain crime rates are sufficiently low overall. They must also be sufficiently low within the various population clusters. Such clusters can be defined quite narrowly, so long as intracluster rates and intercluster inequalities in rates are statistically significant. It may be the case, for example, that poor, black, female, inner-city residents, on account of the incidence of violent crimes committed against them, do not effectively *have* the right to personal integrity, though on paper this right is guaranteed to them as to everyone else. This violation of the first principle would likely place these women among the least advantaged.

Now, surely, some persons outside this cluster will suffer violent crimes, and some persons within this cluster won't. But singling out the persons whose basic rights are actually violated, rather than those whose basic rights are actually ill protected, is implausible. On this proposal the identification of the least advantaged heavily depends on chance factors that have little to do with the prevailing basic structure, which may result in a highly heterogeneous and unrepresentative least advantaged group. The proposal also disregards the fact that those whose basic rights are ill protected live in fear even if they never in fact suffer a violation of their rights.

11.5. His criterion of justice, Rawls says, ultimately requires institutions "to maximize the worth to the least advantaged of the complete scheme of equal liberty shared by all" (TJ 204–5). This requirement presupposes something like the following rationale:

(a) Given their limited general knowledge, the parties find it rational to assume that those they represent have a preeminent interest in the *worth* of their freedom, in being in the best social position to enjoy, exercise, or take advantage of whatever freedom the first principle requires them to have. Hence they want individual shares to be evaluated in terms of worthwhile freedom.

Worthwhile freedom, as we have seen, is a function of three components. Rawls's special conception, however, attaches overriding importance to effective legal freedom, gives lexical priority to the first two components over the third. To make plausible that the parties would accept this priority of freedom over its worth (which stands behind the lexical priority of the first over the second principle), Rawls must invoke a further premise, roughly as follows:

> (b) The parties find it rational to assume that it is (something very close to) a necessary prerequisite to being in a position to enjoy, exercise, and take advantage of one's first-principle freedom that one should have certain publicly recognized and effectively enforced basic rights and liberties that institutionally protect such enjoyment. There is no worthwhile freedom without effective legal freedom.

To be sure, when one does have such basic rights, one's enjoyment of the freedom they protect may still depend on social and economic factors. The extent to which one is in a position to *enjoy* the freedom to own property, to *exercise* freedom of movement, or to *take advantage* of the freedom to have one's opinions published, for example, is a function of one's wealth and income. Still, if one does not *have* the relevant basic rights at all, then enjoying the correlative freedoms is altogether out of the question. This conjectured premise (b) would explain the parties' overriding concern with effective legal freedom. That Rawls must rely on an argument of this sort raises three further difficulties for his position.

11.5.1. Let us begin with the simple case of a single aspect of freedom for which the first principle requires effective institutional protection in form of a basic right or liberty, L. The extent to which persons actually *enjoy* this freedom depends on whether they *have* L (effective legal freedom) and on the further means (money, education, etc.) at their disposal. Now why should having L be incommensurably more important than having those means—so that in nonideal contexts establishing the former always takes priority over increasing the latter? The answer I have suggested Rawls must give is that having L is a *prerequisite* without which the means for the enjoyment come to naught. There are two ways of reading this claim, both problematic. We can take the prerequisite to be conceptual, that is, to hold that it is logically impossible to enjoy or exercise a basic right or liberty that one does not have. In this case we would have to read (a) as asserting that the parties care about freedom only insofar as it is enjoyed *as a matter of right*. But if we read this way, (a) is implausible. Why should persons who in virtue of their socioeconomic position do in fact enjoy some aspect of their first-principle freedom be considered unfree in the relevant respect just because what they enjoy is not the object of an effectively enforced legal right? Why should freedom of movement or freedom from arbitrary arrest, say, have value only insofar as they are enjoyed as rights? Alternatively, we can read (a) as allowing that the parties care even about freedom that is not enjoyed as a matter of right. In this case, we would take the prerequisite to be causal, to hold that if some aspect of one's freedom is not publicly recognized and institutionally protected, then one will not, as a matter of fact, enjoy it. In this construal, (b) is implausible. It is not historically true, for example, that freedom from arbitrary arrest, or freedom of movement, is enjoyed only in societies in which a legal right to these aspects of freedom is publicly recognized and effectively enforced. Either way, the lexical priority of the interest in L over the interest in the means for enjoying the aspect of freedom that L protects jars with the idea of maximizing the worthwhile first-principle freedom of the least advantaged.

11.5.2. This conclusion can be further supported. Just as an aspect of freedom may be enjoyable in some degree even though it isn't legally protected, it may also be in some degree unenjoyable even though it is so protected. A basic right or liberty L, though listed in the constitution, may not in fact be effectively enforced, for certain sectors of society perhaps, so that some find it very difficult to enjoy or exercise L even though they have the money, education, etc., to do so.[27] Now if having L were an all-or-nothing affair, then it might be plausible to assign it the preeminence Rawls postulates over the means for enjoying the correlative freedom. But if the transition from not having L to having L lies somewhere on a continuum, then the priority is no longer plausible, for the transition may then be a small step indeed (no matter where the line is drawn). Thus, it was at some time during the 1960s, perhaps, that blacks in the United States began to *have* certain rights they had formerly had only on paper. In such a case it seems implausible to assume that the decisive incremental increase in their effective legal freedom should have made a greater contribution to their worthwhile freedom than *any* increase in their means of enjoyment could have done.

11.5.3. Let us suppose, contrary to the preceding two objections, that without L (effective legal freedom) the means for enjoying the correlative aspect of freedom are generally of little or no value, so that it *is* plausible to assign lexical priority to the demand for the former over the demand for the latter. Even this supposition would not be enough. Rawls needs to show not merely that for each basic liberty, L, having L is lexically more important than having the means for the enjoyment of the freedom L protects. He must also show that having L is lexically more important than the means for the enjoyment of *any* first-principle freedom. (From the fact that each daughter is younger than her mother it does not follow that all daughters are younger than all mothers.) To see clearly what is at stake, suppose some group has the basic right or liberty L but not K. It may then be false that their worthwhile freedom would gain incommensurably more through their acquisition of K (as

[27]Rawls holds that under certain halfway favorable conditions a restricted set of basic liberties may be justifiable, provided the loss in terms of basic liberties left unrecognized is outweighed by "the greater protection" or "the larger security" of the basic liberties that are recognized (TJ 231, 233), so that the worst first-principle score is superior overall (see §13.1). This statement shows that he would grant that what I have called effective legal freedom is a matter of degree.

an effectively enforced right) than through a significant increase in their means for enjoying L. It is quite possible that a greater gain in the worthwhile freedom of the poor would result from an improvement in their income and education (enabling them better to take advantage of their existing basic rights and liberties) than from additional legal rights (whose effect on their worthwhile freedom may be rather slight so long as they remain poor and uneducated).

11.6. The preceding three objections have assumed (that the parties accept) the exclusive concern for maximizing the worth of freedom as Rawls understands freedom. Before examining that assumption, let us look more closely at this understanding. Rawls explains what aspects of freedom he is especially concerned with by specifying that the first principle requires the institutional protection of a fully adequate package of basic civil and political rights and liberties that covers the following four categories (outlined at TJ 61 and refined in BLP 5 et passim):

(A) The basic political liberties, which are said to be connected with the capacity for a sense of justice (BLP 47). These include the basic right to vote and be eligible for public office as well as basic rights to political speech and assembly (freedom of thought). Rawls includes here as a first-principle requirement that institutions must maintain the fair value of the basic political liberties, though this requirement is left rather vague (BLP 42).

(B) The basic rights and liberties protecting freedom of conscience, said to be connected to the capacity for a conception of the good (BLP 47). These include, in particular, rights to freedom of association as well as basic religious liberties (BLP 56–57).

The remaining two categories contain "supporting" (BLP 50) basic liberties, necessary to the adequate development and full exercise of both moral powers:

(C) The basic rights and liberties protecting the freedom and integrity of the person. These are violated "by slavery and serfdom, and by the denial of freedom of movement and occupation" (BLP 50). They further include the right to be free "from psychological oppression and physical assault" (RAM 640) and also "the right to hold and to have the exclusive use of personal property"—though this latter without certain (capitalist) "rights of acquisition and bequest, as well as the right to own means of production and natural resources" and without certain (socialist) rights "to participate in the control of means of production and natural resources, which are to be socially owned" (BLP 12).

(D) The basic rights and liberties associated with the rule of law, including protections against arbitrary arrest and seizure.

11.6.1. The objection to this account can be formulated by charging Rawls with, alternatively, a truncated conception of fundamental freedom or an overblown view of its importance. Consider, to begin with the first formulation, a basic structure engendering a substantial inci-

dence of severe and unrelieved poverty. The poor under this scheme
are in many obvious ways unfree on account of their poverty. The
existing ground rules provide no legal path on which they can obtain
more than part of what they need. They and their families may be
unfree to purchase a nutritious and healthful diet, sufficient clothing
and heating fuel for the winter, needed medical care and medications,
a decent education, and so forth. Where does Rawls's account take note
of this sort of unfreedom? Granted, Rawls wants his conception of
freedom to be confined to its most fundamental aspects, but is it not
fundamental when social conditions leave one without access to sufficient food and heating fuel while there is plenty of it around? Rawls
may reply that the fundamental aspects of freedom are identified
through the two highest-order interests in the development and exercise of the two moral powers, and that persons who are very poor in a
democracy are much better able to satisfy *these* interests than persons
living under a dictatorship because they are still able to engage in the
activities protected by the basic civil and political rights and liberties.
Even if you and your family freeze through the winter and must feed
yourselves on dog food, you can still attend political meetings and
religious ceremonies. But perhaps such a reply would tend to cast
doubt on Rawls's account of the two highest-order interests rather than
vindicate his list of first-principle goods.

In its second formulation, the objection accepts Rawls's conception
of fundamental freedom as it is and then rejects the claim that the
worth of freedom (so defined) is all that ultimately matters to prospective participants in social institutions. Persons have some basic social
and economic needs. Foremost among these are the needs for a certain
minimum access to food, clothing, shelter, care, culture, and education. Such goods are of much greater urgency and importance than
could be derived by viewing them merely as means for fulfilling a more
urgent need to secure the worth of one's fundamental freedoms. Rawls
does not do justice to this problem by addressing the possibility that
"the basic liberties may prove to be merely formal" (BLP 40). This
phrasing of the issue already presupposes that the importance of social
and economic essentials lies in their function as means to the enjoyment of fundamental (civil and political) freedoms. If the account of
social primary goods is to reflect a plausible notion of human needs
(RAM 643; WOS 15; FG 554; SUPG 172–73), then it cannot deny the
fundamental role basic social and economic needs actually play in a
human life. But insistence on the preeminence of the basic (civil and
political) rights and liberties constitutes just such a denial. To illustrate:
understood as part of a maximin criterion, the account of social primary goods must provide a plausible measure of persons' shares
through which one can *identify* the least advantaged under each institutional scheme and *compare* the social positions of these groups
across schemes. Now suppose basic rights are unequal (in an intra- or
interschemic comparison). For such cases, Rawls's criterion, con-

cerned with the worth of freedom, would always count the social position with the lesser basic rights as worse. Of two groups with scores <90,100> and <100,20>, the former would be viewed as the less advantaged. Thus his conception would entail, for example, that (affluent) persons whose basic rights to freedom of political speech or assembly are (even slightly) restricted ipso facto have a worse share than others who, though free from this restriction, are malnourished and homeless. But this ranking is intuitively implausible. One would be reluctant to employ Rawls's account of social primary goods, with its heavy emphasis on civil and political freedoms, as a guide for choosing "a society in which his enemy is to assign him his place." One would be reluctant to use this account even if one were persuaded that persons have highest-order interests in developing and exercising their two moral powers. It is not credible that in the United States today the lowest prospects for developing and exercising the two moral powers would be raised more by overturning the "profoundly dismaying" (BLP 74–79) precedent of *Buckley* v. *Valeo* (in which the Supreme Court declared unconstitutional various congressional limits on election expenditures) than by improvements in the diet, shelter, or education of the poorest citizens.[28]

12. The Package of Basic Rights and Liberties

The previous section has raised various doubts about Rawls's presentation of "the two principles as the maximin solution to the problem of social justice" (TJ 152). I now discuss some possible responses in Rawls's behalf, including proposals for revisions that would help him cope with the difficulties. Here I don't address the possibility of a radical redescription of the original position with a retraction, perhaps, of the maximin idea. Instead, I discuss four main strategies for making Rawls's proposal attractive to the parties in the original position *as described*. All four strategies have at least some basis in Rawls's texts.

[28]One could respond to this criticism with an empirical claim, that the plight of the poor will not be effectively addressed by the political process unless and until all citizens, whatever their socioeconomic position, have a roughly equal opportunity to influence the outcome of political decisions. *Buckley* stands in the way of precisely such an equalization of political influence. But this response is not available *to Rawls*. His argument for the priority of the basic liberties is based on their *intrinsic* rather than their *instrumental* importance. His claim is that "the interests of liberty . . . become stronger as the conditions for the exercise of the equal freedoms are more fully realized. Beyond some point it becomes and then remains irrational from the standpoint of the original position to acknowledge a lesser liberty for the sake of greater material means and amenities of office" (TJ 542). Moreover, the suggested empirical claim is unavailable in the case of other infringements of the first principle. Removing a restriction on religious freedom, for example, will not improve the situation of those whose prospects for developing and exercising their two moral powers are blocked by severe poverty. Its removal would nevertheless, on Rawls's account, have priority over relieving their poverty.

Before I begin, let me note that most of the problems I have sketched involve the application of the two principles (serially ordered) to situations of injustice, that is, to social systems in which both principles—(§§11.3.1, 11.5.1–3)—or at least the second—(§11.2.1)—are not satisfied. And even the remaining difficulties—though also relevant to the ideal-theoretical question of whether a basic structure fully satisfying Rawls's two principles would indeed optimize the worst share (as intuitively assessed in terms of social primary goods)—become much more pressing when, because of violations of the second principle, social and economic inequalities are very great (§11.2.2) or basic social and economic needs are not met (§11.6.1). Rawls's proposal would be a great deal more plausible, though also much less interesting, if it did not presume to provide guidance for the reform of unjust institutional schemes.

12.1. One might in large part simply deny these difficulties by asserting a weaker version of the empirical claim sketched in note 28. The parties run no risk by adopting the serial ordering because efforts toward satisfying the first principle do not, as an empirical matter, compete with efforts toward satisfying the second. This assertion is doubly implausible. It would seem quite possible that the establishment or strengthening of some basic liberty for all participants or for some group(s) can worsen the worst social position. One can readily imagine or cite from history situations in which major economic reforms toward the eradication of malnutrition, illiteracy, and homelessness and a fairer distribution of income and wealth generally are impeded or blocked by the more affluent (whose interests would be adversely affected by the projected reform) through their concerted use of the media and the political process as guaranteed by basic rights and liberties. Even apart from this consideration, it is quite conceivable that the establishment and strengthening and then the maintenance and effective protection of basic liberties can divert political efforts and social resources from the task of reducing social and economic deprivations. An effective system of equal basic liberties is not cost free but calls for parliaments, a judiciary, administrators, police forces, and much more. It seems clear that the effective improvement of these mechanisms would generally demand a different allocation of efforts and resources than would be required to improve nutrition and basic education for the poor, say. Given these eventualities, the parties must consider that the serial ordering may endanger the satisfaction of the most basic social and economic needs. And if they take these needs as seriously as they take some of Rawls's basic liberties, then they would not risk ranking them lower on the basis of uncertain empirical assumptions.[29]

---

[29]This argument is analogous to one Rawls gives to show that the parties would not "consent to the principle of utility. In this case their freedom would be subject to the calculus of social interests and they would be authorizing its restriction if this would lead

12.2. The failure of this empirically based denial suggests the first strategy: restrict the serial ordering to ideal theory, that is, jettison the implementation priority of the first principle while reaffirming its design priority. Indeed, Rawls says once that "the principles and their lexical order were not acknowledged with [nonideal] situations in mind and so it is possible that they no longer hold" (TJ 245). Consider also how Rawls rejects the idea that the first principle should be amended by the requirement that all participants must have a certain absolute minimum of social and economic benefits (ensuring that their basic social and economic needs are met): "Whatever the merits of this suggestion, it is superfluous in view of the difference principle. For any fraction of the index of primary goods enjoyed by the least advantaged can already be regarded in this manner" (BLP 44). Clearly, this argument can be reassuring only in regard to the design priority of the first principle.

But these passages are drowned out by countervailing evidence. That the parties adopt a priority rule governing what conditions justify unequal basic liberties (TJ §37, §39, 302) shows that they do deliberate about nonideal situations as well.[30] Moreover, Rawls does not merely seek to construct the ideal of a perfectly just well-ordered society and then have us use intuition and instrumental rationality for muddling through toward this ideal. He reiterates again and again that his conception of justice is to guide the course of social change (TJ 520, 263) and that a crucial feature enabling it to do this is the serial ordering of the two principles (TJ 43, 244, 246, 303; BLP 11 et passim). Of course, Rawls may still choose to limit his ambitions, but this limitation would constitute a devastating loss of practical political relevance for his theory.

Now it can hardly be kept secret from the parties that the serial ordering of the two principles is to be relevant to determining which injustices "need to be dealt with first" (TJ 303). If it were, then the original position would be of no use in justifying *to us* (in our nonideal social world) that we should give precedence to the implementation of Rawls's first principle. Thus Rawls must show that the parties would find the serial ordering convincing on the understanding that it is to be applied in nonideal contexts as well. The serial ordering must lead to a plausible ranking of less-than-just regimes and to plausible political priorities for cases in which the principles are not satisfied (with plausibility both times understood by reference to the parties' concern for the worst *ex post* lifetime shares).[31] And this is in fact a crucial test

---

to a greater net balance of satisfaction. Of course, as we have seen, a utilitarian may try to argue from the general facts of social life that when properly carried out the computation of advantages never justifies such limitations, at least under reasonably favorable conditions of culture. But even if the parties were persuaded of this, they might as well guarantee their freedom straightway by adopting the principle of equal liberty" (TJ 207).

[30]In ideal theory, "the question of compensating for a lesser than equal liberty does not arise" (TJ 204; cf. §13.1 herein).

[31]This consideration indicates how Rawls goes wrong when he rejects as superfluous the incorporation of a social minimum into the first principle. Such an additional

because the serial ordering is of comparatively minor significance in the (moreover rather theoretical) event that all principles or all but one are fully satisfied.

12.3. If the difficulties confronting the serial ordering of the two principles cannot be plausibly denied or evaded, we are reduced to finding ways of coping with them. In two minor cases there are relatively straightforward solutions. The problem set forth in §11.2.2 can be resolved through a minor modification. When conflicting specifications of the basic liberties would be preferable from the points of view of different socioeconomic classes, so that the position of the representative equal citizen is ill defined and cannot adjudicate how the basic liberties should be made compatible with one another, then this adjudication should be undertaken from the standpoint of the lowest socioeconomic class.

The problems noted in §11.2.1 and §11.3.1 can likewise be resolved through a modification. Rather than viewing any citizen as occupying two social positions (one within each of the two parts of the basic structure), we can regard each citizen as having just one overall share, which is defined by reference to *both* principles of justice. Here the least advantaged are singled out by first identifying those with the worst first-principle scores. Should this group include everyone or no one or be otherwise too large or too small to qualify as a representative group in Rawls's sense, the second principle is brought in as a secondary criterion. Once the representative group of the least advantaged has been identified in this way, its members' first-principle scores and their second-principle scores can be aggregated so as to determine the worst *representative* share (cf. §17.5).[32] The task of institutional reform is then to raise this worst social position if possible. Here improving the representative first-principle score of the least advantaged takes priority over improving their representative second-principle score, which in turn takes priority over improving even the representative first-principle scores of more advantaged groups. Thus, understood as *implementation* priorities, the priority concern for the least advantaged overrides the lexical priority of the first principle, if these two priorities should ever in nonideal contexts be in competition for scarce resources. This modification leaves intact the lexical *design* priority of the first over the

---

requirement may well be redundant within *ideal theory*. But it makes a great difference in nonideal situations by determining whether his conception of justice assigns a high or a low priority to the political task of meeting basic social and economic needs in comparison to the task of expanding effective legal freedom.

[32]This proposal can work only if the idea of representative groups is extended to the first principle, though this extension may be somewhat implausible in the case of established inequalities in first-principle goods (cf. §10.6). It would be ever so tedious, however, to try to treat these two kinds of first-principle inequalities differently, and so in what follows, I use the idea of representative groups across the board. As for Rawls's view on this matter, it is unclear from his writings (e.g., the (b)-clause of the first priority rule [TJ 302]) whether he wants to evaluate inequalities in first-principle goods by reference to the worst *individual* or the worst *representative* share.

second principle. We can never improve our ideal of a perfectly just basic structure by allowing abridgments of first-principle goods for the sake of raising second-principle scores. Ideally, all participants must have a fully adequate package of basic rights and liberties.

These modifications still leave the important worry that the serial ordering may lead to a misidentification of the least advantaged (by being too concerned with whether persons have effective legal freedom rather than with whether their basic social and economic needs are met) or may demand too much attention to the establishment and protection of their basic liberties at the expense of their basic social and economic needs (§§11.3.1 and 11.5.1–3). We can understand the remaining three strategies as addressing this worry.

12.4. The second strategy consists in puncturing, to some extent, the sharp "distinction between fundamental rights and liberties and economic and social benefits" that Rawls had introduced "to exploit . . . an important division in the social system" (TJ 63).[33] This is done by specifying the first principle so that it forbids radical social and economic inequalities (avoidably involving extreme poverty).[34] Here we can draw upon a socioeconomic provision that is already part of the first principle, namely, the requirement that the fair value of the basic political liberties be protected: "The worth of the political liberties to all citizens, whatever their social or economic position, must be approximately equal, or at least sufficiently equal, in the sense that everyone has a fair opportunity to hold public office and to influence the outcome of political decisions" (BLP 42), or somewhat less vague, "those similarly endowed and motivated should have roughly the same

[33]Rawls wants the differentiation into two principles to reflect three distinct divides: a division in the social system, as the first principle governs its civil and political, the second its social and economic aspects; a different order of importance, as the need for first-principle goods is ranked lexically above the need for social and economic benefits; and a distinction in kind, as the first principle requires certain specific protections while the second merely demands that representative socioeconomic shares be related in certain ways. It would be a remarkable coincidence indeed, if these three divides were to coincide as perfectly as Rawls wants.

[34]Some critics have urged as an ideal-theory revision that certain socioeconomic provisions be elevated to the first principle (perhaps as "welfare rights"). But in ideal theory such an amendment is indeed superfluous for the reason Rawls gives (BLP 44), unless one repudiates his semiconsequentialism for the sake of a fully consequentialist conception of justice. Such a repudiation, not always recognized as such, is endorsed by several critics. Thus Michaelman finds it unacceptable that the parties "are extremely conservative in dealing with the risk that the socially generated basic structure will define some very low socio-economic positions, but not especially conservative about the risk that naturally generated impairments will be very expensive to overcome" (CWR 339). Gutmann insists that it is "rational for individuals in the original position to accept the risk of moderately lower income prospects in exchange for the certainty that their health will be protected and maintained at all but outrageous cost to society" (LE 127). The amendment to the first principle that I am entertaining here has an entirely different rationale. Rawls's exclusive focus on shares of *social* primary goods is retained, and the amendment is suggested in an attempt to vindicate the *implementation* priority of the first over the second principle.

chance of attaining positions of political authority irrespective of their economic and social class" (TJ 225). In *A Theory of Justice* Rawls takes this requirement to entail that "there is a maximum gain permitted to the most favored on the assumption that, even if the difference principle would allow it, there would be unjust effects on the political system and the like excluded by the priority of liberty" (TJ 81). "Disparities in the distribution of property and wealth that far exceed what is compatible with political equality have generally been tolerated by the political system" (TJ 226, cf. 225, 277, 279; BSS 65–66; PFE 5).

By incorporating a limitation on economic inequalities into his first principle, Rawls could reassure the parties that by accepting the proposed priority of the first over the second principle they would not run a serious risk that meeting basic social and economic needs will in nonideal contexts take second place to the establishment of basic liberties (which could hardly be enjoyed by those whose basic needs remain unmet). Rawls's latest writings seem to close the door on this strategy, however. They envision that the fair value of the basic political liberties be protected through the "public financing of political campaigns and election expenditures, various limits on contributions and other regulations" (BLP 73, cf. 42–43). Simultaneously Rawls explicitly rejects, as we have seen, the incorporation of a social minimum into the first principle (BLP 44). The resulting narrow interpretation of the first principle fails to give the parties any assurance that when the difference principle is *not* satisfied, meeting basic social and economic needs won't be deferred for the sake of (efforts toward) establishing basic civil and political liberties.

12.5. A third strategy for addressing the remaining problems of §11 invokes the proviso that the serial ordering applies only in "reasonably favorable conditions" (BLP 11). Rawls writes that the lexical priority of the basic rights and liberties may not apply "when social conditions do not allow the effective establishment of these rights" (TJ 152, 542).[35] And

---

[35]In fact, Rawls suggests that the serial ordering applies *only* when social conditions allow the effective establishment of the basic rights and liberties: "In adopting a serial order we are in effect making a special assumption in the original position, namely, that the parties know that the conditions of their society, whatever they are, admit the effective realization of the equal liberties" (TJ 152). But he cannot mean what he says, because it would make completely obsolete the first priority rule attached to the special conception (TJ 302). And indeed, Rawls adds in the German translation "or, if not, that these conditions are favorable enough so that the priority of the first principle indicates the most urgent reforms and shows the way to a social state in which all basic liberties can be fully realized" (TG 177; my translation). Let me, then, propose these distinctions. *Reasonably favorable* conditions are ones in which the serial ordering applies. These may be either *truly favorable* or *halfway favorable*, depending on whether or not the basic liberties can be effectively established for all. *Unfavorable* conditions are ones that are not reasonably favorable. What Rawls leaves completely vague is how halfway favorable conditions are to be distinguished from unfavorable ones, i.e., how the domains of the general and special conceptions are to be delimited (cf. the quoted addition to the German translation).

he can then reject as irrelevant any implausible implications his serial ordering might have under unfavorable conditions.

But the difficulties arise even in truly favorable conditions in which the basic liberties can be effectively established for all. A social system under truly favorable conditions is presumably advanced enough economically to *render feasible* economic institutions under which the most urgent needs are met, but the feasibility of such institutions hardly entails their existence. Those in the worst socioeconomic position may *in fact* be malnourished, illiterate, and destitute. It is not at all clear why the parties should demand that in such situations political efforts and social resources be devoted to the effective establishment of the basic liberties even though the poor would largely be unable to take advantage of them. H. L. A. Hart has raised this problem in a clear form.[36] But in his response to Hart, Rawls merely reiterates without comment that reasonably favorable conditions include "circumstances which, provided the political will exists, *permit* the effective establishment and the full exercise of these liberties" (BLP 11, my emphasis). Given this definition, it is indeed "evident" (BLP 11) that reasonably favorable conditions obtain in the United States today. The hypothesis that *if* the United States had a just economy then all could fully exercise their basic liberties suffices to trigger the serial ordering, regardless of the extent to which the real existing poor can in fact take advantage of their basic liberties.

Curiously, when Rawls actually tries to substantiate the parties' belief that once certain conditions obtain the interest in the basic liberties is preeminent and the special conception should therefore apply, he suggests a quite different definition of "reasonably favorable conditions." "As the general level of well-being rises (as indicated by the index of primary goods the less favored can expect) only the less urgent wants remain to be met" (TJ 542). "Until the basic wants of individuals can be fulfilled, the relative urgency of their interest in liberty cannot be firmly decided in advance. It will depend on the claims of the least favored as seen from the constitutional and legislative stages" (TJ 543). Despite the "can be," it seems that Rawls is here concerned with the actually least advantaged, thereby suggesting a different interplay between the general and special conceptions that is much more congenial to the parties' maximin concern. The special conception comes into play only when those in the worst *actual* socioeconomic position can exercise basic liberties, and thus are sufficiently well-off rationally to value such liberties above further advances in their material well-being. Otherwise, the general conception applies, demanding that basic social and economic needs be met so as to guide social progress to the point where the special conception can take over. Had Rawls

[36]Hart, RLP 249 n. 13.

adopted this way of delimiting the domains of the general and the special conceptions, the serial ordering in the latter would have been much more plausible as part of a maximin criterion, though it would then be quite uncertain, rather than "evident . . . , that in our country today reasonably favorable conditions do obtain" (BLP 11). This uncertainty in turn would once again frustrate Rawls's hope that his theory can provide definite political guidance for institutional reform under existing conditions.

12.6. Rawls has yet a fourth strategy for dealing with the remaining problems, which involves a partitioning of his project. His main goal for now is to show that the parties in the original position would prefer his proposal (with the serial ordering) over "the first principles associated with the traditional doctrines of utilitarianism, with perfectionism, or with intuitionism" (BLP 6). By concentrating upon this "initial aim" of justice as fairness (BLP 6–8), Rawls leaves room for his "doubt . . . that the principles of justice (as I have defined them) will be the preferred conception on anything resembling a complete list" (TJ 581). He thereby retracts his claim to be presenting *the* maximin solution to the problem of social justice.

One might think that such modesty is uncalled-for. Rawls could easily vindicate his claim to be presenting *the* maximin solution by abandoning the two principles and proposing that the general conception (or some even less specific maximin criterion) be applied across the board, irrespective of social conditions. Yet by leaving open how the various social primary goods are to be weighted vis-à-vis one another, the general conception gives very little guidance for its own application and thus avoids the difficulties associated with the special conception only at the price of imposing significant risks of another sort. Seeking to safeguard the interests of those they represent in a definite and clear-cut way, the parties would prefer a detailed and specific criterion of justice. But given the vast range of subtly varying potential proposals of the appropriate specificity, it must be extremely difficult (if not impossible) to identify precisely *the* most rational choice in the original position as described. It may then be reasonable to aim first for a proposal that beats the traditional criteria of justice, while deferring the question whether this proposal can itself be surpassed.

But does Rawls achieve even his "initial aim"? Relying on the maximin rule, the parties would focus on the worst social position under each of the various alternative proposals. Yet although Rawls discusses at length the worst outcomes possible under competing (especially utilitarian) criteria, a similar scrutiny of his own criterion is lacking. He might have examined, for example, the possibility of an underclass of destitute persons living in a society that is economically advanced enough to bring into play the serial ordering of the two principles. In this context Rawls's criterion would demand that political efforts and social resources be devoted to the establishment of a fully adequate scheme of basic civil and political liberties.[37] But progress in this direction would not substantially better the position of those in the underclass, for whom improvements in basic liberties are of little worth. They would have to watch gains in the positions of those already much better placed (who, unlike themselves, can take advantage of increasing basic liberties), while being aware that their own basic social and economic needs will take center stage only after the first principle has been fully satisfied.

The likelihood of this scenario is not ascertainable and hence irrelevant for the parties, but let me add anyway that the scenario is by no means far-fetched. Rawls apparently believes that it obtains in the United States today. He says that "for us the priority of the basic liberties is required" (BLP 11) and implies that the first principle is not satisfied: "In our society part of the political task is to help fashion . . . the political will" for the effective establishment of the basic liberties (BLP 11, cf. 75–79). Rawls does not attempt to give anything like an exhaustive statement of what remains to be done toward satisfying his first principle. But I assume he would have to concede that such reforms are likely to demand a different allocation of political efforts and social resources than would be demanded for the attempt to improve the worst socioeconomic position (occupied, perhaps, by welfare recipients, the unemployed, and those even more disadvantaged).

The worst-case scenario for Rawls's criterion is very bleak—quite significant death rates in the underclass from malnutrition, trivial diseases, or lack of heating fuels are not ruled out. The worst-case scenario for the principle of utility is very bleak as well—political opponents and hated minorities may have to be persecuted, even eradicated, for the sake of achieving and maintaining a utility-maximizing society. It is possible that Rawls could still find ways of achieving his initial aim.[38] But this achievement is sufficiently difficult and doubtful to motivate the attempt to improve upon Rawls's list of basic liberties even now, in the hope of achieving the initial aim in a clear and convincing manner.

12.7. This thought favors a resuscitation of the second strategy, which alone rescues what Rawls clearly considers highly desirable, namely the practical political importance of his special conception,

---

[37] The first principle is the primary criterion for identifying the least advantaged, and improving the first-principle score of this group has supreme priority. Hence, political efforts and social resources may be devoted to meeting basic social and economic needs only insofar as they cannot be used to expand the effective legal freedoms demanded by the first principle. Cf. Hart, RLP 251.

[38] He could argue, for example, that if his conception of justice is consistently followed, the problem of poverty will eventually take center stage and be reduced to the feasible minimum, whereas the principle of utility might demand that certain minorities be persecuted indefinitely. Members of the underclass can die with the consolation that there will be a time when extreme poverty of the sort they experienced will no longer exist, while members of the persecuted minorities have no analogous assurance. Would this make a difference?

involving the design *and implementation* priorities of the first principle, which is so much more definite in its demands than the general conception. This strategy preserves the judgment that the special conception is widely applicable today, requiring that efforts and resources be allocated to satisfying the first principle even at the expense of satisfying the second. It seeks to strengthen the plausibility of this priority by including within the first principle the requirement that basic social and economic needs must be met.

This first-principle social minimum is best justified, I believe, by showing basic social and economic needs to be entailed by, or by stipulating them as on a par with, the highest-order interests. Rawls would presumably prefer the former kind of justification. One might formulate the amendment as guaranteeing to everyone a bundle of social and economic benefits that is sufficient for normal persons (whose physical and mental constitutions fall within the normal range) to develop and exercise their two moral powers and to be "normally active and fully cooperating members of society over a complete life" (SUPG 168; cf. BLP 85). This formulation allows for variation in basic social and economic needs with age. Infants and the aged need more care, children more education, adolescents more food, and so forth. True to Rawls's semiconsequentialism, the formulation is based on our *standard* needs as human participants in a given social system. It assumes that all participants have the same needs over a complete life and thereby preserves the advantage for stability that I used earlier to explain why Rawls bases his account of social primary goods upon the stipulation of *common* highest-order interests rather than upon the various interests persons have in virtue of their *diverse* needs, endowments, preferences, or conceptions of the good.

Thus, leaving aside interpersonal differences in basic social and economic needs becomes more plausible when—as in Rawls's work—the relevant bundle of social and economic benefits is defined abstractly in terms of social *primary* goods such as income (rather than in terms of rice, linen, etc.). The first principle would then require that an institutional scheme should, if feasible, guarantee to every participant sufficient socioeconomic goods for meeting the basic social and economic needs of a normal human person participating in the relevant social system. When normal persons differ, this minimum—the same for all—is defined so that it suffices for the greater needs (within the normal range).[39] I refer to basic social and economic needs, so defined, as the *standard basic socioeconomic needs* within some social system.

---

[39]The minimum income must then be sufficient to cover the greater caloric requirements associated with higher metabolic rates or pregnancy (cf. Sen, WAF 198–99) as well as the greater clothing needs of the tall, for example. In defending and extending Rawls's semiconsequentialism here, I am not disputing Sen's point that when *measuring* whether (standard) basic needs are actually met, we do best to rely on data about mortality, malnutrition, and illiteracy rather than on income data (cf. Sen, SL 35–36).

What these standard basic socioeconomic needs are is in large part straightforward. Human beings need food and drink, clothing and shelter, as well as some interaction including education and care (for example, in childhood and old age).[40] Hence it is rational in their behalf to require of an institutional scheme that it assure its participants that they can meet these needs. In more traditional societies this requirement might best be satisfied through a solidaristic family or kinship structure coupled with some form of organized charity. In modern societies effective legal rights would presumably be necessary, but these need figure only as a last resort. Basic social and economic needs can be met without an elaborate welfare system or government "handouts"—if economic institutions minimize unemployment, for example, and include adequate insurance provisions for various contingencies and retirement.

The more detailed specification of standard basic socioeconomic needs will to some extent depend upon a social system's natural environment, culture, and level of political and economic development. Thus how much income persons require to meet their standard clothing needs within some social system may depend on this system's natural environment (prevailing climate), on prices, and also on cultural factors if persons must be in a position to appear in public without shame.[41] Similarly, persons will be presumed to need access to *enough* of an education to be able to understand and participate in their society's political, legal, and economic systems and associational life. To this extent the more detailed specification of standard basic needs may have to be left to the constitutional and legislative stages.[42] It should be clear in any case that under somewhat more fortunate conditions the social minimum required by the first principle would be well below the minimum entailed by the second, so that standard basic socioeconomic needs, and first-principle requirements generally, can be met without much strain on the economic system.

12.8. There are further reasons in favor of the amendment.

[40]There is broad consensus on the basic status of these needs, both nationally and internationally, and their incorporation into the first principle (on the highest tier of Rawls's account of human needs) is then particularly appropriate for a moral conception that aspires to be the shared kernel of political morality around which an overlapping consensus can form.

[41]This example is due to Adam Smith, WN 2:399–400 (bk. 5, chap. 2, art. 4).

[42]I say "may" because I am not sure whether these stages, defined through a gradual lifting of the veil of ignorance (TJ §31), aren't an unnecessary shuffle. For already behind the thickest veil the parties can do all the work if what they are given to assess and compare are proposals hypothetical in form: "*If* the social system exists in conditions X and has cultural traditions Y, *then* its basic structure should satisfy requirements Z." Rawls himself uses this expedient. He does not postpone to the next stage the question whether the general or the special conception applies. Rather, he defines the domains of application of these two conceptions in the original position, in terms of hypothetical circumstances of which the parties cannot know whether they obtain. Similarly, it would seem possible for the parties to adopt several specifications of basic social and economic needs, each designed for a particular natural-cultural-economic-political context.

12.8.1. For one thing, it is necessary to round out the package of first-principle goods. Thus Rawls holds that "certain basic liberties are indispensable institutional conditions once other basic liberties are guaranteed; thus freedom of thought and freedom of association are necessary to give effect to liberty of conscience and the political liberties" (BLP 24). I understand him as saying here that the political liberties (for example), though legally completely guaranteed and also effectively protected, might still be close to meaningless without the effective legal freedom to associate and assemble in peace. One can defend the first-principle social minimum analogously, as an indispensable institutional condition necessary for making meaningful the basic rights and liberties associated with the freedom and integrity of the person, the basic political liberties, and the rule of law. When persons cannot afford food or shelter or when they lack access to education or basic care, they can still *have* rights to hold personal property or to run for public office (effective legal freedom) but can hardly begin to enjoy or fully to exercise these basic rights (worthwhile freedom). For them the result may be that the integrity of their person is protected against violence even while it collapses through deprivation of food and shelter. For society at large, it may be that a segment of its population cannot (fully) participate in its legal system, political process, and associational life.

12.8.2. The amendment is necessary, too, to make the fair value of the basic political liberties fully secure, thus preserving an important part of what Rawls had earlier deemed necessary for this purpose, namely, a first-principle limitation on social and economic inequalities (TJ 81, 226, 277). His later discussion of the same issue suggests that it is enough "to keep political parties independent of large concentrations of private economic and social power in a private-property democracy, and of government control and bureaucratic power in a liberal socialist regime" (BLP 42–43), perhaps by means of the "public financing of political campaigns and election expenditures, various limits on contributions and other regulations" (BLP 73).[43] But such measures cannot possibly secure for the poor "a fair opportunity to hold public office and to influence the outcome of political decisions" (BLP 42) unless their basic social and economic needs are met.

12.8.3. A further reason is that the first principle in its amended form makes it plausible to argue that the parties would find the special conception convincing even on the understanding that it will guide institutional reform in situations of injustice. With the amendment Rawls's conception would come much closer to being the maximin solution also to the transition problem. It thereby gains in the features that account for the attractiveness of the maximin idea. In this context

---

[43]But in 1986 (albeit in a new preface to his 1971 book) Rawls speaks again of "large and inheritable inequalities of wealth incompatible with the fair value of the political liberties" (PFE 5). If this statement reflects his considered position, it would facilitate acceptance of my proposed amendment.

the reduction in the strains of commitment is probably most important. Those who, reasonably favorable conditions notwithstanding, cannot meet the most basic social and economic needs of themselves and their families won't be asked to support a program of institutional reform that calls first and foremost for the full establishment of a fully adequate scheme of basic civil and political liberties. Instead, they are assured that meeting such needs is a top priority of institutional reform, coequal with the expansion of effective legal freedom. In this way the envisioned path of institutional reform can elicit the willing cooperation of those in the actually worst social position—surely desirable for a conception of justice that professes supreme concern for the least advantaged.

12.8.4. Once standard basic socioeconomic needs are secured by the first principle, the precise delimitation of the domains of the general and special conceptions becomes much less important—and Rawls's vague reference to "reasonably favorable conditions" thus much less unsatisfactory. Under the proposed amendment, efforts to establish basic civil and political liberties can be limited for the sake of social and economic gains whenever the latter are *themselves* required by the first principle. And this may well be an understanding of the first principle that makes the serial ordering plausible even for a large range of distinctly unfavorable conditions. This reason favors the amendment over the third strategy, which relies much more on the general conception, because the more definite guidance for institutional reform that the special conception provides is now available for a wider range of less-than-just basic structures.[44]

12.8.5. Admittedly, multiplying the guarantees included in the first principle risks weakening the requirement for the most essential ones and recreating within the first principle "the indeterminate and unguided balancing problems we had hoped to avoid by a suitably circumscribed notion of priority" (BLP 10). But being in a position to meet one's basic social and economic needs is itself a fundamental prerequisite for a minimally worthwhile human life and thus on a par with the most essential basic liberties on Rawls's list. Not to include the requirement for such a social minimum within the first principle is itself tantamount to risking what is most essential.

12.8.6. To be sure, efforts toward satisfying the difference principle would under mildly fortunate conditions also tend to raise the worst socioeconomic position above that social minimum, and this tendency may indeed render the proposed requirement "superfluous" *for ideal theory.* Incorporating the requirement into the first principle is nevertheless not redundant, because of Rawls's insistence that the serial

---

[44]Of course, the third strategy could be made equivalent to the second by stipulating that the special conception does not apply unless standard basic socioeconomic needs are met and by specifying the general conception so that it weights basic rights and liberties and standard basic socioeconomic needs very heavily.

ordering is to apply in nonideal situations as well. The proposed first-principle requirement ensures that when unmet basic social or economic needs constitute a violation of the first principle, they cannot (like demands issuing from the second principle) be set aside or deferred for the sake of fully establishing the basic liberties. This assurance would lead the parties as Rawls describes them to prefer the two principles so amended over Rawls's later proposal (in BLP), on which the first principle does not constrain the distribution of social and economic goods at all. The amendment, therefore, strengthens Rawls's claim to have achieved the "initial aim" of his theory (which claim was weakened, I believe, by his deletion of the limitation on social and economic inequalities from the first principle).

12.9. The first-principle goods that constitute what I would call a fully adequate package can then be categorized as follows (cf. §11.6):

(A) basic political rights and liberties, together with the guarantee of their fair value;

(B) basic rights and liberties protecting freedom of conscience;

(C) basic rights and liberties protecting the freedom and integrity of the person, including rights to a socioeconomic position that is suffient to meet the basic social and economic needs of any normal human participant in the relevant social system;

(D) basic rights and liberties covered by the rule of law.

All these must exist not merely on paper but effectively, in practice. A fully adequate package is a package of basic rights and liberties that are both *complete* (so that all standard basic needs are covered) and *well-protected* (so that these basic needs are actually secured).[45]

Even if Rawls's proposal, so amended, achieves the initial aim in a convincing way, it still faces a number of problems. Among these are, in weakened form, some of the difficulties raised in the preceding section, as well as questions about which civil and political liberties to include and how to specify them.[46] These problems cannot be neatly resolved;

[45]Any actual such package is then two-dimensional, its "area" determined by its two "sides." One of these represents its content, the completeness of its basic rights and liberties (formal legal freedom). The other represents the security of the basic rights and liberties covered, how well-protected they are. In the second dimension one needs, though Rawls does not provide, the notion of a *sufficiently* secure or well-protected basic right or liberty. Failing this, the first principle could, realistically, never be satisfied and would then require all available social resources to be devoted to such things as expansion of police forces (to improve protection of the basic right to physical integrity).

[46]Some questions of this sort are: Does, or should, the first principle forbid segregation and apartheid as based on a separate-but-equal doctrine, and if so, how? Should discrimination in hiring and university admissions be ruled out by the first principle or only by the opportunity principle as Rawls suggests? (BLP 79–80). Similarly, should the first principle require that medical providers and other businesses not be allowed to refuse patients and customers on arbitrary grounds such as race? Moreover, is it really "irrational or superfluous or socially divisive" (BLP 44) to incorporate the fair value of any but political liberties into the first principle, or do some basic rights covered by the rule of law also call for a fair-value protection that might limit, in particular, the access costs of

there is no hope that one might "derive" *the* maximin solution to the problem of social justice from the description of the original position, given that the parties' aversion to risk favors various *competing* desiderata. The preferred criterion should have a content that expresses concern for the least advantaged, should engender stability when satisfied, should be clear and straightforward so that it can serve as a public criterion, should be determinate so as to make definite demands upon existing social institutions, and so forth. The problems raised in §11 were formulated primarily by appeal to the first concern, but taking all concerns together, there may be no solution that is clearly superior to the two principles with the amended list of first-principle goods. In any case, seeing the complexities involved, it may be well to follow the fourth strategy. Once the initial aim is achieved, we view this list "as a starting point that can be improved by finding a second list such that the parties in the original position would agree to the two principles with the second list rather than the two principles with the initial list" (BLP 7). We would proceed analogously for all other difficulties and improvements—concerning the second principle, the priority rules, the general conception, or the delimitation of the domains of the general and special conceptions.

13. The Political Process

13.1. I have been assuming that Rawls takes the special conception to consist of two (serially ordered) maximin criteria, governing what he thinks of as two distinct and jointly exhaustive parts of any basic structure. But on the face of it, the first principle is not a maximin criterion. Unlike the difference principle, which requires that institutions should tend to produce social and economic inequalities insofar as doing so would optimize the socioeconomic position of the least advantaged, the first principle requires the basic structure to generate an *equal* distribution of first-principle goods.[47] One may think that

---

poorer groups to the court system? Here, one might argue that in the absence of such provisions poor persons would tend to shun lawsuits because of the prohibitive cost or financial risk involved. They would then be known to be much less likely to seek legal redress, which in turn would make it more likely for decisions affecting them to be made without due regard to their rights. Rawls's argument for incorporating the fair value of the basic political liberties emphasizes that the political process is a "public facility [that] has limited space" (BLP 43). But one could say the same of the judicial process as well. A similar argument might be made, though perhaps with less plausibility, in favor of a fair-value guarantee for freedom of expression through the mass media.

[47]The first principle requires for each person a scheme of equal basic liberties that is compatible with a similar scheme of liberties for all. This formulation has an air of mystery. If there are to be packages of *equal* basic liberties for all, why must not each person's package be compatible with a *like* (and not a similar) package for everyone else, as Rawls's earliest statements of the first principle (JF 166, JR 244) had demanded? One conjecture is that Rawls means to rule out less-than-equal packages while leaving some

Rawls faces a further difficulty here. Wouldn't the parties prefer a criterion that favors inferior packages of basic rights and liberties for some when this improves the worst package?

Rawls barely touches upon this question, but an explanation suggests itself. The first principle requires that a basic structure contain full safeguards for the most basic needs of normal human persons (as Rawls conceives of them). Now, a participant's standard basic needs—unlike his preferences, which might always be better satisfied by means of indefinite increases in income or wealth—can be completely met. Moreover, since there are no inherent conflicts between the standard basic needs of a plurality of participants, truly favorable conditions make it possible for all participants to be assured that they can meet these needs. Rawls can then conclude that an ideal basic structure would protect a fully adequate package of basic rights and liberties for *every* participant. His insistence on an *equal* distribution of effective legal freedom (or of first-principle goods) is then a corollary of the fact that, under truly favorable conditions, everyone's (by stipulation) equal basic needs can be fully met. Here maximin entails equality, because when all first-principle scores can be optimal (*fully* adequate), then no unequal institutional distribution of first-principle goods can be justified as optimizing the worst share.

This explanation is confirmed by what Rawls says about halfway favorable conditions, which, though "reasonably favorable," make it impossible for everyone to have a fully adequate package. He takes the serial ordering of the two principles to entail a "priority rule" according to which basic liberties can be restricted only for the sake of basic liberties. There are two cases: (a) the basic rights and liberties may be equally incomplete for all insofar as this incompleteness (through the better protection of the remaining basic liberties) improves the standard package of basic liberties overall, or (b) they may be unequal insofar as such inequalities improve the worst package of basic liberties.[48] Rawls's willingness to allow such inequalities in the context of

---

room for unequal but equivalent ones. Here, one might think of a constitution conferring somewhat different but equivalent basic rights and duties upon men and women or upon various (named) linguistic, ethnic, regional, or religious groups. Alternatively, Rawls may be suggesting that, while recognized basic rights and liberties should be strictly equal, their protection can hardly be exactly equal for different groups. The first principle would then require packages that protect an *equal* formal legal freedom *similarly* well, and therefore are only *similar* overall (effective legal freedom). Both these conjectures leave in place the question I raise in the text.

[48]TJ 302, revised in accordance with BLP 5–6 and my terminology. In its earlier formulation, the first principle had required that basic rights and liberties be maximally extensive (TJ 302), and the (a)-clause of the priority rule was then also used to guide marginal trade-offs among the fundamental freedoms so as to identify, within ideal theory, "the most extensive system of [mutually consistent] basic liberties" (ibid.). Prompted by criticisms from H. L. A. Hart (RLP 239–44), Rawls has since retracted the idea of extensiveness (BLP 46). On his later account, the notion of "a fully adequate scheme of equal basic liberties" (BLP 5) is developed independently on the basis of the two highest-order interests, and so the (a)-clause of the priority rule no longer plays a role in

halfway favorable conditions shows that the underlying idea for assessing the institutional distribution also of first-principle goods is maximin, and not equality.[49]

It is only with respect to truly favorable conditions, Rawls asserts, that "the question of compensating for a lesser than equal liberty does not arise" (TJ 204).[50] The question can arise in the real world, and here Rawls's concern is to show what would have to be the case for institutions generating unequal basic rights and liberties to be justified: There must be no feasible institutional scheme under which everyone would have a fully adequate package (that is, complete basic rights and liberties, sufficiently well-protected), and leaving some fundamental freedom(s) of some group entirely unrecognized must otherwise augment (the protection of) other basic rights and liberties so significantly that a comparison of feasible institutional schemes with an eye to optimizing the worst package (now and in the future) favors the scheme with unequal basic rights and liberties. In modern developed societies during peace time, it would seem quite difficult to justify institutions under which groups differ in legal rights of categories (B)–(D). It is hard to see how restricting any of these might substantially augment (the protection of) other basic rights and liberties in ways that would otherwise be impossible.[51] Somewhat more formidable is John Stuart Mill's argument for unequal basic *political* liberties if it is understood as follows: some persons are to have inferior political liberties so that the better educated may have a superior opportunity to influence the outcome of political decisions; this practice is justified because under

specifying the list of basic rights and liberties. Now *both* clauses of the priority rule are relevant only to nonideal theory, where they govern how, under halfway favorable conditions, restrictions of basic rights and liberties can be justified as "adjustments to natural limitations and historical contingencies" (TJ 246).

[49]If this claim is correct, then the (a)-clause, too, should really be concerned with the *worst* first-principle score. Basic liberties may be equally restricted only if those whose incomplete package is least well protected have more effective legal freedom than would be had by those with the least well protected package under a scheme of equal complete packages. It is not surprising that Rawls should have overlooked this point in formulating the (a)-clause, given that he also fails to appreciate the parallel point in ideal theory (cf. §11.2.2). Another problem with my claim is that Rawls merely *permits* uniform or unequal restrictions of basic rights and liberties when these are necessary to optimize the worst package (cf. TJ 242, 247, 380). But his reluctance to *require* such restrictions may well be motivated by the idea that under halfway favorable conditions institutions should also be shaped with an eye to facilitating the necessary reforms toward a perfectly just institutional scheme. A fully adequate package for all may be much harder to achieve if certain basic rights and liberties are now not even recognized (for some). I suggest that this rationale fits at least tolerably well with my interpretation of the first principle as a maximin criterion dedicated to optimizing the worst first-principle score.

[50]This assertion is compatible with "the lesser liberty of children" (TJ 244). Though parent and child have unequal basic rights and liberties now, they do not have unequal lifetime expectations.

[51]This possibility seems especially unlikely because those disadvantaged by selective restrictions of basic rights and liberties tend to lose their standing of equal citizenship, the most important social basis of self-respect (TJ §§79, 82). The gains produced by such inequalities will rarely be great enough to compensate these groups for such losses.

the alternative practice with equal basic political liberties the political process would tend to be so ineffective or so liable to abuse that the worst package would be even worse (perhaps the political process itself would then be used to restrict basic liberties).[52] I will proceed with this line of thought once the role of the political process has become somewhat clearer.

13.2. The political process is a paradigm instance of the idea of *procedural justice*.[53] This is primarily an idea for the nonviolent reconciliation of conflicting claims and thus an alternative to (unmediated) persuasion and compromise. It presupposes a procedure of reconciliation to which the relevant claimants are sufficiently committed to accept what this procedure produces by way of settlements, which adjust their claims to a point of mutual compatibility. Examples of such procedures are the toss of a coin, employment of a mutually agreeable expert or arbitrator, courts, markets (bidding), and the political process (voting).

Such procedures come in three ideal-typical varieties, which in practice are often intermixed. Over a certain range of possible outcomes the claimants disagree but are willing to accept whatever outcome the procedure may produce. This is the element of *pure* procedural justice.

But while they disagree about the outcome to be preferred, the claimants will often agree that certain outcomes are unacceptable. When they do, they have a shared (partial) criterion, independent of any procedure, for the acceptability of outcomes. They can use this criterion to design, select, or constrain the procedure in such a way that mutually unacceptable outcomes are, as far as possible, ruled out. Insofar as the procedure reliably excludes certain mutually unacceptable outcomes, it contains an element of *perfect* procedural justice.

Such reliable exclusion is sometimes not achievable, typically because it is less than obvious whether some outcome in fact satisfies the shared criterion. Agreement on the criterion is then to some extent nominal. It coexists with disagreements over whether the criterion is satisfied. Where this is the case, the claimants may still agree that the procedure should have certain features that will tend to make it more likely that the outcomes produced will satisfy (or come close to satisfying) the criterion in question. Such features would embody the element of *imperfect* procedural justice.

---

[52]Cf. Mill, UOLC 283–90; and TJ 232–33. A more topical variant might be the analogous argument purporting to justify continued inequality in the *worth* of basic political liberties, which gives the wealthy superior means for influencing the outcome of political decisions. For example, "If the less affluent and less educated had equal effective political influence, then government personnel would be even more incompetent and corrupt, and adopted legislation and policies would be less just on the whole."

[53]My treatment differs in various ways from Rawls's discussion of procedural justice (TJ 85–86 or KCMT 523). In particular, I view pure, perfect, and imperfect procedural justice not as three clearly distinguishable kinds of procedures but as elements that in actual procedures are often combined.

As an illustration, consider our institution of the criminal trial. This is a case of perfect procedural justice insofar as the procedure firmly excludes outcomes that are universally agreed to be unacceptable (for example, vicarious punishments or the maiming of convicts). It is a case of imperfect procedural justice insofar as everyone agrees that defendants should be convicted only if guilty and be acquitted otherwise. Although this agreement may be merely nominal (so long as there are disagreements about whether some defendants are guilty or not), it will support a shared desire to design the procedure so that it is reasonably likely to produce outcomes sensitive to the facts. It is a case of pure procedural justice, finally, insofar as there is some slippage between even the most complete appreciation of the empirical and legal facts of, and the exact punishment appropriate in, a particular criminal case.[54]

Among the three elements, pure and perfect procedural justice are the most clearly distinct. The other two distinctions are more gradual. Imperfect shades into perfect procedural justice as the reliability of some (feature of a) procedure—the probability that it will exclude certain unacceptable outcomes—approaches 1. It shades into pure procedural justice as the space of possible outcomes grows too large or too dense for any outcome to be precisely connectible to the agreed-upon independent criteria.

There is another way in which the boundary between pure and imperfect procedural justice is problematic. With pure and perfect procedural justice, there can be no conflict between the shared commitment to the procedure and the shared commitment to an independent criterion for unacceptable outcomes. In the pure case, there is no shared commitment to an independent criterion, and in the perfect case this criterion is either satisfied or else the procedure was not correctly followed (though which of these is the case may still be controversial). With imperfect procedural justice, by contrast, such a conflict is possible. It is possible, for example, that a guilty person is declared innocent at the conclusion of a properly conducted trial. If the procedure is to achieve its purpose of reconciling conflicting claims, however, then persons must accept its outcome even when they are convinced that it does not satisfy the relevant independent criterion. Insofar as the procedure is imperfect, it must, in general, be regarded *as if it were pure*.

Yet only in general. Persons who are part of the procedure itself may have to be excepted. Judges and jurors are not to think during their

---

[54]Suppose it is agreed that the punishment of anyone found guilty should fit the gravity and circumstances of his or her deeds, record, character, and so on. However elaborately specified, these factors will underdetermine the punishment—and that not only for a fallible human judge. Even Hercules, who would assess all relevant factors with precise knowledge and perfect understanding (cf. Dworkin, TRS 105–30), would presumably find that these considerations cannot determine the outcome with perfect precision (e.g., the precise length of time, to the second, that various robbers should spend in jail). Within certain limits, the correct punishment is whatever the judge says it is.

deliberations that they can render any verdict they please because their verdict will *define* the correct outcome. Rather they must try in good faith and to the best of their abilities to deliver whatever verdict accords with the facts and the merits of the case. It is only because they are trusted to take this attitude that the procedure is believed to be reasonably reliable. And its reliability in turn supports the shared commitment to the procedure, on the basis of which outsiders are willing to accept its outcomes whatever they may be.

13.3. Some instances of procedural justice are much simpler, but the political process involves the same complexities. There is an independent criterion of justice, and the political process therefore contains elements of perfect and imperfect procedural justice as it satisfies this criterion with certainty or probability. Insofar as outcomes are underdetermined by this independent criterion, the political process contains an element of pure procedural justice. Within some range, any outcome will *count as* correct merely by virtue of having been produced in the proper way. In this instance such leeway is welcome, for it allows more of a social system's institutional features to be shaped in accordance with collective preferences emerging from political debate.

An ongoing political process is then assessed and, if need be, reformed by reference to two requirements: first, the equal basic political liberties together with their fair value must be fully recognized and protected, so that all participants equally have a genuine opportunity for meaningful political participation as demanded by their first highest-order interest; second, the political process must be reliable, that is, must result in legislation and policies that are just (insofar as they are subject to an independent criterion).[55]

In theory, these two requirements leave open a vast range of institutional options. Obviously, a thorough assessment of these options cannot be made in the abstract. Rather, it might start from comparative historical analyses and be further advanced, perhaps, by some social experiments. In view of the great diversity of possibilities and our relative ignorance in regard to them, it is somewhat regrettable that Rawls largely takes for granted a political process resembling the model common to the United States and Great Britain—with a *representative* legislature (TJ 222; BLP 50), a *multiparty* system, and *single-member territorial constituencies* (TJ 222–23).

None of these three assumptions is obvious. Concerning the first, some role might be reserved for direct democracy, which within a reasonably settled institutional scheme may constitute a suitable

---

[55]These two requirements are clearly stated at TJ 197–98 and 221. Sometimes Rawls comes close to saying that the equal basic political liberties and their fair-value guarantee are themselves justified by the requirement for a reasonably reliable procedure (e.g., BLP 45). But I think his considered view is that the basic political liberties have an additional, independent foundation in the first highest-order interest (BLP 47) and the basic need for (the social bases of) self-respect (TJ 234).

mechanism for resolving matters of a fundamental nature. Typically, such matters arise infrequently, are clearly definable and not overly pressing, and therefore permit of extensive debate culminating in a well-deliberated decision by the entire population. Referendums may be especially appropriate for decisions altering or reaffirming the scheme of *in*direct democracy through which "normal" decisions are being made, and thereby may ensure a more meaningful form of self-government.

Against Rawls's second assumption, one might envision a democratic single-party system with a hierarchy of organs, the higher-level ones being composed of delegates from the next lower level, who are perhaps bound by an imperative mandate. Such a political process would seem compatible with Rawls's "principle of (equal) participation" (TJ 221) and the fair value of the political liberties, at least if it is assured "(1) that there is full intra-party democracy, (2) that party membership is open, and (3) that the price of participation in the party is not a greater degree of activity than the average person can reasonably be expected to contribute."[56] Such a democratic single-party system might do better in involving ordinary citizens in the formulation and resolution of concrete political issues than does a multiparty system under which the participation of most citizens may tend to degenerate into an infrequent choice among two or three preexisting party platforms.

Finally, one could argue against Rawls's third assumption that a "winner-takes-all" electoral system tends to overrepresent the larger and more established groups. Under such a system, minority views that are not concentrated in one or a few territorial constituencies may be effectively excluded from the legislative debate, perhaps abridging the fair value of the political liberties of members of such a minority.[57] In any case, it is unclear why some systems of proportional representation should not be acceptable as well.

My objective in briefly raising these issues is not to argue for or against some particular model of a democratic political process but only to emphasize that there is a great deal of space for institutional alternatives about which persons of good will may reasonably disagree. This point is of some importance in Part Three, where I support the ideal of a global basic structure that would embody a certain degree of

[56]Macpherson, RWD 21.

[57]Here, clearly, one cannot object that a member of a minority will not be on the winning side as often as other participants or that a minority will not be on the winning side in proportion to its relative size. The objection is rather that when a minority of 10 percent, say, is widely dispersed so that its candidates lose in every electoral district, then its members don't have a fair opportunity, through arguments put forward by their representatives, to influence the outcome of political decisions. This may or may not be an abridgment of the fair value of their political liberties. Rawls says nothing about how a person's chances to influence political decisions may be affected by the distribution of views among the other participants.

tolerance toward diverse national institutional schemes. It is likely that there are meaningfully democratic forms of self-government that are quite different from those Americans happen to be accustomed to.

13.4. Another regrettable omission is Rawls's complete silence on the subject of federalism. This omission, in conjunction with his almost exclusive concentration on the element of imperfect procedural justice in the political process, may suggest that he finds decentralized organs of self-government superfluous. Following Rousseau and Mill,[58] Rawls views democratic institutions as centering around the ideal that persons vote their conscience rather than their self-interest; everyone is asked to make a *moral*, not a prudential judgment (TJ 357, 284, 230–31).[59] When the task is to formulate just legislation (as defined by some independent criterion), then it may seem that all issues, including local ones, should be discussed and decided by all because "an ideally conducted discussion among many persons is more likely to arrive at the correct conclusion" (TJ 358).

In fact, however, one can still prefer a decentralized procedure for making political decisions of merely local significance. This preference need not be based on the claim that someone's ability to influence a political decision should be proportional to how much it affects oneself. If persons are to be excluded from political decisions of other localities, the reason is not that they stand to gain or to lose nothing either way (that would more likely be an asset) but rather that they are presumably in no position to make an informed, responsible judgment. They cannot possibly know enough about all these matters, nor is it either practicable or morally acceptable to delimit the group of those who are competent otherwise than by rough geographical criteria.

The reasons for the partial decentralization of political decision making become stronger once we qualify Rawls's characterizations of the political process as an instance of imperfect procedural justice (TJ 229, cf. §54). There are many political issues that do not have a uniquely correct outcome. In these contexts and respects the political process is a case of pure procedural justice, and citizens can argue and vote on the basis of their own interests. Issues of this kind are the stuff of day-to-day politics: How much should be spent on maintaining the purity of the public water supply, public recreation areas, or fire, ambulance, and garbage-collection services? How are opening hours, holidays, marriage contracts, broadcasting, consumer protection, and the school

[58]See Rousseau, SC 153, 83, 149; and Mill, UOLC 215–18, 277–79.

[59]Participants in the political process are to debate and decide *as if* their knowledge were constrained by a thinner version of the veil of ignorance (cf. TJ §31). This may well be an appealing ideal, but one cannot simply presuppose it in designing the political process. It must also be shown that the preferred kind of political process would work even while all participants are fully aware of their particular interests and situations. The process must have a certain robustness. It must produce acceptable outcomes even though the two highest-order interests will not be determinative for all its participants all the time.

curriculum to be regulated? Should high-rise buildings be allowed or car congestion be reduced in some particular area and, if so, to what extent and how? Such questions don't have uniquely correct answers, defined by the decision an ideally reasonable and well-informed legislator would make behind some partial veil of ignorance (cf. TJ 196–98, 357). What is important is merely that the persons affected have the power to shape the environment that shapes their lives, that they can, within broad limits, arrange their more immediate social world the way they want it to be. And this value obviously, favors local mechanisms of political decision making.

As these thoughts suggest, justice permits and probably favors federalist institutions that feature decentralized legislative, executive, and judicial organs. This idea might be combined with Rawls's four-stage sequence (TJ §31). Whereas a more abstract criterion of justice governs the ground rules of the self-contained social system as a whole, various different specifications of this criterion might govern practices whose authority is confined to a particular regional division. Thus the requirement of equal basic political liberties can be satisfied even while political processes are designed differently on the various levels (global, national, provincial, municipal) and in the various (territorially defined) divisions on the same level. In fact, why should it not even be permissible that in a representative democracy the delegates from the various political subdivisions are elected in diverse ways, so long as rough equality of political influence is preserved among persons from different constituencies?[60]

Again, these thoughts are of some relevance to the argument of Part Three, for they show that a well-ordered world community need not be a world state in the ordinary sense of "state." Political decision making on the global plane can be confined to issues that are truly transnational in character, and such issues can be settled through a democratic political process that takes account of the different political traditions of the various nations.

13.5. The first principle attends only to standard basic needs, which

---

[60]A semiconsequentialist conception of justice abstracts from natural interpersonal differences and thus presumes that the participants in the relevant social system have the same needs and interests over a complete lifetime. Correspondingly, persons' shares are evaluated in terms of the same metric of social primary goods. It does not follow, however, that the specification of these goods must not be subject to regional variations. This thought may evoke the sad memory of historical separate-but-equal doctrines, but there are two important differences: the regional variations in political structure are to be based upon variations in regional preferences (by contrast, blacks did not get to vote on whether they preferred their separate status), and there is to be full freedom of movement across regional boundaries (by contrast, no black could choose to have the "white" set of rights and opportunities instead). This idea could be generalized. Slight regional variations in how other basic rights and liberties are specified may be permissible, so long as the resulting packages are roughly equivalent and fully adequate everywhere. And something analogous might hold for other (e.g., educational) opportunities as well.

can be completely safeguarded through a definite and limited package of effectively enforced basic rights and liberties. Hence, if the first principle were the only independent criterion for judging political decisions, then the political process of a just basic structure would contain a large element of pure procedural justice. But Rawls proposes that this remaining leeway should be further constricted through the second principle. This proposal can be recommended to the parties through the following rationale: if the design of the second part of the basic structure were left entirely to the political process as a matter of pure procedural justice, then a voting coalition including more affluent classes could easily impose or perpetuate economic institutions under which the poor would be much poorer than is unavoidable (though their standard basic socioeconomic needs would still be met).[61]

The least restrictive way of blocking this considerable danger involves constraining the political process so that the interests of all participants are tied to those of any least advantaged group. This, I think, is the general idea behind the second principle. It ensures that decisions made through the political process are framed in a way that precludes bias against particular persons and groups. While the first principle requires definite and specific safeguards in the form of a package of enumerated basic rights and liberties, the opportunity principle requires nothing about what specific opportunities an institutional scheme is to generate but constrains only the distribution of such opportunities, whatever they may be. Similarly, the difference principle requires only of social and economic inequalities that they must optimize the socioeconomic position of the least advantaged; no such requirement is imposed upon any other features the social system may tend to produce. In this way, the choice of any institutional features that affect socioeconomic positions roughly equally are, insofar as they are not preempted by the first or opportunity principles, left to be governed by the political process as matters of pure procedural justice.[62] These may include features that affect or constrain overall economic activity (working hours, pollution, depletion of mineral resources), the proportion of the social product allocated to education and health care, the provision of public goods, and birth rates.

The constraints added by the second principle make Rawls's criterion more acceptable to the parties. The principle requires more of an institutional scheme with regard to the worst socioeconomic position it permits, without detracting from what is significant about the basic

---

[61]Nozick argues quite persuasively that this actually tends to happen when economic institutions are shaped through democratic procedures: "A voting coalition from the bottom won't form because it will be less expensive to the top group to buy off the swing middle group than to let it form" (ASU 275).

[62]By saying that certain choices are to be *governed* by the political process as matters of pure procedural justice, I always mean to include the option of delegating these choices to households, school boards, administrators, experts, and the like.

political liberties.[63] One might have thought that these additional constraints should also play a role in assessing an existing political process and in guiding its reform. After all, the second requirement upon any political process is that it should be reliable, that is, produce legislation and policies that are just. Here the reliability of the political process with regard to the difference principle is of special concern. Often a large variety of mutually incompatible economic laws and policies can with some plausibility be defended as doing best by the difference principle because in this matter so much "depends upon speculative political and economic doctrines and upon social theory generally" (TJ 199). Still, there is hope that such political rationalizations can be curbed to some extent so as to ensure that the difference principle is at least approximately satisfied. While the equal basic political liberties require social and economic legislation to be created democratically (rather than by a group of upright experts, say, though legislators could of course consult such experts), they are consistent with a system of judicial review that would filter out at least the clearer cases of legislation violating the second principle.

Alluding to "the history of successful constitutions" (BLP 52), Rawls opposes this idea, however, with his remarkable fiat that "the second principle of justice . . . is not incorporated into the constitution" (ibid.).[64] This is remarkable because it would seem to contradict Rawls's official position. The incorporation of the second principle would clearly be compatible with a fully adequate package of basic political liberties for all.[65] But if so, then the question of whether it should be

[63]This general way of understanding the second principle presents Rawls as offering a resolution to the tension between what Amy Gutmann has called participatory and distributive equality (see LE chap. 7), an idea further explored in the next chapter. It also defends Rawls against the charge that he argues fallaciously from the premise that it is rational for each to want more second-principle goods rather than less to the conclusion that it is rational for each to want everyone to have more second-principle goods rather than less' (see §10.5.4).

[64]This is at odds with the fact that some requirements of the opportunity principle do now exist as constitutional guarantees. Thus, as Martin points out, many state constitutions in the United States guarantee the right to a free public education (RR 112–13).

[65]Clark and Gintis deny this, claiming that Rawls cannot allow the second principle to be incorporated into the constitution of a just, well-ordered society, because such incorporation would violate the first principle by making the basic political liberties less extensive. They then argue that neither a capitalist nor a market-socialist society will satisfy the difference principle, because citizens, with their particular moral and personal ends, cannot be expected to vote for the requisite economic institutions (RJES 317–18, 324). Though I essentially agree with their empirical views, I dispute their interpretive claim. I see no reason why the basic political liberties should have to be understood as including the liberty to pass legislation that violates the second principle. That no such understanding is necessary is even more obvious now that the first principle requires all participants to have "a fully adequate scheme" (BLP 5) rather than "the most extensive total system" (TJ 302) of equal basic liberties. After all, such a fully adequate package is also compatible with other constitutional devices that limit the scope of majority rule, by stipulating, for example, that certain legislative changes require a 75 percent majority or the consent of two legislative bodies or of two consecutive parliaments (cf. TJ 224, 229–30).

incorporated must be settled by reference to the two principles themselves. The second principle ought to be part of the constitution if and only if this would tend to improve the worst social position on the whole.[66]

His opposition is further remarkable because Rawls himself suggests that existing institutions are not all that successful, in that they don't even remotely satisfy the difference principle (TJ 87). And how can we expect them to, so long as this principle is not incorporated into the public and official terms of the institutional scheme? How are actual legislators to understand that they are to frame their deliberations in accordance with the difference principle, when it is merely one among many incompatible ideas debated by the academics of the well-ordered society? I would think, then, contrary to Rawls, that if the second principle is a requirement of justice at all, if it is part of that kernel of political morality that is to solve the fundamental assurance problem by lasting through and constraining all institutional changes, then it must be enshrined in the legal order in a way that reflects its permanent and foundational status. It must not be merely an idea that legislators may or may not find attractive and may use on occasion as a preamble to a package of social or economic legislation.

13.6. When it comes to nonideal contexts, the second principle once again gets short shrift, this time, however, for systematic reasons. The question here is whether and on what grounds equal basic political liberties may be restricted for the sake of ensuring juster legislation. Recall the two requirements a political process must satisfy. First, the procedure should be such that all participants have basic political liberties that are equally complete and well-protected and whose fair value is maintained so that all have "a fair opportunity to hold public office and to influence the outcome of political decisions" (BLP 42). Insofar as the political process is an instance of pure procedural justice, this requirement is unopposed. In the remaining "impure" area, however, where an independent criterion exists for judging outcomes of the political process, a second requirement comes into play. The political process should be designed so as to be maximally reliable.

Rawls characterizes this second requirement as one for a procedure whose outcomes are most "likely to accord with the principles of justice" (TJ 198). This formulation slides over an important point. Basic political liberties may be restricted (on the grounds that restriction will lead to juster legislation) only if such legislation constitutes an improvement by the lights of the *first* principle (cf. TJ 229). This shows that the second requirement really consists of two parts: a requirement that output satisfy the first principle, which is on a par with and thus might at the margins override the first requirement for the basic political

---

[66]This point is not undermined by the commonplace, true enough, that no procedure involving human beings could be perfect, could consistently produce optimal outcomes. Reliability matters even where perfection is out of reach.

liberties and their fair value;[67] and a requirement that output satisfy the second principle, which ranks lexically below both first-principle requirements and thus can influence the design of the political process only within whatever leeway they may leave. Not even the slightest restriction of basic political liberties or of their fair value is justifiable when the better legislation it would lead to merely reduces unjust social and economic inequalities, however significantly.

Rawls must show that the risk-averse parties, with their decision rule, would find this result acceptable. This task highlights once again the crucial importance of my proposed amendment of the first principle. The parties must assume that the poor may find it very difficult to persuade a majority to support social and economic reforms required by the second principle. Rawls holds that restrictions of basic political liberties for the sake of satisfying the second principle are nevertheless strictly ruled out (under reasonably favorable conditions). The parties would certainly find this requirement unacceptable unless they are assured that restrictions of basic political liberties may be justifiable when they are necessary to meet standard basic socioeconomic needs. Hence the parties have yet another reason to want a clear and straightforward social minimum to be incorporated into the first principle where it *will* play a primary role in determining how the political process is to be adjusted to natural limitations and historical contingencies.

[67]Unequal basic political liberties such as Mill had proposed may be justifiable in this way when the inequalities would make other basic rights and liberties significantly more complete or more secure (cf. TJ §37). Put in my terms, Mill's claim (as Rawls reconstructs it) would be that under existing halfway favorable conditions, we ought to accept a smaller shortfall in regard to the first requirement in order to avoid a larger shortfall in regard to the second. We are to accept unequal voting rights because the loss in terms of basic political liberties and their fair value is outweighed by the gain, through juster legislation, in (the protection of) other first-principle goods. It is claimed that, given feasibility constraints, plural voting enhances the worst package of basic rights and liberties overall.

C H A P T E R 4

The Second Principle
of Justice

14. Rawls's Opportunity Principle

14.1. The second principle is among the features of his conception that Rawls has tended to deemphasize in recent years. He now believes, as we have seen, that the second principle of justice is to be excluded from the written constitution of a well-ordered society (BLP 52). More recently, he has even declared the difference principle all but dispensable: "The primary aim of justice as fairness is achieved once it is clear that" the parties would prefer average utilitarianism constrained by his first and opportunity principles over average utilitarianism unconstrained (PFE 4). In this area, unsurprisingly, we have nothing like the detailed elucidations Rawls has since provided in support of his first principle and thus must rely more extensively on his account in *A Theory of Justice*. There are some significant revisions, however. The account of social primary goods is now said to be based on the conception of the person as characterized by the two highest-order interests.[1] As we will see in a moment, the doubly ambiguous account of the second principle in *A Theory of Justice* receives some clarification in the course of which Rawls all but deletes what was arguably the most important second-principle good: opportunities.

The second principle (of the special conception) imposes two requirements upon the social and economic inequalities an institutional scheme may generate: the *opportunity principle* and the *difference principle*. These are serially ordered so that the former ranks lexically

[1]See SUPG 165 n. 5 and also JFPM 224 n. 2 (the word "higher-order" there must be a misprint). In TJ and FG, by contrast, the account was more significantly based upon social theory and the thin theory of the good with the Aristotelian Principle (cf. PFE 3, where Rawls discusses this shift).

161

above the latter, just as the first principle ranks lexically above the second principle as a whole. Before discussing these requirements in more detail, I must settle two preliminary matters. One of these concerns the role "the social bases of self-respect" play in the metric of second-principle goods in terms of which socioeconomic positions are to be evaluated. The other preliminary matter concerns the ways in which institutional inequalities might be generated.

14.2. The difference principle governs the distribution of what I call *index goods*—powers and prerogatives of offices and positions of responsibility; income and wealth; and the social bases of self-respect. It requires that the basic structure generate inequalities in index goods if and insofar as these optimize the social position of the least advantaged (or, as I have also said, the worst representative share). Here the inclusion of the third index good, the social bases of self-respect, is puzzling. This good "has a central place" (TJ 62), is "very important" (TJ 92), is "perhaps the most important primary good" (TJ 440), is even "defined as [the] most important primary good" (TJ 604 [index]). If it really is so important, then why does it come in only on the lowest priority level, as an index good whose distribution is to be governed by the difference principle?[2]

Rawls's idea seems to be that self-respect is due to various factors (has various "bases"), some of which are much more important than others. The most important *social* basis of self-respect is (or in a just society ought to be) the equal basic liberties, and Rawls appeals extensively to self-respect in support of his first principle and its lexical priority (TJ §82). He even hopes that social institutions, merely by satisfying the first principle, are immune to complaints invoking self-respect: "The basis for self-esteem in a just society is not then one's income share but the publicly affirmed distribution of fundamental rights and liberties. . . . [We seek] to eliminate the significance of relative economic and social advantages as supports for men's self-confidence . . . [T]he precedence of liberty entails equality in the social bases of esteem" (TJ 544–46).[3]

Still, Rawls recognizes that even a basic structure under which the equal basic liberties are fully protected may, when the economic inequalities it generates are severe, fail to support the self-respect of, and respect for, the poor. They may in effect be second-class citizens and be exposed to feelings of relative deprivation—or, as Rawls prefers to say, "excusable envy" (TJ 546, 534). It may then be implausible to (assume the parties would) require that institutions should be designed so that

[2]This ambiguity in Rawls's notion of the social bases of self-respect is also noted in Michaelman, CWR 345–46.

[3]Rawls suggests that a just society might achieve this end by ensuring that "the various sectors of society [are] non-comparing groups" (TJ 545)—an idea he explicitly rejects in the context of feudal or caste schemes (TJ 547). He might more plausibly have argued that once essential needs are met, the competition for economic status can be made to fade away as associational ties and personal projects come to assume greater importance.

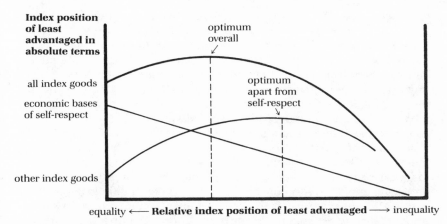

Graph 1. Optimum index inequality according to the difference principle, with and without residual (economic) bases of self-respect

the social and economic inequalities they generate tend to optimize the worst socioeconomic position. The poor might "excusably" prefer a socioeconomic position that, though somewhat worse in absolute terms, is (in relative terms) somewhat less inferior.

Rawls handles this problem by recognizing that a *residual* component of self-respect may have to be included among the index goods.[4] Adding this index good enables the difference principle to take account of abridgments of self-respect that are due to a significantly inferior share of other index goods (see Graph 1).

Rawls's halfhearted offer that "theoretically we can if necessary include self-respect in the primary goods" governed by the difference principle (TJ 546) does not then detract from the great importance he elsewhere attaches to self-respect. He assumes that the need for self-respect (insofar as it is socially based) would be met, at least in very large part, through those institutional features in virtue of which a basic structure satisfies the first and opportunity principles. Vindicating this assumption will be one central goal in my attempt to specify the opportunity constraint that is to be imposed upon the difference principle. I will try to interpret the opportunity principle so that its satisfaction, together with that of the first principle, would ensure that the social bases of self-respect are, as Rawls envisions, at least roughly equal across all sectors of society. My occasional appeals to self-respect in the course of interpreting the opportunity principle refer, then, not to its residual component included among the index goods but to the

---

[4]This point would have been clearer had Rawls spoken more narrowly of the *residual* (or economic) bases of self-respect, one's relative status in production (powers and prerogatives of offices and positions of responsibility) and consumption (income and wealth). The *social* bases of self-respect also include education and, of course, the basic rights and liberties.

full social bases of self-respect that also figure so prominently in Rawls's argument for the priority of the equal basic liberties.

14.3. Coming to the second preliminary, institutions may generate inequalities in various ways. Perpendicular to my earlier distinction between established and engendered inequalities, we must now distinguish between the various kinds of noninstitutional facts to which the inequalities produced by an institutional scheme may be related. What facts about particular individuals explain the lifetime share each comes to have under the institutional scheme they participate in? If shares are unequal, then there must be such facts. These facts are not themselves part of the institutional scheme and are therefore irrelevant to its assessment. What is relevant is which kinds of facts an institutional scheme allows to play a causal role in determining shares and how significant an impact it allows each kind of fact to have. Here Rawls wants to distinguish among "three main kinds of contingencies" (WOS 11): natural contingencies, social contingencies, and "such chance contingencies as accident and good fortune" (TJ 72).

In first explicating the second principle, Rawls puts a good deal of weight upon the distinction between natural and social contingencies. Luck is almost entirely ignored, though inequalities arising through chance are implicitly grouped together with those arising from natural contingencies.

The natural/social distinction is problematic in various ways, and Rawls does not draw it precisely. Concerning inequalities related to differentials in natural talent—his paradigm example for natural contingencies—Rawls suggests that insofar as socioeconomic inequalities are talent-induced, they can be explained by reference to two factors: the natural distribution of talents and the prevailing institutional scheme. This suggestion, however, is too simple. There is a third factor, namely, how valuable the various natural talents are considered to be in the relevant social system. To some extent this third factor will itself be determined by the prevailing institutional scheme. To some extent it will also be due to exogenous determinants, such as the system's natural environment, culture, and level of development. In any case, this third factor ensures that even so-called *natural* contingencies (the distribution of valuable talents) will have a considerable social component.

A dramatic example of this are race- and gender-induced inequalities, neglected in *A Theory of Justice*. In some actual societies a person's prospects for social primary goods are very considerably affected by his or her gender, descent, or skin color. Clearly, such inequalities are related to natural contingencies, in Rawls's sense. Yet, upon reflection, they seem to have more in common with inequalities related to social contingencies, as exemplified by the social class of one's parents. For although it is plausible to say that the lack of a talent is a natural handicap and that the natural diversity of talents is a fact to which social institutions must adjust themselves in some way, it is at least doubtful that being female or black makes one naturally handicapped or that social institutions must adjust themselves to the natural diversity of skin colors and genders (or of height or hair growth, for that matter).[5] These remarks make it appear doubtful that a conception of justice can plausibly place as much weight on the distinction between natural and social contingencies as Rawls does in interpreting his second principle. I will substantiate these doubts more concretely in a moment.

14.4. With this background, let us consider what Rawls takes the content of the opportunity principle to be. He is clear throughout that this principle requires at least *formal* equality of opportunity, that is "equality as careers open to talents" (TJ 65). This requirement is scantily explained. Surely Rawls means to preclude ground rules that call for exclusion of specific persons or groups from certain careers. Presumably he wants to require further that ground rules must positively mandate that opportunities be allocated in certain ways (for example, by firms and schools). I conjecture that to maintain formal equality of opportunity institutions must prescribe that information about openings be reasonably widely available and that no group be excluded wholesale from the competition for an opening, unless this group is defined by its members' (1) inability or unwillingness to pay the access price (tuition, for example), (2) inferior suitability or qualifications as reasonably related to prospects of success in the relevant career, or (3) age. I think discrimination by age need not be prohibited for the sake of maintaining formal equality of opportunity as Rawls would specify it. By not admitting students above the age of thirty-five, law schools would not be affecting persons' *lifetime* shares differentially.

These conjectures still leave important questions open. May other grounds (race, gender, good looks, religious or political affiliation) be used to the extent that doing so merely hampers some groups but does not exclude them altogether? May such criteria be considered components of suitability at least, when patients—to take admissions to medical schools as an example—have more trust in white, male, ugly, Christian, or conservative doctors?

14.5. Rawls clearly believes that mere formal equality of opportunity, associated with the natural-liberty interpretation of the second principle (TJ 65–72), is not enough of a constraint on a market economy. Because of two ambiguities in his account, however, it is much less clear which stronger version of the second principle he means to be endorsing as his own (democratic-equality) interpretation.

Rawls views as an improvement (over natural liberty) the liberal-

---

[5]This thought retains its validity even if it is believed that race and gender correlate with natural endowment, for even then one can question (as Plato did in the *Republic* bk. 5) why institutions should adjust themselves to natural differences in race or gender, rather than directly to the diversity in talents.

equality interpretation of the second principle (TJ 73–74), on which the opportunity principle constraining the principle of efficiency is strengthened into "the principle of fair equality of opportunity." In first introducing this principle, he writes: "The thought here is that positions are to be not only open in a formal sense, but that all should have a fair chance to attain them. Offhand it is not clear what is meant, but we might say that . . . those who are at the same level of talent and ability, and have the same willingness to use them, should have the same prospects of success regardless of their initial place in the social system. . . . Chances to acquire cultural knowledge and skills should not depend upon one's class position, and so the school system, whether public or private, should be designed to even out class barriers" (TJ 73). The index of *A Theory of Justice* lists this as the place where "equality of fair opportunity [is] defined" (TJ 594). There are two roughly parallel passages: fair equality of opportunity requires "equal chances of education and culture for persons similarly endowed and motivated" (TJ 275), and "the second principle . . . requires equal life prospects in all sectors of society for those similarly endowed and motivated" (TJ 301).[6]

This evidence suggests that Rawls's own democratic-equality interpretation of the second principle—"combining the principle of fair equality of opportunity with the difference principle" (TJ 75)—follows the liberal-equality interpretation in invoking the distinction between inequalities of opportunity that an institutional scheme allows to arise from social contingencies and those it allows to arise from natural contingencies (TJ 72–75). The former would be entirely prohibited by the opportunity principle, whereas the latter would be left to "the difference principle [which] would allocate resources in education, say, so as to improve the long-term expectation of the least favored. If this end is attained by giving more attention to the better endowed, it is permissible; otherwise not" (TJ 101).

Conflicting with this understanding of Rawls's own democratic-equality interpretation, there are indications that Rawls wants *all* inequalities of opportunity to be constrained by a maximin criterion. Thus he chooses a class-induced inequality to illustrate his difference principle: "Those starting out as members of the entrepreneurial class in property-owning democracy, say, have a better prospect than those

---

[6]In what follows, I speak not of chances or prospects but of *access*. One reason is that Rawls is concerned with chances or prospects across social classes only for those similarly endowed *and motivated*. Those born into the lowest class may be less motivated to take advantage of their opportunities so that their lifetime shares will tend to be inferior. Such inequalities do not fall under Rawls's opportunity principle, which requires merely that those disadvantaged by social contingencies should *be able* to achieve the same success as similarly endowed members of other classes, and which thus is concerned with inequalities of *access*. Socioeconomic inequalities that arise from (or cause) class-related differences in motivation are not, therefore, violations of the opportunity principle, though such inequalities are constrained, of course, by the difference principle.

who begin in the class of unskilled laborers. . . . [T]his kind of initial inequality in life prospects . . . is justifiable only if the difference in expectation is to the advantage of the representative man who is worse off" (TJ 78). And he writes that "an inequality of opportunity must enhance the opportunities of those with the lesser opportunity" (TJ 303).[7]

The first ambiguity, then, concerns the kind of limitation Rawls wants to impose upon socioeconomic inequalities that institutions allow to arise from social contingencies. Is he requiring rough statistical equality among persons born into different classes who are similarly endowed and motivated, or may the basic structure generate inequalities so long as doing so raises the socioeconomic position of the least advantaged in absolute terms?

The second ambiguity concerns the question 'Equality or inequalities of what?' On one understanding, Rawls was postulating a separate social primary good of intermediate importance, and such a good, opportunities, indeed appeared on the canonical list of social primary goods (TJ 62, 92). It would include access to "cultural knowledge and skills" (TJ 73) and to "education and culture" (TJ 275). Postulating such a good, Rawls could explain the design priority of the opportunity principle over the difference principle as follows: a basic structure under which the least advantaged suffer a shortfall from fair equality of opportunity is always unjust, even when this enables them to have a better index position, because opportunities are incommensurably more important than index goods (just as first-principle goods are incommensurably more important than opportunities). In this vein Rawls writes: "It is not enough to argue . . . that the whole of society including the least favored benefit from certain restrictions on equality of opportunity. We must also claim that the attempt to eliminate these inequalities would so interfere with the social system and the operations of the economy that in the long run anyway the opportunities of the disadvantaged would be even more limited" (TJ 300–1). "An in-

---

[7]He also says that "the difference principle redefines the grounds for social inequalities as conceived in the system of liberal equality" (TJ 511). I don't profess to know what Rawls's point is in this sentence. I tend to think he is suggesting that the democratic-equality interpretation *weakens* the constraint upon socially induced inequalities by substituting the difference principle for that of fair equality of opportunity. This understanding would support what Rawls is seeking to show, namely, that "within the context of the theory of justice as a whole, there is much less urgency" to abolish the family (TJ 511); the weaker constraint is more easily satisfied. But I concede that another reading is possible as well (cf. Martin, RR 75). The democratic-equality interpretation *strengthens* the constraint upon inequalities in rewards by substituting the difference principle for the principle of efficiency. This understanding, too, would lend some support to what Rawls is seeking to show. He would be assuming that once the difference principle is satisfied, inequalities in the rewards attached to the various jobs would not be very great and fair equality of opportunity would be enhanced for those born into the less affluent families, thanks to the more egalitarian distribution of income and wealth among their parent generation.

equality of opportunity must enhance the opportunities of those with the lesser opportunity" (TJ 303)—not merely their index position.[8]

Alternatively, Rawls might have been concerned with the possibility that social contingencies might be allowed to give rise to inequalities in index goods—in income and in powers and prerogatives of offices and positions of responsibility. This view is suggested, for example, by his paraphrase: "Positions are to be not only open in a formal sense, but . . . all should have a fair chance to attain them" (TJ 73). There is no separate social primary good "opportunities".[9]

Cast as questions, the two ambiguities can be summed up this way: First, under the ideal basic structure, are inequalities of opportunity arising from social contingencies [1] permitted insofar as, *ceteris paribus*, they (interschemically) enhance the worst socioeconomic position, or are they [2] strictly ruled out? Second, does the opportunity principle limit how social contingencies may give rise to differentials in access to [A] index goods or to [B] opportunities understood as a social primary good in their own right? These two ambiguities permit (initially) four mutually incompatible readings of Rawls's democratic-equality interpretation of the second principle, including four different versions of the opportunity principle as it constrains the difference principle, as follows:

[1A] Inequalities in index goods are governed by the difference principle, subject only to the condition (OP_{1A}) of formal equality of opportunity.[10]

[1B] Inequalities in index goods are governed by the difference principle, subject to the condition (OP_{1B}) that there must be formal equality of opportunity, and inequalities of opportunity (for example, in access to education) may be allowed to arise from social contingencies only if and insofar as allowing them to arise optimizes the opportunities of the least advantaged.

[2A] Inequalities in index goods are governed by the difference principle, subject to the condition (OP_{2A}) that there must be formal equality of opportunity, and no inequalities in index goods may be allowed to arise from social contingencies (that is, access to index goods must be equal for similarly endowed persons born into different social classes).

[8]Here one might add that under less than truly favorable conditions an inequality of opportunity could, theoretically anyway, also be justified by arguing that it is necessary to optimize the worst package of first-principle goods. But for the time being we do best to simplify matters by restricting the discussion to ideal theory.

[9]Though not a social *primary* good, opportunity (like education) would still be a social good, on a par with the index goods. Opportunity would be among the things that income and wealth make accessible and presumably also among the residual social bases of self-respect.

[10]Though it reads the opportunity principle as requiring merely formal equality of opportunity, [1A] is not the same as the natural-liberty interpretation of the second principle, because it imposes the difference principle, instead of the much weaker principle of efficiency (TJ 66–70), as a secondary constraint upon social and economic inequalities.

[2B] Inequalities in index goods are governed by the difference principle, subject to the condition (OP$_{2B}$) that there must be formal equality of opportunity, and no inequalities of opportunity may be allowed to arise from social contingencies (that is, access to education and the like must be equal for similarly endowed persons born into different social classes).[11]

Since the texts do not clearly favor one reading, let me proceed with a brief analysis, which will show that only version [1A] is tenable.

14.6. Version [1B] involves the idea that opportunities constitute a separate category of social primary goods, intermediate in the lexical hierarchy between first-principle goods and index goods. It implies a preference for the feasible basic structure that optimizes the worst (set of) opportunities. But this requirement makes no sense. For opportunities must be understood either in absolute or in relative terms. If we understand them in *absolute* terms (as reflecting, for instance, how much education one has access to), then [1B] requires that resources must without limit be devoted to the production of opportunities in preference to index goods, because the opportunities of the least advantaged take precedence over their index position. This priority is absurd. On the other hand, if we understand opportunities in *relative* terms (as reflecting how much education one has access to as a percentage of the average, for example), then the second principle allows no inequalities of opportunity at all, and [1B] collapses into [2B]. This dilemma undermines [1B], together with Rawls's idea that the way to justify inequalities of opportunity is to show that they "enhance the opportunities of those with the lesser opportunity" (TJ 303, cf. 300).

Version [2B] presupposes a rationale in which opportunities are conceived in relative terms, as a positional good. What is presumed to be important is not having access to as much education as possible but having no less access to education than others. With the good so defined, the parties, reasoning in accordance with the maximin rule, will adopt an *equality* of opportunity principle. They will not care how much there is by way of opportunities in absolute terms (and thus can allow the political process to govern overall allocations to education). They will prohibit inequalities of opportunity because any such inequalities must (logically) reduce the worst set of opportunities and, therefore—given the lexical priority within the second principle—count as lowering the worst social position overall (even when they raise the worst index position).[12] Although it presupposes such a ra-

---

[11]The parenthetical clauses might also be, for [2A], "prospects for index goods must be equal for similarly endowed and motivated persons born into different social classes," and, for [2B], "prospects for education and the like must be equal for similarly endowed and motivated persons born into different social classes." Compare n. 6.

[12]Again, I am here disregarding that an inequality of opportunity could still be justified by appeal to the first principle, as being necessary to raise the worst representative first-principle score.

tionale, [2B] is also inconsistent with it, because [2B] allows inequalities of opportunity based upon *natural* contingencies, allows, for example, as Rawls clearly wants to allow (e.g., TJ 101), inferior access to education for persons less well endowed.

Version [2A] involves the assumption that opportunities do *not* constitute a social primary good in their own right, that socioeconomic positions are determined by index goods alone. On this assumption, the parties will prefer a criterion of social justice that assesses all social and economic inequalities that institutions tend to produce by reference to the lowest index position. They have no reason to allow this lowest index position to be lowered in order to equalize across classes the index prospects of persons similarly motivated and endowed. So [2A], too, is inconsistent with its suggested rationale. It collapses into [1A], which lets the difference principle govern *all* inequalities of opportunity (whether based on social or natural contingencies), subject only to the one constraint of formal equality of opportunity.

It may seem that if the parties cared only about index goods, then they would go even further and prefer to [1A] a proposal on which the opportunity principle is deleted entirely. But I think Rawls could defend the weakest opportunity principle even if it were not correlated with a social primary good of its own. Formal equality of opportunity requires a universal right to compete for all openings on the basis of one's suitability and qualifications as well as one's ability and willingness to pay the access price. This is a nearly cost-free legal mechanism that, through gains in productivity, is bound to pay its own way, for it ensures that a larger number of qualified applicants are available for the more important jobs. Adopting it, with design and implementation priority over the difference principle, involves negligible risks for the lowest index position and has significant advantages in specificity and also from the standpoint of the parties' concern that institutions should support self-respect, should engender a shared sense of equal citizenship, and should minimize the strains of commitment.

14.7. Having looked at four versions of Rawls's second principle, each with its suggested rationale, we have found that only [1A] is tenable. Indeed, some evidence suggests that Rawls now favors [1A], although he still speaks of the principle of *fair* equality of opportunity. Thus, on the canonical list of social primary goods Rawls replaces, the entry "opportunities" (TJ 62, 92; FG 536) with "freedom of movement and free choice of occupation against a background of diverse opportunities" (KCMT 526; BLP 22; cf. SUPG 162).[13] Moreover, the only substantive passage on the opportunity principle in the later writings seems to

---

[13]This is strangely redundant, for "freedom of movement and free choice of occupation" are also included under the freedom and integrity of the person (BLP 50); their protection is thus already required by the first principle. And a "background of diverse opportunities" would seem a rather odd (public) social primary good. I have the impression Rawls wanted to drop a social primary good from the list without saying so.

suggest a requirement of *formal* equality of opportunity: "Announcements of jobs and positions can be forbidden to contain statements which exclude applicants of certain designated ethnic and racial groups, or of either sex. . . . The notion of fair equality of opportunity . . . has a central range of application which consists of various liberties together with certain conditions under which these liberties can be effectively exercised" (BLP 79).

14.8. We have found no plausible rationale in *A Theory of Justice* for the view that inequalities in access to education ([2B]) or to jobs with associated rewards ([2A]), are acceptable when related to *natural* contingencies, but unjust when related to *social* contingencies.[14] But one might think that this view is nevertheless morally plausible or that it appeals to the parties for other reasons (such as publicity, equal citizenship, or stability). Let me present two reasons for doubting that this is so.

14.8.1. The first difficulty can be illustrated by a social system whose participants are divided into rich and poor, better endowed and worse endowed. So there are four groups: RB, PB, RW, and PW. Suppose this social system has basic structure ONE, which tends to engender significant class-induced differentials in educational opportunities. Admission to the better schools requires little by way of talents and motivation but is mainly regulated by high tuition charges. Many members of RW can and do attend such schools, but most of those born among the poor cannot do likewise, whatever their endowments. Assume further that the tuition barrier is in fact justified on the [1A] reading of the second principle (where it requires only formal equality of opportunity). There are enough RB entrants to fill the most important offices with qualified graduates, even without offering subsidies to members of PB, and the tuition barrier provides a powerful incentive to parents to work especially hard for the sake of financing their children's education. These two factors, by maximizing overall income, make ONE the scheme that optimizes the index position of the least advantaged (PW), as the difference principle requires.

On the [2A] and [2B] readings of the second principle, this social system stands in need of institutional reform. The educational or job prospects between groups RB and PB, and between groups RW and PW,

[14]OP_{2A} is the weaker constraint on the difference principle. It allows what OP_{2B} excludes, namely, an economic system under which the social class one is born into affects one's access to education, say, but not one's access to index goods. Perhaps there are special quotas that give persons born into the lower classes fair access to better jobs, regardless of qualifications, merely on the basis of their talents and motivation. Or perhaps there are special income supplements that compensate such persons for their lesser jobs and self-respect insofar as these are due to the class-induced inferiority of their education. There is a certain remoteness about such possibilities. It seems unlikely that either efficiency or the difference principle would ever favor that OP_{2A} be satisfied in these ways rather than by reducing class-induced inequalities in fair access to education (as OP_{2B} would mandate). I am therefore taking the liberty of treating [2A] and [2B] together in what follows.

must be equalized. Assume there is a feasible alternative basic structure, TWO, under which the intellectual and motivational entrance
requirements are raised and tuition fees made affordable to members
of PB; TWO comes much closer than ONE to satisfying OP_{2A} and OP_{2B}. It
also satisfies the difference principle, which this time, of course, is
subject to a more demanding opportunity principle (OP_{2A} or OP_{2B}).
Now suppose index positions are those given in Table 3. On reading
[1A], ONE is preferred because it generates the higher minimum index
position (20 as against 17). On readings [2A] and [2B], TWO is preferred
because it avoids a higher-order injustice. Under ONE the poor (PB and
PW) suffer a much greater inequality of opportunity.[15]

This preference for TWO illustrates the first difficulty. Yes, thanks to
the much lower prospects in RW, the least advantaged (PW) now enjoy
something approaching "fair equality of educational opportunity." But
their education is not one bit better under TWO than under ONE, nor is
their overall disadvantage at all reduced; they are still effectively excluded from the better schools, which continue to be accessible to
others. It is absurd to regard their position as much better under TWO
than under ONE just because two *other* groups, PB and RW, have (so to
speak) exchanged places.[16] And it would be similarly bizarre to allow
OP_{2A} or OP_{2B} implementation priority over the difference principle, that
is, to hold that efforts toward reversing the prospects of PB and RW are
always more urgent than efforts to mitigate even severe poverty within
PW (as when their index position falls far short of the feasible minimum
of 17).

14.8.2. The second difficulty is that fair equality of opportunity, as
understood in [2A] and [2B], can never be satisfied, at least if the
equality in question really "requires equal life prospects in all sectors of
society for those similarly endowed and motivated" (TJ 301). More
affluent parents can always spend additional resources to ensure that
their children will get ahead vis-à-vis children from poorer backgrounds who are equally well endowed and motivated. And even if they

---

[15]In stating these preferences, I assume of course that other things are equal (particularly as regards the distribution of first-principle goods and *formal* equality of opportunity). I also assume that there are no class-induced differentials in motivation.

[16]This objection can be countered by specifying the [2A] or [2B] notion of fair opportunity in terms of access to index goods or opportunities *consonant with one's endowments*. This specification would entail that under ONE only the members of PB suffer a
higher-order injustice and are therefore the least advantaged group. The members of PW
suffer no higher-order injustice under either ONE or TWO, because, worse endowed as they
are, they have less of a need for better jobs or a better education. This counter provides a
rationale for Rawls's decision to handle inequalities related to social contingencies
differently from those related to natural contingencies. But it is not a promising counter
for at least four reasons. The difficulties of specifying a reasonably sharp notion of
consonance, suitable as part of a public criterion of justice, are overwhelming. The lexical
priority of the opportunity principle, so understood, seems far too risky. The proposed
specification is exposed to the two objections raised in §10.4.2.2 against defining social
primary goods relative to natural attributes. And such a definition is, at any rate, inconsistent with Rawls's semiconsequentialism.

Table 3. Index positions under alternative basic structures

	Representative groups			
	RB	PB	RW	PW
Basic structure ONE	90	24	60	20
Basic structure TWO	75	60	22	17

did not do this, their children would have many intangible advantages in terms of the contact persons they are exposed to in their home, neighborhood, and peer group.[17] A school system that does literally "even out class barriers" (TJ 73)—if possible at all—is bound to be extremely expensive and therefore would reduce index positions (including that of the least advantaged). *Requiring* such an education system is thoroughly implausible and surely unacceptable to the risk-averse parties, especially if the opportunity principle entailing this requirement is to have not only design but also implementation priority over the difference principle. These difficulties show decisively, I think, that [1A] is preferable to [2A] and [2B].

15. Educational and Employment Opportunities

15.1. There is another way of saving Rawls's intuition (at the time of writing *A Theory of Justice*) that the difference principle should be constrained by something stronger than merely formal equality of opportunity. This new version of the second principle addresses our two difficulties by understanding the opportunity principle so that it requires more on behalf of the worse endowed and also requires less than strict equality (though it still understands opportunities in relative terms). Let me begin with the former improvement.

A major defect of Rawls's attempts to formulate an opportunity principle requiring more than formal equality of opportunity is his idea that the distinction between social and natural contingencies is morally significant. If Rawls is right that inequalities of opportunity are too important to be left to the index-good calculus, then this must be true of race-induced and gender-induced as much as of class-induced inequalities. And it would seem to be true of talent-induced inequalities of opportunity as well. In fact, being excluded from education on

[17]See Fishkin, JEOF, who adduces a good deal of empirical evidence to show the infeasibility of implementing this principle, which he calls "equality of life chances," through increased educational expenditure for children born into the lower classes. Fishkin also considers ways of implementing the principle that involve invasions of family autonomy. It is unclear whether Rawls takes the first principle to rule out such measures (see TJ 511). In any case, it would be rather embarrassing if his conception of justice did, in practice, require such invasions of family autonomy.

the ground that one's talents aren't worth developing may well be more devastating to one's self-respect than exclusion on the ground that one's parents cannot afford to pay tuition. Yet all four readings of Rawls that we have considered may support as ideal a basic structure under which very little education and training are available to the less well endowed. In each case their disadvantage is justified by appeal to the difference principle. The cost of offering more education to the worse endowed is a bad investment, is not fully redeemed by their greater productivity later in life. Skimping on their education maximizes over- all income and therefore, given the difference principle, also the in- come of the least advantaged (most of whom may themselves be among the worse endowed). Hence, severe talent-induced inequalities in edu- cational opportunity may well be required by Rawls's second principle, even under the best of circumstances.

Rawls seeks to mitigate this harsh result by emphasizing "the role of education in enabling a person to enjoy the culture of his society and to take part in its affairs, and in this way to provide for each individual a secure sense of his own worth" (TJ 101); "resources for education are not to be allotted solely or necessarily mainly according to their return as estimated in productive trained abilities, but also according to their worth in enriching the personal and social life of citizens" (TJ 107). Stated in proper form, his thought must be this: The severe educational inequalities in question are justified only when they (interschemically) optimize the index position of the least advantaged. But they are un- likely to do this, because any gain in the *income* of the least advantaged they may produce will probably be outweighed by a loss in their self- respect.[18] Hence, only rather mild talent-induced inequalities of educa- tional opportunity will be justifiable by the difference principle.

Of course, lacking any notion of how the various index goods are to be weighted and aggregated, we have no way of evaluating this claim. But if the index does indeed take account of education in this way, then why should the difference principle need to be subjected to a further constraint specifically upon *class*-induced inequalities of opportunity? This question presses toward [1A]. But let me here pursue the inverse question: if we do need a special constraint upon inequalities of oppor- tunity arising from *social* contingencies, then why shouldn't this con- straint need to be extended to inequalities of opportunity related to other kinds of contingencies? This question presses toward a new version of the democratic-equality interpretation of the second princi- ple:

[3B] Inequalities in index goods are governed by the difference principle, subject to the condition (OP_{3B}) that there must be formal equality of

[18]See §14.2. Such educational inequalities may also lower the access the least advan- taged have to powers and prerogatives of offices and positions of responsibility, which Rawls lists as another index good.

opportunity and rough equality of actual opportunity (that is, participants must have roughly equivalent access to education and the like).[19]

OP_{3B} requires, in addition to formal equality of opportunity, that everyone should have access to a roughly equivalent education, with equivalence defined in terms of cost.[20] This does not mean that persons must actually receive such a roughly equivalent education, only that it must be genuinely accessible to them. Perhaps genuine access is incompatible with discouragements of the kind that have been subtly hampering the education of women. Presumably genuine access also does not exist when parents may refuse educational opportunities on their childrens' behalf (which would suggest that the earlier stages of education must be compulsory).

Governed by the opportunity principle, such access is inalienable, cannot be gambled or given or sold away (cf. §10.7). Nevertheless, there may be cases of persons having genuine access to but declining a roughly equivalent education. Such cases do not indicate an injustice in the relevant education system.

Finally, OP_{3B} is insensitive to *how* a basic structure ensures that all have access to a roughly equivalent education. Schools and universities may be publicly financed, or students may have access to sufficient personal or parental funds, scholarships, summer jobs, or loans from public or private sources.

15.2. Version [3B] accords with [B] by conceiving opportunities as a social primary good in their own right. In the other dimension, [3B] is egalitarian, like [2], in understanding opportunities in relative terms (as a *positional* good). In this, it diverges from the assumption implicit in [1], namely, that a person gains by having more access absolutely even if this greater access comes at the expense of having less access than others. Compared to [2], [3B] is *more* egalitarian by having the opportunity principle constrain all inequalities of opportunity—not only those arising from social contingencies but also those arising from natural contingencies or luck. Thus [3B] assumes that a person compares her educational opportunities not only with those had by others whose talents and luck are similar to her own. But then [3B] is also *less* egalitarian than [2] in that it employs a less demanding notion of equality, as I will explain.

Version [3B] avoids the first main difficulty associated with [2A] and [2B]. In the hypothetical case we have considered, [3B] would require

[19]The clause in parentheses might also be "prospects for education and the like must be roughly equal for persons similarly motivated." Compare nn. 6&11 above.

[20]This idea is supported in Galston, JHG 262–63. For there to be rough equivalence, educational opportunities must also be diverse, so as to match the diversity of persons' talents, motivation, interests, and ambitions. The specification of this requirement will in part depend upon each social system's circumstances and, therefore, must presumably be deferred to the legislative stage.

institutional reforms toward yet another basic structure, THREE, under which, because of a stronger constraint upon the difference principle, the index position of the least advantaged (PW) would once again be worse than under ONE. This time, however, the justification for this absolute decline in their index position (from ONE to THREE) is not blatantly implausible. The reform of the education system would greatly improve the educational opportunities of the least advantaged, thereby strengthening one important basis of their self-respect. It would also tend to improve their *relative* index position, because [3B], unlike Rawls's four versions of the second principle, does not allow their handicap in terms of marketable talents to be compounded by the disadvantage of an inferior education.

Moreover, [3B] is a great improvement in simplicity. To determine whether OP_{2A} and OP_{2B} are satisfied, we must be able to delimit the various social classes and, within each of these classes, the subsets of persons similarly motivated and endowed; and we must be able to ascertain the probability-weighted average expectation for educational opportunities ([2B]) or future success ([2A]) within all these relevant subsets. In order to determine whether OP_{3B} is satisfied, we need only understand what educational opportunities the various participants have. This is also much closer to how other social primary goods are understood.[21]

Version [3B] has the same sort of advantage over [1A], which presupposes a complex (and quite possibly unmanageable) index calculus for assessing talent-induced inequalities of educational opportunity—which calculations, Rawls seems to think, would justify only minor talent-induced inequalities in any case (TJ 101, 107). Version [3B] is much simpler than Rawls's versions and therefore more suitable as part of a public criterion of social justice that is to engender stability.

Moreover, Rawls's versions of the second principle are liable to undermine the self-respect of the "worse endowed" by permitting that they have inferior access to education when more can be achieved for them by fostering the development of greater talents. By contrast, [3B] downplays Rawls's distinction between the better and worse endowed. The point of the education system now is to offer roughly equal encouragement and support to the development of *different* talents, whatever they may be, rather than to encourage and promote unequally the development of "better" and "worse" endowments (for the sake of optimizing the index position of the least advantaged).

By departing from Rawls in this way, [3B] does not get too close to an extreme that Rawls wants to avoid. The principle of redress, as he refers

---

[21]Version [3B] also accords with my proposal (§11.6.1) to use the account of social primary goods (enshrined in Rawls's criterion of justice) to identify representative groups, especially the least advantaged. Versions [2A] and [2B] presuppose some *independent* way of identifying relevant social classes. I show later (§17.5) that Rawls has no plausible way of doing this.

to it (TJ 100–1), requires that the "better endowed" have inferior access to education on the grounds that they can still achieve as much as others whose inferior endowments are brought to fruition.[22] This extreme and Rawls's versions of the second principle fail, I believe, for much the same reasons. First, they view education as merely a means for producing some desirable social result, which in both cases is evaluated in terms of index goods. Yet in virtue of its crucial role in shaping not only our index-good prospects but the very persons we are, education is a pivotal social good in its own right, an essential precondition for the development of the two moral powers and of a secure sense of self-respect. These considerations support ranking access to education above index goods, as some passages of *A Theory of Justice* suggest. But if educational opportunities have this elevated status, they must have it in *all* interpersonal comparisons, not just in comparing the social positions of persons similarly endowed. Second, Rawls's versions and the principle of redress allow indefinite inequalities in educational opportunities for persons differentially endowed. On [3B], by contrast, no ranking of natural endowments is incorporated into the public conception of justice. All persons, no matter what their endowments may be, have the same claim upon educational resources. By understanding the second principle in this way, we (or the parties) avoid undermining the self-respect of those whom Rawls treats as the worse endowed and ensure that the opportunity principle (OP_{3B}), like the first principle, is a firm and perspicuous pillar of a shared public notion of equal citizenship.

The argument for [3B] can be further strengthened by attending to the other main kind of contingencies that Rawls exempts from the scope of his opportunity principle—luck. Consider a society in which some 20 percent of all children cannot gain admission to any school. The scheme is defended on the ground that the inequality is not related to social contingencies, since schools select pupils at random. Rawls's versions of the opportunity principle all allow this defense. All individuals and groups compete for admission on equal terms (formal

---

[22]In the way they accommodate natural inequalities, both [3A] and Rawls's versions constitute plausible midpoints between two extremes (cf. §10.4.2). Historical societies have allowed natural differentials in endowment to give rise to considerable inequalities in access to education and index goods. The principle of redress suggests inverting these inequalities. Social and economic inequalities that institutions generate should not *aggravate* but rather *mitigate* natural inequalities. This proposal, however, conflicts with Rawls's semiconsequentialism. As a *natural* primary good (and a natural basis of self-respect), endowments are excluded from the Master Pattern in terms of which feasible basic structures are to be assessed. Still, reforms indicated by the second principle would constitute progress even by the lights of the principle of redress, in that they would reduce the extent to which social inequalities aggravate natural inequalities (cf. TJ 100–1). According to Rawls, inequalities in access to education and index goods across endowment groups are to be constrained by the difference principle. Version [3B] goes somewhat farther. It requires roughly equal access to education for all and only *subject to this condition* lets index inequalities be governed by the difference principle.

equality of opportunity), and similarly endowed and motivated persons born into different social classes have equal prospects for education (OP_{2B}) and achievement (OP_{2A}). Rawls's assessment of this scheme would then turn upon whether it satisfies the difference principle—and this it might well do, because it is cheaper and might yield an equally suitable work force. OP_{3B}, by contrast, prohibits this scheme; and this is surely plausible, seeing that the 20 percent who are excluded from education will be marked off for life as a distinct social group whose inferior status cannot be outweighed by any gain in the minimum index position.

15.3. Version [3B] has at least two main weaknesses. It is exposed to an analogue of the second difficulty with versions [2A] and [2B]. The disposition of more affluent parents to spend more on the education of their children may necessitate an implausibly expensive education system that makes accessible to all an education equal to the best. Moreover, [3B] requires that roughly equal resources be available for the education of all, even where such resources would have a negative net impact on available index goods. This constitutes a risk for the (absolute) index position of the least advantaged.

These weaknesses can be mitigated in two ways. First, one should narrow the definition of *educational* opportunities so as to exclude many expensive but not so central items (flying, music, and skiing lessons; educational travel; a home telescope or laboratory; etc.). It seems difficult to put this idea into more principled form so that it can be evaluated behind the veil of ignorance (and does not strike us as ad hoc), but it surely must be employed to some extent.

Second, one can try to define *rough* equivalence in a way that is both somewhat liberal *and* especially sensitive to the parties' concern for those with the worst educational opportunities. What is needed is not a measure for the overall equality of cost (like the Gini coefficient), but a measure specifically focused upon the extent to which the worst opportunities fall short of the middle range. The intuitive idea is that everyone must have access to some reasonably high proportion of what others actually have. This idea may be specified as follows: The *standard* (per capita) cost of education in a social system is defined not as an average but in terms of some percentile(s), whereby the more extravagant educational privileges enjoyed by a few children of very rich or very committed parents are simply disregarded; and a *minimally adequate* education is then defined as one the cost of which does not fall short of the standard by more than some fixed percentage.[23] For exam-

---

[23]Clearly, specifying this second idea (partly perhaps at the constitutional or legislative stages) will again be ad hoc to some extent, but this is not a strong reason for the parties to reject [3B] in favor of [1A]. If rough equivalence of educational opportunities really is crucially important (in light of equal citizenship, self-respect, and the two highest-order interests), then the parties will want it protected even by a definition that is in some degree arbitrary, rather than not have it protected at all. Let me add that such arbitrari-

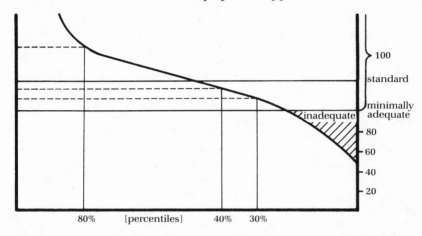

Graph 2. Specifying what is "minimally adequate" under the opportunity principle

ple, one might define the standard as the mean of per capita educational costs at the 80th, 40th, and 30th percentiles and an education as minimally adequate when its cost does not fall short of the standard by more than 25 percent. Obviously, the details of this proposal, as given here and in Graph 2 are for purposes of illustration only. Version [3B] thus subjects the difference principle to the requirement that all participants are to enjoy formal equality of opportunity and minimally adequate educational opportunities (that is, access to at least a minimally adequate education).

15.4. My proposed specification of [3B] puts no weight on Rawls's distinction between social and natural contingencies. Hence, just as it is not (very) sensitive to whether a few rich parents hire private tutors for their children, it is also not (very) sensitive to whether there are some small but expensive educational programs designed to improve the applicant pool for some economically crucial set of jobs. Such tolerance is congenial to the maximin rule, which focuses the parties' attention less on how far those at the very top are above, than on how far those at the very bottom fall below, the middle range. It allows leeway for institutions to generate whatever minor educational inequalities are most strongly favored by the difference principle (that is, make the greatest contributions to raising the lowest index position).

My specification of [3B] also accords with the idea—which I see as animating the second principle (§13.5)—of not overconstraining the

---

ness is unavoidable in many other important cases, such as the definition of representative groups and of the fair value of the political liberties or the specification and weighting of index goods. It is unavoidable also for Rawls's versions [2A] and [2B]. The prohibition of (class-induced) inequalities of opportunity cannot require literal *equality*.

political process. When the standard cost of education is defined in terms of some suitable percentile(s), then it cannot easily be forced into escalation by the determined efforts of some parents to give their children a head start. This standard cost remains largely under the control of the political process, which, though it must not permit significant educational advantages and (especially) disadvantages for particular persons or groups, can raise or lower the overall allocation of social resources to the education system.

Unlike Rawls's versions [2A] and [2B], [3B] contains, I believe, a principle of *fair* equality of opportunity whose priority over the difference principle is plausible. I have not tried to decide whether the opportunity principle should take this form or be cast as a requirement for merely formal equality of opportunity (as in [1A]). Here a crucial question is whether the parties would accept the implementation priority of OP_{3B} over the difference principle. Is it plausible to reform an institutional scheme that generates severe socioeconomic inequalities by beginning from the lower age groups, with the equalization of educational opportunities? Should political efforts and social resources be primarily devoted to mitigating not the excessive poverty of the least advantaged group but the educational disadvantages suffered by its younger members? Are excessive educational inequalities a higher-order injustice than excessive index inequalities? Affirmative answers to these questions are made at least possible by my proposed amendment to the first principle. We can assume that basic social and economic needs are satisfied or would in any case have implementation priority over reforms of the education system.

The ultimate tenability of [3B] also depends on whether it can be plausibly extended to other areas in which the idea of fair equality of opportunity might be appropriate. I will discuss two such extensions.

15.5. Rawls takes the requirement of *formal* equality of opportunity to govern not only access to educational facilities but also access to jobs throughout the economic system: "Announcements of jobs and positions can be forbidden to contain statements which exclude applicants of certain designated ethnic and racial groups, or of either sex" (BLP 79). This formulation suggests the idea of constraining the difference principle by a requirement also of *fair* equality of employment opportunity.

One may think that no such requirement is necessary because fair equality of educational opportunity and formal equality of employment opportunity together entail fair equality of employment opportunity. But though it is perhaps true for inequalities of employment opportunity related to social contingencies, this entailment clearly fails for the other main kinds of contingencies. Handicapped by less marketable talents or bad luck, some of those willing to work may face long-term unemployment, even though they had (access to) a minimally adequate education and formal equality of employment opportunity is maintained.

Ranking fair access to employment above the index goods is not an implausible idea, given the special significance of such access for self-respect, for the realization and exercise of the two moral powers, and for a shared sense of equal citizenship. Those who are involuntarily unemployed for long periods tend to become a separate and disadvantaged social group whose disadvantage cannot be compensated by a better index position (by generous unemployment benefits, for example). This reason in favor of a requirement of *fair* equality of employment opportunity raises the question whether OP$_{3B}$ can be extended to include such a requirement. Here we might introduce a notion of *standard* participation in social cooperation (such as median number of hours worked in some life phase), with *minimally adequate* employment defined as some fraction of this standard.[24] OP$_{3B}$ would then require that social institutions must safeguard minimally adequate employment opportunities (access to minimally adequate employment) for all. Once again, the detailed specification of this requirement focuses on those who fall *below* the middle range and leaves some latitude so as not overly to constrain the difference principle and the political process. Thus it leaves the political process free to adjust the overall level of economic activity, subject only to the condition that such adjustments must not selectively impose severe hardships. Laws and policies may decrease jobs available in some profession with consequent short-term unemployment and may affect working hours (through annual vacations, a retirement age, or such like), but they must not produce significant long-term unemployment, except when this can be justified by appeal to the first principle or to other parts of the opportunity principle.

16. Medical Opportunities

16.1. Rawls simply leaves medical needs aside, apparently in the belief that the distribution of health care is of only marginal significance for the appraisal of a conception of justice (e.g., KCMT 546; SUPG 168). He seems far too sanguine in this respect, however. The fact of differential medical needs casts doubt upon a cardinal tenet of his conception of justice by posing a critical challenge to his semiconsequentialism. This is reason to look for a plausible Rawlsian response to the problem of medical needs.

By itself, the difference principle would justify inequalities in access to health care when these optimize the index position of the least advantaged. The difference principle might then favor a scheme under

---

[24]Again, the notion of adequacy must be enriched by the idea that some of the employment opportunities available to a person must be minimally appropriate to her interests and abilities, and again, it seems impossible to specify this notion of appropriateness in the abstract.

which access to medical care is used as an incentive or channeled to where it will most effectively enhance patients' economic productivity. Such a scheme violates central commitments of Rawls's conception of justice, however, for it palpably values the life and health of different participants unequally and thus undermines the self-respect of those having less access as well as the hope for a shared public notion of equal citizenship. These are strong reasons for believing that medical care, like education and employment, is special vis-à-vis the index goods and that the difference principle should not govern inequalities in access to health care by itself but should be constrained in this regard by some fair-equality requirement.

But how can such a requirement be part of the opportunity principle? How is access to health care an opportunity? Rawls seems to use the term *opportunity* restrictively, to refer to access to goods that are useful in the competition for the better jobs. Nevertheless, his emphasis on the highest- and higher-order interests and his concern for the least advantaged favor a broader understanding of the term. The first principle alone cannot fully secure our opportunity—fundamental to the spirit of Rawls's conception—to participate in human interaction, to form (and revise) a conception of the good in the context of the political, cultural, and associational life around us. Rawls should, therefore, see the importance of education at least as much in the fact that it enables one to understand, cherish, and participate in many diverse forms of human good as in the fact that it may give one a shot at occupying a leadership office. He should appreciate, similarly, that the importance of being employed consists not just in the chance to gather the skills and experience necessary to rise through the ranks but at least equally in the chance to collaborate with others and to share responsibility for the continuance of humankind. These considerations broaden the notion of opportunity sufficiently for it to cover access to medical care as well. This good is of great strategic importance; its distribution crucially affects persons' access to nearly all forms of human good—including, but by no means limited to, the better jobs.[25] Let us then explore whether another extension of OP_{3B} can yield a constraint upon the difference principle that copes with the problem of medical needs in a plausible way.

So extended, OP_{3B} would require, first of all, *formal* equality of medical opportunity. No group can be excluded wholesale from any available medical procedures, medications, and other health-relevant goods. There are three exceptions, analogous to those in the case of educational and job openings. The medical system may exlude wholesale from certain medical goods and services groups defined by their members' (1) inability or unwillingness to pay the access price, (2)

[25]See also Daniels, JHC 27–28, and chap. 3.

medical unsuitability (as when the procedure would be unnecessary or ineffective), or (3) age.[26]

16.2. What more does *fair* equality of medical opportunity require? In outlining my answer, I first make the simplifying assumption that medical needs occur *naturally*, that is, are due to factors beyond human control. Once a reasonably clear specification for this central case is on hand, it will be easier to fit in medical needs of other kinds.

While Rawls brackets the entire subject of medical needs, he is otherwise a thoroughgoing semiconsequentialist. He defines and compares relevant positions solely in terms of *social* primary goods, irrespective of natural differentials in endowments, needs, good looks, tastes, and desires. Now one may think that semiconsequentialism is clearly untenable for the assessment of a medical system. What must be fair, in this area, is the distribution not of health *care* but (roughly) of *health*, that is, the distribution of medical care relative to medical needs.

Contrary to this view, I will here provisionally preserve Rawls's semiconsequentialism also in respect to medical care, even though Rawls himself, of course, is not committed to its tenability in this area.[27] There are two main reasons for taking this approach. Denying semiconsequentialism in one area would have enormous repercussions for Rawls's conception of justice as a whole. Suppose an exception is made in respect to medical needs—a natural primary good plays a role in measuring distributive shares for purposes of assessing the justice of social institutions, and the social good of health care is used to compensate for differentials in this natural primary good. It would then be quite difficult to reject other exceptions in a principled way. If we take differences in persons' native medical needs into account in interpersonal comparisons, then why shouldn't we have regard to other congenital differences too? Once the original position is redescribed so that the parties care not merely about *social* positions (representative *shares*) but also about medical needs, then why would they not be concerned with the worst overall situation? Why would they not, in assessing the distribution of income, bear in mind that appealing clothes are more important for the ugly or instruments for those espe-

---

[26]Discrimination by age is acceptable, once again, because it does not differentially affect persons' *lifetime* shares of medical care. This account leaves open the questions I have raised about Rawls's account of formal equality of opportunity (§14.4): may other grounds (e.g., race, gender, religious or political affiliation) be used to some extent so long as doing so merely hampers some groups but does not exclude them altogether?

[27]In an aside Rawls once says that "disease and illness support claims to medicine and treatment" (WOS 14), but he may here be suggesting not claims of justice but claims of morality, correlative, perhaps, to our natural duty of mutual aid (cf. n. 32 herein). I want to read him in this way, because I find the semiconsequentialist element attractive and am interested in what it leads to. Still, I fully realize that Rawls may now be on the point of abandoning his semiconsequentialism by retreating to higher levels of abstraction on which he could altogether avoid taking a stand on this issue (cf. Chap 3, n. 11).

cially musical? Why wouldn't they, in assessing the distribution of education, also take account of the fact that some learn more slowly and thus need more education to acquire the same knowledge or skills?[28] Taking a fully consequentialist approach in one area would exert considerable pressures toward a fully consequentialist approach across the board, toward utilitarianism or a conception like Sen's.

The other main reason is that if medical care is to compensate for medical needs, then a just medical system would presumably have to maintain rough equality of result, which could be enormously expensive. If health is the good with respect to which fair equality of opportunity must be maintained, then—subject only to the proviso that sufficient resources be devoted to ensuring fully adequate packages of first-principle goods—any shortfalls from good health must be reduced as much as possible, no matter what the cost may be in terms of index goods.[29] This result, however, is implausible. If existing medical (and educational) systems are unjust, then this is not, it would seem, because some medical (or educational) needs remain unmet but because some have so much less access to medical care (and education) than others with comparable needs.

These reasons motivate my attempt to sketch a semiconsequentialist notion of fair equality of medical opportunity that fits with how OP_{3B} was specified in the areas of education and employment. As far as justice is concerned, medical need as such does not then support a valid claim to medical care. It is not an injustice, even in a very affluent society, if little is spent on health care (or education).

[28]This is a serious problem, I think, for the way Norman Daniels extends Rawls's opportunity principle to the institutional distribution of medical care. He affirms that medical care should be unequally distributed so as to compensate for "needs which are not equally distributed among individuals" (JHC 46). Yet he *denies* the analogue of this claim for education—health care must compensate for natural handicaps insofar as "disease and disability restrict an individual's opportunity relative to that portion of the normal range his skills and talents would have made available to him were he healthy" (JHC 34). But why even out *some* natural inequalities but not others? Consider two (groups of) persons whose opportunity ranges are similarly restricted, excluding them from worthwhile pursuits that they greatly value. In one case the restriction is due to congenital medical problems; in the other to a congenital lack of talent. In both cases the restriction can be overcome by expensive compensatory medical/educational programs. Why must the former programs be available but not the latter? It's not, I hope, because we intellectuals and composers of theories might be needing the former but hardly the latter.

[29]Daniels in fact draws this conclusion, requiring equal access *at least* to the "basic tier" of health-care services, comprising "services needed to maintain, restore, or compensate for normal species-typical functioning" (JHC 79). Besides various preventive programs, he requires institutions to "maintain persons in a way that is as close as possible to the idealization" and to provide "extended medical and social support services for . . . those who can in no way be brought closer to the idealization" (JHC 48). One may wonder whether any existing society can afford to make available to all its citizens *whatever* such restoring and compensatory services might bring them closer to species-typical functioning, irrespective of the cost-benefit ratio involved (cf. Fried, RW chap. 5). But my doubts concern the separate question whether a basic structure really *must*, as a matter of justice, embody so heavy an emphasis on health care.

16.3. In view of the great differences in natural constitutions, it would be bizarre to require that persons, over their lifetimes, should receive roughly equivalent bundles of health care. Such an equal distribution would waste resources on those lucky and robust enough not to need much medical attention at all, and it would also waste resources in cases where somewhat more than an equal bundle would be needed to make the difference. I propose instead that we conceive the social good that is to serve as the analogue to education and employment as *health protection*, defined as access to medical care *when needed*. The stipulation is that persons have an equal need to have, and to have the assurance that they will have, such access. OP_{3B} requires, then, that everyone should have access to roughly equivalent health protection. My interpretation and specification of this requirement will be guided by the idea that, as with education, overall allocations to the medical system should be governed by the political process as a matter of pure procedural justice, and that this method is plausible so long as rough equivalence in access to health protection is preserved.

It may seem that fair equality of access to health protection would in practice demand a considerable expansion of existing medical systems, which would constitute a grave risk to the index position of the least advantaged. But this can be avoided by utilizing two ideas already sketched in the context of education. First, needed medical care should be defined narrowly as care that directly alleviates an existing medical condition (which, by definition, impairs a person's capacity for normal participation in social interaction). This definition would exclude vacations in a health spa, first-class hospital beds, cosmetic surgery, and the like.[30]

Second, in assessing the distribution of health protection one should be concerned not with overall inequalities but with how far those at the very bottom fall below the middle range. The intuitive idea is, once again, that everyone should have access to some reasonably high proportion of what others actually have. No doubt, this idea can be implemented in many different ways, but I will here, somewhat arbitrarily, select one of these for purposes of illustration. I begin with a delimitation of the various natural medical conditions, each defined by reference only to medical factors (affecting the urgency or effectiveness of various treatments) and the age of the patient, without reference to the patient's race, gender, social status, and the like. We then find the cost of needed medical care that persons in various population clusters (defined by any statistically relevant parameters, such as income, race, gender, place of residence) tend to receive in the event of some particular medical condition. Defining a *medical history* as a lifetime combination of medical conditions, we can similarly find the cost of needed medical care that persons in various population clusters tend to re-

[30]Compare Daniels, JHC chap. 2.

ceive in the event of some particular medical history. We can then estimate a person's expected lifetime cost of needed medical care by averaging the cost of needed medical care that persons in his population cluster receive in the event of various medical histories. This is a weighted average based on (what one might call) "the average medical history," a realistic probability distribution over medical histories based on their relative frequencies in the relevant social system. The expected lifetime cost of needed medical care is higher for those who, for the same medical histories, would receive more or better care than others. Given the distribution of expected lifetime cost of needed medical care within the social system, we can define standard medical care in terms of some percentiles for expected lifetime cost and minimally adequate medical care as some fraction of standard medical care. Finally, we can define *minimally adequate health protection* as access to minimally adequate medical care. OP_{3B} requires that every participant be able to ensure that the expected lifetime cost of his needed medical care is at least X percent of the cost of standard medical care (that is, of the cost of medical care that the standard participant is expected to receive).

While the first of these two ideas limits the scope of OP_{3B}, the second ensures that it won't be (very) sensitive to the extravagant medical care that a few rich (or hypochondriacal) persons may secure for themselves or to the special medical care perhaps enjoyed by a few prominent individuals. (And there is then no reason to impose legal limits upon the health protection enjoyed at the very top, even if the first principle allowed such limitations.) Presumably, most existing societies do not secure access to minimally adequate health protection for all, and overall medical expenditure would undeniably increase if they did. But the necessary increase is quite limited. It is not required that everyone have access to health protection close to the very best enjoyed by anyone—which would be quite similar to the requirement, rejected earlier, that all medical needs must be met. The principle demands only that access to health protection be improved for those in the bottom quintile or so, to bring them up (or close) to the middle range (cf. Graph 2). It is this demand, in behalf of those whose access is much inferior to that of most, that is strongly supported by considerations of self-respect and equal citizenship. Because the proposed principle entails no more than this demand, the parties may give it implementation priority over the difference principle.

16.4. OP_{3B} is insensitive to *how* access to minimally adequate health protection is secured for all. Participants may have sufficient income and wealth so that all can purchase nearly as much medical care as the standard participant is in fact purchasing. Another possibility is a tax-funded medical system that provides minimally adequate health protection to all or at least to those who cannot afford it on their own. Alternatively, the requirement might also be satisfied through a competitive market for health insurance. In this case, if medical expenses are generally paid through insurance and if lifetime premiums are roughly proportional to expected lifetime medical expenses, then everyone would have to be able to afford some health insurance coverage costing at least X percent of standard health insurance coverage. If, for example, the cost of health insurance for the standard citizen (defined in terms of percentiles) is $2,000 per year, then everyone must be able to afford health insurance coverage costing at least (say) 75 percent of this amount, that is, $1,500 annually. In a just scheme of this sort, adults may still be at liberty not to insure themselves (so long as they *can afford* minimally adequate health insurance), just as they may normally forgo needed medical care to which they have access. The principle is formulated so as to require *access to* minimally adequate access to needed medical care, which is compatible with institutions under which persons have the option to decline on either level.[31] Obviously, the three possibilities I have sketched can be combined in various ways.

By focusing on overall health protection measured in terms of cost, OP_{3B} is also insensitive to *which* medical conditions one is protected against and to what extent. One may be able, through health insurance or personal funds, to meet all health-care expenses up to a certain ceiling, or one may have, through insurance or a publicly financed medical system, quantitatively unlimited protection that is confined to certain medical conditions or medical procedures. The political process can be left free to make decisions affecting these matters and also the overall allocation of resources to medical care. It will no doubt be guided by considerations of efficiency. It will ensure, for example, that medical care for each medical condition is accessible at least insofar as

---

[31]Thus, I think Charles Fried's proposal represents one plausible idea for how fair equality of medical opportunity could be maintained. Let incomes be fair, and let persons be free to purchase as much health insurance and as much medical care as they wish (RW 126–28). This proposal is, *pace* Daniels (JHC 20–21), quite unobjectionable, assuming, as is highly probable, that when the difference principle is satisfied (incomes are fair) the minimum income suffices to buy minimally adequate health protection. Further reducing income inequalities under such conditions would be irrational, because it would lower the minimum income (and the health insurance that can be purchased from it). But why should fair equality of medical opportunity be required at all if the difference principle is highly likely to secure the same end by itself? The answer is familiar from the defense of my amendment to the first principle. Incorporating a requirement of fair equality of access to health protection into the opportunity principle is probably superfluous in ideal theory. So the requirement's design priority over the difference principle is quite possibly insignificant. What must be secured—if health protection is indeed, like education and employment, special vis-à-vis the index goods (cf. Daniels, JHC chap. 1)—is the requirement's *implementation* priority. This priority entails that, when the difference principle is *not* satisfied, Rawls's criterion of justice will urgently demand institutional reforms ensuring that excessive inequalities in income do not, at least, engender excessive inequalities in access to health protection. This demand might support, for example, the institutionalization of something like the U.S. Medicaid program, which, as Fried suggests, may indeed be unnecessary within a just economic scheme.

its marginal cost is outweighed by its marginal benefits in terms of increased productivity, because such medical care will tend to raise all index positions. This desideratum would strongly support preventive measures in the areas of public hygiene, prophylaxis (vaccinations), and the like. But then [3B] also allows the political process to go far beyond what efficiency mandates by allocating a very large proportion of the social product to medical care at the expense of index goods.

Now some persons, at (almost) any level of health protection, will be unlucky enough to encounter a combination of medical conditions for which they cannot obtain the medical care they need. Indeed, some may even be born with medical problems that exceed any level of health protection they can afford. Such cases introduce radical inequalities in persons' quality of life. But, not being *social* inequalities, these are not, on a semiconsequentialist approach, viewed as indicating an injustice. Rather, they are *natural* inequalities for which, or for the eradication of which, social institutions bear no responsibility. Nevertheless, such natural inequalities are at least mitigated by defining the relevant social good so that it is sensitive to differentials in medical needs. Among persons with the same health protection, those with worse medical histories should receive more medical care—*up to a certain point*.

16.5. Insofar as medical conditions are unpredictably distributed (so that everyone faces roughly the same probability distribution over lifetime medical histories), the allocation of social resources among the various natural medical conditions poses no distributive problem. Suppose, for example, that minimally adequate health protection is provided through a state-sponsored medical system and is defined through a list of medical conditions for which specified treatment is universally available free of charge. Here drawing up the list of covered medical conditions, with corresponding treatments, can be left to the political process as a matter of pure procedural justice. When participants (and their elected representatives) are exposed to a roughly equal risk that they, or someone close to them, will develop any given medical condition, then the interests of those who will be afflicted with the condition are represented in everyone's deliberations, and the political process operates under (what one might call) a natural veil of ignorance. This is still plausible in the case of medical conditions that affect children in particular. Although those participating in the political process are not and never again will be children, one can take for granted that a large and permanent majority of them care for at least some members of the youngest generation, for example, their own descendants.

But then many natural medical conditions are not unpredictably distributed. There are medical conditions that only persons in certain determinate genetic categories have or are susceptible to. It is thus possible for the political process—dominated by a majority of persons certain that they (and their loved ones) will never suffer the medical condition in question—to define a state-sponsored package of minimally adequate health protection so that such conditions are excluded. It may seem promising to rule out this possibility through the requirement that minimally adequate health protection must be defined in terms of cost only, so that each person is to have access to health protection that secures access to *all kinds* of available medical care (for natural medical conditions) up to a certain overall cost. But this is at best a partial solution because the problem recurs in the allocation of social resources to various areas of medical research, which influences what medical procedures are available and at what price. Again, the political process may tend to allocate few, if any, resources to researching medical conditions that only affect genetically handicapped minorities.

On a semiconsequentialist approach we cannot criticize a medical system guided by such majority decisions as unjust even though it is unresponsive to the medical needs of such minorities. One may think that semiconsequentialism is therefore implausible here, but this is at least not obvious. Our hypothetical medical system would secure roughly equal health protection for natural medical conditions that everyone is roughly equally likely to have. If more is required on behalf of those who, through no fault of their own, are genetically handicapped, then why should not more be required also on behalf of those who, through no fault of their own, have run out of health protection? The fully consequentialist alternative approach involves the dubious view that an institutional scheme, rather than generate a fair distribution of benefits and burdens for its participants, should operate in a remedial way, should distribute benefits and burdens so as to balance things out among its participants for the sake of the overall fairness of the universe. Correlatively, the fully consequentialist alternative approach abandons the attractive idea that justice does not mandate very large allocations to the medical or education systems but requires only that these systems function in accordance with some plausible principle of fair equality of access.[32]

This way of dealing with medical conditions involving genetic predispositions may be radically transformed through contemporary ad-

---

[32]To say that *justice* demands no more is not to say that when persons have medical conditions for whose treatment they lack personal funds, health insurance, and other entitlements, they may just be cut off entirely from all (further) medical care. To do so would in many cases be a violation by the other participants of the natural duty of mutual aid (cf. Martin, RR 189–90). This duty can be discharged collectively through the political process by appropriating some resources for humanitarian care. The duty of mutual aid presumably does not mandate the provision of expensive long-term treatment and therefore cannot significantly affect overall allocations to an extensive medical system. The appropriations at issue would nevertheless slightly reduce the index position of the least advantaged. I think such reduction is permissible on the ground that the difference principle is subject to our collective natural duties.

vances in medical technology toward making genetic handicaps avoid-able. Once such technologies have come into wide use, a genetic handi-cap will reflect a social disadvantage (rather than a natural handicap). This scenario would suggest yet another extension of OP_{3B}, which I won't discuss—a requirement of roughly equal access to available procedures for ensuring the conception of children who are not genet-ically handicapped—which requirement might cover not only genetic handicaps relevant to health, but also those relevant to education and employment.[33]

16.6. So far we have at best a first approximation to the [3B] require-ment of fair equality of medical opportunity. We must yet consider medical conditions that are *socially produced*, that is, due to actions of and interactions among participants in the social system. Socially pro-duced medical conditions fall under the "benefits and burdens of social cooperation" (TJ 4–5), whose institutional distribution Rawls's criterion of justice is meant to govern. Such diseases and disabilities, unlike natural medical conditions, are part of the participants' shares and thus do play a role in identifying and evaluating the worst social position by reference to which an institutional scheme is to be as-sessed. I will argue that OP_{3B} should therefore require *full* health pro-tection against socially produced medical conditions.

Let us begin with socially produced medical conditions that are unpredictably distributed, diseases caused by general pollution, for example. One may think that these at least can be accommodated just like natural medical conditions. The circumstances causing them and the medical response to them can both be left to the political process as matters of pure procedural justice because everyone has a roughly equal chance of suffering the medical conditions in question. This argument fails for the reason I noted earlier in connection with the education system that randomly excludes 20 percent of all children (§15.2)—those actually afflicted with the medical condition, even if they are not identifiable in advance, suffer disadvantages that place them below the best minimum social institutions can secure. This would happen if, through obtaining medical care for a socially produced medical condition, their entitlements (personal funds, potential insur-ance benefits, or whatever) decline to a point at which they (or mem-bers of their family) fall below the best feasible minimum share of social primary goods. It might also happen if they simply could not obtain needed medical care for a socially produced medical condition. In

[33]One major problem here is to decide whose opportunities are at stake. To speak of the opportunity of a child to be born unhandicapped would raise questions of personal identity. If I had not been born genetically handicapped, then I would not have been born at all (but at best a sibling or corrected version of myself). So how can one say that *I* lacked a certain opportunity? To ascribe the opportunity to the parents would seem to permit them to decline the opportunity, in which case they could conceive genetically handi-capped children. For an interesting discussion of such complexities, see Ackerman, SJLS chap. 4.

such cases, the unlucky can validly complain that the institutional distribution of the benefits and burdens of social cooperation has left them at an excessive disadvantage vis-à-vis others. The same potential complaint shows that reasonable efforts must be made to produce the knowledge, facilities, and medications necessary to care for socially produced medical conditions.

So extended, OP_{3B} would require that needed medical care for socially produced medical conditions must be made available. Moreover, (the cost of) such medical care is not considered part of persons' shares for purposes of any other requirement of Rawls's criterion of justice. Persons must have a fully adequate package of first-principle goods, minimally adequate health protection for natural medical conditions, minimally adequate educational and employment opportunities, and a fair index position *apart from* whatever needed medical care they receive for socially produced medical conditions. Such care is viewed as mitigating or offsetting these medical conditions.

The cost of caring for socially produced medical problems may still be privatized, but only insofar as no shares of social primary goods are thereby reduced below the best feasible minimum. Perhaps it is preferable, however, not to privatize such costs at all. This way at least the measurable externalities of political decisions are fully internalized. The political decision about whether, to what extent, and on what terms pollution should be permitted is made on the understanding that the medical costs of pollution cannot be shifted off upon an unlucky few but must be imposed upon the polluting firms and households or else be borne by society at large—and similarly with medical costs arising from crimes and traffic accidents, whose incidence is affected by political decisions about police deployment and traffic regulations.[34]

Insofar as socially produced medical conditions are not unpredictably distributed, the same considerations apply, but they apply with greater stringency. While victims of unpredictably distributed medical conditions are (thanks to the natural veil of ignorance) adequately represented in the political process, this is not true of special risk groups (those living near a dam, factory, or power plant, for instance). This consideration provides another reason against imposing the costs of socially produced medical conditions upon their victims insofar as they can afford them.

---

[34]It does not matter, in my view, whether such effects of political decisions on socially produced medical conditions were foreseeable. If they were not, then imposing the resulting medical costs upon the (private) producers of harm may be impossible (as these costs exceed their assets and insurance coverage) and unreasonable (as they acted with due care and within legal constraints). It may also seem unreasonable to impose these costs upon the population at large, which, through the political process, adopted the relevant legal constraints. Still, the costs may not just be left where they fell, with the unlucky victims—at least not insofar as such victims cannot afford them without falling below the best feasible minimum share of social primary goods. Here justice requires a kind of strict liability, borne ultimately by society at large.

Moreover, the imposition of considerable medical risks upon small groups, even if the costs of treatment are fully covered, will often run afoul of the first principle. The political process need not be constrained to adopt laws and policies that reduce the rate of crime or of pollution-induced medical conditions as far as feasible. An institutional scheme under which higher rates are being allowed through the political process (treating crime/pollution victims may be cheaper than crime/pollution-prevention programs) may be just, so long as the basic right of all to the integrity of their person is still sufficiently well-protected. When the risks are concentrated upon small groups, however, this constraint will often not be satisfied. In some such cases, special risks may be reduced by offering risk groups full information about known dangers and help in relocating or otherwise protecting themselves. In other cases, proposed laws and policies may have to be abandoned altogether.[35]

OP_{3B} would then also require full health protection against socially produced medical conditions (modulo feasibly providable medical care). Unlike the requirement of minimally adequate health protection against natural medical conditions, this requirement will materially constrain the difference principle even in ideal theory by mandating the allocation of social resources to medical care at the expense of index goods. But this requirement is not implausible, for what it demands is not that independently existing social resources be diverted to medical care but that alternative regulations and policies be evaluated on the understanding that their (impact on) medical costs must be fully covered. If some social project, policy, or regulation is not, by and large, collectively beneficial enough to cover the cost of treating any (additional) medical conditions it engenders, then it should not be undertaken in the first place. The difference principle is then understood as governing only the *net* benefits of social cooperation, that is, its benefits minus its burdens. This reasoning is plausible because the higher minimum index position attainable in the absence of this requirement would be achieved at the expense of a group of medical

[35]May principles of justice, especially ones that require persons to have certain *inalienable* goods (§10.7), be revised by consent? May a population decide not to count certain socially produced risks as inconsistent with rights to personal integrity, decide to give certain socially produced medical conditions the lesser status of natural medical conditions? Even when circumstances conducive to informed consent obtain, such revisions must, I think, be rejected, if only on account of those who cannot consent (e.g., children) or who do not consent (being outvoted does not constitute consent). As regards medical care for socially produced medical conditions, these two groups could be accommodated. When the members of a car-loving society mutually release one another from responsibility for the medical costs arising from car traffic (thereby reducing gasoline taxes or insurance rates that would otherwise cover such costs), they can exempt children and nonconsenters (e.g., the poor who, besides being least likely to drive cars, are least able to cope on their own with socially produced medical conditions). But if such car enthusiasts dislike speed limits, drunk-driving laws, or unleaded gasoline, how can they shield children and nonconsenters from violations of their personal integrity?

victims of social cooperation whose social position, though it would look acceptable on paper, is eroded by medical costs imposed upon them by others (if indeed they are able to obtain adequate treatment at all). The burdens imposed upon such victims must be taken into account in any intuitively plausible criterion for identifying the least advantaged and evaluating their social position.

16.7. There are, finally, *self-caused* medical conditions, defined as ones that *foreseeably* arise from an agent's own *reasonably avoidable* conduct. I assume that [3B] places such diseases and disablities on a par with ordinary tastes and desires and thus counts demand for treatment of these medical conditions as on a par with demand for ordinary commodities and services.[36] Inequalities in access to treatment of, or health protection against, self-caused medical conditions are then governed not by the opportunity principle but by the difference principle. Thus the political process may not allocate funds to researching and treating lung diseases caused by smoking except insofar as such allocations pay for themselves (for example, through the improved productivity of treated smokers). This constraint precludes a majority of smokers from using the political process to impose medical costs arising from their habit upon society at large. Use of the political process in this way would give smokers an unfair advantage vis-à-vis nonsmokers and also vis-à-vis persons who choose to run other, less popular, special risks. Groups choosing to run special risks of incurring self-caused medical conditions are, then, in large part themselves responsible for arranging (or not arranging) the additional health protection they need. They may organize themselves to finance pertinent medical research, either on their own or through appeal to charity; they may work more or consume less so as to be able to afford insurance against or treatment of self-caused medical conditions; and so forth.[37]

16.8. On [3B], then, fair equality of medical opportunity requires minimally adequate health protection for natural medical conditions and full health protection for socially produced medical conditions. In view of the great difficulty of developing an even halfway satisfactory (principled and plausible) criterion for assessing institutional distributions of medical care, I find the implications of [3B] for this area theoretically and morally convincing enough to merit further exploration.

---

[36]Such medical conditions may still trigger our duty of mutual aid, though this duty is perhaps weaker here than in the case of natural medical conditions.

[37]Yet imposing in this way the responsibility for medical conditions caused by smoking upon the smokers themselves may well be unacceptable so long as adolescents face strong peer pressures toward smoking or information about the health hazards isn't widely disseminated. To count as self-caused, a medical condition must foreseeably result from conduct that is reasonably avoidable. Imposition of these two conditions (foreseeability and avoidability) provides useful incentives to the political process to ensure that they are satisfied, which in turn will tend to reduce such senseless health problems.

Here the question is, in particular, whether the distinction between natural, self-caused, and socially produced medical conditions can be made sufficiently precise to be able to cope with the tremendous complexities of the medical cases that actually arise. Though I cannot possibly discuss this question thoroughly, I will briefly indicate some of the complexities. I think these can be summarized under three main headings: first, it will sometimes be unclear how given causes of medical conditions should be classified; next, there arise problems about how to classify a given medical condition when several causes of different kinds combine to produce it (for example, some form of pollution that affects only persons with a certain genetic trait); last, ascertaining what caused a given medical condition also involves difficulties, compounded by the undesirable incentives toward cheating that a medical system structured in accordance with my proposal may provide. Let me offer a few remarks on the first two kinds of complexities in the hope of showing that at least a large range of ordinary medical conditions can straightforwardly and plausibly be classified in accordance with my proposed extension of OP_{3B} to health care.

Injuries from motor vehicle accidents will sometimes have a natural cause (such as a heart attack) but are normally either self-caused (negligence, drunkenness, etc.) or socially produced (when someone else is at fault). In the latter case, accident victims must be in a position to cover their medical costs without falling below the best feasible minimum share of social primary goods. This condition might best be met by imposing (excess) costs not upon society at large (including nondrivers) but primarily upon those causing accidents and secondarily upon all drivers (through mandatory insurance, gasoline taxes, or whatever). This way of internalizing medical costs is applicable to a wide range of activities and projects through which persons or associations create special health risks, from industrial facilities to firearms.[38]

Medical conditions suffered by victims of crimes are generally socially produced. Hence crime victims must be in a position to cover their medical costs without falling below the best feasible minimum share of social primary goods. It may be infeasible to impose such costs fully upon criminals, and they must then in part be borne by society at large. This result seems plausible in that it provides incentives to the political process to reduce crime rates even below what is required by the first principle. When costs are borne by all, the political process is more likely to extend adequate police protection to minority areas, say, because not doing so will also be expensive.

In exceptional cases, medical conditions caused by crime may be

[38]If the first principle is compatible with legislation creating a right to own firearms (which may depend upon statistical information about the marginal effect of such legislation upon rates of firearm related crimes and accidents), then the medical cost such a right engenders is best covered through taxes on gun ownership, fines imposed upon criminals, or strict liability by gun owners.

considered self-caused, namely, when the victim foreseeably placed himself in a high-risk situation. Such exceptions are likely to exist for almost all medical conditions with given natural or social causal components. Persons who know they are allergic to certain kinds of food can reasonably be held responsible for avoiding such food; pedestrians may reasonably be held responsible for staying clear of busy superhighways; and so forth.

Infection in the course of an epidemic such as AIDS would in general be considered to have a natural cause (assuming, of course, that the virus did not originate in some industrial or military experiment). But it may come about through causes of the other two kinds as well. When information about the disease is widespread, a case of AIDS contracted through a high-risk activity (reused hypodermic needles, unprotected intercourse) is presumably self-caused, at least when alternatives (clean needles, condoms) are readily available. And if the infection occurs in the course of medical treatment (blood transfusion) or through a crime (rape) it would be socially produced.

Occupational health problems, when arising from risks that are fully understood and consented to, are self-caused (and socially produced otherwise). It may seem, to the contrary, that occupational hazards should be minimized even if the cost of doing so is much greater than the savings due to reduced risk incentives. This view, however, is vulnerable to the charge of paternalism. If workers prefer the higher risks and higher incomes (part of which they can spend on additional health insurance) then why prohibit? This charge seems plausible at least in ideal theory, assuming that an institutional scheme satisfying Rawls's criterion of justice would provide the circumstances for genuine consent (especially by precluding dire poverty and long-term unemployment).[39]

16.9. My proposed version of the opportunity principle requires formal equality of educational, employment, and medical opportunity. It also requires that all participants have access to a minimally adequate education, to minimally adequate employment, and to minimally adequate health protection for natural and full medical care for socially produced medical conditions.

To conclude, let me restate the three principal objectives of this discussion. First, in specifying what I take to be the strongest tenable version of Rawls's opportunity principle, I hope to have provided a reasonably clear conceptual framework within which alternative speci-

---

[39]These remarks are compatible, I think, with a defense of the U.S. Occupational Safety and Health Administration requirement that medical conditions arising from toxic and other harmful materials at the workplace must be avoided "to the extent feasible" (see Daniels, JHC 144). At present such medical conditions can still count as socially produced on the grounds that workers are either not fully informed about relevant health risks or cannot reasonably avoid jobs imposing such risks (given the current extent of unemployment and poverty).

fications of the opportunity principle can be discussed. Such specifications may vary in strength in at least three dimensions: the opportunity principle may range over education and/or employment and/or health care; in any of these areas it may require either merely formal or fair (including formal) equality of opportunity; and any of its requirements may have either merely design priority or both design and implementation priority over the difference principle.[40]

Second, I have maintained that Rawls's notion of formal equality of opportunity is rather vague and that he offers no tenable specification of fair equality of opportunity at all. He seems now to favor a variant of [1A], requiring merely formal equality of (presumably educational and employment) opportunity. As an alternative, I have tried to outline a tenable specification of fair equality of opportunity. In doing so, I have, third, been concerned to defend a semiconsequentialist approach in areas where initially it would seem least plausible. Attainment of these last two objectives ultimately depends upon the practicability of [3B] and upon the availability of potentially superior alternatives.

17. The Difference Principle

17.1. Rawls's three principles differ not only in respect to the social primary goods they cover but also in the way they constrain the institutional distribution of these goods. First-principle goods are by and large defined in absolute terms.[41] They are definite protections of the basic needs of normal persons as Rawls conceives them. When some participants (avoidably) have a less than fully adequate package of these goods, then this is an injustice quite irrespective of what packages of these goods the others have.[42]

[40]Allowing mixtures, these three parameters permit at least 124 possible specifications (more, if different priorities may attach to the two components of fair equality of opportunity). Let F = fair (with formal), f = formal, 0 = the principle does not apply; and let P = design and implementation priority and p = design priority only. Then there are at least five possibilities in each area: FP, Fp, fP, fp, and 0. For three areas, this yields $5 \times 5 \times 5 = 125$ possibilities. Subtract one because if it applies in none of the three areas (0/0/0), the principle disappears. If the opportunity principle is one of either fair or formal equality of opportunity throughout and if it has design and implementation priority over the difference principle, then there are only $2 \times (2 \times 2 \times 2 - 1) = 14$ possibilities, ranging from the strongest principle requiring fair equality of educational, employment, and medical opportunity (F/F/F), to the three weakest principles requiring merely formal equality of opportunity in only one area (f/0/0). How strong an opportunity principle the parties would adopt depends to some extent upon general empirical information (available in the original position)—for example, about the marginal effects of alternative specifications upon the lowest index position.

[41]Though there are relative elements in the definition of some first-principle requirements, as with the *fair* value of the political liberties and the cultural variability in the notion of *standard* basic socioeconomic needs.

[42]This is not to deny that even if a requirement is formulated in clearly absolute terms, an inferior package may still be especially intolerable. It may be more damaging to self-respect (as when women are denied the vote under a scheme of universal male suffrage), and it may involve a competitive disadvantage (as when the adherents of some religions may not organize or advertise themselves while others are permitted to do so).

The second principle imposes two relative constraints upon the social and economic inequalities an institutional scheme may tend to generate. These constraints allow the political process to govern overall levels of education, health care, and economic activity,[43] so long as such political decisions affect roughly equally the opportunity and index positions of the various representative groups (the least advantaged in particular). Thus the opportunity principle is largely insensitive to whether persons have much access or little, requiring only that no one's opportunities fall significantly below the middle range. The difference principle imposes an even less definite relative constraint upon the institutional distribution of index goods. It requires that social institutions, insofar as they produce index inequalities, be structured so as to optimize the index position of the least advantaged. Here even the degree of inequality is left entirely open, to be determined, however, not by the political process but by empirical facts (for example, concerning the effectiveness of various incentives).

It has sometimes been overlooked that the difference principle entails no general demand to raise the index position of the least advantaged by all feasible means as far as possible—even by strip-mining national parks, by shortening lunch breaks, or through subliminal messages piped to work stations. It is only insofar as they generate social and economic *inequalities* that social institutions must be designed to optimize the index position of the least advantaged. The political process is allowed to govern, as matters of pure procedural justice, those other features of the institutional scheme that affect index positions roughly equally—such as restrictions on time worked, resource depletion, and pollution. These restrictions may be quite tight; to be just, a society need not be affluent or aim to be (cf. FG 545).

17.2. Before discussing this point further, let me make a few comments on the index. Rawls often discusses the difference principle in its simplest form, where it governs the institutional distribution of only income and wealth (SUPG 162–63). Here it is important for purposes of the index that shares of income and wealth be corrected for any expenses connected with the first and opportunity principles. Whatever entitlements persons have to minimally adequate educational opportunities or whatever funds they need to gain access to first-principle goods (including goods to meet their standard basic socioeconomic needs), for example, are not to be included in their income and wealth as evaluated under the difference principle. Persons cannot be said to enjoy fair equality of opportunity *and* a reasonable amount of disposable income, if in fact they face a choice between having only one *or* the other. This point is only marginally important when such higher-order expenses (for example, the cost of meeting one's standard socioeco-

---

[43]There are lower limits on these levels. There must be enough economic activity (with whatever education and health care this presupposes) to cover the costs of a just society, especially the costs of satisfying the first principle, and there must be enough education to ensure the proper functioning of legal and political institutions.

nomic needs) are roughly the same for everyone. But they may not be. There may be great differences, for instance, in the expenses persons incur for socially produced medical conditions.[44]

With regard to an ongoing economic scheme, the difference principle requires that institutional features affecting relative index positions (income tax rates, for example) should be designed, insofar as feasible, so that they, *ceteris paribus*, optimize the index position of the least advantaged in absolute terms. This requirement involves the assumption that in assessing institutional inequalities, persons (as represented in the original position) take an incommensurably greater interest in their *absolute* than in their *relative* index position. For the simplest case of income and wealth this assumption is quite clearly implausible. Some of "the good things in life" are positional goods. Access to them is scarce and therefore competitive. Whether I can own a secluded lakefront property, see a famous orchestra perform, show generosity toward friends and relations, or buy my children the toys owned by their peers, depends in part on how much money others can devote to these same purposes. If such positional goods are of some importance or if persons are susceptible to feelings of relative deprivation (or excusable envy), then it may be plausible to attach some commensurate importance to *relative* economic positions. To deflect such criticisms, Rawls can bring in the other two index goods—the residual social bases of self-respect (accommodating excusable envy) and powers and prerogatives of offices and positions of responsibility—which are, at least in large part, intrinsically positional (or constant-sum) goods and will therefore limit the sacrifice of relative for the sake of absolute income and wealth. But since Rawls says nothing about how these other two goods are to be specified and weighted within the index, I won't discuss this issue further.

It seems clear that the index must also include *leisure time* as a distinct social primary good. This good can be defined simply as the inverse of time worked, which is a burden of social cooperation.[45]

---

[44]Also, some persons raise more children than others and may then face additional higher-order expenses connected with this task. I believe, however, that such expenses may be, but do not have to be, fully subtracted from their index position. Especially in a context of overpopulation, it would not be unjust to assign to parents a primary responsibility for these expenses (provided birth-control information and devices are widely available and so on). In this case, the decision to have children would be treated like any other consumption decision. The difference principle would require only that index positions calculated *ex ante* (without taking child-raising expenses into account) must not fall below the best feasible minimum index position (also calculated *ex ante*). Of course, this responsibility may be assigned to parents only insofar as neither parents nor children suffer a shortfall of first-principle or opportunity-principle goods, which are always measured *ex post*.

[45]This was first proposed in Musgrave (MULT). Rawls, characteristically, responds that "if necessary the list of primary goods can in principle be expanded" (PRIG 257 n. 7). Jeffrey Reiman advocates an understanding of the difference principle on which it governs *only* work time. This proposal seems implausible, however. Not everything money can buy is produced by other persons' labor. Land is a very important salable

Leisure time must play a role in interpersonal comparisons through which the least advantaged within an existing social system are identified. Even though their annual or lifetime income is rather low, those who choose to do only a few hours of well-paid work each week cannot plausibly be considered less advantaged than others who work many more hours per week in a lower-paying job.[46]

Leisure time must be taken into account in interschemic comparisons as well. To see why, consider that one prominent way in which a relative reduction can lead to an absolute improvement in the lowest index position is through *incentives*. These may be used to improve the matching of persons to careers and also to elicit greater efforts from persons already committed to a certain career. To satisfy the difference principle, the resulting increases in productivity must suffice to finance the incentives *and also* to raise the index position of the least advantaged. The introduction of such incentives worsens the relative but improves the absolute index position of those who fail to win them. In the spirit of this Rawlsian idea, effective leisure-time incentives should be equally welcome. Promising an extra month of vacation to those willing to enter a certain profession or to those willing to make special efforts may enhance efficiency so that (holding production constant) everyone will gain a few extra vacation days. The desirability of this institutional change will register on Rawls's index only if leisure time is included.[47]

---

good in most societies, and offices have been sold or auctioned off in many. Moreover, different kinds of work often differ greatly—in being more or less prestigious, healthful, dirty, dangerous, interesting, tiring, and the like. Surely, such differences must be taken into account in assessing the justice of an economic scheme. If one accepts "time labored" or "effort expended" (Reiman, LTDP 143) as an interpersonally invariant measure for the burdens of social cooperation, however, then one is constrained to view as the appropriate equalitarian baseline a scheme under which hours of work are rewarded equally, whether the work is that of a gardener, miner, executive, or musician (cf. LTDP 143–44). Rawls provides at least the headings under which these complexities can be taken into account. The difference principle governs the institutional distribution not only of income and wealth (including what is obtainable therewith) but also of powers and prerogatives of offices and of positions of responsibility and of the (residual) social bases of self-respect. So Rawls leaves room for the plausible idea that persons' index position may differ merely because their jobs are differentially prestigious or demanding.

[46]This conforms to Rawls's suggestion that "twenty-four hours less a standard working day might be included in the index as leisure. Those who are unwilling to work would have a standard working day of extra leisure. . . . So those who surf all day off Malibu must find a way to support themselves and would not be entitled to public funds" (PRIG 257 n. 7). Unlike the other two index goods Rawls proposes, leisure time can be measured and made commensurable with income and wealth in a straightforward way. Here one idea is to define an exchange rate of income vs. work time by reference to the relevant social system's aggregate rate of productivity (the rate at which the population at large transforms work time into income and wealth). Though the details are complicated, this task is clearly manageable.

[47]A further reason for the inclusion of leisure time is that it can make the index sensitive to socially important but unpaid work. In assessing the economic position of parents, for example, one may take into account not merely their expenses in raising and educating children but also the time they spend on these activities. Whether such time is to be

17.3. With these rough ideas about the index, let us see how the difference principle may be applied. Graph 3 represents how the lowest (*absolute*) index position varies as a function of its *relative* status. This relative status can be given as a percentage of the mean (absolute) index position so that the leftmost vertical line represents 100 percent or perfect equality.[48]

In order to elucidate the force of the difference principle, as I propose to understand it, let me distinguish four ideal-typical kinds of institutional choices. First, there are choices that affect neither relative nor absolute index positions, for example, decisions about how the law specifies freedom of the press or regulates marriage and divorce. Insofar as such choices are not preempted by prior principles of justice, they can be governed by the political process as matters of pure procedural justice. The difference principle has no bearing on them.

Second, there are choices that—through their impact on available index goods overall—affect the vertical location of the curve. They do not affect relative index positions but result only in parallel transformations up or down. Of this kind are choices about limits on working hours and production (intended, perhaps, to conserve resources or to protect the environment), about allocations to and within the education and medical systems, about the rate of investment, about the production of public goods, and so on. The difference principle, governing only (institutional) index *inequalities*, does not constrain such choices at all. They, too, insofar as they are not preempted by the first and opportunity principles, can be left to the political process as matters of pure procedural justice. There is no significant risk of bias against the least advantaged because all representative index positions are affected roughly equally.

Third, there are choices of institutional features of the economic system that affect relative index positions, such as the choice of income tax rates. Such choices, representable as movements along the curve, are paradigmatically governed by the difference principle, which favors whatever unified solution to the issues of this kind would optimize the lowest index position in absolute terms.

The most difficult are institutional choices of the fourth kind, which affect the shape of the curve. Suppose, for example, that in a capitalist

---

counted as work will depend on contextual factors. If birth rates are high enough (/too high), raising children presumably need (/should) not be considered a contribution. But I suppose that in other circumstances it would not be unjust to recognize such time as a burden of social cooperation, a contribution to the reproduction of society. (In this case optimizing the lowest index position might require such measures as subsidized day-care services for large, poor families.) The inclusion of leisure time in the index provides a way in which such matters *can* be accommodated.

[48]The graph cannot show how changes in the relative status of other positions that leave the relative status of the lowest index position unchanged may also raise or lower the lowest index position. Rawls excludes this possibility by assuming that engendered index positions are close-knit (TJ 80–82), so that institutional changes affecting any one index position will affect every other index position as well, especially the lowest.

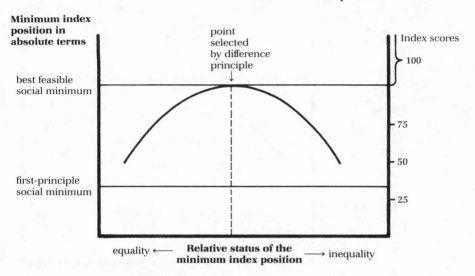

Graph 3. Lowest index position as a function of its relative status

economic system the minimum index position is highest when index inequalities are fairly large, while in a socialist economy the minimum index position is highest when index inequalities are less significant. Can the difference principle be brought to bear upon a choice of this kind?

For a comparative assessment to be meaningful, we must make strong *ceteris paribus* assumptions. The two schemes must not differ in the extent to which and manner in which they do and can satisfy the first and opportunity principles, and institutional choices of the second kind must also be the same as far as possible. Suppose these assumptions are satisfied. Does it then follow, in analogy to choices of the third kind, that Rawls's criterion of justice requires capitalism (in Graph 4) because it makes feasible a higher social minimum? Or may, in analogy to choices of the second kind, socialism be chosen through a democratic political process on the ground that the adverse effect of this choice upon the absolute index position of the least advantaged is no greater than its adverse effect upon the other representative index positions?

Rawls seems to prefer the latter answer: "The theory of justice does not by itself favor either form of regime" (TJ 280; also BLP 12 n. 13). But it is unclear what "by itself" is supposed to mean. Does his theory favor one form of regime once the empirical information contained in the graph is supplied? It seems not, for he continues: "Which system is best for a given people depends upon their circumstances, institutions, and historical traditions" (TJ 280, cf. 274). This statement suggests that Rawls wants the capitalism/socialism issue to be determined by the

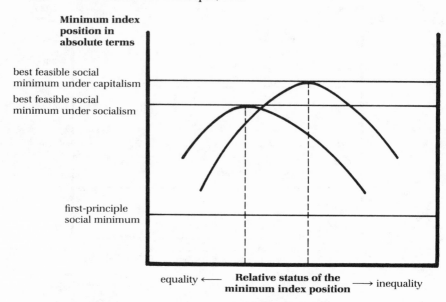

Graph 4. Minimum index positions under different economic systems

fictional parties to a "constitutional convention" (as he calls it), who "now know the relevant general facts about their society, that is, its natural circumstances and resources, its level of economic advance and political culture, and so on" (TJ 197). This idea of a gradual lifting of the veil of ignorance seems to arise from Rawls's tendency to think of the political process as exclusively an instance of imperfect procedural justice, a tendency from which I have departed. I find the idea of a hypothetical constitutional convention (and hypothetical legislature) unpalatable because it suggests that the participants must choose their constitution, laws, and policies, down to the minutest detail, in reference to what it would be rational to choose (by Rawls's standards) for the particular circumstances of their social system. These circumstances, traditions, etc., fix the "correct" political decisions, regardless of the participants' own concerns and preferences.[49]

My discussion of the political process (constitutional decisions included) suggests the idea that the participants of a social system may decide the capitalism/socialism issue democratically *in light of* their circumstances and historical traditions. Like choices of the second kind and unlike those of the third, this decision between socialism and capitalism is protected by the political liberties and therefore treated as a matter of pure procedural justice. This answer is of course still

[49]Rawls's gradual lifting of the veil of ignorance is not only motivated by the implausible ambition to let justice settle everything (cf. §13.2.3 herein) but also (and independently) constitutes an unnecessary shuffle—or so I have argued (Chap. 3, n. 42).

conditional upon the assumption (incorporated into Graph 4) that neither of the best feasible minimum index positions (under capitalism and socialism, respectively) is, *ceteris paribus*, worse than the other *both* in relative and in absolute terms.

My view agrees with Rawls in holding that the difference principle can settle the capitalism/socialism issue only in special cases. This result will be welcome in Part Three, for it promotes international stability by narrowing the grounds on which compelling another people to change their form of regime from capitalism to socialism or vice versa might be justified by appeal to Rawls's criterion of justice.[50]

17.4. These considerations indicate how an ideal economic system, presumably utilizing the market mechanism at least for purposes of resource allocation (cf. TJ 273), can be viewed as an instance of procedural justice whose ground rules are governed by Rawls's criterion of justice and by collective preferences as expressed through the political process. Such an economic system would embody an element of perfect procedural justice insofar as it, for example, reliably maintains fair equality of opportunity and ensures that everyone's standard basic socioeconomic needs are met. It embodies an element of imperfect procedural justice insofar as there will presumably always be some room for error about how to design the institutions that generate socioeconomic inequalities so as to optimize (*ceteris paribus*) the absolute index position of the least advantaged. And it embodies an element of pure procedural justice insofar as it regulates how individuals get "distributed" over the various index positions.

17.5. Let me conclude Part Two with a brief sketch of the interpersonal and interschemic comparisons involved in Rawls's criterion of justice (as I have developed it)—which comparisons serve, respectively, to identify the least advantaged group within each scheme and to compare the prospects of least advantaged groups that would exist under feasible alternative schemes.

Rawls defines the least advantaged in terms of index goods alone, making the ideal-theory assumption that the first and opportunity principles are fully satisfied. If his criterion is to guide the course of social change, however, then it must also rank feasible basic structures that do not satisfy this ideal-theory assumption. My attempt to extend the definition accordingly is based on the idea of specifying the size of the least advantaged group as an interschemically invariant percentage of total population.

Rawls proposes to define the least advantaged under the difference

[50]Such a justification could still appeal to the difference principle when, under the other form of regime, the minimum feasible index position would be, *ceteris paribus*, higher *both* in relative and in absolute terms. Or it might appeal to the first principle when the other form of regime is preferred by the participants themselves and would not violate the difference principle. A similar burden of proof must be met in the case of other choices concerning economic institutions (e.g., between income-tax and proportional-expenditure-tax schemes [cf. TJ 278–79]).

principle as "all those with the average income and wealth of [unskilled workers], or less," or as "all persons with less than half of the median income and wealth" (TJ 98). But, so defined, the least advantaged group may turn out to be very large or very small or even nonexistent. It is hardly rational to demand that institutional reforms should aim to improve the position of a fictional social group.[51]

Somewhat more promising is the idea of searching out whatever least advantaged representative groups, reasonably homogeneous but of varying sizes, would emerge under the feasible alternative institutional schemes. With this idea, as with Rawls's earlier definitions, however, interschemic comparisons involving a smaller and worse-positioned versus a larger but better-positioned least advantaged group become indeterminate.[52]

There is surely some arbitrariness in stipulating the size of least advantaged groups in advance, especially in the case of institutional schemes that would in fact produce a reasonably homogeneous "natural" underclass. But this is not a serious problem. The fraction to be chosen must fall within a certain range—must be large enough to appeal to the parties' interest that their criterion should issue in definite and significant demands for situations of injustice and must be small enough to appeal to the parties' interest to aim these demands specifically at improving the worst shares. Half a percent is too small and 60 percent too large, though both 4 percent and 20 percent may be arguable.[53] Fortunately, the precise fraction size (within the reasonable range) is not too important, because different stipulations would lead to the same or nearly the same practical demands. Institutional reforms devised to optimize the position of the least advantaged as defined will either have a strong tendency to improve the general

[51]More recently, Rawls has defined the least advantaged "very roughly" as those "persons whose family and class origins are more disadvantaged than others, whose endowments have permitted them to fare less well, and whose fortune and luck have been relatively less favorable" (WOS 11). Since "the relevant measures are based on social primary goods" (ibid.; cf. SUPG 164), this proposal supports the idea of defining the least advantaged as those with the lowest lifetime share of social primary goods and is at least compatible with my suggestion to delimit this group by some percentile (to be kept fixed for purposes of interschemic comparisons).

[52]This point is suggested by Scanlon (RTJ 195). One may think that on a contractarian view the size of a group should not matter, so long as it really is representative within "its" institutional scheme, but ignoring group size leads to paradox. Suppose we are comparing two basic structures under which the two least advantaged groups (defined as narrowly as possible while still preserving their representativeness) comprise 2 percent and 4 percent of population, respectively. The second group is very slightly better off. Still, we cannot presume that the parties would base their comparative assessment on this fact if it is reasonably obvious that the lower half of the second group, though not itself a "representative" group, is worse off than the first group. This consideration supports the idea of defining an interschemically invariant notion of representativeness.

[53]To some extent, the choice of a larger fraction size can be compensated by defining the group scores of the least advantaged in a way that is especially sensitive to the worst scores within this group. Thus one may use the *geometric* mean, for example, to aggregate individual scores within groups.

prospect of a smaller or invariably improve the general prospects of a larger actual underclass. The parties' interests are accommodated either way. Within the reasonable range, the proportion of the least advantaged to total population does then not matter very much, though it matters, of course, that this proportion be kept fixed for purposes of interschemic comparisons.

Once the relative size of the least advantaged group has been stipulated, the members of this group are identified through the staggered application of three measures corresponding to the lexically ordered account of social primary goods. We may represent each participant's share as an ordered triplet or *triscore*, $<X,Y,Z>$. Here X measures first-principle goods, Y opportunities, and Z index goods. All three scores are capped at 100.[54] The formula $X = 100$ represents a fully adequate package of basic rights and liberties; $Y = 100$ represents (taking the strongest version of OP_{3B}) formal equality of educational, employment, and medical opportunity, plus access to at least a minimally adequate education, minimally adequate employment, minimally adequate health protection for natural medical conditions, and full medical care for socially produced medical conditions; $Z = 100$ represents an index position that does not fall below the best feasible social minimum modulo institutional choices of the second and fourth kinds.[55] Z-scores—unlike X- and Y-scores—are inherently comparative in an interschemic sense. To score the index position of the least advantaged, we must be able to estimate how much better it could be under feasible alternative basic structures that differ only in their production of social and economic inequalities.

Once the social positions under some institutional scheme have been coded in this way, the resulting triscores can then be ordered like the words in a dictionary: X-scores lexically override Y-scores, which in turn lexically override Z-scores. The least advantaged are those in the tail portion (of the stipulated relative size) of this ordering. When the first principle is not satisfied, X-scores alone will often suffice. In that

---

[54]It is because they are capped that triscores do not represent what I have called shares or social positions. When two persons or groups have identical triscores, their shares may still be unequal. A Y-score or Z-score of 100 signifies only that opportunities are *no worse* than minimally adequate or, respectively, that an index position is *no worse* than the feasible minimum. In a perfectly just society socioeconomic positions might be quite unequal, while triscores would be uniform at $<100,100,100>$.

[55]Defined in this way, a just social minimum is not required to be much above what is necessary to meet standard basic socioeconomic needs. The level of affluence of a just social system is determined through individual and collective choices of its members, such as their leisure, savings, or consumption patterns or their environmental concerns. It is then possible that the index position of the least advantaged under a just basic structure ONE is much lower, in absolute terms, than the excessively low index position of the least advantaged under basic structure TWO. This is the case when the economic system of TWO, but not that of ONE, can be reorganized *in respect only to the index inequalities it tends to produce* in a way that raises the lowest index position (in absolute terms).

case the least advantaged are those whose package of basic rights and liberties—incomplete or ill protected—is least adequate. They may suffer excessive exposure to violent crime, be unable to meet their standard basic socioeconomic needs, be significantly disadvantaged as regards (the fair value of) basic political liberties, or suffer abridgments of their civil liberties.

The next step consists in aggregating the X-scores, the Y-scores, and the Z-scores of the least advantaged individuals. Here, I think, one can simply use the geometric (or arithmetic) mean to derive the lowest *representative* triscore, which is the primary measure for assessing the basic structure as a whole. Basic structures can then be ranked by their lowest representative triscores, just as shares within a basic structure were ordered on the basis of their triscores.[56]

To attain a perfectly just basic structure, we should then aim at institutional reforms that raise all representative triscores toward <100,100,100>. Here the course of social change is guided by two implementation priorities: the priority of the least advantaged (the worst triscore) and, secondarily, the priority of X-scores over Y-scores over Z-scores. Thus political efforts and social resources must be devoted first and foremost to improving the representative X-score of the least advantaged, followed by their Y-score and Z-score, which in turn are followed by the X-score, the Y-score, and the Z-score of the second least advantaged group, and so on.[57]

The discussion of Part Two has, I hope, made the Rawlsian criterion of justice clearer and more specific. Still, a great deal remains to be done before we can arrive at something like a workable notion of representative triscores that could really serve as a public criterion of social justice. One needs the size of representative groups and a clearer idea of intrapersonal aggregation of social primary goods. More important, the various basic rights and liberties must be defined more precisely, and weights must be assigned to various ways in which a package of basic rights may be incomplete or ill protected. My schema for understanding fair equality of opportunity must be further specified by sharpening the notions of education, employment, medical condition, standard, minimally adequate, socially produced, and so on. It must be sketched how "powers and prerogatives of offices and positions of responsibility" and the (residual) social bases of self-respect can be made commensurable with the other index goods, income/wealth and leisure time. These tasks are less philosophical than the ones I have here undertaken and would seem to require considerable expertise in

[56]Should lowest triscores be equal, the triscores of more advantaged representative groups may have to be brought in as tie breakers. Compare here Rawls's lexical difference principle (TJ 83).

[57]This formulation incorporates my proposal (§12.3) that the priority concern for the least advantaged group must override the lexical priority of the first over the second (and of the opportunity over the difference) principle, when these are understood as *implementation* priorities.

other fields. I hope this discussion has at least made clearer how such expertise might be employed. I also hope that my development of Rawls's criterion of justice has reached a level of specificity on which we can gain at least a reasonably precise idea of the institutional reforms that this criterion, as applied to a particular institutional scheme, would likely demand if it were fully spelled out.

PART THREE

GLOBALIZING THE RAWLSIAN CONCEPTION OF JUSTICE

CHAPTER 5

From Modus Vivendi
to Value Overlap

18. The Practical Importance of Justice

18.1. When a philosopher spends his life developing and refining an elaborate theory of justice, it may be interesting to ask about the importance of his work and about its author's view thereof. Insofar as Rawls writes for an academic audience, the answer is straightforward: he has shown how central strands of Kant's moral and political philosophy can be restated in a way that makes them independent of Kant's transcendental philosophy with its pervasive dualisms (WOS 18). He has made a contribution to moral theory, the comparative study of substantive moral conceptions, by bringing the neglected contractarian paradigm up to date.[1] He has surely achieved many other valuable things besides, such as developing new ideas for theory construction (model conceptions) and justification (reflective equilibrium). But my question here concerns the practical political message of Rawls's philosophy, which is concerned, he says, with the indefinite future, whereas the politician looks only "to the next election, the statesman to the next generation" (IOC 24). What is the moral import of his work for a wider readership of persons of good will who also have the indefinite future at heart?

Rawls's suggestions on this score go in two directions. Around the time of writing *A Theory of Justice* he emphasizes our "natural duty to remove any injustices" in existing institutions. His theory shows how

[1]"My aim is to present a conception of justice which generalizes and carries to a higher level of abstraction the familiar theory of the social contract as found, say, in Locke, Rousseau, and Kant" (TJ 11). "The main conceptions in the tradition of moral philosophy must be continually renewed . . . by noting the criticisms that are exchanged and by incorporating in each the advances of the others (IMT 22).

we are to identify "the most grievous" injustices in developed Western societies (TJ 246). Where such suggestions are at all concrete, they refer to the first principle and in particular to the fair value of the political liberties (TJ 226; BLP 74–79). Remarks on what needs to be done for the sake of the second principle are rare and cursory.

In his later writings, Rawls is more prone to emphasize the importance of his work for enhancing the legitimacy of our social institutions. He wants to develop a conception of justice that, through appeal to commonly held convictions, strengthens citizens' moral allegiance to their institutional scheme: "The real task [of political philosophy] is to discover and formulate the deeper bases of agreement which one hopes are embedded in common sense, or even to originate and fashion starting points for common understanding by expressing in a new form the convictions found in the historical tradition by connecting them with a wide range of people's considered convictions: those which stand up to critical reflection" (KCMT 518). Rawls calls this a "practical social task" (KCMT 519), but not in allusion to our political task to bring existing social institutions into line with the requirements of justice. Rather, he is expressing a view of the criteria for adequacy within political philosophy, which should not "search for moral truth" (KCMT 519) but seek a conception of justice that the present citizens of the United States find convincing. If "our history and the traditions embedded in our public life," "our disputes since, let's say, the Declaration of Independence," or "people's considered convictions" (KCMT 519, 518) were different, the real task of political philosophy would be correspondingly different as well.

Lest this thought be misunderstood, let me distinguish two senses in which a moral conception may be parochial. On the one hand, it may be parochial by basing itself upon the values and considered moral judgments prevalent in one society at a certain period. Rawls's conception of justice is self-consciously parochial in this sense. Its criterion of justice and the justification of this criterion are chosen for their supposed appeal to the reflective common sense of (primarily) present-day Americans. Rawls wants to have presented in a developed and idealized form the way thoughtful contemporary Americans would see the world, would assess their own past and present institutions and the institutions of other historical societies. This he sees as his practical social task. His conception fails if it does not appeal to the moral consciousness of his compatriots.

On the other hand, a moral conception may claim a limited domain. Thus it may view itself as applicable only to certain kinds of social systems under certain kinds of empirical circumstances, or embracing some version of cultural relativism, it may see itself as applying only within a certain culture and epoch, much like a set of rules of etiquette. Rawls's conception in *A Theory of Justice* is only slightly parochial in this sense. Though it is in some ways adaptable to various empirical and cultural conditions, it is nevertheless applicable to all essentially self-contained social systems existing under the circumstances of justice (TJ §22).[2]

On the view stressed in the later writings, the importance of Rawls's work consists then in finding a way of arranging prevalent considered judgments on all levels of generality into a unified and perspicuous whole, giving due weight to the values alive in this culture—to the liberty of the ancients and that of the moderns (TJ 201); to freedom, equality, and fraternity (TJ 105); to the ideas of Hobbes, Locke, Rousseau, Kant, and Sidgwick; to rational choice theory and the perspective *sub specie aeternitatis* (TJ 587). Here the principal task is to resolve "an impasse in our recent political history. . . . The requisite understanding of freedom and equality . . . , and the most suitable way to balance the claims of these notions, have not been expressed so as to meet general approval" (KCMT 517). If this impasse could be resolved, we would perhaps feel differently about some of our current institutions and change them, but it is primarily the hope for broad public consensus, and not for such changes, that lends urgency to Rawls's work.

Recently (JFPM; and esp. IOC), Rawls has tried to explain more fully why this justificatory task is so important. It matters that citizens have a *moral* (rather than a merely prudential) allegiance to the institutions of their society. The task of political philosophy is to develop a kernel of political morality that can be at the center of an overlapping consensus and hence can permanently resolve the fundamental assurance problem. Such a kernel of political morality must first and foremost settle what it is politically urgent to settle: how to choose now among feasible institutional alternatives. But stability requires that citizens should also agree in broad outline upon the ground of such settlements, that is, upon a criterion of justice. Such a criterion identifies and evaluates the morally salient properties and features of institutional schemes and thereby anticipates how such a scheme may and (especially) how it may *not* be adapted to changing circumstances. If such a shared political morality assures the various social groups that there will continue to be room for their particular values and way of life, then each such group can develop a moral allegiance to the basic institutions (as they are and will be), including a willingness to uphold these institutions

---

[2]I think this is how we must interpret Rawls's remarks that the original position represents a perspective *sub specie aeternitatis* (TJ 587) and that his conception of the person constitutes an Archimedean point (TJ 584, §41). He was not claiming to present a "universal theory . . . which people in different circumstances, particularly people in different cultures, would have equal reason to accept" (Pettit, TJ 311). Yet he was also not prepared to admit that the parochial basis of his theory limits its applicability to societies in which our dominant liberal paradigm prevails: "A theory of justice must work out from its own point of view how to treat those who dissent from it" (TJ 370), domestically as well as internationally. For this antirelativism, Rawls has been criticized by Gutmann (LE 169), among others, and it seems that he has now come around to Gutmann's view, for he has dramatically shrunk, since TJ, the domain of social systems to which he takes his conception to be applicable (cf. Chap. 6, n. 31).

even when it is able to change, subvert, or bypass them to its own rational advantage. Thus a shared political morality is a prerequisite for a widespread categorical sense of justice, which in turn is an important component of a well-ordered social system.

To some extent, the two views are harmonious and mutually reinforcing. Rawls's conception of justice is to provide a better understanding and appreciation of our values and their relation to one another. Such appreciation deepens the moral allegiance to our social institutions (insofar as they are just) and also guides and facilitates institutional reforms that can be shown to enhance the justice of our basic structure. And institutional reforms for the sake of justice tend to bolster moral allegiance to our values and institutions.

One may think that the practical political importance of this twin project is nevertheless quite limited. The political competition in the United States already takes place in the context of an overlapping consensus that assures the major interest groups that shifts in the political balance of power will not be exploited in an attempt to shift the very terms of the political competition against them. In fact, compared to other developed Western countries, so much has been taken off our political agenda (cf. IOC 14 n. 22) that one may be excused for finding American political debates positively dull.[3] Moreover, the emphasis on overlapping consensus limits the importance of attaining the kind of deeper philosophical agreement Rawls envisions in favor of agreement on just a criterion of justice. We need not agree on the merits of various doctrines by Kant and Sidgwick or on the meaning of freedom and equality but only "on the way basic social institutions should be arranged if they are to conform to the freedom and equality of citizens as moral persons" (KCMT 517). Again, it seems that U.S. citizens—sharing a rhetorical commitment to these values—already agree, by and large, that their basic institutions conform to those values.[4]

Still, Rawls might think it worthwhile to extend and deepen agreement on *how* and *why* they so conform, for such deeper agreement would make the consensus about institutions more resilient to changing circumstances. And he may, of course, want to extend the existing

[3]Rawls may disagree. At least he seriously considers (and then denies) the objection that "the idea of an overlapping consensus is utopian." Unfortunately he leaves this objection ambiguous—what is supposedly utopian is "either to bring about an overlapping consensus (when one does not exist), or to render one stable (should one exist)" (IOC 18). And his ensuing reply to the objection is so abstract that one can't tell what he thinks about the political life of the society that is the primary object of his reflections.

[4]This is not said to criticize Rawls. One can hardly fault his theory for the unexcitingness of its conclusions, if this is due to the fact that there is so little left to do for the sake of justice. I should add, though, that some would not view the narrowness of the American political debate as reflecting an overlapping consensus but would regard this debate as conducted and controlled by a small elite, who see to it that many significant issues never get on the political agenda in the first place. The lack of disagreement reflects resignation and consequent political apathy, not consensus.

overlapping consensus by incorporating into it some demands tradi-
tionally raised by segments of the Democratic party: the reform of legal
regulations governing the financing of election campaigns, increased
taxation on the inheritance of large estates, and improved educational
opportunities for children born into disadvantaged environments.[5]

18.2. This rather mainstream program of institutional reform becomes a little more definite and exciting if one thinks through the
deeper philosophical commitments of Rawls's conception. One may be
led, in reflecting upon the first principle, to look beyond the letter of the
constitution, important legislation, and Supreme Court decisions. A
high crime rate in urban ghettos may, for example, force the conclusion
that their residents lack a right (in the relevant sense) to personal
integrity. I have also argued that involuntary malnutrition and homelessness, when avoidable, must be considered injustices of the first
order of priority, and I have discussed other modifications, especially
in regard to how Rawls's conception should treat the unemployed, the
"worse endowed," and those suffering from socially produced medical
problems.

Yet all these matters pale in comparison to an inquiry of truly mo-
mentous urgency and importance. Suppose Rawls has correctly recon-
structed the criterion by which sincere and thoughtful Americans
would assess the justice of social institutions and the ideal of a well-
ordered society that they would affirm upon reflection. Then how
would such Americans reflect upon the justice of the prevailing *international* institutional scheme; what vision might they form of a well-
ordered *global* social system; and how would they evaluate U.S. foreign
policy insofar as it will have (and has had) any bearing on the structure
of global institutions? The third part of this essay is devoted to these
issues.

I proceed by discussing in reverse order the international analogues
of the two views of the importance of Rawls's work. Thus I explore in
the next chapter what the substance of Rawls's conception of justice

---

[5]Though Rawls has scrupulously avoided associating himself with any political party
in the United States, he tentatively and reluctantly suggests that in England his conception "has been seen as social democrat, and in some ways as labour" (PFE 1—draft:
"might be referred to"). In the same preface, Rawls usefully indicates his preference for
economic institutions that, as far as possible, maintain the requisite degree of economic
equality (as mandated by the difference principle and perhaps the fair value of the
political liberties) through an equalization of starting positions, rather than through a tax-
funded welfare scheme that continually counterbalances the centrifugal tendencies of
market forces. "Basic institutions must from the outset put into the hands of citizens
generally, and not only of a few, the productive means to be fully cooperating members of
a society. The emphasis falls on the steady dispersal over time of the ownership of capital
and resources by the laws of inheritance and bequest, on fair equality of opportunity
secured by provisions for education and training, and the like, as well as on institutions
that support the fair value of the political liberties. To see the full force of the difference
principle it should be taken in the context of property-owning democracy (or of a liberal
socialist regime) and not a welfare state" (PFE 6).

might imply for the assessment of the existing world order and of various possible efforts toward global institutional reform. But before looking at the content of such a conception of global justice, I try to show *that* (and why) we must achieve an overlapping consensus upon such a conception in the first place. So the present chapter argues for the great importance, and the possibility, of working toward an international community that is well-ordered, at least in the sense of sharing a kernel of political morality together with a categorical allegiance to it.

18.3. Let me begin by explaining how the ideal of a well-ordered world society differs from the (broadly Hobbesian) ideal of an effective world government, featuring central mechanisms of adjudication and, especially, enforcement. In the course of this explanation, I will try to support the hypothesis that the absence of world government is *not* the central problem with our current global order, so lacking in peace and justice.

The conventional question of whether there should be a world government is misleading. By presenting the issue in stark either/or terms, it reflects a deep and historically influential mistake. The traditional form of this mistake might be called the dogma of absolute sovereignty, the belief that a *juridical state* (as distinct from a lawless state of nature) presupposes an authority of last resort. This view arises (in Hobbes and Kant, for example) roughly as follows. A juridical state, by definition, involves a recognized decision mechanism that uniquely resolves any dispute. This mechanism requires some *active authority* because a mere written or unwritten code (a holy scripture, set of legal documents, or whatever) cannot settle disputes about its own interpretation. A limited or divided authority would not do, however, since conflicts might arise over the precise location of the limit or division. There must then exist one ultimate, supreme, and unlimited authority if civil peace is to be possible at all.[6]

This dazzling reasoning is now safely buried beneath the historical facts of the past two hundred years, which show conclusively that what cannot work in theory works quite well in practice. Law-governed societies are possible without a supreme and unlimited authority. There is, it is true, the possibility of *ultimate* conflicts, of disputes in which even the legally correct method of resolution is contested. One need only imagine how a constitutional democracy's three branches of government might engage in an all-out power struggle, each going to the very brink of what, on its understanding, it is constitutionally authorized to do. From a theoretical point of view, this possibility shows that we are not insured against constitutional crises, and thus

---

[6]This dogma—prefigured in Aquinas, Dante, Marsilius, and Bodin—is most fully stated in Hobbes's *Leviathan*, chaps. 14, 26, 29. For Kant's statements of it, see KPW 75, 81, 144–45. The dogma maintained its hold well into the twentieth century, when it declined together with the Austinian conception of jurisprudence. Cf. Marshall, PSC pt. 1; Benn and Peters, SPDS chaps. 3, 12; and Hart CL.

live in permanent danger of them. But this danger no longer undermines our confidence in a genuine division of powers. We have learned
that such crises need not be frequent or irresolvable. From a practical
point of view, we know that constitutional democracies can endure,
can ensure a robust juridical state.[7]

Now all this is hardly seriously in dispute. What is perhaps not
generally understood is that the same point applies on the "vertical"
axis as well. Just as it is nonsense to suppose that (in a juridical state)
sovereignty must rest with one of the branches of government, it is
similarly nonsensical to think that in a federalist scheme sovereignty
"must" rest either on the federal level or with the member states.
Making this assumption, one is bound to conclude that it must rest on
the federal level, for if it rested with the states, then there wouldn't be a
federalist scheme at all. But then the assumption is philosophically
unsound, descriptively inaccurate of existing federalist constitutions,[8]
and (as I will show) politically disastrous for the prospects of world
peace and global justice.

18.4. Once we dispense with the traditional concept of sovereignty
and leave behind the silly all-or-nothing debates about world government, there emerges a clear preference for an intermediate solution,
which provides for some central organs of world government, though
organs that lack any ultimate sovereign power or authority. It is just
such an intermediate solution, of course, that we have now, in the form
of some international law with some mechanisms of adjudication and
enforcement (such as the International Court of Justice and the United
Nations Security Council).

Admittedly, these existing institutions have not exactly been successful, and one may well claim that their failure, even by their own
standards, must be explained by the weakness of existing mechanisms
of adjudication and enforcement, that the violence and injustice per-
vading our world result from there being *not enough* world government.

Proponents of this view can use the weakness of international adjudication mechanisms to explain the pervasive ambiguity and vagueness of international law. So long as only a small fraction of intergovernmental disputes are ever settled impartially, there will be a dearth of
authoritative precedents, and major disagreements about the inter-

---

[7]Quite apart from the (anachronistic) historical objection raised in the text, I also
believe that the argument for absolute sovereignty is theoretically flawed and should
never have been taken so seriously. Even the most unified scheme of supreme authority
involving a monarchical sovereign does not provide a complete decision mechanism. It is
still *possible* for disputes to arise about whether this is the king or an impostor, whether
yesterday's king has transferred authority or is dead (or insane), or if he is dead, who his
successor is. A "logically" complete decision mechanism is a mirage. If that were what it
takes, then we could not in principle transcend the state of nature.

[8]The U.S. Supreme Court, for example, is *not* empowered to review the application of
state law.

pretation of international laws and treaties will persist unresolved. Moreover, so long as governments can presume that, in all likelihood, they will be able to avoid an authoritative rebuke, they will be tempted to put forward surprising (and even ludicrous) interpretations of international laws and treaties in justification of their conduct.

Similarly, one can use the weakness of international enforcement mechanisms to explain disregard of (and cynicism about) international law. So long as international laws and treaties are rarely enforced for their own sake, governments will be tempted to violate, abrogate, or reinterpret them if the net benefit of doing so is considerable. This tendency will affect even governments strongly committed to the ideal of a law-governed world order. Without assurances that other governments will fulfill their international obligations, they cannot find it either responsible or morally requisite that they alone should make major unilateral sacrifices for the sake of law.

Though there is some truth in such (essentially Hobbesian) accounts, I do not think they get to the heart of the problem. Our global institutional order is shaped by intergovernmental agreements and, more important, by government practice and acquiescence—all of which are based on prudential deliberations informed by the current distribution of power. In such an environment, statesmen and citizens are left without a *moral* reason for wanting their state to support this order, which is seen as merely the crystallization of the momentary balance of power. I would like to explore the possibility that this fact about international institutions, if it animates the dominant attitude toward them, is the cardinal obstacle blocking moral progress in international affairs. In suggesting this hypothesis as an alternative to Hobbesian accounts, I don't mean to imply that stronger prudential restraints wouldn't be a good thing, only that they will be difficult to establish without changing this dominant attitude. My hope is then that the analysis of the next section, if it could be fully worked out, would offer a deeper understanding of our predicament, including an explanation of why progress toward more effective central mechanisms of adjudication and enforcement has been so elusive.[9]

19. International Relations as a Modus Vivendi

19.1. In providing a basic analysis of the fundamental assurance problem as it arises in international relations, my objective is twofold: I want to suggest a partial explanation of what is plainly morally objectionable in the present international order, and I want to show, partly

[9]The analysis to be sketched is intended to fit with the contrast Rawls develops (in IOC) between two models of institutionalized coexistence. I do not claim, however, that Rawls has thought about or would approve my extension of this contrast to international relations.

on the basis of this explanation, why it is of such critical importance to achieve a global order that embodies shared values.

In the Hobbesian dimension of progress, a first step beyond un-limited and universal war is an element of coordinated self-restraint. Two parties (persons, tribes, states, or whatever) understand that each of them is restraining itself in some way in order to elicit some recipro-cal self-restraint from the other side. Such a mutual understanding need not be explicit, nor does it require any value commitments. Mu-tual assurance can rest entirely upon each party's appreciation that the other party—given its interests, capabilities, and situation—would be irrational to destroy the arrangement.[10]

The Hobbesian *ideal* is an extension of this model. Peace is to be achieved by inaugurating a mode of coexistence that, once in place, perpetuates itself by ensuring that each party has sufficient incentives to participate so long as most others are participating as well. Presum-ably, large-scale arrangements of this sort are too complex to be tacit, but no matter how complex, the model is supposed to work without shared values. Each party's continued participation is to be assured by the plain fact that it would be foolish to quit.

When the relations among parties center around (tacit or explicit) agreements along this Hobbesian axis—from the most narrow, fragile, and transitory bilateral understandings to the most comprehensive, robust, and enduring universal accord—we can characterize their co-existence as a *modus vivendi*. Let me develop this idea a little in the abstract.

The participants in a modus vivendi are primarily motivated by their own self-defined interests and do not much care about one another's interests as such. Yet each has reason to support a shared institutional scheme—that is, a system of rules and conventions, practices and procedures, organs and offices—that accommodates the interests of other parties to the point were they find it in their best interest to participate as well. On the surface, a modus vivendi is then an agree-ment among a plurality of parties to restrain their competitive behavior in certain ways. Since the scheme is to be designed so that continued participation is in each party's best interest, the terms of the scheme must satisfy the condition of *prudential equilibrium*, that is, must be such that all parties have reason to participate on the going terms.

Whether a given party, P, views the going terms as acceptable, how-ever, depends upon a number of *variables*, such as P's self-defined interests and, most important, the general distribution of power (which affects P's vulnerabilities and opportunity costs of participation). Which terms satisfy the prudential equilibrium condition is then sub-ject to fluctuation. Suppose, for example, that P's power has increased, so that P now has more to gain and less to lose from a (partial) break-

---

[10]For a more elaborate account, see Hobbes, *Leviathan* chaps. 13, 17.

down of orderly relations. It may then be prudent for P to press for more favorable terms, and other groups will prudently accede to P's demand, weakened groups being obliged to accept less favorable terms because of their increased vulnerability or decreased threat advantage. If a modus vivendi is to endure, the distribution of benefits and burdens may then have to be adjusted so that participation continues to be each party's rationally preferred option. This possibility generates, below the surface, a competition over the *terms* of the modus vivendi, and *this* competition is not restrained at all. There is no limit to how weak a party may become through shifts in the distribution of power (compounded by shifts in the terms of the modus vivendi), and there is no limit to what a weak party may prudently acquiesce in within a modus vivendi, in preference to quitting.

Contrary to this conclusion, it may seem that there *is* a limit to such shifts. The terms of a modus vivendi must at least be mutually advantageous in the sense that each party derives a net benefit from participation as compared to total isolation. But this is not so. How well off a party would be in splendid isolation is irrelevant to the bargaining equilibrium if this party cannot secure such isolation for itself. Even when accepting tributary status in a modus vivendi is clearly less attractive than isolation, it may still be the prudent thing to do when the expected alternative is not isolation but attack and enslavement, for example.[11]

19.2. The great virtue of a modus vivendi is that it can work, can prevent all-out war, even among parties who have no faith in one another and believe they have nothing in common by way of shared values. In order to assure one another's continued compliance, the parties need only continually adjust the ground rules governing their interactions so that participation and compliance continue to be each party's preferred option. In a non-constant-sum world, orderly coexistence is possible even without shared values and mutual trust.

Nevertheless, precisely this virtue, which makes the modus vivendi model so wonderful a remedy against war, renders it unsuitable for achieving peace and justice. On the one hand, the indefinite malleability of its terms is needful to a modus vivendi's endurance through changes in the power, interests, and situation of its participants. Yet, on the other hand, this malleability is a source of instability and great danger. A modus vivendi can persist through such changes only if its participants can, at each time, agree on terms appropriately reflecting the current distribution of power. Moreover, the long-term malleability of a modus vivendi engenders short-term instability; each participant must be afraid of getting into a vicious cycle in which its decline in

---

[11] I am here implicitly rejecting David Gauthier's conclusion that self-interested parties would find it rational to honor his version of the Lockean proviso (MA chap. 7, sect. 5). His argument for this conclusion seems to me plainly mistaken, though I cannot show this here.

power reinforces and is reinforced by a deterioration in the terms of its participation. If it anticipates such a trend, it may prefer to fight now rather than await a further decline in its power. Or if others suspect that this might be its evaluation, they may find it prudent to preempt by attacking it first. Such disturbances can lead to a partial or complete breakdown of ordered relations. And even if the modus vivendi survives, some of its participants may not (or may see their freedom and values destroyed). There is no lasting protection against even the very worst outcomes.

Therefore, values, however deeply held, will have only a marginal impact upon the participants' conduct and (through this) upon the terms of the modus vivendi. Since the parties are fearful of one another, each will give precedence to its survival and to the long-term security of its values over their short-term instantiation. No party is likely to impose serious ethical constraints upon its pursuit of power through which alone it can hope to *survive* and (ultimately) *prevail*. And each will want to prevail so as to eradicate the threat from others, who must be suspected of wanting to prevail for just this reason.

Let me illustrate each party's reasoning with a hypothetical train of thought: Others may be seeking to shift the balance of power against us, which, in the long run, might enable them to eradicate us or our values altogether. We cannot eliminate this danger for the time being. Thus our best counterstrategy for now consists in trying, within a modus-vivendi framework, to stem any advances on their part and to weaken their position. Since this is a matter of survival, we must not constrain these efforts by our values, for if we do, we will be competing at a disadvantage. They will certainly not constrain their conduct by our values, and since they are fearful (and perhaps bent upon prevailing), they are unlikely to constrain it even by their own values. In this situation, we must not endanger our survival and that of our values by allowing these values to hamper our efforts to block and neutralize the threat from others.

I conclude that relations within a modus vivendi will be neither peaceful nor just. The long-term dangers to which a modus vivendi exposes its participants are boundless and permanent, demanding their persistent and utmost vigilance; the competition over the distribution of power and over the terms of association will be ferocious. Moreover, even if the parties to a modus vivendi have deep and sincere value commitments, it is likely that their values will not have a significant impact upon their external conduct, will not figure prominently in their decisions about compliance or in their efforts to shape the terms of the scheme. Since each participant cares primarily for its relative position, the terms of a modus vivendi will essentially reflect a dynamic bargaining equilibrium which—based upon the participants' power and strategic interests—is largely detached from any values they may have. The inconstant terms of a modus vivendi are likely over time to violate *any* ethical conception (unless the belief in "the right of the stronger" counts as one such conception).

19.3. Let me try to bring these abstract observations to bear upon international relations. Here the explanatory part of my account centers around two hypotheses: current international relations are in essence a modus vivendi, and the chief reason why international institutions are so much less successful than the institutions of well-established national societies is that the latter enshrine shared values (and not that they include more central government).

In applying the modus-vivendi model to international relations, I take for granted a global background convention. The land of the world is divided up into clearly demarcated territories. Each territory has one government, the person or group wielding overwhelming power (ultimately, controlling irresistible means of coercion) within the territory, and each government is recognized by others as having full jurisdiction over all persons and resources within its domain. Given this background convention, the actors shaping international institutions are, first and foremost, *governments*, and my hypothesis postulates then an *intergovernmental* modus vivendi.

My first hypothesis can now be stated, more specifically, as follows. Governments are engaged in a competition that is regulated by whatever institutions the main adversaries find it advantageous to agree upon or to acquiesce in from time to time. Yet they also see their rivalry, on a deeper level, as *unlimited*. No society's values, institutions, or way of life are beyond the threat of violent subversion by existing enemies outside the national territory. At bottom, international relations are a struggle to the death. That they are provides at least a partial explanation of the absence of peace and justice in the world today, an explanation that, in particular, need make no reference to the *content* of the values affirmed by the competing governments. I cannot here provide the detailed political analysis that might defend my first hypothesis but must settle for a brief illustrative outline.

19.3.1. The modus-vivendi analysis of the status quo explains the absence of genuine peace by viewing us as trapped in a vicious cycle. The very fact that governments fear and distrust one another gives them good reason for such fear and distrust. There are no realistic prospects of establishing peace through a world state, because no national government can come to rule the world without a global war, and the strongest governments won't allow the creation of independent effective mechanisms of adjudication and enforcement. Given their averseness to risk (their greater concern for surviving than for prevailing), it would be irrational to accept powerful organs of world government, which, although designed to curb each government's power, could affect its security in either direction. This is true in a world of competing interests, and it is even more true in a world of disparate values, in which each government must fear that central organs may come to be dominated by those who believe that its domestic institutions and national form of life *ought* to be eradicated.[12]

Weaker governments, of course, may want central mechanisms of adjudication and enforcement and may be forced to submit unilaterally to such mechanisms, but the strongest ones cannot be forced and will not submit. The strongest governments may agree to *dependent* central mechanisms, which require unanimity or lack enforcement power of their own, but such mechanisms will not be *effective*, because they are impotent in regard to the principal problem. They cannot bring the competition among the major powers firmly under the rule of law. To see why, consider a modus vivendi whose five strongest participants are authorized to adjudicate any dispute by simple majority vote,[13] and suppose the distribution of power is such that any three are actually strong enough to enforce their judgment even against a coalition including the other two. Here each of the five must—and will know that the others must—try to join a dominant coalition, if only from fear that such a coalition would otherwise form against itself. Far from affording long-term security, this sort of arrangement is merely another version of the ferocious competition to the death, with the five principals bargaining over one another's support in the attempt to be part of a dominant coalition.

19.3.2. Governments generally will not honor individual provisions of an ongoing modus vivendi when the net benefit of noncompliance is substantial, and they understand and expect as much of one another. Since mutual trust and other assurances of future compliance (through effective mechanisms of adjudication and enforcement) are lacking, each government must assume that others may "reinterpret," violate, renegotiate, or abrogate international laws and treaties when they perceive this to be in their best interest (taking account of loss of others' self-restraint toward oneself, propaganda and credibility costs, etc.). Given this assumption about others, it will itself act in this fashion. Doing so seems both permissible and necessary. It seems *permissible* because international laws and treaties reflect only self-interested bargaining (have no inherent ethical standing) and because most other governments take the same attitude and surely do not rely on one another's good faith. It seems *necessary* because a government that allows itself to be seriously hampered by imprudent respect for the official rules of the game runs a grave risk of being taken advantage of by others and thereby endangers the long-term survival of itself and its values.

---

[12]Hobbes clearly appreciated how disparity of values, even more than competing material interests, may block acceptance of a central supreme authority. Vast stretches of the *Leviathan* (in parts 3 and 4) are devoted to showing through scriptural exegesis that good Christians ought to accept and obey the sovereign even when he commands acts and observances they consider blasphemous.

[13]One might think here of a strengthened version of the United Nations Security Council.

This dominant attitude engenders wars as governments exploit perceived opportunities to gain through (illegal) aggression, through preempting supposedly impending (illegal) aggressions, or through punishing supposed violations of international laws or treaties. The ground rules of an intergovernmental modus vivendi can therefore furnish only weak prudential restraints upon government conduct. Their infringement or abrogation is considerably more likely than significant violations of domestic ground rules, which are backed by shared ultimate values (and more effective sanctions).[14]

Moreover, this attitude fosters a permanent climate of tension and insecurity, as governments must always reckon with noncompliance by others and thus can never take full advantage of the freedom of action they might have if adherence to international laws and treaties could be taken for granted. No declaration of neutrality, peace treaty, mutual-defense alliance, or nonaggression pact, for example, can relieve a government of the fear of finding itself alone in the face of a foreign military attack.[15]

19.3.3. The enduring climate of insecurity and hostility is aggravated by two additional tendencies. First, the (bargaining) power of governments within a modus-vivendi framework is mainly a function of the distribution of *military* strength (roughly, the comparative unacceptability of war), with *economic* strength playing an important—partly subsidiary, partly independent—role. Any government whose military strength is greater than its economic strength (each relative to other governments) enjoys increased bargaining power during periods of heightened tension because of the greater importance of military (in comparison to economic) strength. A period of crisis, for example, makes it easier for a military giant to exact concessions from an economically strong but militarily weak ally. Of course, governments whose relative economic strength is greater than their relative military strength may much prefer a more relaxed global environment, but their

[14]The dominant attitude of governments toward international laws and treaties is then, on my hypothesis, like the prevalent domestic attitude toward parking regulations: international agreements are treated as moralized rules in government rhetoric, but as unmoralized rules in government conduct. It is generally thought acceptable that decisions about compliance should be based on a self-interested calculation of (probability-weighted) costs and benefits. This claim is evidently compatible with the fact that many treaties (covering copyrights, patents, postal cooperation, and such like) are rarely or never violated. In these matters the strains of commitment are minimal, and weak prudential restraints are therefore fully sufficient. (Moreover, these treaties would seem to be too marginal in any case to qualify as being part of the global basic structure.)

[15]Even while it is understood that any government will break any international law or treaty when the net benefit of doing so is substantial, such ground rules can still have great value. They serve to coordinate expectations and to make certain future events less likely and less frequent. In this role international laws and treaties help keep the ongoing modus vivendi in equilibrium. I should add that I am here addressing the current *global* institutional framework. In some local contexts, such as Western Europe, international relations are beginning to acquire a value-based character.

preference is of little moment insofar as it is very much easier to augment than to reduce international tension.

Second, the tendency toward tension is further strengthened by each government's interest in increasing its support from its own population, which will enhance its international bargaining power. Vilifying opponents and inducing crises is one method of increasing domestic support, exploiting the predictable tendency of populations "to rally around the flag" in response to a heightened sense of insecurity. Obviously, a government may be tempted to employ such methods in the interest of less patriotic purposes as well—to improve its chances for reelection perhaps, or to consolidate its position at home. Though the motives for fueling such crises arise domestically, the *opportunity* to do so depends on the hostility endemic to current international relations.

19.3.4. In a modus vivendi among hostile powers, the pressures toward strategic (amoral) government conduct are overwhelming. Even if some statesman sees himself as committed to his nation's values and as competing with others (partly) *in behalf of* these values, he cannot allow himself to be seriously hampered by these values in the competition. He must leave such values behind when he enters the foreign-policy arena, where surviving and prevailing ("national security") take precedence over all else. Thus values are unlikely to play much of a genuine (as opposed to a propagandistic) role in the conduct of foreign policy and in the emergence of international institutions (through explicit or tacit bargaining).

This account explains, on the one hand, the prevailing disregard for the poorest and strategically least significant societies and regions. No government will show much unilateral concern for foreigners, for such concern tends to weaken its own bargaining position. Moreover, governments are unlikely to agree to incorporate such concern into the shared institutional scheme—being risk-averse, each will be reluctant to accept even a distribution of burdens that seems to weaken itself no more than it weakens its relevant competitors.

On the other hand, this account also explains two prominent aspects of the terms of an intergovernmental modus vivendi: First, these terms tend to embody little concern for how persons are treated within their own society. Each government's interest in controlling some particular matter within its own territory normally vastly outweighs its interest in influencing how the same matter is dealt with abroad. Perhaps the value commitments on all sides would favor clear, internationally supervised rules against government abuse, but since it is unpredictable how such rules would affect the balance of power, risk-averse players are unlikely to create effective, independent mechanisms for the authoritative application of such rules. Nor will they make unilateral sacrifices for human needs and welfare. Under the exigencies of competition, governments must be extremely concerned with their own and their allies' international (bargaining) power, which depends to a significant extent upon their strength at home. They may then have to use—and support their allies when they use[16]—repressive measures (such as secrecy, disinformation, surveillance, infiltration, intimidation, and worse) to stifle domestic dissent and to maximize domestic control.[17]

Second, the terms of an intergovernmental modus vivendi are likely to include an understanding that each great power has special claims to regions that are geographically or economically more important to its security than to that of any other great power. Within its sphere of influence ("hemisphere"), a great power may operate without serious interference from other great powers. It may force weak states to change their government or political system; to "request" or accept its military bases and advisers (even invasion); to open their doors for its exports, its credits, and its acquisition of their resources and productive facilities; and so forth. Such an understanding is, again, mutually advantageous for risk-averse players.

19.4. This concludes my outline of how some of the less appealing features of our contemporary world might be explainable, in part, in terms of tendencies endemic to an intergovernmental modus-vivendi framework. Even if these tendencies are not always strong or dominant, they do add up to a firm expectation regarding a global order that primarily reflects the common interests of, and bargains among, deeply hostile governments: So long as this order persists, our world will be pervaded by violence (and the threat and danger of violence), political repression, and extreme poverty of strategically worthless populations. This is not to deny that values sometimes do have a real impact upon foreign policy and upon international institutions (over and above their propagandistic employment to justify self-interested conduct). It is enough that the systemic explanation is approximately true, that the current mode of coexistence is essentially a modus vivendi, that it engenders roughly the tendencies I have outlined, and that these tendencies account for a good deal of current human misery.

And this misery is significant. Up to one-fifth of humankind spend their entire lives in poverty and on the edge of starvation—politically impotent, malnourished, and without reserves for the event of even a minor natural or social misfortune. Millions of children die every year from malnutrition and easily curable diseases—the vast majority of them under everyday conditions in the midst of plenty rather than in

[16]One may be obliged to support brutal allies when they might otherwise damage one's position by becoming less tractable or by switching sides. Some of the world's worst tyrants have been quite adept at expoiting this fact.

[17]These methods, as well, governments will be tempted to employ in the interest of less patriotic, purely domestic purposes, and again, their opportunity to do so depends on the hostility and insecurity endemic to current international relations.

well-publicized famines. Simultaneously, roughly a trillion dollars are spent annually on "defense" worldwide, on attempts to shift or preserve the existing distribution of power. Through this preoccupation, further millions of persons are trapped in wars, civil wars, and campaigns of repression and insurrection (often incited and abetted by third parties), with their methodical massacres, destroyed homes and livelihoods, organized starvation, torture, rapes, and disappearances.

Such horrors are too pervasive to be explained, ultimately, by reference to powerful actors who have perverse values or none at all. Rather, I submit, they are in large part engendered by the reigning modus-vivendi framework, within which the fear for one's security and that of one's values is paramount. This is not to deny that a good number of powerful actors are evil, but we cannot, I think, explain the prominence and success of such actors without reference to the current intergovernmental modus vivendi, in which they have an excellent chance to receive recognition and support in the name of some national interest, and in which concerted action against them is highly unlikely.

20. A Value-Based World Order

20.1. If the analysis of current international relations as an intergovernmental modus vivendi could be successfully completed, it would provide a systemic explanation of the sordid realities just sketched. Now it might be thought that such an explanation tends to condone prevalent government conduct, and thus lets statesmen off the hook too easily. But this need not be so. For suppose there is another kind of institutional scheme, feasible on a global scale, that would not engender the violence and injustice endemic to our modus-vivendi framework. Then the account I have sketched would merely reconceive the political task and responsibilities. We must transcend the prevailing modus vivendi and aim to establish that superior form of institutional scheme.

We have seen how the modus-vivendi model contrasts, on the one hand, with the total absence of restraints, as in a state of unlimited war (though a modus vivendi is surely compatible with limited violence, excluding certain times, targets, or methods in warfare). I will now explore how this model contrasts, on the other hand, with another conception of mutual accommodation—envisaging another way for a shared institutional scheme to emerge and be sustained even while its participants have divergent interests and values.

The central idea is to seek institutions that are based not upon free bargaining informed by the changeable distribution of power but upon some values that are genuinely shared. Such shared values do not exist if all participants seek security or if each wants its religion or form of regime to survive or to prevail in the end, for they may still differ about *whose* security or *which* religion (form of regime) they care for. Nor can we speak of shared values when the parties have a common interest—in peace, for example—that is *instrumental* to their disparate deeper commitments and projects. They are then not committed to peace as such. Each merely, for its own reasons, prefers peace under current conditions. So their coexistence is still a modus vivendi, because they do not share one another's ultimate values, which in a different context might lead them to war. An institutional scheme is value-based only if its participants hold in common some important *ultimate* values (including some principles for balancing or ordering them) that are significantly embodied in the institutions regulating their interactions.

20.2. It may seem that such reliance on shared values presupposes a shared value system, such as Catholicism in the Middle Ages, and that in a world of diverse fundamental outlooks appeal to values can only be divisive. But this objection is based upon a false dichotomy. We need not envision for the world what is lacking in every national society, namely, a *comprehensive* agreement on values (cf. IOC 14–15). Instead, we can start from what we already have, a world in which *some* values are shared. Our primary predicament is not that there is no value overlap, or even that there is too little, but that even those core values that are widely shared play too marginal a role in the design of international institutions and in the conduct of foreign policy (including the prevailing attitudes toward existing international agreements).

Moreover, shared values need not be all-pervasive. In a national society resources may be allocated to the highest bidder, and many legislative issues may be decided by self-interested bargaining (logrolling and so on). Still, in a well-governed society *some* matters are nonnegotiable—for example, that none will be slaves or be left to starve and, in particular, that the basic terms of the political competition may not be shifted against those whose strength declines. These matters are protected not by an enduring majority *preference* but by the citizens' sense of justice, which here supersedes their particular interests. In the international arena, by contrast, the dominant assumption—and wellgrounded fear—is that *everything* is negotiable, that any law, treaty, charter, or declaration may be "reinterpreted," violated, renegotiated, abrogated, abandoned, or simply forgotten.

The progress I envision begins, then, from some consensus on values, however narrow, that allows the establishment of institutional fixed points that stand above ordinary negotiation and bargaining and thus are immune to shifts in the power, interests, and opportunities of the major parties. The foremost prerequisite of such a transformation is that societies should accept—*morally* rather than only prudentially (as a vexing necessity imposed by the present distribution of power)—the continued existence of one another and of the values central to their domestic social contracts. Beyond this prerequisite, the prospects for a value-based institutional scheme will depend upon what, concretely, their values and attitudes are, and upon the following three conditions. First, the parties are convinced that there *ought to be* a scheme that through a fair distribution of benefits and burdens accommodates all of them to the point where each can make a sincere and reliable commitment that will withstand tempting opportunities as well as shifts in relative power and self-defined interests. Second, the parties can identify and perhaps extend some common values—a starting point for a shared conception of justice, for example, or some mutually valued institutional reforms. Third, the parties are willing for the sake of what is itself a valued goal to modify their values to some extent. Here the pivotal question is whether they can see their way to embracing an institutional scheme that is more tolerant of some broader range of diverse values than each would have liked, and tolerant enough to guarantee that the (similarly modified) values of others can, in their essentials, survive forever.

If such a transition succeeds, the typical participant may well come to value the resulting order in its own right rather than continue to wish for less tolerant institutions built upon its own values alone. The commitment to a mutually acceptable scheme would then further deepen as a consequence of the transition itself (through the experience of mutual trust and cooperation), while the overlap of genuinely shared values expands. This, at least, would be the favored outcome of the transition.

20.3. The hope that there could spread a shared preference for a heterogeneous world, including capitalist and socialist democracies, over the global imposition of one's own form of regime may sound utopian. That it *can* happen is shown, however, by historical experience—for example, by how relations among the Christian faiths developed after the Protestant Reformation (cf. IOC 18). From decades of bloody warfare emerged a modus vivendi. Though neither side gave up its goal to reunify the church on its own terms, both sides realized that they were for now unable to impose such a reunification and thus accepted a fragile bargain in preference to continued warfare. Since power was held by autocratic princes on both sides, the bargain struck, not surprisingly, reflected their *common* interests: *cuius regio eius religio*, each lord may force his religion upon his subjects without outside interference.[18] Still, this temporary convenience was gradually transformed into a genuinely shared value commitment with quite a different content, religious toleration with deference to the individual's freedom of thought and conscience. No authority whatever may enforce religious beliefs. This *moral* conviction is now at the very core of Western political thought, whether academic or popular, and is widely taken for granted among members of the relevant denominations.

---

[18]This settlement parallels the two last-mentioned aspects of the intergovernmental modus vivendi (§19.3.4).

The decisive condition for an analogous transformation in our current world is, I believe, widespread acceptance of what one might call *international pluralism*, the idea that knowledgeable and intelligent persons of good will may reasonably favor different forms of (national) social organization. There are two main grounds for wanting this idea as a shared basis from which to work toward a better world.

20.3.1. The first is realism. Attaining a world of peace and justice *requires* widespread acceptance of international pluralism, at least if the more violent avenues of progress ("prevailing over the other side") are morally excluded. It is a minimal demand upon political ideal theory that it develop an ideal of a *future* world, that is, of a world that is connectible to the status quo by a morally admissible route (one that does not pass through World War III, for example). This demand is not met by an ideal that envisions the abolition of capitalist states or socialist states or both. A useful contribution to the political task at hand, to overcoming violence and starvation, just *cannot* consist in arguing that all national societies must conform to the writer's favored social ideal.[19]

In fact, such arguments *contribute* to our predicament, our imprisonment in an intergovernmental modus vivendi. Today, powerful factions in each of several major societies are committed to the belief that their form of regime is plainly superior to that of some opposing societies and that it would not be wrong in principle to destroy the opponents' domestic institutions by force (so as to liberate the people they oppress). There is, in fact, some eagerness to "turn around" regimes on the other side because they, too, may recognize no ultimate restraints against "liberating" a system of our type and are liable to do so when they can in order to remove threats to *their* long-term survival. But then, under the present distribution of power, neither side can be confident to survive an all-out attempt to liberate the societies on the other side. And this military stalemate among the superpowers is, and is widely understood to be, the vital condition for continued coexistence. Neither side believes that were it significantly weaker, its values would be allowed to survive. Rather, each side must assume and will take its opponents to assume that the other side stands ready to use any means at all, including global war, even for its secondary goal of prevailing, so long as its preeminent goal of survival is not significantly endangered thereby.

The essential *fragility* of this status quo is clear from its complex

---

[19]There are countless advocates of homogeneous worlds in the socialist tradition, typically disagreeing quite warmly over the correct brand of socialism that ought to be globalized. But homogeneity has its capitalist advocates as well. Thus Michael Doyle wants a world of "liberal" states, defined as democracies with "market and private property economies" (KLL 212, cf. 208). Doyle shows how the number of capitalist democracies has increased over the past two centuries and extrapolates that all states will be "liberal" by the year 2113 (KLL 352). The worthy political scientist neglects to calculate an analogous projection based on the proliferation of *socialist* states, which, by the same argument, are similarly destined to cover the world.

preconditions. At least the great powers (know one another to) care much more for their own regime's survival than for the eradication of opposing regimes. They are risk-averse, in part because the status quo is, for now, quite satisfying to them. Moreover, these governments have and know one another to have rational prudence and a cool appreciation of the current distribution of power. Finally, the dominant governments also are, and know one another to be, convinced that this distribution (the bargaining equilibrium) is not about to shift dramatically against any one of them in the medium term (which would make that power a likely aggressor and a likely target for preemption). We have no right or reason to hope that these fortunate conditions will last forever. And while there is every reason to welcome the existing intergovernmental mode of coexistence insofar as it *postpones* global war, we must use the time to work for institutional reforms that will bring *peace.*

Widespread acceptance of the idea of international pluralism would make possible a world in which certain value clusters, with their coordinate national forms of regime, are *morally* accepted and permanently protected against violent extinction. Once societies know of one another that they sincerely accept the continued existence of one another's national constitutions, then it becomes reasonable to order one's preferences concerning a shared *global* institutional scheme by considering how well various alternatives reflect one's values, rather than by how they affect the capacity of one's society and values to survive and prevail in a ferocious competition.[20] Thus international pluralism enables a shared institutional scheme based not upon a fickle power equilibrium but upon a firm core of values. If such a scheme can be established, then it is much more reasonable to comply with its terms, even when noncompliance would yield a net benefit, because the scheme better reflects one's own values and because the long-term survival of one's society and form of regime is no longer at stake.

The realist argument for accepting international pluralism has at bottom an ethical character. It appeals to those who, concerned about the long-term danger of global war, reject the option of fighting it out. It also appeals to those who are willing to revise their vision of a just global order to the point where it can be implemented, rather than insist on an "ideal" vision that will exist only on paper in a world pervaded by violence and injustice. On the realist argument it is, then, for the sake of our values themselves that we should modify these values in the direction of greater tolerance (cf. §9.4.4).

---

[20]This is the next best thing to a piece of "perfect technology of justice" that would make it permanently impossible for values to be altered or extinguished by force (cf. Ackerman, SJLS esp. 82). Note that such an analogue to a perfect technology of justice would not only make it impossible to destroy the values others hold; it would also cancel the most important reason for wanting to do so in the first place—the fear that *they* may seek to destroy *our* values.

20.3.2. The second ground for accepting the idea of pluralism is its plausibility. In fact, the idea is robustly plausible, in that it can be accepted for various and even incompatible reasons. It accommodates those who, though convinced they know what a just and humane society would look like, realize that they cannot establish the superiority of their ideal from shared premises. It accommodates those who doubt that they can now (or that anyone can ever) be reasonably certain to have found *the* best way of organizing a human society. It accommodates those who believe that the best social world would contain a variety of forms of national organization. It accommodates those who are convinced that different institutional ideals may be appropriate to societies that differ in natural environment and level of development. And it accommodates those who think that each national community must be left free (within broad limits) to work out its own constitution in light of its history and culture, which it alone is able and entitled to interpret and to extend into the future. No doubt, some of these reasons can be combined, and new ones could be added to the list, but perhaps these five are enough to show that international pluralism is plausible—and more plausible than its opposite, the claim that someone is in possession of a complete blueprint for a just and humane society whose superior merits could be denied only by the morally corrupt and the dim-witted.

Of course, I am not claiming that one may reasonably favor *any* form of social organization. On the contrary, it is *not* reasonable to advocate, say, slavery, colonialism, apartheid, or autocracy. So the idea of pluralism that should be widely shared is by no means tantamount to a general agnosticism with regard to the justice of national institutions. What is needed is the recognition that knowledgeable and intelligent persons of good will may reasonably disagree about the fundamental issues dividing the world today. For example, should the means of production be controlled by national governments, or locally by workers or by private owners? Is the best forum for democratic discussion and decision making afforded by a single-party, two-party, or multiparty system? Which is more important in the appraisal and reform of social institutions, the protection of civil and political liberties or the satisfaction of basic social and economic needs? If only we could understand our disagreements about such matters as *reasonable* disagreements, then we could jointly work toward a world in which alternative answers to these questions could coexist in a peaceful, friendly, and supportive international environment. Insofar as we see attempts to realize national institutional ideals different from our own as neither evil nor deluded (and need not fear from them violence against our domestic values and institutions) we have no good reason to resist such attempts. We could come to respect and even to learn from the variety of national regimes existing beyond our borders. At least the mere fact that the people of another society live under social institutions different from those we favor gives us no ground at all to interfere in their affairs.

20.4. It will certainly be said that there is very good reason for rejecting international pluralism. The reason is our historical experience with the adherents of those other values, which includes an abundance of horrendous crimes committed or supported by them. Even a cursory glance at the opponents' record of military aggression, economic exploitation, or political repression, it is said, should convince any reasonable person that either their values are intolerable or their professed commitment to these values is nothing but a cynical exercise in bad faith. Hence we must not compromise our values to the point of accepting their right to exist, for to do so would amount to a wholesale betrayal of our most venerable commitments.

But the fact that our historical experience supports such an argument against one or both main forms of regime—and I will not deny this—does not show that any acceptable global order would have to exclude regimes of this sort. What our historical experience shows is how capitalist and socialist governments design global institutions and how they behave (within and outside their borders) *in the context of a modus-vivendi framework*. This may teach us very little about how capitalist and socialist governments would design global institutions and how they would interact if surviving and prevailing were no longer at issue. Let us at least entertain the thought that the horrors of this world are not, or at least not primarily, the horrors of capitalism and/or socialism per se but the horrors of an inconstant modus vivendi among deeply hostile governments, each fearing the eventual destruction of its values.

This thought balances the tragically self-perpetuating character of the existing modus-vivendi framework with a corresponding reason for *optimism*. Just as a climate of mutual fear and distrust makes it more rational to fear others and distrust them, so a climate of mutual trust and confidence would make it more rational to have trust and confidence in others. Small increases in the mutual assurance afforded by firm value-based institutional fixed points would lead to much greater increases in overall mutual assurance.[21] Being caught in a circle of fear and distrust does not show that the parties are inherently untrustwor-

---

[21]This multiplier effect can be illustrated as follows: A thinks that B is less inclined to seek to destroy A's values; hence A has less reason to fear that B may try to destroy A's values; hence A has less reason to seek to destroy B's values; hence B has less reason to fear that A may try to destroy B's values; hence B has less reason to seek to destroy A's values; hence A has even less reason to fear that B may try to destroy A's values. And so forth. In discussing the prospects for moral progress of the human race, Kant writes that even while its success is not assured, the French Revolution "has aroused in the hearts and desires of all spectators who are not themselves caught up in it a *sympathy* which borders almost on enthusiasm, although the very utterance of this sympathy was fraught with danger" (KPW 182). Perhaps this has a parallel in our time in the sympathy, however skeptical, evoked by the impulses that have recently been emanating from the Soviet Union.

thy or that their values are intrinsically so irreconcilably opposed that institutions based on value overlap are out of the question. Rather, their untrustworthiness is, quite predictably, engendered by the situation they perceive themselves to be in (and therefore really *are* in), a situation in which each participant is preoccupied with ensuring that its values will survive and prevail.

Whether a value-based global order is attainable and what it might look like are, I think, still open questions. It has never yet been tried, for existing agreements are, and are understood to be, based upon strategic bargaining. While the participants in a modus vivendi often *use* appeal to values (to justify their own conduct or to condemn the conduct of opponents), they do not engage one another in a serious ethical discourse about the institutions that ideally *ought* to regulate their interactions.

20.5. So on my view as well, governments and statesmen bear a special responsibility for the injustice and (actual and imminent) violence permeating our world today. Yet I see them as primarily responsible not vis-à-vis an existing global order, which they all too often violate, but vis-à-vis a possible future order, which they lack the will and vision to help bring about. This is the ultimate crime against peace and justice because it perpetuates the modus-vivendi character of international relations, which is incompatible with genuine peace and with justice however conceived.[22]

This crime is especially serious because it would not be so hard to make progress. I am envisioning nothing extravagant, only the gradual establishment, one by one, of firm value-based institutional fixed points that stand above ordinary negotiation and bargaining and are immune to shifts in the power, interests, and opportunities of governments. Even institutions that once began as negotiated bargains could slowly and undramatically develop into such fixed points. This could happen through the gradually escalating willingness on the part of different

[22]My primary emphasis here is on governmental efforts toward institutional reform rather than on government conduct within an ongoing institutional scheme. Thus, I am not urging a unilaterally "moralistic" as opposed to a "realistic" foreign policy (in Hans Morgenthau's sense). Rather, my point is that within a modus-vivendi framework, foreign policy will always be realistic in substance (though it may, in addition, be moralistic in rhetoric). If we want to see our values embedded in international institutions and in our government's conduct of foreign affairs, then we must transcend the modus-vivendi framework, within which the concern with the surviving and prevailing of national constitutions is paramount. In the absence of perfect technologies, this requires a shared sense of tolerance and an effort to base global institutions upon an overlap in ultimate values rather than upon the shifting balance of bargaining power among parties that consider themselves to have nothing ultimate in common. Still, achieving such a transition may require that states take some moral steps on their own, which must, at least in the beginning, be acceptable from a prudential standpoint. Here a state might, for example, unilaterally signal its willingness to contribute to the transition to a value-based order by designing foreign policies that (without endangering its own survival and security) demonstrate its willingness to forgo advantages that would be incompatible with a just global order (as it itself envisions it).

governments to make genuine sacrifices for them, to honor a law or agreement even when doing so is against the government's interests, all things considered. Yet over and over again, governments create the opposite precedent; they ignore laws, charters, treaties, and declarations that they had once inaugurated with great shows of commitment and thereby reinforce the dominant conception of international relations as amoral.

A case in point is the condemnation of war crimes and (especially) crimes against humanity, which, at Nuremberg, were said to shock the conscience of humankind. In situations where their own military actions or those of their allies were at stake, the relevant powers have since been willing, for the sake of even minor objectives, to ignore the war-crimes statutes they formulated. This is not a case where shared values are sadly absent. What is lacking is the political will to *make effective* the values that are shared, by embodying them as fixed points into a global institutional order where they would be maintained through the *moral* allegiance they evoke among the peoples of the world. This is a moral failure, primarily of politicians, who thereby subvert the very idea that international documents couched in the language of fundamental law and supreme morality could ever be anything more than temporary bargains reinforced by propaganda penalties.

Value-based institutional fixed points might also develop, more formally, through an international ethical dialogue. Just as teams of nuclear-weapons experts are asked to negotiate a draft agreement on arms control, so teams of political philosophers and international lawyers might be asked to identify, codify, and extend the area of shared value commitments. Such discussions would lead nations to a better understanding of one another's more comprehensive values, which is bound to broaden and deepen the commitment to the value of tolerance—and tolerance of alternative forms of national organization in particular. They might also lead to agreement on some path of institutional reforms that are genuinely valued by both sides and eventually, perhaps, to a shared conception of justice that could guide the appraisal and gradual reform of the global institutional order.[23]

At least in the beginning (before much mutual confidence has been built up), the agreements emerging from such a high-level ethical dialogue will have to affect the participant states in a balanced way, so as to minimize the strains of commitment. For instance, the superpowers might be unable at present to give a reliable mutual undertaking to tolerate the apostasy of a major ally because this undertaking would

[23]In Chapter 6, I argue for a particular globalization of Rawls's conception of justice, which seems to me to be an especially appropriate position with which to enter such an international ethical dialogue. Though distinctively Western, it is based on a small family of widely accepted values and also tolerant of some range of diverse national institutional schemes, including, in particular, schemes with a socialist economy.

impose severe strains upon whichever side would be called upon to honor it first. This does not mean that the discourse must aim (like negotiations of the arms-control type) for agreements that are mutually advantageous. Such agreements might, and perhaps should, rather be mutually *dis*advantageous.[24] The governments of the more affluent nations might, for example, agree to create and fund an agency, independent from themselves, that is charged with promoting the economic development of the world's poorest countries and regions (combatting malnutrition, illiteracy, disease, and economic dependence). With some good will, such a reform should be feasible (in a period of reduced tension) by finding a mutually acceptable distribution of burdens that preserves the relative bargaining position of the relevant governments. While such a scheme would reduce the benefits these governments derive from their superior position, it would reduce them proportionately and hence not (dis)advantage any one of them vis-à-vis the others. The moral significance of such tangible concern for the world's most disadvantaged populations would go far beyond its immediate effects. By demonstrating their willingness to give increasing weight to values at the expense of concern for the preservation and expansion of national power, the relevant governments would build up, through the experience of nonprudential collaboration, the mutual respect and trust that are necessary for the gradual transition to a value-based world order.[25]

20.6. So far, this chapter has sketched a systemic analysis of one feature of a global institutional scheme, determining the degree to which it has a modus-vivendi or value-based character. I have argued that this feature has a tremendous impact on the ordinary level of day-to-day human misery as well as on the shared risk of extraordinary catastrophe (through another world war, for instance). These thoughts are straightforwardly generalizable to other world-order features. The idea is to understand the existing framework of international relations as a basic structure in the sense of Chapter 1, and then to investigate how various morally significant macrophenomena vary with variations in the features of the global basic structure.

This sort of investigation is obviously more difficult when the domain is the world at large. For one thing, it is more difficult to work with

[24]Yet, even if they are mutually disadvantageous, the mere fact of having achieved stable agreements is likely to benefit both sides, e.g., by fostering trade and economic cooperation.

[25]This transition would be facilitated through jointly established adjudication and enforcement mechanisms that are independent of any of the participants and firmly committed to the transformation process so that they will tend to counterbalance any strains of the transition. As the strength of independent forces increases, they would add weight to the reasons in favor of continued compliance and thus would tend to allay fears of noncompliance on the part of others. On the other hand, the creation of enforcement mechanisms (in particular) may also appear risky to the protagonists, and it is thus of some importance that progress is possible without them.

comparative statistical information because there are no simultaneous alternative worlds to be observed. Still, social theory would seem to provide enough of an understanding to support some significant, though general, conclusions. The centrifugal tendencies endemic to laissez-faire market schemes, for example, are well enough documented in the context of various national and regional economic schemes to allow generalization to the global plane. This generalization enables a systemic explanation of the fact that international inequalities are vast, and still increasing, as the poorest countries tend to have the lowest (often negative) rates of economic growth.[26] The current distribution in national rates of infant mortality, life expectancy, and disease and the global incidence of starvation and poverty can then be accounted for, in large part, by reference to the existing world market system with its lack of distributional constraints.[27]

Again, such macroexplanations cannot be fully preempted by the corresponding microexplanations. Having explained various particular wars and insurrections by reference to intrinsic factors, we must yet account for the overall *rate* of internal and external government violence, which (I have suggested) requires reference to an international modus vivendi that perpetuates military competition and the absence of effective mechanisms for the creation, application, and enforcement of international law. Similarly, microexplanations of why this or that less developed country has or has not "taken off" economically do not add up to an explanation of the centrifugal tendency in per capita gross national product.[28]

And again, the two levels are separable not only for purposes of explanation but also from a moral point of view. In my homicide example (§2.3), it was consistent to hold each and every murderer fully responsible for his act *and* to criticize the legal system (lacking effective handgun legislation) on account of some percentage of these murders. Similarly, here, we should surely hold the Somozas and Marcoses fully accountable for the plight of their compatriots. But, consistent with this, we can also criticize the prevailing international order on account of current misery, so long as the prevalence of corrupt military dictator-

[26]Yes, growth differentials are partly due to differential birth rates, but then high birth rates are themselves caused partly by poverty.

[27]See Nagel, PF, for a clear and eloquent elaboration of this point.

[28]Thus, it is fallacious to infer that all poor societies could have taken off from the fact that some (e.g., South Korea and Taiwan) have. It is at least likely that the sustained success of the few was conditional upon the competitive niche they occupied between a large number of more developed societies (over which they enjoyed a labor-cost advantage) and a large number of less developed societies (over which they enjoyed an advantage in capital and technology). If some such macroexplanation is true, it follows that it was impossible for *all* Third World countries to succeed in this way (for greater competition within the niche would have greatly reduced the advantages for its occupants). At best, the success stories can show that *each* Third World country could have taken off by occupying the niche (and that microexplanations are therefore needed to show why *these* rather than *those* countries succeeded).

ships in Third World countries is itself explainable in terms of systemic factors—if it is the reigning modus-vivendi framework, for example, that explains why typically even the most murderous tyrant can induce some powerful governments to give him political and military support (against his domestic and foreign opponents) by appealing to or agreeing to serve their larger strategic interests.

20.7. That social institutions are implicated in this way makes it morally urgent to investigate whether there are realistic possibilities for institutional change, for a New Deal, on the global plane. Suppose we believe that, other things being equal, (1) there is moral reason to prefer a world with lower rather than higher rates of malnutrition, infant mortality, and government violence and (2) there is a feasible alternative global basic structure under which such rates would be significantly lower. Then we have reason to view the existing world order as unjust and to hold those collaborating in its perpetuation morally responsible for the imposition of this order upon (in particular) those who are most likely to be massacred, tortured, or starved under the current regime. At stake here are not merely positive but negative rights and duties. Positive duties (of mutual aid, for example) establish a direct link between persons in distress and those able to alleviate their plight, irrespective of any further facts about the social context. Considerations of justice establish an indirect link, presupposing further contextual features, as follows: Certain deprivations and disadvantages are understood as established or engendered by an institutional scheme. This scheme is unjust against the background of at least one feasible alternative scheme that would not give rise to similarly severe deprivations and disadvantages. And the more advantaged participants in the prevailing institutional scheme are collectively responsible for the injustice of the scheme insofar as they actively perpetuate it and resist its reform.[29] Such considerations of justice are here at stake. By ignoring the misery of the world's poorest populations, we are disregarding not merely our positive duty of mutual aid but our negative duty not to make others the victims of unjust institutions. As citizens of the developed nations, we have created and are perpetuating by use of our economic and military power a global institutional order under which tens of millions avoidably cannot meet their most fundamental needs for food and physical security.

The next chapter attempts to specify and support the foregoing remarks by outlining a Rawlsian conception of global justice. These remarks may be summarized as claims about how, in general terms, we should answer two questions. The first is the analogue to "who is my neighbor?" in morality: how far should my moral concern for social institutions extend? Here one might be tempted to deny that such

---

[29]As before (Chap. 1, n. 26), I am leaving aside the complicated question of when such coresponsibility for injustice is blameworthy, but I will say a little more about the relation of injustice and responsibility in the concluding section (§24.3).

responsibility extends beyond national borders: "We share responsibility only for our national institutional scheme, in which we participate as citizens, and which we can most immediately affect (e.g. through voting)." I reject this view because it treats the existing global institutional framework as a natural or God-given fact. If we, the citizens of powerful and approximately democratic countries, do not share some responsibility for this global order, then no one does. And this is implausible, given that we are advantaged participants in this order, who help maintain and are (collectively) capable of changing it. My affirmation of the moral salience of (and of a collective moral responsibility for) the global basic structure, amounts to a partial defense and development of §28 of the *Universal Declaration of Human Rights*: "Everyone is entitled to a social *and international* order in which the rights and freedoms set forth in this Declaration can be fully realized" (my emphasis).

The second question is how we should assess a global institutional framework from a moral point of view. Here I favor a broadly consequentialist assessment that is concerned, first and foremost, with its least advantaged participants, those in our world who lack well-protected fundamental rights and liberties (as stipulated, for example, by the *Universal Declaration* or by Rawls's first principle in its amended form).

C H A P T E R 6

A Criterion of
Global Justice

21. The Traditional Law of Nations

21.1.1. Rawls recognizes the cosmopolitan character of his theory by sketching, at least, how his criterion for assessing the institutions of a national society might be complemented by additional principles of justice governing international relations. This brief outline jars, however, with central commitments of his theory, chiefly his focus on the basic structure and his conception of all human beings as free and equal moral persons. These commitments would instead, I will argue, lead one to abandon Rawls's primary emphasis on domestic institutions in favor of globalizing his entire conception of justice.

Such a globalization is not incompatible with the essential elements of Rawls's work thus far. It is only for the purpose of "a first approximation" (BSS 70 n. 8), that he wants to "leave aside here the problem of justice between nations" (BSS 57) and begin with the idealized case of a self-contained society. "At some level there must exist a closed background system, and it is this subject for which we want a theory. We are better prepared to take up this problem for a society (illustrated by nations) conceived as a more or less self-sufficient scheme of social cooperation and as possessing a more or less complete culture. If we are successful in the case of a society, we can try to extend and to adjust our initial theory as further inquiry requires" (BSS 70 n. 8; cf. TJ 8).

21.1.2. I concede that a criterion of justice for domestic institutions would be sufficient if modern states were indeed closed schemes. In this case there simply would not *be* a global basic structure for principles of global justice to apply to. Of course, the natural distribution of assets (climate, soil, mineral resources) among a plurality of self-contained societies may be radically unequal, and it would thus not be

240

difficult to show that Rawlsian parties would adopt something like Charles Beitz's international resource redistribution principle, even for a world of truly self-contained societies.[1] But this does not suffice to demonstrate that Rawls is really committed to requirements of global distributive justice that make demands even in the absence of international interaction. It remains to be shown that the construct of the original position is relevant to the question whether members of truly self-contained societies have an obligation to establish contact and to develop joint institutions with other such societies. This Rawls seems to deny: He restricts the relevance of the original position to questions of *justice* and conceives (in)justice as a property of social institutions (which, by hypothesis, are absent on the global plane). There are certain "relations of individuals to one another which set the stage for questions of justice" (TJ 130). I surmise Rawls would agree with Kant's more precise formulation that (just) institutions are required "among human beings . . . who cannot avoid mutually influencing one another."[2] Within his theory as a whole, there are grounds for bringing his contractarian device to bear on the global plane only if there is significant global interdependence.[3]

Fortunately, the concession and the debate surrounding it are entirely academic, since all agree that there is and will be extensive global interdependence. If modern societies are not closed, we must at some point go beyond Rawls's "first approximation" and ask how his conception of justice might best be adapted to the complexities of the real world. Rawls has not yet seriously addressed this issue. The central place of domestic institutions in his work up to now rests on nothing deeper than his (entirely plausible) hunch that making the simplifying assumption of national isolation has significant expositional advantages for introducing his broadly consequentialist approach.

21.1.3. How one adapts Rawls's conception to more complex realities will evidently affect how the deliberations of the parties in the original position will eventually be presented and interpreted. I will argue for viewing the parties as immediately addressing the world at

[1]Cf. Beitz, PTIR 136–43.

[2]Kant, KPW 73 (cf. MEJ §§8–9). Yet Kant does once formulate a broader requirement, addressed to "all men who can at all influence one another" (KPW 98n).

[3]Scanlon makes the same point, relying on the fact of "systematic economic interaction" or "regularized commerce" (RTJ 202). In his book, Beitz agrees (PTIR 131, 151) and argues elaborately for the extensiveness of current global interdependence (PTIR 143–53). Yet, prompted by criticism from David Richards (IDJ 292), Beitz has since come to the opposite view—that making the validity of a criterion of global justice dependent upon the factual question of global interdependence "would arbitrarily favor the status quo" (CINS 595, and cf. n. 8). I fail to see this danger, for whether the members of different societies can or cannot avoid mutually influencing one another is, though an empirical matter, surely not up to them. At this stage of world history we cannot realistically avoid international interaction, and so the members of rich societies have no incentive to exploit the fact that the criterion of global justice would not apply if societies were self-contained.

large and as dealing with the organization of national societies only within the context so provided. Taken seriously, Rawls's conception of justice will make the social position of the globally least advantaged the touchstone for assessing our basic institutions.

This conclusion needs defense on two levels. In this section and the next, I show how my global interpretation of Rawls's criterion of justice is plausible *within* his framework, how it is supported, especially, by his individualism and his arguments for the focus on the basic structure. In §23 I argue that on this, its most unified and elegant interpretation, Rawls's conception is still plausibly applicable to our world—despite, in particular, significant intercultural diversity of convictions even about justice. Drawing on arguments from all parts of this book, the concluding section addresses the practical meaning of a Rawlsian conception of global justice in our world.

21.2. In discussing how the construct of the original position should be brought to bear upon the problem of global justice, I will concentrate upon three main alternatives, two of which are suggested by Rawls's own brief remarks on international relations.[4] These remarks are clear insofar as they propose that *after* a criterion of domestic justice has been chosen, the contractarian device should be reused on the international level. Beyond this, Rawls's description of the second, global session of the original position permits two competing readings, which he does not keep distinct. On the first—henceforth R_1—the global parties are viewed as representing *persons* from the various societies, who, once again, are "to make a rational choice to protect their interests" (TJ 378). They must do so, however, even though "they know nothing about the particular circumstances of their own society, its power and strength in comparison with other nations, *nor do they know their place in their own society*" (TJ 378, my emphasis).

On this reading, the parties will again be guided by their clients' imputed desire for social primary goods, and since their place in their own society and that of their society among others are unknown, the parties will, by maximin, choose a criterion that makes the globally least advantaged the preeminent touchstone of global justice, no matter which societies they may belong to. Global institutions will then be assessed by how well they satisfy Rawls's criterion interpreted globally.[5]

This claim—that the parties would choose essentially the same criterion in the second session as in the first—is supported by Rawls's endorsement of a *thick* veil of ignorance. The parties do not know "the

[4]TJ 377–79. Rawls offers these two pages as part of a discussion of conscientious refusal. It would therefore be unfair to regard this passage as a considered proposal for how his first approximation should be adjusted to take account of global interdependence.

[5]Evidently, I am here keeping fixed Rawls's arguments to the effect that his criterion (the combination of the general and special conceptions) is the maximin solution (cf. §11.1.1).

general configuration of society, its political structure and economic organization, and so on"—including presumably its size and the degree of its ethnic, cultural, and geographical diversity—because such knowledge would at best "obscure how intimately the principles adopted are tied to the conception of the person" (KCMT 550; cf. BSS 58; WOS VI). Moreover, in formulating the parties' task, Rawls refers only vaguely to the basic structure of an inclusive, self-contained system. For aught they know, the parties might be deliberating about the world at large.

On the other reading of Rawls's remarks—R_2—the second session involves a more dramatic adjustment of the original position, since the parties are now conceived as "representatives of *states*" (TJ 378, 379, my emphasis). Rawls tells us that such representatives would be concerned to further "their national interest . . . [as] defined by the principles of justice that have already been acknowledged. . . . [A] nation will aim above all to maintain and to preserve its just institutions and the conditions that make them possible" (TJ 379). So the parties' ideal of a just world would be, essentially, a world of just states. For a world falling short of this ideal, the parties, assuming they again employ the maximin rule, would adopt a priority rule focused upon the states whose domestic institutions are least just. So R_2 entails weaker constraints than R_1 on international inequalities. In this regard, a just global basic structure need merely ensure that no states are too poor to be able to satisfy Rawls's criterion domestically.[6]

Despite this difference, the two readings agree that first-principle goods are paramount.[7] Those farthest from having a complete and well-protected package of basic rights and liberties ipso facto count as the globally least advantaged under R_1, and those societies whose least advantaged suffer the greatest shortfall from such a fully adequate package ipso facto count as the least just under R_2. However inconsistently Rawls may have described the parties' second, global session, it will quite clearly yield a criterion that assesses global basic structures by the severity of the first-principle violations each tends to produce.

21.3. It is then astonishing that Rawls takes this global session to

---

[6]There may be readings or extensions of the text that fall between the two I discuss, perhaps envisaging a criterion sensitive to the per capita income in the poorest societies. I skip such complexities, assuming that my arguments against R_1 and R_2 defeat intermediate interpretations as well.

[7]Unless, of course, the lexical ordering of the two principles is suspended in favor of the general conception. I neglect this complication in my argument in the hope that my amendment to the first principle allows us to expand the range of (only "halfway favorable") conditions under which the special conception can plausibly apply. In any case, even if the general conception applied to today's world (R_1) or to some of its poorer societies (R_2), Rawls's criterion would still have radical implications for the assessment of the current global basic structure, especially if, as Rawls asserts, the special conception determines the long-range demands of justice (TJ 152, 542). How these radical implications could be developed will be clear enough by analogy to the actual argument I present in the text.

result in a reaffirmation of the "familiar" principles of international law, for which he relies on the seminal but dated account in James Brierly's book *The Law of Nations*. Under this regime, "states have certain fundamental equal rights . . . analogous to the equal rights of citizens in a constitutional regime" (TJ 378). As examples, Rawls mentions (TJ 378–79) the rights to self-determination, nonintervention, and self-defense; the rules of *jus in bello*; and the principle that treaties consistent with these constraints are to be kept (the remaining treaties being void *ab initio*).

The parties, on either R_1 or R_2, have various reasons for rejecting this proposal. To begin with, it is wholly insensitive to distributional concerns. International economic relations shaped by free bargaining (among governments and other economic agents) afford no assurance that national societies will not avoidably lack "a sufficient material base for making the equal liberties effective" (FG 545). But the parties would urgently want a global institutional framework that provides such assurance.

Next, a world of great international inequalities will give rise to considerable strains of commitment. Many a government will be bound by very burdensome treaties, whose terms, negotiated perhaps by some predecessor government, reflect a bygone and unfavorable distribution of bargaining power. The commitment to keep such treaties will frequently come under severe stress.

Moreover, there are, on Rawls's proposal, no effective mechanisms of adjudication and enforcement that could offset these considerable strains of commitment and thereby keep the situated assurance problem from arising. In the absence of such recognized mechanisms, governments have no assurances that others will comply with the going ground rules even when the net costs of compliance (including opportunity costs) are high. The lack of such assurances makes it more often advisable and also morally more acceptable not to comply oneself when compliance is costly or even risky. This climate of actual and potential noncompliance, together with "honest disagreements" among governments that are equally entitled to judge and enforce international laws and treaties, ensures that the perennial scourge of war will continue, as Rawls implicitly acknowledges by concentrating most of his further discussion upon the rules of warfare.

This permanent danger from noncompliance and war (and the fear, hostility, and suspicion associated with it) will in turn actualize the fundamental assurance problem. Each government will, and will deem itself morally entitled to, shift the ground rules in its favor when it can, so as to make itself and its domestic population less vulnerable to noncompliance or attack by other governments.

Taken together, these four considerations show that under the rules of international law Rawls endorses even an initially well-ordered (stable) international system would tend to degenerate into a modus vivendi in which compliance with these ground rules and thus their endurance would be problematic. In other words, it is not the case that the familiar law of nations (at Brierly's time or our's) would work well if only there were mutual trust. Rather, the prevailing modus-vivendi framework is the equilibrium state toward which an international system governed by this law of nations will tend regardless of initial governmental attitudes and good will. A world order based on these ground rules is *inherently* unstable, as can be shown by extending Rawls's own observations about the strains of commitment and the two assurance problems.[8]

We have seen how the parties have important reasons for rejecting the traditional international-law regime Rawls endorses. The inequality and instability (fostering noncompliance and wars) such a regime tends to engender would jeopardize the parties' aspiration for a world in which first-principle goods are universally secure. These reasons apply even if we assume that all of the world's societies are firmly committed to protecting first-principle goods within their borders (at least insofar as their respective levels of development permit). Since this assumption is highly unrealistic, however, one should also consider whether proposed ground rules for international relations are plausible when some societies are less than just and whether they will exert some influence upon national regimes to gravitate toward domestic justice. Rawls's proposal of equal state rights fails on these two counts as well. Societies and their governments are to be accepted as equals under those rules, even if their internal constitutions are characterized by tyranny, repression, exploitation, and radical inequalities. Persons abused by their own governments have no official remedies and must rely on the willingness of other governments or agents to intercede in their behalf. Moreover, since each state is sovereign over its internal affairs, this international order generates no countervailing forces that would resist the degeneration of a national basic structure. Such institutional indifference to the domestic (in)justice of national regimes aggravates the instability of the proposed world order because it undermines the *moral* reasons for unconditional compliance with international laws and treaties.

21.4. These Rawlsian criticisms of Rawls's endorsement of the traditional international-law regime indicate three main directions of institutional reform toward a global order under which basic rights and liberties would be more complete and better protected. First, the parties would favor an organization of the world economy that makes it sensitive to distributional concerns, so that all societies have at least a sufficient material base to satisfy the first principle domestically. Second, they would want (more) international disputes to be settled

---

[8]On the strains of commitment, see TJ 176–78; RAM 653; RMC 144. On what I have called the situated and fundamental assurance problems, see TJ 270 and 336; and IOC 11 and 19–20, respectively.

through mutually recognized legal procedures rather than through war or threat advantage—a reform that in due course might be complemented by central enforcement mechanisms. Progress toward this second goal would reduce or eliminate the incidence of war and make it much more likely for right rather than might to prevail in international conflicts. Third, the parties would prefer international law to afford some remedies to persons against abuse by their own governments, some incentives for societies to reform themselves—minimally by providing for diplomatic and economic sanctions (when these would be effective) against unjust national regimes. Seeing that progress has been made since Brierly's time, on the latter two fronts,[9] and that the parties, on any textually tenable construal of their second session, would adopt a criterion that favors such reforms, I am at a loss to explain Rawls's quick endorsement of a bygone status quo. Given the genesis of the international-law regime as an instrument developed by governments to serve their own special interests, it would seem a surprising coincidence indeed if it (in any of its historical versions) were the most suitable institutional framework for realizing basic rights and liberties.

In one concrete case Rawls himself shows a concern for basic liberties that radically departs from traditional international law. He writes that an army of conscripts rather than mercenaries may be "demanded for the defense of liberty itself, including here not only the liberties of the citizens of the society in question, but also those of persons in other societies as well. Therefore if a conscript army is less likely to be an instrument of unjustified foreign adventures, it may be justified on this basis alone despite the fact that conscription infringes upon the equal liberties of citizens" (TJ 380). This demand goes far beyond his conservative endorsement of the law of nations. One might, therefore, best discount this endorsement, rather than recognize it as evidence against any reasonable understanding of how Rawls describes the parties' second, global session.

22. The Internal Argument

Let me then return to the two ideas Rawls has suggested for extending the original position to the subject of international relations and field against these ideas my own alternative, G. Instead of two separate

[9]For example, the International Covenant on Civil and Political Rights and the International Covenant on Economic, Social, and Cultural Rights both involve specific legal obligations, though only a minority of states have acceded to them. The former of these envisions jurisdiction by the U.N. Human Rights Committee (ICCPR §41) and also contains an optional protocol recognizing the right to individual petition to this U.N. body. Similar provisions are contained in the European Convention on Human Rights. Reflecting the parties' concern for first-principle rights and liberties, a criterion of global justice acceptable to them would demand substantial further reforms along these lines.

sessions in which the parties adopt criteria for national and then for international institutions, G envisions a single, global, original position. This modification, again appealing to the thick veil of ignorance, leaves intact Rawls's whole argument for the two principles, directing it however at our entire social world. The relevant "closed scheme" is now taken to be the world at large. This section will first show how R_2 is incompatible with Rawlsian commitments and then present a number of arguments that favor G over R_1 (and R_2).

22.1.1. One main reason Rawls gives for taking the basic structure as the primary moral subject is that institutional inequalities, at least insofar as they are based upon natural or social contingencies, are inescapable and present from birth. They deeply shape our character and interests, goals and aspirations, even talents and abilities (BSS V; TJ 7, 259). Thus they affect our lives much more profoundly and call more urgently for moral reflection than inequalities arising from what individuals choose to do (including participation in associations such as firms, churches, or universities) and from how their activities happen to turn out.

Nationality is just one further deep contingency (like genetic endowment, race, gender, and social class), one more potential basis of institutional inequalities that are inescapable and present from birth. Within Rawls's conception, there is no reason to treat this case differently from the others. And so it would seem that we can justify our global institutional order only if we can show that the institutional inequalities it produces tend to optimize (against the backdrop of feasible alternative global regimes) the worst social position.

Now one may think that there is another kind of justification peculiar to the global case, where the claims of *states* must also be given their due. Such a thought is suggested by R_2, on which the parties are viewed as representatives of states. Even conceding that there are feasible alternative institutional schemes that would generate a superior minimum share, one can still argue that any such alternative scheme would infringe more important rights and interests of states. I cannot envisage a plausible instance of such a justification, but in any event, it would not fit into a Rawlsian framework, because it would be incompatible with Rawls's individualistic conviction that in matters of social justice only *persons* are to be viewed as ultimate units of (equal) moral concern: "We want to account for the social values, for the intrinsic good of institutional, community, and associative activities, by a conception of justice that in its theoretical basis is individualistic. For reasons of clarity among others, we do not want to rely on an undefined concept of community, or to suppose that society is an organic whole with a life of its own distinct from and superior to that of all its members in their relations with one another. . . . From this conception, however individualistic it may seem, we must eventually explain the value of community" (TJ 264–65).

Consequently, Rawls recognizes only persons as "self-originating sources of valid claims" (KCMT 543) and so commits himself to basing his criterion of social justice exclusively upon data about individual shares. This commitment favors an interpretation of the original position that, like G and R_1, consistently conceives the parties as representing *persons*, never associations or states as in R_2. In any case, how associations, communities, and states are to be conceived and what roles they are to play within a self-contained social system must for Rawls depend only upon how alternative solutions would affect this social system's individual human participants.[10]

22.1.2. Let us turn to Rawls's second main reason for beginning with the subject of basic social institutions and for asserting that the inequalities they tend to produce must be governed by nothing less demanding than a maximin criterion. Interpersonal agreements can carry moral weight only if they are *freely* entered into under conditions that are *fair* (cf. BSS 52–53). This, Rawls believes, is often not the case when some participants' basic rights and liberties, opportunities, or economic positions are grossly inferior. The attractive idea of "interaction among consenting adults" can be morally appealing only if differentials in bargaining power do not exceed certain limits. A tendency to generate excessive inequalities is a particularly deep moral defect in a social system because many of the voluntary interactions taking place within it will be morally flawed as a result. It is then of considerable moral importance that social systems be so structured that those limits are maintained, or (as Rawls puts it) "background justice" is preserved. This is given as one main reason for the preeminence, within moral reflection, of the quest for a conception of justice for the basic structure.

This reason, too, extends to the global plane because, even if each state maintained a distributional background ensuring that interactions among its citizens are free and fair, international (including intergovernmental) inequalities in information and bargaining power may still be so great as to render international interactions unfair and coercive[11]—hence the need for a conception of *global* background justice.

---

[10]This constraint is still compatible with the claim that the most fundamental right of *persons* is the right to live in a state that has the kind of state rights accorded by international law. If this were true, then the present order might indeed be the best we can hope for. At least the foremost right of persons is fairly secure. Given all Rawls has said about the basic liberties, this piece of conservative ingenuity will not fit into his conception of justice, but it is popular with others, most notably Walzer (JUW 53–54; MSS).

[11]Here, we should think not merely of individual transactions, such as a treaty establishing a foreign military base or an agreement between a Western tourist and a Bangkok prostitute. There are more complex cases, as when, in some poor country, local demand for grain and beans competes with foreign demand for cotton and coffee. Even if the coffee consumers are no more affluent than the relevant landowners and never have any dealings with the (much poorer) would-be consumers of grain, grossly unequal bargain-

The current law of nations is a complete failure in this respect because it is entirely insensitive to such differentials in bargaining power.

On R_2 the global parties would adopt a criterion that assesses the terms of international interaction by how they tend to affect the internal justice of (especially the least just) states. This criterion might support some important institutional reforms in the current international-law regime. In particular, it would require a reorganization of the world economy so as to ensure that, as far as possible, each society has "a sufficient material base for making the equal liberties effective" (FG 545). Still, this criterion does not offer an acceptable conception of global background justice in Rawls's sense, because it could be fully satisfied despite indefinite international inequalities. Let me elucidate this point by discussing somewhat more concretely two issues with respect to which R_2, though supported by ordinary prejudice, conflicts with Rawlsian commitments (which are accommodated by G and R_1).

22.1.2.1. One conflict concerns the *relative* requirements of the first principle, which (beyond specific "threshold" safeguards) envision rough *equality* in regard to some basic liberties. Thus decisions through the political process are required to be made in such a way that those significantly affected by them have equal rights and roughly equal opportunities to participate in the deliberations and to influence their outcomes (cf. TJ §36). Should this requirement extend also to political choices significantly affecting the citizens of more than one society?

R_2, viewing the parties as representing *states* and thus yielding a criterion that assesses international institutions exclusively in terms of the internal justice of states, would lead here to a break in continuity. The right to equal political participation extends up to but not beyond the national level. Political matters of supranational significance could then be decided by one state unilaterally, provided only that the decision is sanctioned through the domestic political process and does not undermine or endanger the internal justice of other societies. Foreigners, if unable to exact a treaty, would be obligated to acquiesce in decisions from which they are by right excluded.[12] This result is consis-

---

ing power may yet play a pernicious role. By displacing local food production, foreign demand for coffee tends to raise food prices, which in turn reduces the ability of the poorest locals to transform their need for food into effective market demand. (Such scenarios of declining "exchange entitlements" are discussed in Sen, PF.) If starvation results in this case, we cannot hold the consumers of coffee responsible for it under a principle of morality. Market participants cannot possibly be required to anticipate such remote effects of their transactions (cf. BSS 54–55). Only a conception of (global) *justice* that attends to the effects of institutions can correctly locate the root of such problems and thus perhaps help eradicate them.

[12]Political choices, including supranational ones, may be matters of pure procedural justice that for reasons of fairness or collective rationality cannot be settled through the cumulative result of uncoordinated decisions by governments, corporations, and individuals. Or they may involve a more significant element of imperfect procedural justice, as they may accord more or less well with moral criteria—with social justice, justice

tent with the status quo, but it conflicts with Rawls's individualistic commitment, which links the first principle, in particular, to the status of all human beings as free and equal moral persons. This commitment, which makes the restriction of political equality to the national and subnational levels appear arbitrary, is honored by both R_1 and G, which support a right to equal participation (for those significantly affected) in the making also of supranational political decisions.

22.1.2.2. The other conflict concerns the understanding of Rawls's second principle. According to R_2, international institutions should encourage and support the fulfillment of this principle *within each state*. The terms of international interaction might then be perfectly just, even if they tend to produce vast international inequalities in access to health care and education and in income and wealth. The criterion of global justice, as Rawls's representatives of *states* would fashion it, demands only that global conditions be maximally support-ive of each society's attaining its national interest "to maintain and to preserve its just institutions and the conditions that make them possi-ble" (TJ 379). Yet if excessive social and economic inequalities are unjust domestically, how can like inequalities arising internationally be a matter of moral indifference? The grounds on which Rawls holds that fair equality of opportunity and the difference principle constitute requirements of background justice militate against confining these requirements within national borders.

Let me explicate this idea of a globalized second principle somewhat more concretely by examining the natural and social contingencies that international socioeconomic inequalities may be based upon or related to (cf. §14.3). Let us begin with a reflection upon the moral status of the natural assets (such as mineral resources, fertility, climate, etc.) of the various states. The geographical distribution of such assets is cer-tainly morally arbitrary in Rawls's sense.[13] The natural assets in a state's territory are not a reflection of the moral worth of—are not Deserved by—either this state or its citizens. The moral arbitrariness of the distribution of natural assets supports (within a Rawlsian framework) the conclusion that those whose territory includes exceptional natural assets have no claim that a just global economic scheme should offer any particular rewards for making these assets available. Just as Genius

---

between generations, or our natural duties (including those toward other forms of life). Gross inequalities in political influence are unjust in both these cases, albeit for some-what different reasons. Possible examples of supranational political choices are policies pertaining to the installation and proliferation of nuclear technologies; disease control; genetic engineering; the preservation of historical and cultural treasures; the storage, use, and dissemination of information; exploitation of natural assets (air and water pollution, use of oceans and outer space, destruction of tropical forests and ozone layer); decima-tion and extinction of biological species; experimentation with animals; global capital accumulation; ground rules for international trade and investment (operation of interna-tional financial institutions and multinational corporations).

[13]As argued in Beitz, PTIR 136–42—though Beitz does not use "morally arbitrary" in (what I think is) Rawls's sense.

has no prior claim that she be offered any specific income advantage for the development and exercise of her greater talents (cf. §6.3), so the Saudis have no prior claim to being offered any specific income advantage for producing and delivering crude oil. The terms of international cooperation may and should therefore be designed so that the social inequalities they allow to arise from natural contingencies (the distribution of natural assets) tend to optimize the worst representative individual share (cf. §6.4). In this way, a globalized second principle would constrain but not preclude income inequalities that reflect skewed terms of trade (for example, crude oil versus cotton) arising, via patterns of supply and demand, from the morally arbitrary geographical distribution of natural assets.

Beitz wants to derive more from the parallel between natural endowments and natural assets, namely a global resource redistribution principle (which he believes should apply even in the absence of any international interaction). He wants the criterion of global justice to govern not merely the terms on which states can develop and market their natural assets but also rights over these assets themselves. But Beitz's argument for his global resource redistribution principle crucially depends upon Nozick's mistaken interpretation of how Rawls treats natural endowments. If social institutions may be designed to rectify inequalities in natural endowments—perhaps through organ transplants or through collective ownership of (or a head tax on) special gifts—then we can indeed conclude that social institutions may also redistribute natural assets (provided these are relevantly similar to natural endowments). But then, as we have seen (§5.1.1), Rawls is not committed to the premise of this argument. There is no reason within his semiconsequentialist conception of justice—not even a reason overridden by considerations of personal freedom—to interfere with the natural distribution of special gifts and handicaps. Each person is to have a right to her natural endowments and is to control their development and exercise. What would follow from Beitz's suggested parallel of natural assets with natural endowments is therefore quite different from what he concludes. Each state is to have a right to its natural assets and thus may freely decide not to develop them, to use them domestically, or to market them abroad on the terms offered within a just global economic scheme. Under the terms of such a scheme states rich in natural assets (like especially gifted persons) could derive advantages from their good fortune, although the magnitude of these advantages is limited by the scheme's being designed so as to optimize the social position of the least advantaged individual participants.[14]

[14]These limits would probably be less significant in the case of states and their natural assets than in the case of individuals and their natural endowments because states can more easily reduce their economic participation by becoming more self-reliant. The terms of an economic scheme designed to elicit optimal levels of cooperation would then probably be relatively more favorable to asset-rich states than to gifted persons.

But then Beitz's parallel between natural assets and natural endowments is mistaken. Yes, the geographical distribution of natural assets is just a natural fact or contingency, but having a property right or eminent domain over natural assets is very much a *social* fact. Such rights are among the benefits and burdens ·of social cooperation, and their institutional distribution, unlike the natural distribution of endowments, does then stand in need of justification.[15] Part of the distribution of income and wealth, the institutional distribution of natural assets is included in the master pattern in terms of which a Rawlsian criterion of global justice would assess any particular global basic structure. This does not mean that—assuming global interdependence—Beitz's resource redistribution principle can after all be derived from Rawlsian commitments. Rather, how a just global institutional scheme would regulate ownership and control over natural assets depends upon the *empirical* question of which institutional design would optimize the worst social position.

The parallel between individuals and states, which the parallel between natural assets and natural endowments is parasitic upon, will not fit into a Rawlsian moral conception. For Rawls, individual human persons, and they alone, are the ultimate units of moral concern. While persons, together with their natural attributes, are the fundament of his semiconsequentialist conception of justice, all other units (firms and families, states, churches, and universities) and their attributes are viewed as dependent on and regulated by social institutions, which are to be designed for the sole benefit of persons, viewed as potential participants in these institutions.

It may seem that a globalized second principle is much less plausible as a constraint on inequalities based upon *social* contingencies. But I don't think this is so. For suppose, on the contrary, that some national society is poor owing to a greater aggregate preference for leisure time and consumption, depressing the rate of savings. Even then, the relative neglect of the health and education of its children cannot be justified merely by the fact that others in this society did not make adequate savings. With its emphasis on individual lifetime shares, Rawls's criterion of justice would favor institutions designed so that persons who by choice enjoy more leisure time or consumption must normally bear the consequences by receiving less of (other) goods, simultaneously or at other times. Beyond this provision, Rawls requires

---

[15]It may be helpful (though slightly misleading in light of the next paragraph) to recall here what I have said about Rawls's distinction between natural and social contingencies. Social inequalities related to the distribution of natural assets do not really arise either from a natural contingency (as do talent-induced inequalities) or from a social contingency (as do class-induced inequalities). They are closest to gender- and race-induced inequalities. They are based on natural facts that, absent certain social facts, might never have had the slightest social importance. It is a social fact that human beings came to attach such enormous moral importance to skin color, and it is a social fact that they divided the world into national properties.

domestic institutions to distribute whatever burdens remain in ways satisfying the second principle, and he should thus require international institutions to distribute such burdens analogously. Persons should suffer from the unproductiveness of their parents or compatriots only insofar as (because of the resulting incentives) their social position would still be better than the worst social position under all feasible alternative economic schemes (including ones that do not permit selective penalization at all). Rawls's individualistic perspective never allows burdens to be imposed upon someone *merely* on account of the conduct of her relatives or compatriots. Their propensities toward leisure time and consumption are inappropriate determinants of her social position—no less morally arbitrary than the geographical distribution of natural assets.

22.1.3. One may think, despite the arguments presented, that the description of the global parties as representatives of states can yet be saved on some other interpretation. The global parties could be described, for example, as concerned for the (political, economic, military) strength of the states they represent, so that they would choose a criterion that is sensitive to the wealth and bargaining power of the worst-off states. But such modifications of R_2—besides simply *assuming* a morally fundamental role for the state—still do not adequately cope with the relative aspects of justice. If the problem is split up so that inequalities among compatriots and inequalities among states are dealt with separately, then no excessive inequalities may come into view even though enormous inequalities exist across national borders. To give a simple example, suppose income inequalities are constrained by a ratio of 30:1. Allowing the separation of levels would substantially weaken this limit. Income in the poorest state (with a per capita gross national product of 200) might vary between 360 and 12, while in the richest state (with a per capita gross national product of 6,000) the spread is between 60,000 and 2,000. Imposing two separate 30:1 limitations comfortably permits inequalities of 5,000:1 (a spread of 60,000 to 12). This thought can be adapted to more complex measures of inequality (such as the Gini coefficient) or to nonquantifiable dimensions of comparison (such as political influence). It undermines, in particular, the idea of two separate maximin criteria, one formulated in terms of individual shares and applying to domestic basic structures, the other formulated in terms of national shares and applying to the global institutional framework. Even if both are satisfied, the position of the globally least advantaged could still be far worse than is unavoidable.

The unacceptability of such a dual criterion emerges clearly when one observes that it would provide an *incentive* to "just-ify" otherwise excessive interpersonal inequalities (in political influence, socioeconomic position, and the like) through the interposition of national borders. An unjust state can conveniently be split into two just ones, inhabited, respectively, by the rich and the poor. This "reform" would be essentially cosmetic, removing the injustice (as defined by the proposed dual criterion) without mitigating the gross inequalities in bargaining power and social position between the two groups. Such incentives are not a farfetched possibility. They may well be at work in South Africa, where the whites are pursuing such "reforms" by creating a number of separate "homelands"; and one may also argue that the First World's reorganization of a formerly colonial periphery into sovereign states was partly motivated by incentives of this sort. In our world, national borders function as welcome blinders for our moral sensibilities.[16]

The individualistic basis of Rawls's theory as embodied in his concern for background justice supports, then, an interpretation of the original position on which the global parties represent persons and therefore assess a global institutional scheme by the worst representative individual share it tends to produce. Ideally, they would want such a scheme to be maximally supportive of basic rights and liberties, to foster fair equality of opportunity worldwide, and to generate social and economic inequalities only insofar as these optimize the socioeconomic position of the globally least advantaged persons. Hence R_1 provides the systematically more satisfactory reading of Rawls's remarks, and to it I will now turn.

22.2.1. One argument favoring G over R_1 is continuous with the issues just discussed. On R_1 the parties, conceived as representatives of *persons*, learn at the beginning of the second session that their society is not really closed and self-sufficient but part of a multinational scheme. This brings out an incoherence in R_1, for the parties (to put it dramatically) would come to regret their prior choice of a criterion of domestic justice. They would now, by maximin, favor a criterion by which *all* basic institutions are assessed by reference to the globally worst social position. Only principles for international institutions remain to be chosen, however, since each national basic structure is already pledged to its own domestic least advantaged group. And international institutions devised for the maximum benefit of the globally least advantaged may not benefit them very much.[17] In any case, to whatever extent the damage can be contained, the parties would at this point want to undo their first agreement, substituting the stipulation that *all* basic social institutions should be governed by the two principles, interpreted globally.

[16]I elaborate this thought in a forthcoming essay on moral incentives.

[17]For example, the more favorable the terms of international trade are to the globally least advantaged, the less such trade there would tend to be. Overly favorable terms undermine their own purpose and therefore will not be favored by the global difference principle. Thus, even in a world that fully satisfies both criteria adopted on R_1, institutions may not sufficiently mitigate the effects of contingencies—may allow excessive inequalities present from birth or may fail to ensure the fairness of individual transactions.

22.2.2. My second argument targets more generally the priority of the domestic case. Suppose we finally begin (as Rawls does provisionally) with a national session of the original position, yielding a criterion of domestic justice, and then complement this result with perhaps quite elaborate international ground rules for preventing global injustice. This procedure involves an implausible and unnecessary assumption, namely that the favored model of the national basic structure can be developed without paying any attention to the international environment in which national societies exist.

This assumption is implausible because the fact of a plurality of nations cannot be accommodated simply by adding further rules. One difficulty, which Rawls raises in regard to domestic institutions, is that "the rules governing agreements and individual transactions cannot be too complex, or require too much information to be correctly applied" (BSS 54). In the global context, it is even less reasonable to impose upon the various interacting agents the responsibility to conduct their transactions so as to preclude, say, the emergence of excessive discrepancies in bargaining power. Such agents "cannot comprehend the ramifications of their particular actions viewed collectively, nor can they be expected to foresee future circumstances that shape and transform present tendencies" (ibid.). There are thus no practicable rules that could reliably prevent that "the invisible hand guides things in the wrong direction and favors an oligopolistic configuration of accumulations that succeeds in maintaining unjustified inequalities and restrictions on fair opportunity" (ibid.). Hence there is a need for "institutions that define the social background and . . . continually adjust and compensate for the inevitable tendencies away from background fairness" (ibid.).

This difficulty is heightened by the fact that if an international institutional scheme is to endure, it must engender in national governments and populations sufficient compliance with and a basic moral allegiance to its ground rules. Whether it will engender such compliance and allegiance, however, depends in large part on the internal institutional organization of national societies. Reflections on national institutions should therefore be conducted with an eye to such considerations, rather than on the counterfactual assumption of national isolation. This problem, again, corresponds to one Rawls discusses on the national level. He holds that it would be pointless to address the internal organization of associations or to describe various roles in social cooperation with the prerogatives and obligations attached to them, before developing a conception of background justice which stipulates what features the society as a whole should preserve (TJ 110; BSS II). For analogous reasons one should attend to the problem of global background justice from the start. Models for the internal organization of societies must be developed together with the preferred ideal of a global basic structure with whose stability and optimal functioning they are to harmonize.[18]

In view of the apparent complexity of the problem of background justice, it is thus imperative to take a global perspective from the start, to adjust our moral reflections about the internal organization of societies and associations and about the appropriate constraints upon individual conduct in light of our aspiration for a stable and just global basic structure.

A look at institutional interdependence in the opposite direction confirms this result. As is plain from our historical experience, the stability and optimal functioning of a society's domestic institutions are heavily dependent upon its global environment. Or in Kant's words, "The problem of establishing a perfect civic constitution is dependent upon the problem of a lawful external relation among states, and cannot be solved without a solution to the latter problem" (KPW 47).

Since national and global basic structures strongly affect each other's stability and are closely interrelated in their effects upon individual lives, we should think about our basic social institutions *in general* and from a global point of view, thereby aiming for an integrated solution, a just and stable institutional scheme preserving a distribution of basic rights, opportunities, and index goods that is fair both globally and within each nation. Such an institutional scheme, if constructed along Rawlsian lines at all, would be developed through a single unified original position global in scope.

22.2.3. Let me reinforce the preceding two arguments through a parallel point that can be made without reference to global institutions. If we follow Rawls's brief sketch (in TJ §58) and apply his conception of justice for a self-contained social system to the states of our closely interdependent world, then we repeat a failing that is common to all historical social-contract doctrines. In assessing the institutional structure of a society by looking merely at how it affects (distributes benefits and burdens among) *its members*, we fail to come to terms with how our society affects the lives of foreigners (and how our lives are affected by how other societies are organized)—we disregard the (negative) externalities a national social contract may impose upon those who are *not* parties to it.[19] The institutional structure the parties would prefer for their clients' own society need not coincide with the one they would rationally want in the other societies of an interdependent

---

[18]National democratic control over a given territory and its natural assets, say, seems obviously desirable in itself and yet may have distributive effects that tend to subvert the fairness of international economic relations. This consideration is analogous to Rawls's point that rules permitting free transfer and bequest, though unobjectionable in themselves, would tend to disrupt a fair distribution of opportunities and bargaining power (BSS 54). Background justice might be preserved in the face of differential national assets through some form of shared control over, (or an extraction tax upon) nonrenewable natural assets.

[19]Rawls is sometimes aware of this point, as I have shown in §21.4 (TJ 380).

international system. And since impartiality (/the veil of ignorance) precludes us (/the parties) from making an exception of our (/their clients') own society, the criterion of domestic justice must then be adopted from a point of view that combines both perspectives—from the suitably constrained standpoint of persons who are both insiders and outsiders of (different) national societies. Precisely such a standpoint is afforded by the global original position I have proposed.

22.2.4. Furthermore it would seem difficult in a context of tight global interdependence to maintain the sharp distinction between national and international institutions that R_1 and R_2 presuppose. How does one decide whether such institutions as "competitive markets, private property in the means of production, and the monogamous family" (TJ 7) are national or international, and therefore are to be governed by the domestic criterion adopted in the first or by the global criterion adopted in the second session of the original position? By recourse to their history, by the amount of international interaction they involve, or by some conceptual criterion? Or can we follow Rawls, who simply declares that the task of the global parties is confined to choosing "the fundamental principles to adjudicate conflicting claims among states" (TJ 378)?[20]

But even this stipulation only highlights the most intractable issue— the *institution of the modern state* as a particular form of political and economic organization centering around governments that have eminent domain in a demarcated territory, control overwhelming force within it, and interpret and enforce international law beyond its borders. This institution would simply be taken for granted.[21] In Rawls's sketch, the mere existence of the states system in its current form reduces the agenda of the parties' global session to dealings between governments and motivates the priority of domestic over global princi-

[20]Presumably Rawls here has conflicting claims among state *governments* in mind. Constricting the agenda for the global session in this way would certainly make it easier to have the parties adopt something like the familiar principles of international law. It would ensure in advance that the adopted criterion could not possibly assess, one way or the other, what many believe to be the most significant injustice of our time, the opportunities for international exploitation that the world market affords to powerful economic agents operating in impoverished Third World environments.

[21]The claim that absolute military and territorial sovereignty constitutes a *definitive* characteristic of states, and hence must be taken for granted in any attempt to develop a conception of global justice, would go counter to Rawls's repeated insistence that substantive questions cannot be settled by definition or conceptual analysis (TJ 51, 579). Even accepting the proposed definition, we should have to ask why states so defined ought to exist. Let me also note how transcending the prevailing states system fundamentally differs from abolishing the institution of the family (cf. TJ 511–12, 462–63, 301, 74). I would think that the latter goal, unlike the former, is ruled out by "the elementary facts about persons and their place in nature," which are to be taken for granted in Rawls's theory and in the original position (TJ 257). There are two relevant differences, each singly sufficient: first, the nation-state is a comparatively recent historical development and thus certainly unconnected to any essential human need and, second, what is at issue is not the abolition of states but the reform of their internal institutional organization and (especially) of the ground rules regulating international interaction.

ples of justice. His endorsement of this institution can have force, however, only if it has been subjected to moral examination (like other social institutions). Otherwise Rawls would be begging a crucial question, provided we allow, as reasonably we must at the outset, that justice may *fail to require* the states system in its present form. Here Rawls, given his individualism, cannot respond that states or the traditions and communal life they protect have in their own right a claim to exist. And while the institutions of any isolated state might be justified by reference to its *least advantaged* members, a *system* of sovereign states requires a global justification, which, within a Rawlsian conception, must involve a criterion of justice that embodies a priority concern for the social position of the globally least advantaged persons.

22.2.5. My final argument in favor of G is that it offers a significant expositional advantage. Not only can the description of the original position, particularly the motivational assumption characterizing the parties as representing *persons* whose share of social primary goods they seek to optimize, remain the same on the global level. (R_1 also has this advantage.) But in addition we secure the coherence and harmony of our conclusions in advance. *All* institutional matters, including the ideal extent of national sovereignty, are now systematically addressed within a single framework.[22] There is no competition between institutional desiderata issuing from the deliberations of parties differently defined, nor are specific institutional features presupposed ad hoc prior to the original position. By not taking the present states system for granted, by letting the parties decide (as it were) among criteria that accommodate ethnic and cultural diversity in different ways, we can then considerably deepen Rawls's conception, make it more unified and elegant. This gain is significant in its own right, especially in view of Rawls's constructivism, which aims to systematize our moral consciousness into a principled and surveyable whole. Rawls holds that what moves us to accept a conception of justice over others is first its comprehensiveness in accommodating our considered judgments (the aggregate initial plausibility of its various elements) and, second, the unity and elegance achieved in their synthesis (cf. KCMT 518–19). G is a marked improvement in both these respects.

22.2.6. Let me add that G is also in greater harmony (than R_1 and R_2) with an ideal to which Rawls seems to be quite attracted, the ideal of a community of humankind. Thus, in his discussion of stability, he maintains that our "sense of justice is continuous with the love of mankind" (TJ 476) and adds that we would ideally develop a "devotion to institu-

---

[22]This greater unity is also reflected in nonideal contexts where, for instance, national borders may be controversial. What looks like the repression of a local disturbance from one perspective may appear to be denial of the right to self-determination from another. Given the proposed modification, one can systematically tackle such questions through a specification of the basic political liberties, whereas conceiving justice as within and between societies presupposes that their borders are already beyond dispute. Cf. D'Amato, J 268.

tions and traditions . . . which serve the general interests of mankind"
(TJ 489, cf. 501). In enlarging upon Humboldt's ideal of a social union of
social unions, Rawls again finds himself "led to the notion of the
community of humankind the members of which enjoy one another's
excellences and individuality elicited by free institutions, and they
recognize the good of each as an element in the complete activity the
whole scheme of which is consented to and gives pleasure to all" (TJ
523).

23. The External Argument

So far I have shown only that Rawls's idea of a global interpretation of
the original position, on any of the three specifications I have considered, yields a criterion of global justice that is unlikely to vindicate the
traditional international-law regime, which Rawls also endorses. The
incompatibility can be dissolved in two ways. We might say that despite
this endorsement, Rawls is really committed to supporting global institutional reforms toward a regime under which radical inequalities
and deprivations (especially of basic rights and liberties) would be less
widespread and severe. Alternatively, one might hold that such a criterion of global justice is so implausible that one should rather reaffirm
Rawls's endorsement of the law of nations and then modify drastically,
or even withdraw his idea of globalizing the original position. I will
defend the former solution.

In making this defense, I will not worry about the charge that a global
order satisfying Rawlsian principles would be morally unacceptable in
itself, for this would be an objection to Rawls's entire conception and
not to its globalization. His conception centrally involves the claim that
any self-contained social system satisfying the two principles *is* morally
acceptable.

My concern is with objections asserting that in the world as it is there
are special factors, relevant on the global but not the national plane,
that make it inappropriate to apply Rawls's maximin criterion to the
global basic structure. It is convenient to sort such objections into four
categories, depending on whether they appeal to (A) realist or (B) moral
considerations, and on whether they concern (1) the ideal of a just
world order or (2) the transition toward such an order. This section
proceeds in three steps. I will first (§23.1) show that only objections in
category (B1) can seriously endanger my main thesis—namely, that
given Rawlsian commitments, we should assess the justice of our
global institutional scheme by reference to the worst representative
share it tends to generate. I will then (§23.2) discuss three less important objections in this category, before (§23.3) turning to what I consider the most serious objection, the argument from cultural diversity.

23.1. We might still conclude in the end, after the most thorough analysis of institutional options with their coordinate paths of transition, that there is no feasible and morally viable avenue of institutional reform toward a juster global regime. Perhaps our world, so full of oppression, starvation, and war, provides the best feasible minimum share.[23] Or perhaps juster global basic structures are out of reach from where we are. If this were really true, it would go some way toward showing that the world is as just as we now can or may make it, but it would *not* show that a Rawlsian criterion is inappropriate on the global plane. It still "can serve as a standard for appraising institutions and for guiding the overall direction of social change" (TJ 263), to be carried "as far as circumstances permit" (TJ 246). Such a standard would no more be refuted by the fact that it cannot be fully satisfied than an achievement test would be refuted by the fact that no one can answer all the questions in the allotted time. It is not a necessary truth about justice that a just world is attainable through morally permissible institutional reforms.

It is also possible, though never knowable, that whatever improvements are feasible will never take place. Perhaps it is naïve or utopian to hope that any future world will better accord with a Rawlsian conception of global justice. But this is an indictment not of that conception but of ourselves. Realism hardly requires that principles of justice must conform themselves to the prevailing sordid realities. We don't feel justified to give up our ideals of domestic justice or personal honesty just because we despair of achieving them fully. We cannot reasonably demand of moral principles that they vindicate the status quo. All we may ask is that a conception of justice provide a criterion for assessing our global order that allows us to choose from among the feasible and morally accessible avenues of institutional change and thus specifies our moral task gradually to *improve* the justice of this order.

Though they defend my central thesis, these remarks are in an important sense a weak defense, leaving open whether the existing global basic structure can be criticized as unjust. Whether it can depends on general empirical facts that I cannot establish: Is there a feasible alternative global basic structure that would tend to generate less severe deprivations in first-principle goods? Is there a feasible path of institutional reform toward such a world order? The Rawlsian criterion of global justice still makes it possible to justify the prevailing international order by demonstrating that all feasible alternative schemes would tend to produce even greater deprivations and inequalities.

[23]Such a demonstration would be akin to the "slaveholder's argument" in Rawls (TJ 167–68). Yet this justification of the scheme would still leave open whether we are entitled to the particular positions we occupy within the scheme. Even if the argument justifies slavery (the institution), the slaves might still argue that *this slaveholder* is not entitled to his advantaged position, a point Rawls does not take notice of. Likewise, even if the prevailing institutional scheme were as just as we can or may make it, it could still be true that because of past crimes or injustices, many persons and groups are now more (dis)advantaged than by right they ought to be.

Alternatively, one can argue that all feasible ways of working for or implementing institutional reforms are blocked by moral considerations. Yet this is a hopeless claim. There surely are important moral constraints on how to promote institutional change, centrally including constraints on violence, but these constraints still leave us, the more advantaged, many options (though they limit what the less advantaged may do when the more advantaged resist institutional reforms that justice demands).

Similarly spurious (though convenient and therefore popular) are claims to the effect that though we *may* promote institutional reform, we also *may* insist on the perpetuation of our advantaged position. Let me briefly discuss two claims of this kind. First, it is said on behalf of the advantaged participants in an unjust institutional scheme that they formed "legitimate expectations" guiding their choice of a profession, their decisions to found a family, to save money, and so forth and that it is *unfair* that they should have to change their lives now, after having made consequential decisions on the basis of sincere, albeit false, moral beliefs. To begin with, such a view is questionable in that it would increase the incentives toward persuading others (for example, our children) that prevailing institutions are just even when we are not at all convinced that they are. By inculcating such legitimate expectations in them, we insure them against institutional reforms that would reduce their advantaged position. Moreover, the view clashes with what is widely affirmed for morality, that you have no moral claim to stolen property bequeathed to you by your mother, no matter how (innocently) attached you may have become to it in the meantime. Why should matters be different when what is bequeathed to you is an excessively advantaged position in an unjust institutional scheme? Finally, the appeal to fairness can be raised much more plausibly for the other side. For it is hardly fair that those who have been harmed and disadvantaged by unjust institutions should continue to suffer so that those who have been unjustly advantaged by them will not have their expectations disappointed.

Second, it is often said that persons have an indefeasible right (strictly: privilege) to spend most of their income and wealth as they please, that we enjoy, as James Fishkin puts it, a "cutoff for heroism" and a "robust zone of [moral] indifference" (LO chaps. 3–4). Let us grant (for the sake of argument!) that there is such an overriding privilege, perhaps limiting morally mandated expenditures to 2 percent of what we own. We may "sacrifice" more but cannot be morally required to do so. Again, such a fundamental privilege can apply only to what we are morally entitled to. It need not apply to what (directly or indirectly) was acquired through crimes or within an unjust institutional scheme. So, even if we grant the overriding moral privilege Fishkin claims, his argument leads nowhere if it is true that we are advantaged participants under prevailing institutions and these institutions are unjust against the background of at least one accessible alternative scheme under which persons could enjoy their (*ex hypothesi*) preeminent Fishkinian privilege, while lesser rights (to be free from violence and starvation) are also better protected.

A parallel response applies to those who invoke other values—such as our compatriotic fellow feeling or our deep loyalties and commitments, constitutive attachments and friendships, and essential projects—to argue that we may resist progress toward global justice. Within a just world order, all persons, and not just a small minority, could lead lives that embody and are enriched by these values. Therefore, those concerned for such values have reason to support global institutional reforms. Yet all too often what such critics care about is not that such values should thrive but that *they* (perhaps with their family, friends, community, or nation) should enjoy them. Yes, progress would entail that we would have less of a chance to pursue our more expensive projects, but then the question is again why the existing commitments of those greatly advantaged by unjust institutions should take precedence over the interests of those who, at the margins of survival, are in large part deprived of the opportunity to form and pursue such commitments in the first place.

My responses to claims of this general kind are somewhat tangential to my main goal. Even if there were significant moral obstacles to institutional reforms (be they entitlements of the more advantaged or further constraints on action), they would not count against the Rawlsian *criterion* of global justice. They would merely show that it is more difficult to make progress toward satisfying this criterion.

23.2. Let me now discuss three objections of category (B1), which, by appeal to special factors present on the global plane, seek to deny the applicability of Rawls's maximin criterion to the world at large.

23.2.1. Consider the view that whereas Rawls's criterion of justice is meant to apply to the institutions of a self-contained social system whose parts are closely interdependent, international interaction is in fact rather insignificant. Coming, as it does, from the more affluent citizens of the First World, this objection is marred by historical considerations. Perhaps *our* history, economy, and social life have not been affected very much by exogenous influences, but consider the inverse viewpoint. The North Atlantic states have, rather brutally, imposed a single global system of military and economic competition, destroying in the process the social systems indigenous to four continents. Our political and economic transactions, even those internal to the developed West, continue to exert an overwhelming influence on national institutions and social positions in Third World countries.

My point here is not that we must make good for colonial plunder, slavery, and exploitation. Nor am I arguing that these historical events contributed to our advantaged position within today's radically unequal global distribution of social positions and that we are therefore beneficiaries of past crimes and injustices (though it seems difficult to deny that we are). It is enough that the lives of the vast majority of human beings are profoundly shaped and affected by events reverberating through an international scheme of trade and diplomacy in which we are highly advantaged participants.[24]

But could we not go back to a world of closed, self-contained societies in which, as I have already conceded, a Rawlsian criterion of global justice would be out of place, since there would *be* no global basic structure for them to apply to? Or couldn't we move toward a world of minimal international interaction in which straightforward rules of rational cooperation might be appropriate?[25] I am not denying such possibilities, but they are academic. The world is not, and hardly will be again, one in which a criterion of global justice is unnecessary or undemanding.

23.2.2. Still, such academic speculations are relevant for a second objection to globalizing Rawls, which asserts that a criterion of justice is to be rejected if the scheme it favors would not be mutually beneficial. The more prosperous states, the objection continues, would do better without any international cooperation than within a global institutional scheme satisfying a Rawlsian criterion. This objection is raised by Brian Barry against Beitz: "I do not think that [a global difference principle] can plausibly be said to be advantageous to rich as well as poor countries" (HJGP 232, cf. 233–34).

Barry's objection can be construed in two ways. He can be taken to assert that the *transition* to a just global scheme must benefit even those now unjustly advantaged. Barry would then be insisting that existing advantages in capital, technology, education, and the like, need not be relinquished voluntarily. This is the construal to which David Richards responds: "When . . . John Stuart Mill . . . criticiz[ed] injustices to women, he conceded that men, as a class, would suffer some losses when they surrendered their unjust domination, just as slaveowners did when slavery was ended; Mill's argument is quite clear that the gain is not one of actual reciprocal advantage to men (indeed, they lose), but the gain in justice when men regulate their conduct by principles they would reasonably accept if they were women on the receiving end" (IDJ 277–78).[26]

But Barry may also be interpreted as claiming that the new institu-

---

[24]Even apparently domestic events, such as changes in U.S. interest rates or speculative trades in commodity futures, can have a tremendous impact in poor states that have a significant foreign debt, rely on the export of mineral resources or cash crops, or require food imports. Or consider the direct influence exerted by Western governments and their organs (such as the International Monetary Fund) or the immediate impact of arms sales and foreign investments. At issue here is not whether these effects are, on the whole, good or bad. What matters is how profound they are. For many persons they make the difference between life and death, e.g., through starvation, (civil) war, or government repression.

[25]See Beitz, PTIR 165, for the idea of minimal interaction (trading apples and pears). A theory of global justice as rational cooperation is suggested in Danielson, TIP.

[26]See also my last note to Chap. 2.

tional scheme, *once in place*, must be a mutually beneficial one. He could then reply to Richards that, whereas men do better with sex equality than if they did not interact with women at all, the United States, say, would do *worse* in a Rawlsian world order than in splendid isolation.[27]

This objection may rest on a misunderstanding of the maximin criterion. The terms of social cooperation are required to optimize (interschemically) the worst social position, and they will do so only if they engender a good deal of cooperation. Cooperation, however— between persons or collectivities—cannot be coerced; it must be elicited. Participants will be prepared to conduct interpersonal/intercollective transactions only insofar as these benefit them under the prevailing terms. Here the equalizing tendency of the maximin criterion is checked. Though an egalitarian scheme ensures for the least advantaged (the populations of less developed countries) a large *relative* share of the benefits of social cooperation, it makes such cooperation less attractive to others and thus less extensive. For this reason, it may be less just than a more inegalitarian scheme.[28] In any case, a global order that is just by Rawlsian lights is one under which persons and collectivities are free to shun economic transactions of specific kinds. The populations of more developed countries and regions, in particular, would be free to trade only domestically and with one another and hence can be presumed to benefit from whatever further transactions they would conduct. In this sense one can say, barring externalities, that a national or global basic structure satisfying the Rawlsian criterion is, *by the very construction of this criterion*, mutually beneficial for individuals and collectivities as against a benchmark of noncooperation (though presumably no participants would benefit as much and as disproportionately from their international economic relations as we in the developed West do at present).

Nevertheless, Barry's objection may be renewed one last time. A global difference principle may justify not merely a general adjustment of market prices but a different specification of property rights over natural assets—involving, for example, an international tax on (or international ownership and control of) natural assets. It is then quite possible that an asset-rich society or group of societies would do worse under a just global basic structure than in perfect isolation, namely, when the benefits of cooperating are outweighed by the costs of sharing natural assets.

But is this a problem? Should one, in constructing the hypothetical isolation scenarios that are to serve as benchmarks, take as given the

---

[27]Barry's objection, so construed, arises not only in the global context. It can equally be raised within a state, on behalf of a wealthy province, for example, or by a group of such provinces seeking to exclude a poor one. Quite apart from the issue of globalization, then, it is crucial for Rawls's theory that this objection be met, as I hope to do in the text.

[28]Cf. Rawls's distinction between "perfectly just" and "just throughout" (TJ 78–79).

natural assets of the various societies (territories with their mineral resources, fertility, climate, etc.)? Doing so involves two presuppositions, both of which seem questionable and difficult to defend. First, one would be presupposing that the institution of states should be understood as including full national ownership of all natural assets within the national territory, regardless of the distributional effects of this understanding. Here little is gained by simply declaring in the style of Nozick that this principle of national sovereignty "is fundamental." Arguing for the principle would presumably involve the claim that it is morally imperative that states or national communities, perhaps conceived as ultimate units of moral concern, should fully own some territory. It would not be enough to show that they should fully *control* some national territory, because such control would be compatible with, for example, an international tax on the extraction of national mineral resources through which at least the distributional effects of the morally arbitrary geographical distribution of natural assets could be mitigated. Since the premise that there ought to be full national control of natural assets does not support the desired conclusion, the complaint does then involve the presupposition that nations have a moral claim fully to *own* the natural assets within their territory. It seems doubtful that this full-ownership claim has sufficient plausibility to furnish (part of) an independent constraint against which a criterion of global justice can be checked.

The second presupposition is that the currently existing distribution of natural assets among states is morally acceptable. I find this implausible in light of how such assets were in fact acquired in a history involving genocide, colonialism, slavery, unjust wars, and the like. These historical facts cannot be corrected for. We cannot know what natural (and social) assets we would now have if the relevant crimes and injustices of the past had never occurred. Who would "we" even be, in such a counterfactual world? This consideration suggests a different specification of Barry's benchmark, yielding a constraint that a Rawlsian maximin criterion meets easily. Each society, or group of societies, must be more prosperous cooperating within a just global basic structure than it/they would be if existing in perfect isolation with a share of the world's natural assets proportionate to its/their population.[29]

23.2.3. A third objection contends that our global social system, in contrast to some developed Western societies, falls so far short of being well-ordered in Rawls's sense that we cannot apply to it the same

---

[29]So understood, the constraint, rather than shielding resource-rich societies against a Rawlsian criterion of global justice, would tend to protect some of today's poorest societies, those falling far below the modified benchmark. We would conclude, on non-Rawlsian grounds, that the existing global order is unjust insofar as some societies or groups of societies would be more prosperous if, other things equal, they existed in isolation with a proportionate share of the world's natural assets.

criterion of justice as we might apply to the latter.[30] Rawls, however, wants his conception of justice to be more widely applicable.[31] His notion of a well-ordered society is normative, not descriptive: "It embodies . . . certain general features of any society that it seems one would, on due reflection, wish to live in and want to shape our interests and character" (RAM 634). Thus, when the parties are said to choose a criterion of justice for a well-ordered society, this cannot mean that their criterion is applicable *only* to well-ordered societies, that a different criterion should be used for assessing societies that are not well-ordered. (If it meant this, then Rawls's principles would be entirely irrelevant because most of his twelve conditions for well-orderedness [RAM 634–36] are not satisfied by any existing national society either.) Rather, it means that the chosen criterion of justice must harmonize with a cluster of our considered judgments that Rawls collects together into the "model conception" of a well-ordered society. It must be satisfiable under the ideal conditions of a well-ordered social system. Beyond this, however, it must also guide us toward such ideal conditions, must "provide an Archimedean point for appraising existing institutions . . . an independent standard for guiding the course of social change" (TJ 520). Precisely this function of Rawls's criterion would be jeopardized if the Archimedean point itself shifted in response to changing conditions, for example, our changing distance from a well-ordered social system.

This point is clear on the national level. When a constitutional democracy lapses into totalitarianism or authoritarianism (as Germany did in the 1930s or Chile in the 1970s), we are hardly led to think that now a different criterion of justice should be used to appraise the new regime and to guide our efforts to effect change. Similarly, I would think, we cannot conceive of our criterion of global justice, our ranking of alternative global institutional schemes, as changing in response to varying international conditions. Of course, many institutional mechanisms crucial for anything like a well-ordered world community are presently lacking, but how does this lack undermine the belief that in a

---

[30]I owe this objection, forcefully stated, to Robert Fullinwider of the University of Maryland Center for Philosophy and Public Policy.

[31]Originally Rawls's conception was to have been applicable to all self-contained social systems existing in the circumstances of justice (TJ §22). Rawls has since been narrowing the scope he claims for his conception. He now says that "justice as fairness is framed to apply to what I have called the 'basic structure' of a modern constitutional democracy.... Whether justice as fairness can be extended to a general political conception for different kinds of societies . . . [or] to a general moral conception . . . are altogether separate questions. I avoid prejudging these larger questions one way or the other" (JFPM 224–25). He does not mean, I am afraid, that the ideal of a just basic structure he seeks to specify is to envision a constitutional democracy. Rather, he seems to be delimiting what is now the scope of his theoretical concern. His conception is to apply to constitutional democracies; it may or may not be relevant to social systems that are structured differently. It is thereby left open whether it is still applicable even to Great Britain, which does not have a constitution.

just world such mechanisms would exist and that they ought to be established? The creation of political and legal institutions on both the national and global levels would seem paradigmatic instances of our natural duty "to assist in the establishment of just arrangements when they do not exist" (TJ 334, cf. 115).

23.3. The final objection I will consider is that the ideal of a global regime that is just by Rawlsian lights may cohere well with *our* cultural heritage and *our* considered judgments but is nevertheless inappropriate on account of existing intercultural diversity of traditions and moral judgments. We must not impose our values upon the rest of the world, must not pursue a program of institutional reform that envisions the gradual supplanting of all other cultures by a globalized version of our own culture and values.[32]

This is, I think, the most serious objection to globalizing Rawls and the one that seems to have influenced Rawls himself.[33] Consider this passage:

> We take our examination of the Kantian conception of justice as addressed to an impasse in our recent political history; the course of democratic thought over the past two centuries, say, shows that there is no agreement on the way basic social institutions should be arranged if they are to conform to the freedom and equality of citizens as moral persons. . . . [W]e are not trying to find a conception of justice suitable for all societies regardless of their particular social or historical circumstances. We want to settle a fundamental disagreement over the just form of basic institutions within a democratic society under modern conditions. . . . How far the conclusions we reach are of interest in a wider context is a separate question. [KCMT 517–18]

It is worth noting, to begin with, that in the rather agnostic final sentence Rawls is careful not to prejudge the question of an eventual global extension (as he says explicitly at JFPM 225). Moreover, by appealing to such landmarks of "our" political culture as the Declaration of Independence, Immanuel Kant, and the French Revolution, Rawls

[32]The plea not to ride roughshod over the values of other cultures certainly has moral weight. But it can be amusing to observe who is making such pleas. Many of the more emphatic protestations against pursuing our ideals of justice in the international arena come from members of our own culture, and from the more advantaged ones at that. There is no comparable outcry from that global majority living without protection from hunger and oppression. Asserting that tyranny and exploitation in an allied country are accepted parts of its culture is often convenient but less often true. There may well be much less genuinely intercultural (and thus morally significant) disagreement than is often taken for granted. See Berger, ATHR for some ideas on cultural diversity from a sociologist.

[33]The later Rawls, that is, who is withdrawing from the topic of global justice and no longer asserts that his conception of justice is appropriate to all national societies. The spatiotemporal domain that he claims his conception to be applicable to seems to have undergone substantial shrinkage toward the central instance—the United States in the 1960s and '70s. Those uneasy with this shrinkage have another reason for following my interpretation. G does not sidestep cultural divergence but accommodates it.

implies that he takes this culture to extend well beyond our national borders.[34]

More important, Rawls's hesitations affect only one aspect of the global extension. They indicate some doubt as to whether he should take a stand on how societies culturally different from our own should be organized and on how to assess the justice of their domestic institutions. Concerning this question, there may seem to be a morally attractive alternative, namely, to leave this up to the members of that society. No such alternative is available, however, with regard to the deeper question of how the global basic structure should be assessed and reformed. This question we cannot evade short of renouncing international interaction altogether. Nor can we adequately respond to it except through a conception of background justice. There is no recognized *natural* criterion of justice. Nor can there be a *neutral* criterion equally congenial to all values and cultures—minimally because there is outright disagreement about what forms of national organization a just global order should allow. Some will advocate tolerance for as many diverse forms of national regime as can coexist, while others will insist on the global proliferation of some narrowly defined form of regime.[35]

But if these two approaches fail and if global interdependence poses a genuine problem of background justice, then how can Rawls even hesitate to globalize the two principles—*his* criterion for assessing basic institutions? How can he decline to take a stand, a *Rawlsian* stand, on a global order in which the social position of the least advantaged is unimaginably worse than that of the least advantaged in the developed West, in whose behalf Rawls has criticized the domestic basic structures of advanced Western societies?

The answer has to do, I believe, with Rawls's constructivist mode of justification. Reflective equilibrium is achieved among, and relies upon, our considered judgments, at least some of which are moral ones: "There is an appeal to intuition at the basis of the theory of justice" (TJ 124–25). Rawls does not speak of intuitions in the traditional sense, however, as a priori and shared by all rational beings. He recognizes that our moral consciousness evolves historically and ontogenetically and that its fixed points, though we have nothing else to go on, lack any

---

[34]See also his references to "the course of democratic thought over the past two centuries, say" (KCMT 517), to "a democratic society under modern conditions" (KCMT 518, 537), and to "a modern constitutional democracy" (JFPM 224).

[35]Another flaw in the ideal of neutrality is that alternative global basic structures differ in the extent to which they would support any particular form of national organization. This is analogous to a point Rawls makes when he says that the choice of a domestic basic structure will differentially affect the chances of alternative religions and conceptions of the good to gain adherents (FG 549). The idea of institutional arrangements under which all values flourish equally is deeply incoherent. *Any* institutional scheme can be opposed on the (accurate) ground that it is comparatively inhospitable to some particular value or form of life.

ultimate foundation—rational or empirical (cf. JFPM 235). Rawls's explicit strategy is therefore to convince others of the criterion he proposes by bringing their own considered judgments to bear upon the issue of social institutions. The idea of globalizing Rawls's conception of justice is then challenged by the great international diversity of considered judgments, which rules out any "appeal to intuition" in the global setting.[36]

But I don't think this problem defeats the idea of globalization, at least when the "search for reasonable grounds for reaching agreement . . . replaces the search for moral truth," and "the practical social task is primary" (KCMT 519). To attain this practical goal on the global plane, an agreement need not specify a particular derivation of or rationale for the criterion of justice; "there can, in fact, be considerable differences in citizens' conceptions of justice provided that these conceptions lead to similar political judgments. And this is possible, since different premises can yield the same conclusion. In this case there exists what we may refer to as overlapping rather than strict consensus" (TJ 387–88; cf. JFPM 246–51; IOC). What counts, then, regardless of the considered judgments and other reasons that may motivate a particular person, is convergence upon the criterion itself. The present objection to the globalization of Rawls's criterion must then show more than cultural diversity; it must at least show that agreement on such a criterion of global justice is out of reach.

I say "at least" because we might envision an even narrower kind of overlapping consensus. Even those who endorse different criteria of justice and a different long-term vision of a juster world order may still agree about the first stretch of the road. This is not a merely theoretical possibility. Many proposals for institutional reforms, politically supported by Third World nations and arguably favored by Rawlsian principles, have been blocked in recent years by governments of the developed West. Here the fact of cultural diversity is exploited to complement the tedious appeal to our collective self-interest (euphemistically, the "national interest") with a *moral* justification for such resistance. Such a justification is perverse. It would allow us to resist institutional reforms demanded by justice as we ourselves understand it and to exploit what we ourselves recognize as unjust advantages we enjoy within the current international order, on the grounds that other cultures do not (fully) share our moral convictions. (This is analogous to the familiar if outdated belief that as good Christians we may colo-

---

[36]Though cultural diversity in moral conceptions is certainly great, it isn't entirely clear how great it is. Here one should not, I think, pay too much attention to government behavior. In adopting high-sounding national constitutions or international documents, governments may be catering to a foreign audience, and such documents may then not show intercultural consensus. In torturing political prisoners, on the other hand, governments may well be violating, rather than expressing, the moral commitments of their culture.

nize and enslave our neighbors so long as they are not Christians themselves.) If we may not, then we need a conception of global justice at least for the critical assessment and guidance of our own government's policies, which may constitute very significant obstacles to global institutional reform today—obstacles, moreover, for which we would be most immediately responsible.

However narrow a moral overlap we may aim for, I admit we won't get it. There are bound to be persons who disagree with us, in good faith, even about the very first steps of institutional reform. To them, the Rawlsian framework poses a challenge to work out their own conception of justice or at least to expound the grounds of their disagreement. Perhaps some of their criticisms can be undercut internally, or Rawls's main conclusions can be preserved by justifying and explaining them in the objectors' terms to their satisfaction. Maybe the Rawlsian conception will have to be revised in light of their critique. Such things cannot be known in advance. Only the ensuing discussion can show where convergence is attainable and where agreement on particular reforms can indeed not be achieved.

Even if disagreement persists, we may still conclude that a competing position is wrong, and we may then work for a juster world without or even against our opponents, insofar as doing so is morally permissible by our lights. This is what happened in the American Revolution, in the Civil War, and in the New Deal. Social institutions derive no special moral sanctity from the mere fact that they now exist. If we are convinced on reflection that they are unjust, then we ought to work toward feasible improvements, even if some genuine moral disagreements cannot now be resolved. The fact of disagreement is no reason not to act in light of whatever (factual and) moral beliefs we now think are best supported. Our considered judgments support a conception of justice whose scope is universal, even though its present appeal is not.[37] And we are surely not morally required to acquiesce in *any* conduct or practice backed by the (sincerely held) considered judgments of others. As Rawls says, "A theory of justice must work out from its own point of view how to treat those who dissent from it" (TJ 370). Why should *liberals* shun the political struggle over institutional arrangements, leaving their determination to the nonliberal disputants?

The central point of the last two paragraphs is that the difficulty is not unique to the global plane. Intercultural diversity is only a special case of diversity of considered judgments in general. Thus, predictably, critics of Rawls have rejected his ideal of a well-ordered society by refusing allegiance to the "requisite understanding of freedom and equality" (KCMT 517) that he claims is implicit in our public culture. Rawls was not deterred by the certainty that other thinkers in the West would, in light of their moral convictions, come to reject his conclu-

---

[37]Cf. Beitz, CINS 596.

sions. He could not and did not achieve even the narrowest overlap within a single national society. He could hope to (and, I think, *did*) express the convictions of a segment of the intelligentsia in the United States and some other countries, but can he claim to speak for the black, Hispanic, and native American subcultures or even for ordinary farmers, clerks, housewives, or factory workers? Rawls left such questions open, attempting merely to systematize "one (educated) person's sense of justice" (TJ 50). He has thereby initiated a discourse about justice from which greater clarity and convergence may emerge in due course.

The idea of globalizing Rawls aims for no more and no less. We must not be disheartened—or feel absolved!—by pessimistic expectations about the appeal and political success of our considered conception of justice or of the institutional reforms it may call for. Rather, we should develop and propose this conception and then deal with objections and counterproposals from other cultures or from within our own as they actually arise. A cross-cultural discourse about a substantive moral issue of great common concern will broaden the vision of its participants and will tend to make the moral conceptions involved less parochial as each tries to accommodate what it finds tolerable or even valuable in other cultural traditions.[38]

A globalized version of Rawls's conception of justice is an especially suitable one with which to enter such a cross-cultural discourse. It is based upon a small set of widely accepted values and ideas, and it can offer a good deal of flexibility for acknowledging and incorporating cultural diversity. My proposal G, though in some ways more radical, has most to offer by way of such flexibility. Rawls's own sketch of global justice—on either R_1 or R_2—envisions a world in which every national society progresses, in light of the same two principles, toward a predetermined institutional ideal. Rawls allows some variation in national constitutions by letting each of them be determined through a hypothetical "constitutional convention" featuring parties behind a thinner veil of ignorance, who "know the relevant general facts about their society" including its "political culture" (TJ 197). But the flexibility afforded by this gradual lifting of the veil of ignorance is quite limited. Though Rawls allows some variation in how his criterion of domestic justice may be specified, he does not allow this criterion itself to vary from society to society.[39]

[38]There is another important reason for believing that an international discussion of the topic of global justice can be a catalyst for moral progress. Many persons in the West acquiesce in the foreign policy of their government not because they believe that—thanks to cultural diversity, perhaps—it is justified but because they have no settled moral beliefs about this matter one way or the other. In view of the enormity of prevailing deprivations and disadvantages, however, this is an issue that one *ought* to reflect upon. If anything academics might do can really make a substantial moral difference, then a discourse about global justice may well be it.

[39]Moreover, because of his tendency to think of the political process as an instance of only imperfect procedural justice (§13.2–3), Rawls ties even the limited international

G is more liberal in this respect. The global parties are not constrained by any prior criterion of domestic justice; and they will then specifically decide how much room to leave for differences in national institutional arrangements and in national conceptions of domestic justice. Seeing how the original position is described, the parties decide this question by balancing two desiderata (cf. §13.3 and §13.5): They want to enable citizens to choose and revise their own domestic constitution, even their own conception of domestic justice, so long as such choice results from and guarantees for the future free and informed decisions. Yet they also want to preclude institutions that tend to produce severe deprivations or disadvantages for some participants.

The resulting criterion of global justice might be similar to the criterion I have developed in Part Two. Assuming the special conception applies, the globalized first principle might be viewed as requiring a "thin" set of basic rights and liberties (analogous to the *Universal Declaration of Human Rights* and including an effective right to emigrate), which each national society could, in light of its national conception of domestic justice, "inflate" and specify into its own bill of rights. This suggestion is in line with our current moral beliefs. While we firmly believe that the constitutions of our (Western) societies ought to prohibit the establishment of days of government-enforced religious fasting, we can still accept as just a global institutional scheme in which such legislation is not unconstitutional in some (non-Western) societies. (Yet we cannot accept as just a global order in which torture is not ruled out in *all* societies, whatever their culture.)

Similarly, while the global second principle would constrain how societies may arrange their economies, these constraints would be less stringent than Rawls's requirement that each society must satisfy the difference principle internally. This may be so because a country's choice among various forms of economic organization (more or less egalitarian than Rawls's national difference principle would require) does not affect the globally worst representative share of social primary goods or because this choice is protected by the basic political liberties which allow the citizens of each nation to choose, within certain limits, their own mode of economic organization. The resulting global institutional ideal would then allow each society a good deal of choice as regards its internal practices (and moral principles), so long as such choices are supported by most of its citizens and are consistent with the basic rights of all human beings, citizens as well as outsiders.[40]

---

variation he allows to the diversity of national circumstances, rather than to the diversity of national collective preferences (§17.3). Even where constitutional and political choices may differ from country to country, he requires such differences to be rationally related to differences in national conditions. Actual citizens and legislators are required to accommodate these conditions in their deliberations and decisions through the thought experiment of how Rawlsian rational parties (placed behind a veil of ignorance of the appropriate thickness) would accommodate them.

[40]Rawls may now actually agree with this view. At least this is one possible way of making sense of this cryptic remark: "The political liberties, assured their fair-value and

Of course these details are only illustrative speculation. What matters is that by balancing the liberty interest in collective autonomy against other liberty interests, G goes beyond R_1 and R_2 in the liberal quest to allow for "opposing religious, philosophical, and moral convictions" (KCMT 542).

24. Conclusion

24.1. Let me recapitulate the main steps through which I have come to doubt the appealing moral conviction that there is nothing seriously wrong, morally speaking, with the lives we lead. I should say in advance that steps 1, 2, 3, and 6 are essential to my argument; steps 4 and 5 merely broaden and strengthen its conclusion.

24.1.1. There are the abundantly documented facts of widespread extreme deprivations and disadvantages. Large segments of human-kind suffer severe oppression and poverty. They have no effective civil and political rights and are helplessly exposed to violence and abuse by soldiers and guerrillas, landowners and officials. Moreover, they are excluded from the natural and social resources of this planet: they are so poor as to be chronically exposed to malnutrition and outright starvation; they lack access to even minimal health care, and are liable to die early from the most trivial diseases; they rarely have enough education even to be able to read, write, or do elementary arithmetic. Finally most are in no position to improve their situation or to escape from it. Such widespread human misery provides the occasion for moral reflection, which must examine two ways in which we might be connected to this misery: Why do such radical inequalities persist, and what role (if any) do we play in their production? And how might such radical inequalities be overcome, and what role (if any) can we play in their eradication?

24.1.2. There are true macroexplanations of such extreme depriva-tions and disadvantages. These do not compete with true microex-planations, such as: this villager is killed by a death squad because its leader believes his village to be sympathetic to the rebels, this baby is starved because her father lost his job, this student is raped and tor-tured because she participated in a demonstration against the reigning military junta. Macroexplanations aim for an understanding of what microexplanations leave unexplained: Why does our world have such high *rates* of malnutrition, illiteracy, and infant mortality? What ac-counts for the *incidence* of torture and poverty; for the *frequency* of wars, death squads, and military juntas; for the *increasing* gap between rich and poor? The true macroexplanations of these aggregate phe-nomena prominently involve reference to basic global institutions. The

---

other relevant general principles, properly circumscribed, may of course supplement the principles of justice" (BLP 49–50).

frequency of wars and military juntas cannot be understood apart from the fact that our global political order reflects an intergovernmental modus vivendi. Accounting for the prevailing rates of malnutrition and infant mortality requires in addition reference to how the existing global economic scheme assigns eminent domain over natural assets and how it regulates international cooperation through unconstrained market mechanisms. Such macroexplanations may be highly complex, but what is important here is only that our global framework of basic institutions figures prominently in the true macroexplanations of morally significant phenomena and that reforms of this framework could lead to substantial improvements in respect to these phenomena. I do not pretend to have provided satisfactory macroexplanations or to have sketched in any detail paths of institutional reform toward a world order that would not tend to produce radical inequalities.

24.1.3. In thinking about the assessment and reform of basic institutions, we must not ignore their effects and, in particular, the benefits and burdens they tend to *engender*. By denying the relevance of engendered phenomena, one could insist that our global institutional framework is perfectly just already: "The ground rules do not directly call for deprivations and disadvantages. On the contrary, states are officially assigned equal rights against one another and equal sovereignty to regulate their own internal affairs. (Even permanent membership in the United Nations Security Council is based on engendered inequalities in power.) Any inequalities in the political and economic strength of states and in the rights and affluence of their citizens, however radical and predictable they may be, are not established but only engendered by the prevailing global order and hence cannot be held against this order." In contrast to such a strongly deontological conception of justice, I have interpreted Rawls as committed to a broadly consequentialist (more specifically, a semiconsequentialist) approach to the subject of social justice, which established and engendered benefits and burdens are considered on a par. Although I have myself defended this approach, my main conclusion does not presuppose so strong a claim. So long as engendered deprivations and disadvantages count for anything at all in the assessment of social institutions, a good case can be made that the current global order is unjust against the background of feasible institutional alternatives that would not engender such radical inequalities. Even a mildly deontological conception of justice would support this conclusion.

24.1.4. The worst position that the existing global institutional scheme tends to produce affords an appropriate vantage point for assessing the justice of this order as a whole. In assessing the existing global order in comparison to its feasible institutional alternatives, one should be preeminently concerned with the worst-off participants under each institutional scheme. Now it may be denied that the concern for the least advantaged should have the absolute priority it has for

Rawls. One may say that, while terrible poverty and oppression are certainly prevalent and widespread, humankind has made great progress, as witnessed by the security and affluence enjoyed by the citizens of the developed Western nations. Although the least advantaged are as badly off as ever, at least the better positions (the top quintile or so of world population) have been improved considerably. But such progress, which certainly exists, also raises the problem of justice in sharper form. Because we are so affluent and powerful, almost everything we do has a significant impact upon living conditions elsewhere, and because we are so affluent and powerful, we are in a unique position to take up the theoretical and practical task of institutional reform. In any case, it seems quite impossible to deny that the position of its least advantaged participants is at least *one* important measure of the justice of an institutional scheme. If some feasible institutional reform is expected to lead to a significant improvement in the worst position, then this is surely an important reason in its favor.

24.1.5. A plausible evaluation of the morally significant consequences of feasible institutional schemes must give a prominent place to the satisfaction of basic social and economic needs. Here it may be too much to require that an institutional scheme be so designed that even the special needs of its naturally handicapped participants are met. Perhaps such special needs raise issues of morality rather than justice (as Rawls suggests by favoring a semiconsequentialist over a fully consequentialist approach). When even the standard basic socioeconomic needs of some participants are not met, however, we have a most urgent reason to think about, and promote, institutional reforms. This claim is often opposed by the assertion that it is more important that social institutions recognize and protect basic civil and political rights and liberties than that they ensure that basic social and economic needs are met. Even if this assertion could be sustained (and I have argued extensively that it cannot), my main conclusion would remain largely intact. The current global distribution of basic civil and political rights and liberties is extremely uneven. While we, through exercising control over a very powerful government, can play a significant role in shaping the common future of humankind, others either lack political rights altogether or exercise some democratic control within a state that is too poor and impotent to have any real influence. While our freedom and independence are secure, others must live under institutions and rulers installed or approved by foreigners, subject to threats, subversion, or invasion from abroad. And while the basic rights and liberties recognized here are well-protected in most population clusters, such basic rights and liberties are often not effectively enforced abroad even where they are officially on the books. The true macroexplanation of these international inequalities in effective civil and political freedom will again prominently involve features of the existing global order.

24.1.6. A global institutional scheme is imposed by all of us on each of us. It is imposed *on* us in that we cannot simply drop out and renounce participation. This fact is most significant in the case of the scheme's most disadvantaged participants, who are literally being forced, ultimately with resort to violence, to abide by the going ground rules. Thus a mother, unable to find employment and desperate to feed her children, will be punished if she tries to take food from a shop, will be chased away if she tries to grow food on land that is not hers, will be arrested if she tries to demonstrate, will be turned away if she tries to cross into another country (such as ours, for example)—and this not by crooks and thugs but by "the law," by judges, immigration inspectors, and the police, who, backed by our recognition or acquiescence, do their "duty" in the name of human justice.[41] This reflection reveals how unjust institutions embody not only the deepest and most consequential form of human wrong but also (independently) the most intolerable. At least in the modern era, injustice appears in official clothing, under the name of justice, openly before the eyes of the world. It subverts not merely what is right but the very idea of right and leaves its victims without any recourse or appeal.

A global institutional framework is imposed *by*, especially, its more advantaged, more powerful participants. Institutions are not only "staffed" and enforced by human beings (are complex patterns of human conduct); they are also created, shaped, perpetuated, or changed by us. Property and promises, money and markets, governments and borders, treaties and diplomacy—all these do not occur naturally but are invented by human beings and continuously evolve through human conduct. Such institutions are "up to us," collectively, and we therefore have a collective *causal* responsibility for existing institutions. Together we change them or preserve them as they are. Since social institutions are more or less just depending on how they distribute morally significant benefits and burdens among their human participants, this causal responsibility gives rise to a *moral* responsibility, which is a collective responsibility for our collective role in imposing existing institutions upon, in particular, their most disadvantaged (and involuntary) participants. This responsibility may be of great moment when we find ourselves to be (advantaged) participants in an unjust institutional scheme. We have a *negative* duty not to collaborate in the imposition of unjust institutions; and we must then reflect upon and promote institutional reform.

24.2. Taken together, these considerations support two conclusions:

[41]Such recognition is not confined within national borders; the practices in another country are not "a different ballgame." We do not just take notice of foreign governments, laws, judges, and policemen (as empirical facts); we recognize them *as* governments, laws, judges, and policemen. The plausibility of the idea of a global basic structure derives not only from the worldwide existence of states with national governments, laws, judges, and policemen but from their international recognition and their role in international practices and interactions.

our current global institutional scheme is unjust, and as advantaged participants in this order we share a collective responsibility for its injustice. The injustice means, in human terms, not merely that many persons today are very badly off—are unfree, uneducated, powerless, starving, and poor—but that they are *disadvantaged by existing institutions*, deprived of freedom and education, oppressed, starved, and impoverished. The responsibility means that those who uphold and perpetuate these institutions, all of us together, are collectively doing what is done to (in particular) the least advantaged. We have a negative duty to desist; we ought to use our more advantaged political and economic position to work for global institutional reforms.

The plausibility of these conclusions does not materially depend on steps 4 and 5 (the priority concern for the least advantaged and the amendment to the first principle). If they had to be withdrawn or modified, then the current global order might be less unjust (and we collectively responsible for less deprivation) than I am presently inclined to believe. Nevertheless, the failure of these two ideas would not entail the collapse of my argument.

To reach its conclusions, my argument must assume that there are feasible paths of institutional reform whose pursuit would substantially raise the globally worst representative share, particularly in regard to the satisfaction of standard basic needs (as accommodated by the first principle). That there are such feasible paths of reform is something that, however likely it may seem, I have made no attempt to establish.

In one respect, this is not a serious gap. For suppose my argument were accepted. We would then have gained a reasonably clear and determinate idea of what a *plausible* defense of the status quo must look like. My argument leaves room for the attempt (by some social scientists, perhaps) to provide such a defense by showing, for example, that the globally worst representative share cannot be raised through institutional reforms. The chance that such a claim could survive collegial scrutiny seems slight, given the severity and extent of current human misery. Still, there is a remote possibility that some such argument will turn out to be convincing, and so we may yet be amazed (though hardly elated) to learn that our global order is now as just as we can make it and that there is nothing by way of institutional reform that we ought to undertake.

In another respect, the gap is quite serious. I would much like to be in a position to offer concrete and realistic ideas for how the political and economic reforms justice demands might actually be achieved. As it is, I can only hope that the interdisciplinary development of such ideas (involving politicians, jurists, and economists) is more likely once it is clearer what justice requires of our basic institutions.

24.3. I have argued that we advantaged participants share a collective responsibility for the existing global order (specifically for the worst social position we produce through its imposition) and that we have a negative duty to help reform this order insofar as it is unjust. But I do not mean this conclusion to entail an attribution of blame or guilt. It would be (not only counterproductive but also) plainly implausible to claim of most ordinary citizens of developed Western countries that they are blameworthy on account of all the existing human misery. An analogous point could be made about past institutional schemes involving slavery or a radically inferior status for women. Many of those who collaborated through the centuries in the perpetuation of such unjust institutions cannot fairly be blamed, because they could not reasonably have appreciated the wrongness of their conduct. Still, as is now agreed, their conduct was wrong, and they ought to have worked toward institutional reforms insofar as they were able to do so. It is in this kind of situation, I believe, that most ordinary citizens of the developed West are today with respect to the prevailing global institutional framework. It would be moralistic and somewhat silly, perhaps, to blame such persons for violence and starvation abroad. But this does not devalue the attempt to explain to them how, to the best of one's understanding, they do in fact share responsibility for such wrongs and ought to reflect upon and help work toward institutional reform. This attempt is not silly or moralistic, because, insofar as they are moral persons, they would themselves want to be challenged to reflect upon such potential responsibilities and duties. My concern, then, is not with blame or guilt. I merely want to show what, I think, is not easily appreciated—that our global institutional order is unjust, that we do wrong in simply collaborating in the perpetuation and imposition of this order, and that we should therefore explore new ways of acting for ourselves (who can help in the reform of institutions) and for those who will come after us (who, thanks to the juster institutions we will leave behind, should find it easier than we did to live well).

24.4. Despite this qualification, my conclusion may provoke some incredulity (if not annoyance). Please remember that even the injustices we now recognize as the most conspicuous (slavery and the inferior status of women) were once entirely taken for granted. Those advantaged by them found it easy not to think about them or, at best, to invoke some shallow rationalizations, especially since those subjected to severe deprivations and disadvantages typically lack the resources fully to understand and protest their condition. Are we today any more immune to comfortable errors of moral judgment?

Moreover, not all the features that make the prominent injustices of the past so conspicuous are present in what I have portrayed as the principal injustices of our time (and it is therefore perhaps even less appropriate to attach blame and guilt to them). Here two factors are of special importance. The preeminent injustices of our time typically involve radical inequalities that are *engendered* rather than established, and they are injustices in the *global* structure of human interaction rather than in the internal structure of relevant social units (a family, city, or state). There are two ways in which these two factors tend to obscure injustice and responsibility for it.

On the one hand, both factors make injustice harder to diagnose and institutional reforms harder to conceive and to implement. The question whether an institutional scheme establishes excessive deprivations or disadvantages can be answered rather straightforwardly. But suppose we want to find out whether existing hardships, though not called for by the ground rules of an institutional scheme, are nevertheless engendered by it and whether there are feasible institutional reforms through which the incidence of the relevant deprivations could be reduced. Before one can answer these questions affirmatively, one must have gathered a great deal of empirical information, developed estimates about what deprivations and disadvantages feasible alternative institutional schemes would tend to produce, and constructed and tested various macroexplanations. These tasks are obviously even more difficult on the global plane because of the greater size and complexity of the global social system and also because of the lesser accessibility of comparative data.

On the other hand, when excessive deprivations and disadvantages clearly are avoidable consequences of the prevailing institutional scheme, both factors also tend to make it harder to appreciate that the relevant scheme is therefore unjust and that we, as advantaged participants in it, share a moral responsibility for such injustice. Here the injustice of *national* institutions that *establish* radical inequalities and the responsibility of citizens for such injustice were easiest to understand (and historically the earliest to be widely understood). The widespread appreciation of these points in the United States was a main precondition for the abolition of slavery in the 1860s and the introduction of women's suffrage in the 1920s. Meanwhile we have (one might say somewhat simplistically) advanced to the point where one factor alone no longer obscures our vision. It is now widely understood that *national* institutions may be unjust on account of radical inequalities they *engender* and that citizens may share a moral responsibility for such injustice. The widespread appreciation of these points helped achieve the institutional reforms of the New Deal in the 1930s. It is now also generally understood that a *global* institutional scheme may be unjust on account of radical inequalities it *establishes*, and that its participants ought to contribute to the reform of such unjust institutions. This appreciation was instrumental in abolishing the colonialism based upon racial superiority that was a central feature of our global order up until the middle of this century.[42] The plausibility of my

[42]It is probably the general understanding, however, that the citizens of countries that did not have colonies had merely a positive rather than a negative duty to work for global

conclusion combines these two widely accepted points—a *global* institutional scheme may be unjust on account of excessive deprivations and disadvantages it *engenders*.

---

institutional reform. On my view, the duty would be a negative one—provided colonialism is correctly understood as a global institution rather than a set of separate but similar crimes.

Bibliography

Ackerman, Bruce. *Social Justice and the Liberal State*. New Haven: Yale University Press, 1980.

Amdur, Robert. "Rawls' Theory of Justice: Domestic and International Perspectives." *World Politics* 29 (April 1977), 438–61.

Arrow, Kenneth. "Some Ordinalist-Utilitarian Notes on Rawls' Theory of Justice." *Journal of Philosophy* 70 (May 1973), 245–63.

Audard, Catherine, et al. *Individu et justice sociale*. Paris: Seuil, 1988.

Barry, Brian. "Do Countries Have Moral Obligations?" In S. M. McMurrin, ed., *The Tanner Lectures on Human Value, 2*. Salt Lake City: University of Utah Press, 1981.

——. "Humanity and Justice in Global Perspective." In J. R. Pennock and John W. Chapman, eds., *Ethics, Economics, and the Law*. New York: New York University Press, 1982.

——. *The Liberal Theory of Justice*. Oxford: Clarendon Press, 1972.

Beitz, Charles. "Cosmopolitan Ideals and National Sentiment." *Journal of Philosophy* 80 (October 1983), 591–600.

——. *Political Theory and International Relations*. Princeton: Princeton University Press, 1979.

——, et al., eds. *International Ethics*. Princeton: Princeton University Press, 1985.

Benn, S. I., and R. S. Peters. *Social Principles and the Democratic State*. London: Allen and Unwin, 1959.

Berger, Peter. "Are There Any Human Rights?" In B. Rubin and E. Spiro, eds., *Human Rights and U.S. Foreign Policy*. Boulder, Colo.: Westview Press, 1979.

Berlin, Isaiah. *Four Essays on Liberty*. Oxford: Oxford University Press, 1969.

Blocker, H. G., and E. H. Smith, eds. *John Rawls' Theory of Social Justice*. Athens: Ohio University Press, 1980.

Brierly, James L. *The Law of Nations*. Oxford: Clarendon Press, 1963 [1928].

Buchanan, Allen. "Revisability and Rational Choice." *Canadian Journal of Philosophy* 5 (November 1975), 395–408.

Clark, Barry, and Herbert Gintis. "Rawlsian Justice and Economic Systems." *Philosophy and Public Affairs* 7 (Summer 1978), 302–25.

Cohen, G. A. "Capitalism, Freedom, and the Proletariat." In Alan Ryan, ed., *The Idea of Freedom*. Oxford: Oxford University Press, 1979.

——. "Robert Nozick and Wilt Chamberlain: How Patterns Preserve Liberty." In John Arthur and William H. Shaw, eds., *Justice and Economic Distribution*. Englewood Cliffs: Prentice Hall, 1978.

D'Amato, Anthony. *Jurisprudence*. Dordrecht: Nijhoff, 1984.

Daniels, Norman. *Just Health Care*. Cambridge: Cambridge University Press, 1985.

Danielson, Peter. "Theories, Intuition, and the Problem of World-Wide Distributive Justice." *Philosophy and the Social Sciences* 3 (1973), 331–40.

Demarco, Joseph P. "International Application of the Theory of Justice." *Pacific Philosophical Quarterly* 62 (1981), 393–402.

Doyle, Michael. "Kant, Liberal Legacies, and Foreign Affairs." *Philosophy and Public Affairs* 12 (1983), 205–35, 323–53.

Dworkin, Ronald. *Taking Rights Seriously*. Cambridge: Harvard University Press, 1978.

Feinberg, Joel. "The Interest in Liberty on the Scales." In A. I. Goldman and J. Kim, eds., *Values and Morals*. Dordrecht: Reidel, 1978.

Fellner, William. *Probability and Profit*. Homewood, Ill.: R. D. Irwin, 1965.

Fishkin, James S. *Justice, Equal Opportunity, and the Family*. New Haven: Yale University Press, 1983.

——. *The Limits of Obligation*. New Haven: Yale University Press, 1982.

Fried, Charles. *Right and Wrong*. Cambridge: Harvard University Press, 1978.

Galston, William A. *Justice and the Human Good*. Chicago: University of Chicago Press, 1980.

——. "Moral Personality and Liberal Theory." *Political Theory* 10 (November 1982), 492–519.

Gauthier, David. "Justice and Natural Endowment: Toward a Critique of Rawls' Ideological Framework." *Social Theory and Practice* 3 (1974), 3–26.

——. *Morals by Agreement*. Oxford: Clarendon Press, 1986.

Gibbard, Allan. "Disparate Goods and Rawls' Difference Principle: A Social Choice Theoretic Treatment." *Theory and Decision* 11 (1979), 267–88.

Griffin, Keith. *International Inequality and National Poverty*. London: Holmes & Meier, 1978.

Gutmann, Amy. "Communitarian Critics of Liberalism." *Philosophy and Public Affairs* 14 (Summer 1985), 308–22.

——. *Liberal Equality*. Cambridge: Cambridge University Press, 1980.

Hare, R. M. "Rawls' Theory of Justice." In Norman Daniels, ed., *Reading Rawls*. New York: Basic Books, 1974.

Harsanyi, John C. "Can the Maximin Principle Serve as a Basis for Morality? A Critique of John Rawls' Theory." *American Political Science Review* 69 (1975), 594–606.

Hart, H. L. A. *The Concept of Law*. Oxford: Oxford University Press, 1961.

——. "Rawls on Liberty and Its Priority." In Norman Daniels, ed., *Reading Rawls*. New York: Basic Books, 1974.

Hobbes, Thomas. *Leviathan*. Harmondsworth, Eng.: Penguin. 1981 [1651].

Höffe, Otfried. *Politische Gerechtigkeit*. Frankfurt: Suhrkamp, 1987.

Hoffmann, Stanley. *Duties beyond Borders*. Syracuse: Syracuse University Press, 1981.

Humboldt, Wilhelm von. *The Limits of State Action*. Cambridge: Cambridge University Press, 1968.

Johnson, Conrad D. "The Authority of the Moral Agent." *Journal of Philosophy* 82 (August 1985), 391–413.

Kanbur, Ravi. "The Standard of Living: Uncertainty, Inequality, and Opportunity." Appended to Amartya K. Sen, *The Standard of Living*. Cambridge: Cambridge University Press, 1987.

Kant, Immanuel. *Kant's Political Writings*, ed. Hans Reiss. Cambridge: Cambridge University Press, 1970.

———. *The Metaphysical Elements of Justice*, trans. J. Ladd. Indianapolis: Bobbs-Merrill, 1965.

Larmore, Charles. *Patterns of Moral Complexity*. Cambridge: Cambridge University Press, 1987.

Lauterpacht, H. *International Law and Human Rights*. New York: Praeger, 1950.

Locke, John. *The Second Treatise on Government*. Indianapolis: Bobbs-Merrill, 1952.

Lyons, David. "Utility and Rights." In J. R. Pennock and John W. Chapman, eds., *Ethics, Economics, and the Law*. New York: New York University Press, 1982.

MacCallum, Gerald. "Negative and Positive Freedom." *Philosophical Review* 76 (July 1967), 312–34.

MacIntyre, Alasdair. *After Virtue*. Notre Dame, Ind.: University of Notre Dame Press, 1981.

Macpherson, Crawford B. *The Real World of Democracy*. Oxford: Oxford University Press, 1966.

Marshall, Geoffrey. *Parliamentary Sovereignty and the Commonwealth*. Oxford: Oxford University Press, 1957.

Martin, Rex. *Rawls and Rights*. Lawrence: University Press of Kansas, 1985.

Michaelman, Frank I. "Constitutional Welfare Rights and *A Theory of Justice*." In Norman Daniels, ed., *Reading Rawls*. New York: Basic Books, 1974.

Mill, John Stuart. *Utilitarianism, On Liberty, and Considerations on Representative Government*, ed. H. B. Acton. London: Dent, 1972.

Morgenthau, Hans J. *Politics among Nations*, 5th edition. New York: Knopf, 1973.

Musgrave, R. A. "Maximin, Uncertainty, and the Leisure Trade-Off." *Quarterly Journal of Economics* 88 (November 1974), 625–32.

Nagel, Thomas. "Moral Conflict and Political Legitimacy." *Philosophy and Public Affairs* 16 (Summer 1987), 215–40.

———. "Poverty and Food: Why Charity Is Not Enough." In P. Brown and H. Shue, eds., *Food Policy*. New York: Free Press, 1977.

———. "Rawls on Justice." In Norman Daniels, ed., *Reading Rawls*. New York: Basic Books, 1974.

Nardin, Terry. *Law, Morality, and the Relations of States*. Princeton: Princeton University Press, 1983.

Nozick, Robert. *Anarchy, State, and Utopia*. New York: Basic Books, 1974.

Parfit, Derek. *Reasons and Persons*. Oxford: Oxford University Press, 1984.

Paul, Jeffrey, ed. *Reading Nozick*. Totowa, N.J.: Rowman and Littlefield, 1981.

Pettit, Philip. "A Theory of Justice?" *Theory and Decision* 4 (February and April 1974), 311–24.

Plato. *The Republic*, trans. G. M. A. Grube. Indianapolis: Hackett, 1974.

Raz, Joseph. *The Morality of Freedom*. Oxford: Oxford University Press, 1986.

Reiman, Jeffrey H. "The Labor Theory of the Difference Principle." *Philosophy and Public Affairs* 12 (Spring 1983), 133–59.

Richards, David A. J. "International Distributive Justice." In J. R. Pennock and

John W. Chapman, eds., *Ethics, Economics, and the Law*. New York: New York University Press, 1982.

——. *A Theory of Reasons for Action*. Oxford: Oxford University Press, 1971.

Rorty, Richard. "The Priority of Democracy to Philosophy." In Merrill D. Peterson and Robert C. Vaughan, eds., *The Virginia Statute for Religious Freedom*. Cambridge: Cambridge University Press, 1988.

Rousseau, Jean-Jacques. *The Social Contract*. Harmondsworth, Eng.: Penguin, 1968.

Sandel, Michael. *Liberalism and the Limits of Justice*. Cambridge: Cambridge University Press, 1982.

Scanlon, T. M. "Preference and Urgency." *Journal of Philosophy* 72 (November 6, 1975), 655–69.

——. "Rawls' Theory of Justice." In Norman Daniels, ed., *Reading Rawls*. New York: Basic Books, 1974.

——. "The Significance of Choice." In S. M. McMurrin, ed., *The Tanner Lectures on Human Value*, 8. Salt Lake City: University of Utah Press, 1988.

Sen, Amartya K. *Collective Choice and Social Welfare*. San Francisco: Holden Day, 1970.

——. "Equality of What?" In *Choice, Welfare and Measurement*. Cambridge, Mass.: MIT Press, 1982, 353–69.

——. *Poverty and Famines*. New York: Oxford University Press, 1981.

——. *The Standard of Living*. Cambridge: Cambridge University Press, 1987.

——. "Well-being, Agency, and Freedom: The Dewey Lectures, 1984." *Journal of Philosophy* 82 (April 1985), 169–221.

Sher, George. *Desert*. Princeton: Princeton University Press, 1987.

Shue, Henry. *Basic Rights*. Princeton: Princeton University Press, 1980.

——. "The Burdens of Justice." *Journal of Philosophy* 80 (October 1983), 600–8.

Simon, Robert L. "Global Justice and the Authority of States." *Monist* 66 (October 1983), 557–72.

Singer, Peter, ed. *In Defense of Animals*. Oxford: Blackwell, 1985.

Smith, Adam. *The Wealth of Nations*. Chicago: University of Chicago Press, 1976.

Taylor, Michael. *Community, Anarchy, and Liberty*. Cambridge: Cambridge University Press, 1982.

Tuck, Richard. *Natural Rights Theories*. Cambridge: Cambridge University Press, 1979.

Tucker, R. W. *The Inequality of Nations*. New York: Basic Books, 1977.

Universal Declaration of Human Rights, cited by article number.

van Dyke, Vernon. "The Individual, the State, and Ethnic Communities in Political Theory." *World Politics* 29 (April 1977), 343–69.

——. "Justice as Fairness: For Groups?" *American Political Science Review* 69 (1975), 607–14.

Walzer, Michael. *Just and Unjust Wars*. New York: Basic Books, 1977.

——. "The Moral Standing of States." *Philosophy and Public Affairs* 9 (Spring 1980), 209–29.

Wellbank, J. H., Dennis Snook, and David T. Mason, eds. *John Rawls and His Critics—An Annotated Bibliography*. New York: Garland, 1982.

Williams, Bernard. *Moral Luck*. Cambridge: Cambridge University Press, 1981.

Wolff, Robert Paul. "The Derivation of the Minimal State." In Jeffrey Paul, ed., *Reading Nozick*. Totowa, N.J.: Rowman and Littlefield, 1981.

——. *Understanding Rawls*. Princeton: Princeton University Press, 1977.

Index